Noam Mizrahi
Witnessing a Prophetic Text in the Making

Beihefte zur Zeitschrift für die alttestamentliche Wissenschaft

Edited by
John Barton, Nathan Mac Donald, Carol A. Newsom,
Reinhard G. Kratz and Markus Witte

Volume 502

Noam Mizrahi

Witnessing a Prophetic Text in the Making

The Literary, Textual and Linguistic Development of Jeremiah 10:1–16

DE GRUYTER

ISBN 978-3-11-052259-4
e-ISBN [PDF] 978-3-11-053016-2
e-ISBN [EPUB] 978-3-11-053000-1
ISSN 0934-2575

Library of Congress Cataloging-in-Publication Data
A CIP catalog record for this book has been applied for at the Library of Congress.

Bibliographic information published by the Deutsche Nationalbibliothek
The Deutsche Nationalbibliothek lists this publication in the Deutsche Nationalbibliografie;
detailed bibliographic data are available on the Internet at http://dnb.dnb.de.

© 2017 Walter de Gruyter GmbH, Berlin/Boston
Printing and binding: CPI books GmbH, Leck
♾ Printed on acid-free paper
Printed in Germany

www.degruyter.com

MIX
Papier aus verantwor-
tungsvollen Quellen
FSC® C083411

Contents

Acknowledgments

The compositional history of the present book, as that of any other work of its kind, is a long and complex one. The approach presented in this study naturally developed along several years of learning, teaching and thinking of the ancient texts discussed herein, while attempting to define and fine-tune the most adequate methods for their critical investigation. Various aspects of the topic discussed here were first presented in lectures delivered during the last five years at various conferences and workshops, and I have benefitted from the generous advice, constructive critique and unceasing encouragement of family, mentors, colleagues, and students. They are too numerous to be listed, so I thank them here collectively, from the bottom of my heart.

Still, I must single out a few individuals, without whose immense help this project would not have materialized at all. First and foremost, I am particularly grateful to Reinhard G. Kratz for his unfailing support and many thought-provoking discussions on a whole range of scholarly issues. The dear friendship and warm hospitality of Dorothea M. Salzer and Stefan Schorch as well as that of Vera Meyer-Laurin in Berlin enabled me to make significant progress at a crucial juncture of the work. Meira Poliack, Chair of the Department of Biblical Studies at Tel Aviv University, made special efforts to ease my teaching burden so that I would be able to finally bring this project to completion.

Some chapters originally took an article form in Modern Hebrew, but they were all revised when taking their final place within the overall matrix of the present synthesis. An early version of Chapter 2 was published under the title "From Wisdom to Hymn: The Literary, Textual and Linguistic Development of Jer 10:12–13," *Shnaton* 25 (2017): 59–95; I thank the Mandel Institute of Jewish Studies at the Hebrew University of Jerusalem for permission to integrate here an English version of this piece. An early version of Chapter 4, under the title "מלך עולם (Jer 10:10): A Poetic Fragment and its History," is due to be published in a forthcoming *Festschrift*. A precursor of Chapter 5 is "'For None is Like You' (Jer 10:6–7): A Prayer of Praise and its Place on the Map of Biblical Literature," *Beit Mikra* 61/2 (2016): 239–175; I thank the Bialik Institute for permission to include here a revised English version of this paper. I also wish to record my gratitude to readers and reviewers of these papers, especially Dr. Ronnie Goldstein, for making instructive comments and helpful suggestions.

Thanks are also due to Ms. Hephzibah Levin, who skillfully and efficiently edited the language of all chapters. Needless to say, any mistake, weakness or ill judgment that remains is my sole responsibility.

My students, Matan Oren and Adam Lloyd-Alfia, were of invaluable assistance at the stages of proofreading and preparing the index. I am very grateful to them for their painstaking and careful work.

I am thankful to the Editorial Board of the BZAW series – Professors John Barton (University of Oxford), Reinhard G. Kratz (Georg-August-Universität Göttingen), Nathan MacDonald (University of Cambridge), Carol A. Newsom (Emory University), and Markus Witte (Humboldt-Univeristät zu Berlin) – for accepting my book to this distinguished flagship of Old Testament scholarship.

Finally, it is a pleasure to thank the professional staff of de Gruyter – particularly Dr. Sophie Wagenhofer and Ms. Lena Ebert as well as Stefan Diezmann and Aaron Sanborn-Overby – for their patience and skilled handling of the production of the book.

Introduction

§1 Prolusion

The Book of Jeremiah poses one of the greatest challenges to biblical scholarship in terms of its literary composition and textual fluidity, both of which are reflected in the plethora of discrepancies between the Book's Hebrew, Masoretic text (𝔐) and the Greek, Septuagint version (𝔊), both of which are supported by different Jeremiah scrolls from Qumran.

This study traces the intricacies of a range of formative and transformative processes by analyzing the textual manifestations of an instructive case study: the prophecy contained in Jer 10:1–16. Since this prophetic unit notoriously epitomizes many of the typical problems inherent in the textual and literary evidence, it has drawn much scholarly attention due to a range of theoretical and exegetical issues it raises both in itself and in the broader context of the compositional history of the Book of Jeremiah as a whole. Moreover, the prophecy contained in Jer 10:1–16 serves as an example of the genre of idol parodies, also attested in other biblical sources that seem to participate in a broader ancient Near Eastern discourse.[1] The analytical model presented herein is intended primarily to advance our understanding of the particular case study under scrutiny by closely investigating its literary, textual, and linguistic aspects. In so doing, however, this study also aspires to make a contribution to the ongoing, collective effort of critical scholarship towards better comprehension of the complicated compositional history of Jeremiah.[2] Modern study of this issue is heavily indebted to the seminal observations

---

1 For instance, Levtow 2008 highlights the political aspect of iconic cult, following previous discussions about the relationship between biblical idol parodies and the Mesopotamian ritual of induction of cult images; e.g., Berlejung 1998: 369–411, esp. 315–413; Dick 1999; Lundberg 2007. Ammann 2015 explores the relation between idol parodies and the world of wisdom, following the seminal study of von Rad 1972: 177–185.

2 The enormous scope of scholarly literature on Jeremiah – which continues expanding as I write these lines – cannot be surveyed adequately in a focused study such as this one. In order to keep my analysis intelligible, I opted for a highly selective policy of reference, concentrating on the most pertinent publications for the particular issues discussed herein, bearing in mind that the history of scholarship as well as more general aspects of the issue have been repeatedly summarized in some very recent publications (e.g., Adcock 2017; Ammann 2015) and updated critical commentaries. I also preferred to refrain from extended debates with previous studies for the practical sake of producing a monograph that centers on the text itself while maintaining some degree of readability, despite delving into condense philological analyses. An informed picture of the current state of Jeremiah studies may be attained from the various contributions to Najman and Schmid 2016.

DOI 10.1515/9783110530162-001

of Bernard Duhm, adapted and amplified especially by Sigmund Mowinckel.[3] The analytical trajectory marked by their work fertilized numerous subsequent studies, but it also yielded a counter trend, characterized by profound skepticism concerning any possibility to reconstruct the various stages by which Jeremiah assumed its current form, thus preferring to treat its text as a literary unity, thereby reverting back to a pre-critical view of the book.[4] While I do not share this skeptical view of our critical abilities to discern the 'prehistory' of the book, the present inquiry is independent of any particular theory concerning the compositional history of Jeremiah.[5] Most importantly, I do not presuppose the *a priori* primacy of any specific literary component, for instance, by assuming that poetic passages should be regarded, in principle, as older (and more genuine) than passages formulated in prose. Rather, each textual element is examined in and of its own, thus establishing its degree of authenticity and relative chronology vis-à-vis other elements. This is done regardless of theoretical assumptions made on the basis of abstract generalizations, which, as attractive as they may appear to be, do not necessarily conform to the actual evidence furnished by our extant sources.

§2 Demarcation

The delimitation of the prophecy poses no special problems.[6] Its beginning is patently marked by a superscription in v. 1, "Hear the word that the LORD speaks to you, O house of Israel," the likes of which are found throughout the Book of Jeremiah. This passage defines all pertinent dimensions of the communicative situation: the initiator (YHWH), the addressee (the "house of Israel"), the content and relevance of the message ("the word" spoken "to you," or rather "about you"), and the oral/audial medium of communication ("*hear* the word that the LORD *speaks* to you"). As such, it serves as a fitting statement for opening a prophetic message.

> NB. While the redactional nature of v. 1 is evident in all versions of the text, notably, its Deuteronomistic features are more pronounced in 𝔊 than in 𝔐. The main difference between the two versions seemingly concerns only the

---

3 Duhm 1901; Mowinckel 1914.
4 Carrol 1986; Fischer 2005.
5 It should be noted, however, that the result of this study generally confirms the "rolling corpus" model, developed by McKane 1986–96.
6 For the general issue of delimiting the prophetic units contained in Jeremiah, see Lundbom 2009.

syntactic issue of the place of YHWH's name: it is located within the relative clause in 𝔐 (שמעו את הדבר אשר דבר יהוה עליכם, "Hear the word *that the Lord* spoke concerning you"), but outside of the relative clause in 𝔊 (Ἀκούσατε τὸν λόγον κυρίου, ὃν ἐλάλησεν ἐφ᾽ ὑμᾶς = שמעו את דבר יהוה אשר דבר עליכם, "Hear *the word of the Lord* that he spoke concerning you"). However, this variation results in exhibiting different redactional formulae in the passage:

(a) The construct phrase דבר יהוה is popular in Jeremiah as a designation of prophecy, and it is commonly used as the object of the verb שמע in other superscriptions.[7] The phrase דבר יהוה אשר דבר is not employed elsewhere in Jeremiah as a redactional superscription, but rather in narrative descriptions (Jer 36:4; 37:2). It is a common formula in Kings for emphasizing that historical events are realizations of previous prophecies.[8] This is a typically Deuteronomistic emphasis, and the function of this formula is to create a redactional link between originally discrete sources. Thus the formulation of Jer 10:1 according to 𝔊 bears a Deuteronomistic imprint.[9]

(b) 𝔐's reading, שמעו את הדבר אשר דבר יהוה, conflates the common introductory formula שמעו את דבר יהוה (as reflected by 𝔊) with the rarer construction הדבר אשר דבר יהוה, whose attestations in Jeremiah are restricted to the oracles against the nations (Jer 46:13; 50:1).[10] This usage suggests that 𝔐's reading betrays an interpretation of Jer 10:1–16 as a prophecy dealing mainly with the nations. This ideological concern is indeed underscored in 𝔐 – much more than in 𝔊 – and it also corresponds well with the duplication of a subsection of this prophecy (vv. 12–16) in prophecies that concern Babylon (Jer 51:15–19), found among the other oracles against the nations. It appears, therefore, that 𝔐's reading reflects a late rewriting of the superscription in light of the compositional development that the prophecy underwent as a whole.

The end of the prophetic unit is less clearly marked, but it is not seriously doubted nevertheless. The peculiar contents of the prophecy, comprising of a polemic against idolatry on the one hand and hymnic praises of YHWH on the other, do

---

7 Jer 2:4; 7:2; 9:19; 17:20; 19:3; 21:11; 22:29; 29:20; 31:10; 34:4; 42:15; 44:26.
8 1 Kgs 2:27; 13:26; 14:18; 15:29; 16:12, 34; 17:16; 22:38; 2 Kgs 1:17; 10:17; 15:12; 20:19 (=Isa 39:8); 24:2.
9 If this is indeed the case, one must consider the possibility that the formula is employed here – similarly to its function in Kings – in order to link the text back to a previous prophecy. Assuming that the core of the prophecy lies in its polemic against idolatry, the intended antecedent might be the prophecy in Jer 2:26–28, which similarly condemns the worship of idols (cf. Chapter 1, §5.2).
10 Cf. Isa 16:13; 37:22 (=2 Kgs 19:21). The latter passage is not part of Isaiah's collection of oracles against the nations, but it is thematically similar in concerning Assyria.

not continue beyond v. 16.[11] Moreover, v. 16 serves as a fitting conclusion for the argument inherent in the combination of both aforementioned topics: "Not like these [i.e., like the idols] is the LORD, the portion of Jacob, for he is the one who formed all things, and Israel is the tribe of his inheritance; the LORD of hosts is his name."[12]

§3 Preliminaries

From a literary-historical point of view, there are clear indications that Jer 10:1–16 is not an original literary unity but rather a composite text. Most conspicuously, following the superscription of v. 1, the prophecy consists of two major literary strands that differ from each other in almost every respect.[13]

The first strand is a satirical presentation of idolatry. The speaker depicts, with considerable detail, the chain of production of cult images, underscoring their material properties and human-made nature. This colorful depiction culminates in a theological argument that the worship of such idols is senseless: how can humans believe that a cult image really has divine powers, even though they have just produced it by their own hands and are thus acutely aware of its

---

11 Weis 2016a agrees that v. 16 is the conclusion of the prophecy according to 𝔐, but argues that 𝔊 exhibits a different demarcation. In his view, 𝔊 for Chapter 10 divides into three subunits (vv. 1–11, 12–21, 22–25), and vv. 16–17 are taken jointly as a single constituent within this overall structure. However, v. 17 in its Greek garb is quite unintelligible, and all translations and previous attempts to make sense of it are very forced. Perhaps the least radical assumption is that the translator's *Vorlage* was damaged in these verses, and he did his best to salvage something from the few intelligible words and letters that he was able to decipher (cf. Streane 1896: 126–127). Adcock 2017 assumes that vv. 17–18 form an inseparable part of the prophecy (in 𝔐, which in his view represents the original form of the text); but the content, style, imagery and discursive situation of vv. 17–18 are very remote from vv. 1–16, so that they can hardly belong together.
12 For a more detailed discussion of v. 16, see Chapter 1, §7 (pp. 68–70). Kaufmann (1937–63: 3/2.463) suggests that v. 25 ("Pour out your wrath on the nations that do not know you, and on the peoples that do not call on your name; for they have devoured Jacob; they have devoured him and consumed him, and have laid waste his habitation") was originally placed after v. 16 and was intended as a conclusion for the prophecy against idolatry. In conjunction, he considers v. 25 to be cited from psalmic literature (Ps 79:6–7), so that the issue of its place in Chapter 10 is more redactional than compositional. For Kaufmann's unique view of the prophecy under discussion, see Margaliot 1972–74: esp. 87–88.
13 Another conspicuous indication of the composite nature of the text is furnished by its discursive incoherence, marked by sudden and frequent changes in deictic references that "make the reader lose his orientation in the organization of the discourse of the chapter" (Glanz 2013: 227–229; the quote is taken from p. 228).

artificial and perishable nature? The prophecy contains three paragraphs that belong to this strand (vv. 2–5, 8–9, 14–15, hereafter referred to as the "satirical passages").

Interwoven into this strand are other passages whose literary nature is patently distinct. These are hymnic, psalm-like passages that do not refer at all to idolatry but rather focus exclusively on YHWH, glorifying him as the divine sovereign of the entire universe. They too are clustered as three paragraphs (vv. 6–7, 10, 12–13, hereafter the "hymnic passages"). The swing between the satirical and hymnic modes is interrupted once by an additional component: a passage formulated in Aramaic (v. 11). But this passage neatly assimilates into the satirical passages, as it reads as a continuation of the polemic against idolatry.

The form-critical differences between the two major strands are so striking, and the shifts from one strand to the other are so abrupt, that one can easily isolate each constituent without affecting the others. They are combined together only in v. 16, which concludes the prophetic unit. Thus, the internal structure of the prophecy can be presented as following the logic of *alternation:*[14]

Opening	1 שמעו את הדבר אשר דבר יהוה עליכם בית ישראל	[1] Hear the word that the LORD speaks to you, O house of Israel.
S₁	2 כה אמר יהוה אל דרך הגוים אל תלמדו ומאתות השמים אל תחתו כי יחתו הגוים מהמה 3 כי חקות העמים הבל הוא כי עץ מיער כרתו מעשה ידי חרש במעצד 4 בכסף ובזהב ייפהו במסמרות ובמקבות יחזקום ולוא יפיק 5 כתמר מקשה המה ולא ידברו נשוא ינשוא כי לא יצעדו אל תיראו מהם כי לא ירעו וגם היטיב אין אותם [פ]	[2] Thus says the LORD: Do not learn the way of the nations, or be dismayed at the signs of the heavens; for the nations are dismayed at them. [3] For the customs of the peoples are false: a tree from the forest is cut down, and worked with an ax by the hands of an artisan; [4] people deck it with silver and gold; they fasten it with hammer and nails so that it cannot move. [5] Their idols are like a wrought palm tree, and they cannot speak; they have to be carried, for they cannot walk. Do not be afraid of them, for they cannot do evil, nor is it in them to do good.

14 The abbreviation "S" stands for the satirical passages, and "H" for the hymnic ones. The English translation of biblical passages – both here and throughout this study – generally follows the NRSV, but often with modifications of my own.

H₁	6 מאין כמוך יהוה גדול אתה וגדול שמך בגבורה 7 מי לא יראך מלך הגוים כי לך יאתה כי בכל חכמי הגוים ובכל מלכותם מאין כמוך	[6] There is none like you, O LORD; you are great, and your name is great in might. [7] Who would not fear you, O King of the nations? For that is your due; among all the wise ones of the nations and in all their kingdoms there is no one like you.
S₂	8 ובאחת יבערו ויכסלו מוסר הבלים עץ הוא 9 כסף מרקע מתרשיש יובא וזהב מאופז מעשה חרש וידי צורף תכלת וארגמן לבושם מעשה חכמים כלם	[8] They are both stupid and foolish; the instruction given by idols is no better than wood! [9] Beaten silver is brought from Tarshish, and gold from Uphaz. They are the work of the artisan and of the hands of the goldsmith; their clothing is blue and purple; they are all the product of skilled workers.
H₂	10 ויהוה אלהים אמת הוא אלהים חיים ומלך עולם מקצפו תרעש הארץ ולא יכלו גוים זעמו [פ]	[10] But the LORD is the true God; he is the living God and the everlasting King. At his wrath the earth quakes, and the nations cannot endure his indignation.
Aramaic	11 כדנה תאמרון להום אלהיא די שמיא וארקא לא עבדו יאבדו מארעא ומן תחות שמיא אלה [ס]	[11] Thus shall you say to them: The gods who did not make the heavens and the earth shall perish from the earth and from under the heavens.
H₃	12 עשה ארץ בכחו מכין תבל בחכמתו ובתבונתו נטה שמים 13 לקול תתו המון מים בשמים ויעלה נשאים מקצה ארץ [הארץ] ברקים למטר עשה ויוצא רוח מאצרתיו	[12] It is he who made the earth by his power, who established the world by his wisdom, and by his understanding stretched out the heavens. [13] When he utters his voice, there is a tumult of waters in the heavens, and he makes the mist rise from the ends of the earth. He makes lightnings for the rain, and he brings out the wind from his storehouses.
S₃	14 נבער כל אדם מדעת הביש כל צורף מפסל כי שקר נסכו ולא רוח בם 15 הבל המה מעשה תעתעים בעת פקדתם יאבדו	[14] Everyone is stupid and without knowledge; goldsmiths are all put to shame by their idols; for their images are false, and there is no breath in them. [15] They are worthless, a work of delusion; at the time of their punishment they shall perish.
Closure	16 לא כאלה חלק יעקב כי יוצר הכל הוא וישראל שבט נחלתו יהוה צבאות שמו [ס]	[16] Not like these is the portion of Jacob, for he is the one who formed all things, and Israel is the tribe of his inheritance; the LORD of hosts is his name.

The alternating structure is a remarkable feature, virtually unparalleled else-where in Jeremiah or even in prophetic literature as a whole.[15] But the methodo-logical interest in this case lies primarily in the fact that the form-critical analysis is independently corroborated by text-critical evidence.[16]

It is well-known that in Jeremiah, 𝕲 and 𝔐 differ extensively from each other.[17] The prophecy in Jer 10:1–16 comprises a particularly condensed selection of a variety of typical discrepancies between the two textual witnesses. Most notably, 𝕲 is much shorter than 𝔐, as it contains no representation of vv. 6–8 and 10 in their entirety, and it also exhibits shorter readings in other, individual passages. Furthermore, 𝕲 presents a peculiar sequence of the passages comprising the prophecy vis-à-vis 𝔐 by having v. 9 *within* v. 5 rather than following it (i.e., vv. 5a→9→5b). Finally, 𝕲 presents a full range of differing readings of various sorts throughout the prophecy.

While this assortment of differences seems dazzling at first, its significance becomes apparent when mapped against the form-critical analysis presented earlier:[18]

Opening	1 שמעו את הדבר אשר דבר יהוה עליכם בית ישראל	[1] Ἀκούσατε λόγον κυρίου, ὃν ἐλάλησεν ἐφ' ὑμᾶς, οἶκος Ισραηλ·
$S_1 + S_2$	2 כה אמר יהוה אל דרך הגוים אל תלמדו ומאתות השמים אל תחתו כי יחתו הגוים מהמה 3 כי חקות העמים הבל הוא כי עץ מיער כרתו מעשה ידי חרש במעצד 4 בכסף ובזהב ייפהו במסמרות ובמקבות יחזקום ולוא יפיק 5 כתמר מקשה המה ולא ידברו	[2] τάδε λέγει κύριος Κατὰ τὰς ὁδοὺς τῶν ἐθνῶν μὴ μανθάνετε καὶ ἀπὸ τῶν σημείων τοῦ οὐρανοῦ μὴ φοβεῖσθε, ὅτι φοβοῦνται αὐτὰ τοῖς προσώποις αὐτῶν. 3 ὅτι τὰ νόμιμα τῶν ἐθνῶν μάταια· ξύλον ἐστὶν ἐκ τοῦ δρυμοῦ ἐκκεκομμένον, ἔργον τέκτονος καὶ χώνευμα· [4] ἀργυρίῳ καὶ χρυσίῳ κεκαλλωπισμένα ἐστίν· ἐν σφύραις καὶ ἥλοις ἐστερέωσαν αὐτά, καὶ οὐ κινηθήσονται· [5a] ἀργύριον τορευτόν ἐστιν, οὐ πορεύσονται·

---

15 This peculiar feature was observed aptly in early Jewish exegesis, for instance: ארבעה פעמים בדף אחד הראה ירמיהו גנותה של ע"ז ושבחו של הקב"ה (*Exodus Rabbah* 16:2), "Four times on one page will you find that Jeremiah exposed the shame of idolatry and revealed the praise of God" (tr. Lehrman, in Freedman and Simon 1939: 3.207–208), continuing to specify how the two themes alternate. Cf. *Lamentations Rabbah* 1:1 (tr. Cohen, in Freedman and Simon 1939: 7.69–70). See further Chapter 2, §8 (p. 107, n. 91). For the reception of Jer 10:1–16 in rabbinic literature see Lavee 2016 (cf. Rosen-Zvi 2017: esp. 581–582).

16 Ben-Dov 2000 in particular emphasizes the convergence of both types of evidence.

17 For the state of the art, see Weis 2016b.

18 The text of 𝕲 analyzed in this study is the basic text of Ziegler 1976: 201–202 (Jer 10:1–16) and 294 (Jer 51[28]:15–19). The English translation generally follows NETS (A. Pietersma and M. Saunders), albeit sometimes with modifications of my own. Cf. Walser 2012: 58–59, 260–261.

		↓ 9 ἀργύριον προσβλητὸν ἀπὸ Θαρσις ἥξει, χρυσίον Μωφας καὶ χεὶρ χρυσοχόων, ἔργα τεχνιτῶν πάντα· ὑάκινθον καὶ πορφύραν ἐνδύσουσιν αὐτά·
	נשוא ינשוא כי לא יצעדו אל תיראו מהם כי לא ירעו וגם היטיב אין אותם [פ]	5b αἰρόμενα ἀρθήσονται, ὅτι οὐκ ἐπιβήσονται. μὴ φοβηθῆτε αὐτά, ὅτι οὐ μὴ κακοποιήσωσι, καὶ ἀγαθὸν οὐκ ἔστιν ἐν αὐτοῖς.
H_1	6 מאין כמוך יהוה גדול אתה וגדול שמך בגבורה 7 מי לא יראך מלך הגוים כי לך יאתה כי בכל חכמי הגוים ובכל מלכותם מאין כמוך	—
S_2	8 ובאחת יבערו ויכסלו מוסר הבלים עץ הוא	—
	9 כסף מרקע מתרשיש יובא וזהב מאופז מעשה חרש וידי צורף תכלת וארגמן לבושם מעשה חכמים כלם	↑
H_2	10 ויהוה אלהים אמת הוא אלהים חיים ומלך עולם מקצפו תרעש הארץ ולא יכלו גוים זעמו [פ]	—
Aramaic	11 כדנה תאמרון להום אלהיא די שמיא וארקא לא עבדו יאבדו מארעא ומן תחות שמיא אלה [ס]	11 οὕτως ἐρεῖτε αὐτοῖς Θεοί, οἳ τὸν οὐρανὸν καὶ τὴν γῆν οὐκ ἐποίησαν, ἀπολέσθωσαν ἀπὸ τῆς γῆς καὶ ὑποκάτωθεν τοῦ οὐρανοῦ τούτου.
H_3	12 עשה ארץ בכחו מכין תבל בחכמתו ובתבונתו נטה שמים 13 לקול תתו המון מים בשמים ויעלה נשאים מקצה ארץ [הארץ] ברקים למטר עשה ויוצא רוח מאצרתיו	12 κύριος ὁ ποιήσας τὴν γῆν ἐν τῇ ἰσχύι αὐτοῦ, ὁ ἀνορθώσας τὴν οἰκουμένην ἐν τῇ σοφίᾳ αὐτοῦ καὶ ἐν τῇ φρονήσει αὐτοῦ ἐξέτεινε τὸν οὐρανὸν 13 καὶ πλῆθος ὕδατος ἐν οὐρανῷ καὶ ἀνήγαγε νεφέλας ἐξ ἐσχάτου τῆς γῆς, ἀστραπὰς εἰς ὑετὸν ἐποίησε καὶ ἐξήγαγε φῶς ἐκ θησαυρῶν αὐτοῦ.
S_3	14 נבער כל אדם מדעת הביש כל צורף מפסל כי שקר נסכו ולא רוח בם 15 הבל המה מעשה תעתעים בעת פקדתם יאבדו	14 ἐμωράνθη πᾶς ἄνθρωπος ἀπὸ γνώσεως, κατῃσχύνθη πᾶς χρυσοχόος ἐπὶ τοῖς γλυπτοῖς αὐτοῦ, ὅτι ψευδῆ ἐχώνευσαν, οὐκ ἔστι πνεῦμα ἐν αὐτοῖς· 15 μάταιά ἐστιν, ἔργα ἐμπεπαιγμένα, ἐν καιρῷ ἐπισκοπῆς αὐτῶν ἀπολοῦνται.
Closure	16 לא כאלה חלק יעקב כי יוצר הכל הוא וישראל שבט נחלתו יהוה צבאות שמו [ס]	16 οὐκ ἔστι τοιαύτη μερὶς τῷ Ιακωβ, ὅτι ὁ πλάσας τὰ πάντα αὐτὸς κληρονομία αὐτοῦ, κύριος ὄνομα αὐτῷ.

As the table clearly shows, 𝔊 lacks two of the three hymnic passages (vv. 6–7, 10), while two satirical passages (vv. 2–5, 8–9) are combined therein into a single, continuous paragraph (which does not contain v. 8). It is quite unlikely that any scribe or translator would have omitted passages the praise God as the divine king; on the other hand, it is inherently reasonable to suppose that such passages could be supplemented to any religious text along its textual transmission. The simplest conclusion, therefore, is that 𝕾's shorter version testifies to an older stage in the compositional history of the prophecy compared to 𝔐, whereas 𝔐 represents a later formation, enriched with hymnic passages.[19] Thus, 𝕾 generally affirms the results of the form-critical analysis to a surprising degree, affording an independent validation of the composite nature of the prophecy under scrutiny.[20]

While sustaining the basic distinction between the satirical and hymnic passages, 𝕾 also suggests – albeit indirectly – that at least some components of the prophecy had an independent existence prior to their integration into the text. Furthermore, 𝕾 alerts our attention to the possibility that the hymnic strand is not a literary unity of its own – otherwise, it would be difficult to comprehend why vv. 12–13 are shared by both 𝕾 and 𝔐, whereas vv. 6–7 and v. 10 are not witnessed by 𝕾 and remain peculiar to 𝔐 and its congeners. The suspicion that the three hymnic passages do not converge but rather stem from different sources is confirmed by literary and philological analysis, which demonstrates their original independence of one another. Both philological and textual evidence further indicates that the hymnic passages were not added *en bloc,* but rather were added to supplement the prophecy incrementally. Such a development trajectory cannot be reconciled with reading all three passages as a continuous strand.[21]

If this analysis is correct, it also has an important implication for understanding the textual relationship between 𝕾 and 𝔐. Most importantly, the long text of 𝔐 cannot be taken as a direct descendent of the short text represented by 𝕾 (and 4QJer[b]). Rather, one ought to hypothesize intermediate stages, in which the various components were added, bit-by-bit, before accumulating to the

---

19 See especially Bogaert 1981 (1997) (cf. Bogaert 2013: esp. 230–237). Cf. McKane 1985. The relative lateness of 𝔐, however, should not be overstated; for instance, the Hasmonean dating of the so-called "long recension" – asserted by Amphoux, Aussedat and Sérandour 2009 – ignores the fact that it is already recorded in 4QJer[a], copied at the end of the third (or beginning of the second) century BCE, i.e., before the Hasmonean period.

20 This presentation of the evidence presupposes that 𝕾 is a not the product of a free translator but rather a faithful rendition of a deviant Hebrew *Vorlage*. While early critics debated this assumption, it was fully vindicated with the publication of 4QJer[b] (4Q71), a fragment that preserves parts of Jer 9:22–10:20 and closely matches the text underlying 𝕾. This finding renders obsolete all speculations about the allegedly free translation technique of 𝕾. 4QJer[b] was published preliminarily by Janzen 1973: 181–182, followed by the full and official edition of Tov 1997: 171–176 (cf. Tov 1989). Saley 2010 offers an alternative reconstruction of the missing parts. For a survey of the Jeremiah scrolls from Qumran, cf. Lange 2009: 297–324 and 2016.

21 For a different opinion, see Finsterbusch 2013.

conglomerate represented by 𝔐. For this reason, I do not share the common assumption that the Book of Jeremiah circulated in antiquity in (only) two so-called "recensions": a short recension represented by 𝔊 and 4QJer[b] and a long recension represented by 𝔐 and the other ancient versions.[22] Rather, I consider 𝔊 and 𝔐 to be better viewed as a random selection of two witnesses out of a greater number of textual formations that should be surmised in order to account for the textual discrepancies between the extant versions.[23] Put differently, the textual history of Jeremiah is that of an "open recension."

§4 Complicating factors

The above conclusions supply a solid foundation for any critical inquiry of the prophecy in Jer 10:1–16. On this basis, one can analyze further the individual strands and speculate about their distinct histories before, during, and after being integrated into the prophetic unit as it now stands in the extant versions, primarily 𝔐 and 𝔊. Several factors, however, have proved to complicate the study of this prophecy, pushing its scholarly discussion in different – sometimes contradictory – directions:

(1) The seemingly sophisticated literary structure of the prophetic unit led to a harmonistic reading of the prophecy as an original unity.

(2) Attempts yielding opposite results were made to discern different strata even within the most solid part of the prophecy; namely, the satirical passages.

(3) A subsection of the prophecy (Jer 10:12–16) is duplicated elsewhere in the book (Jer 51:15–19), thus comprising one of the many cases of textual doublets so characteristic of the Book of Jeremiah. This situation prompted the assumption that originally, the duplicated section was an independent unit – an assumption that had a decisive effect on all attempts to reconstruct the compositional history of the prophecy.

---

22 Cf. Tov 1981.

23 Cf. the theoretical framework formulated by Tov 1982. Note that the Jeremiah scrolls from Qumran might supply a confirmation for this hypothesis. The oldest copy of Jeremiah from Qumran, 4QJer[a] (dated, on paleographic grounds, to the late third or early second century BCE; cf. Yardeni 1990) is often adduced as supporting the long, proto-Masoretic recension. But even if this is true for Jer 10:1–16, one should take care to distinguish, in this scroll, between the text of the original scribe and the many textual corrections added at a later stage. Most significantly, Jer 7:30–8:3 is missing from the main text, and it was added only by a later corrector. Although the editor eventually preferred to explain it is an omission due to a scribal lapse (Tov 1997: 152–153), the opposite option of considering it as a testimony of an older formation of the text remains an attractive alternative. If so, the text of the original scribe is shorter than 𝔐 but still longer than 𝔊, thus fitting as representing a sort of an intermediate stage between the two.

(4) There are striking parallels between our prophecy and Deutero-Isaiah, which are not limited to the shared theme of a polemic against idolatry but extend to very specific verbal contacts. Such similarities motivated the treatment of Jer 10:1–16 jointly with Deutero-Isaiah's idol parodies, amounting to denying any connection between this prophecy and Jeremiah's *oeuvre*.

I submit, however, that all these arguments rest on a methodologically shaky ground and do not stand up to criticism. Indeed, in my view, none of them is able to subvert the basic contentions presented above regarding the composition of the prophecy and the literary relation between the textual witnesses. Let us consider these points one by one.

§4.1 Literary structure

The identification of an alternating pattern in Jer 10:1–16 exerted much influence over scholarly discussions, as it created an imposing impression of literary cohesion of this prophecy. Many scholars have construed the peculiar alternating structure accordingly as a decisive argument for the literary unity and original integrity of the prophetic unit.[24]

Such a view, however, does not accord with the fact that no alternating pattern is visible in 𝔊.[25] If this version indeed reflects an older stage of the prophecy, the alternating structure should be regarded as a secondary development rather than a feature of the *Urtext*. The only way to defend the alternating pattern as original is to argue for the authenticity of 𝔐 – for instance, by rejecting 𝔊 as the product of a literary technique of reworking an older and longer text by way of excerption.[26]

Indeed, even for scholars admitting the composite nature of the prophecy, the alternation between satirical and hymnic passages could still be interpreted as the result of purposeful redaction.[27] However, this position is not a necessary conclusion from the evidence either. It is just as possible to construe a

---

24 See, e.g., Ackroyd 1963; Overholt 1965; Margaliot 1980; Krašovec 1984: 76–85; Clendenen 1987; Holladay 1986–89: 1.321–337.
25 Cf. Scholz 1875: 60–62.
26 See, e.g., Vonach 2009; Adcock 2017. The extreme view that 𝔊 reflects a heavily corrupted text, the cumulative result of numerous cases of haplography – over 330 instances throughout Jeremiah, consisting of some 1,715 words (!), according to Lundbom 2005 – is based on abuse of textual criticism.
27 As my own previous discussion of this unit implied (Mizrahi 2014: 120–121).

different scenario, which focuses on the fact that most textual segments suspected as late interpolations (vv. 10, 11, 12–13) are actually concentrated together at the same locus. The only passage that appears to violate this rule is the hymnic vv. 6–7, which is separated from v. 10 by the satirical passage of vv. 8–9. But this exception disappears in 𝔊 (where v. 8 is absent and v. 9 is integrated into v. 5), thus pushing vv. 6–7 to the very same locus of the all the other supplementations.

If so, the impression of an alternating structure can be replaced by an alternative view, identifying a compilation of interpolations, all placed on top of each other, within a single structural slot in the prophecy, between vv. 1–5 (including v. 9) on the one hand and vv. 14–16 on the other. In other words, the alternating structure is in the eye of the beholder, and although commentators and scholars repeatedly observed this structure since Late Antiquity through the modern age, it is not necessarily the intended configuration of the text; it may well be the random result of a gradual process of literary accretion.

§4.2 Compositional analysis

While structural features of the prophecy have motivated its harmonistic reading, another complicating factor resulted in an opposite trajectory, yielding a hypercritical approach. More specifically, questioning the literary integrity of the satirical strand led to a radical reevaluation of the originality of most of textual segments contained in the prophecy.[28]

The starting point for this approach has been the argument that v. 2 ("Thus says the Lord: Do not learn the way of the nations, or be dismayed at the signs of the heavens; for the nations are dismayed at them") and v. 3a ("For the customs of the peoples are false") duplicate each other while differing in their phraseology. Thus, v. 2 denotes the nations twice by the term הגוים, whereas v. 3a refers to them as העמים. Furthermore, the passages contrast in the expressions they employ for the false customs of the nations: v. 2 evinces "the *way* (דרך) of the nations," while v. 3a prefers "the *customs* (חֻקּוֹת) of the peoples." These facts were taken as betraying signs of literary complexity, leading to the hypothesis that v. 3a is

---

28 The most influential analysis in this direction is that of Wambacq 1974. The following paragraph describes the essentials of Wambacq's thesis, but its underlying logic is shared by other studies that accepted his analysis.

a redactional addition meant to radicalize the message of v. 2, arguing that the astrological beliefs of the gentiles are completely false (הבל).[29]

It was further speculated that vv. 3b-4 form an even later redactional addition, which reflects a misinterpretation of the term הבל (v. 3a) as a reference to idols, following a usage attested elsewhere in the Book of Jeremiah;[30] these passages were later supplemented by vv. 5, 8, 9, etc. According to this supplementary theory, the original kernel of the prophecy is restricted to v. 2 alone. This is the only passage ascribable to Jeremiah, and it addresses refugees of the northern kingdom, who survived the destruction of Samaria and were not deported by the Assyrians. All the other segments of the prophecy are judged to be subsequent additions made much later, around the beginning of the third century BCE.

Unfortunately, the literary evidence adduced in support of this complicated reconstruction is very slim, and it may well be interpreted in alternative, even contradictory ways. Most importantly, the terms גוי and עם form a word-pair in Biblical Hebrew, so that a single author could have easily employed them within a single context (see, e.g., Deut 4:27 in prose; Deut 32:8 in poetry). Indeed, such a usage is documented elsewhere in Jeremiah (Jer 6:22; cf. 50:41). Similarly, the terms חֻקָּה and דרך are jointly employed, in an overlapping sense, especially in

---

29 The idea that the phrase אֹתוֹת השמים, "the signs of the heavens," refers to astronomical phenomena that were given astrological interpretation is very common among commentators of Jeremiah. Cf. already Targum Jonathan (𝕿), which renders the phrase as "signs which are changed in the heavens," and similarly in rabbinic literature, e.g., b. Shabbat 156a: "R. Joḥanan said: How do we know that Israel is immune from planetary influence? Because it is said, 'Thus saith the Lord, Learn not the way of the nations, and be not dismayed at the signs of heaven, for the nations are dismayed at them': they are dismayed but not Israel" (tr. Freedman, in Epstein 1935: 2/1–2.156a, col. ii, c). Cf. the Syriac commentator Ishodad of Merv (van den Eynde 1972: 1.12, 2.13). Critical scholars sometimes distinguish between the argument against astrology presumably expressed in v. 2 and the polemic against idolatry manifested in the rest of the prophecy. However, the term אות "sign" in v. 2 is better interpreted as denoting a material object (cf. Num 2:2); in that case, אֹתוֹת השמים may be the astral symbols of the deities comprising "the host of heavens," whose worship was common in Judah in the seventh and sixth centuries BCE (2 Kgs 21:3, 5; cf. Deut 4:19; 17:3; 2 Kgs 23:5; Jer 8:2; 19:13; Zeph 1:5), probably under Syrian and Assyrian influence; cf. Cogan 1974: 84–87. (Koch 1982–83: 2.48–54, esp. 52, did not distinguish carefully enough between these two interpretations, and he discussed the whole issue in too general terms; for a different opinion, see Ben-Dov 2000: 106–108.)
30 According to Barstad 1978, the occurrence of הבל in Jer 10:3 is a proper noun, the name of a Canaanite god related to the deity Hubal, known from sources that concern the Arabian peninsula in the pre-Islamic period. However, Becking 1993 persuasively rejected this interpretation (cf. Becking 1999).

Deuteronomistic passages (Deut 30:16; 1 Kgs 2:3; 11:33, 38; 2 Kgs 17:13).[31] Thus, the sharp distinction made between v. 2 and v. 3a is unjustified. Moreover, the very same data may be utilized to argue the exact opposite; namely, that vv. 2–3a belong together, revealing a Deuteronomistic-like hand.[32]

Noteworthy is the methodological lesson that transpires from this discussion. The attempt to distinguish between two literary components – v. 2 vis-à-vis v. 3a – was based largely on the presumed existence of a doublet, while the more traditional criteria pointing to the obvious presence of distinct literary strands in the prophecy – such as differences in theme, stylistic mode, and ideological outlook that distinguish between the satirical and hymnic passages – were played down.[33] In principle, however, redactional activity may fuse together several sources or traditions that will necessarily *differ* in their content and form; yet they need not *duplicate* each other. For this reason, the primary criteria of differences in content, form, and worldview must take precedence in literary-historical analysis; doublets may or may not exist in a composite text, so that their existence is not a prerequisite for its analysis. Finally, internal doublets should not be assumed if other – especially easier – ways to explain the evidence are equally available.

§4.3 Parallel within Jeremiah

A third element that complicated previous discussions of our prophecy is the fact that a subsection of the prophetic unit, Jer 10:12–16, has a verbatim doublet in Jer 51(𝕲 28):15–19. The latter is embedded in a structurally and generically different part of the Book of Jeremiah; namely, as part of the Oracles against the Nations:[34]

---

31 Compare the related word-pair חֹק // דרך (Deut 26:17; 1 Kgs 3:14; 8:58; cf. Exod 18:20; Ps 119:33). Note Job 28:26, בעשתו למטר חק ודרך לחזיז קלות, "when he made a *decree* for the rain, and a *way* for the thunderbolt," as this passage employs the word-pair of חֹק // דרך in the context of God's control over meteorological phenomena.

32 Indeed, Deuteronomistic-like features are not limited to this passage but rather typify a specific stratum within the prophecy (see Chapter 1). Intriguingly, Thiel (1973: 135–138) disregarded such elements contained in Jer 10:1–16. He may have ignored them given his presupposition – inherited from previous scholars (e.g., Mowinckel 1914: 48–49) – that the entire prophecy of Jer 10:1–16 is a late, post-Deuteronomistic addition (e.g., Thiel 1973: 12, 282). It seems to me, however, that the evidence does not support this line of thinking.

33 The decisive weight of the notion of duplication in Wambacq's theory suggests that despite its supplementary results, the critical sensitivity underlying his approach is actually akin to documentary models.

34 The only major difference between 10:12–16 and 51:15–19, according to 𝔐, pertains to the name of Israel, which is included in Jer 10:16 but absent from 51:19. Other than that, there is only

Jer 51:15–19	Jer 10:12–16

15 עשה ארץ בכחו מכין תבל בחכמתו
ובתבונתו נטה שמים 16 לקול תתו המון מים
בשמים ויעל נשאים מקצה ארץ ברקים למטר
עשה ויצא רוח מאצרתיו

17 נבער כל אדם מדעת הביש כל צרף מפסל
כי שקר נסכו ולא רוח בם 18 הבל המה מעשה
תעתעים בעת פקדתם יאבדו

19 לא כאלה חלק יעקוב כי יוצר הכל הוא
ושבט נחלתו יהוה צבאות שמו

12 עשה ארץ בכחו מכין תבל בחכמתו
ובתבונתו נטה שמים 13 לקול תתו המון מים
בשמים ויעלה נשאים מקצה ארץ [הארץ]
ברקים למטר עשה ויוצא רוח מאצרתיו

14 נבער כל אדם מדעת הביש כל צורף מפסל
כי שקר נסכו ולא רוח בם 15 הבל המה מעשה
תעתעים בעת פקדתם יאבדו

16 לא כאלה חלק יעקב כי יוצר הכל הוא
וישראל שבט נחלתו יהוה צבאות שמו

This case is but one example of a much wider phenomenon, as Jeremiah is replete with textual doublets of this kind.[35] Nonetheless, our particular case has led many scholars to view vv. 12–16 as comprising an originally independent literary unit that had its own compositional and textual history, independent of vv. 1–11 (or at least vv. 2–10, if one excludes the redactional superscription of v. 1 and the Aramaic passage of v. 11).[36]

However, such a conclusion is contradicted by basic facts of the literary evidence afforded by both Chapter 10 and Chapter 51. As far as Chapter 10 is concerned, vv. 12–16 cannot be isolated from the rest of the prophecy, because one finds

---

a slight orthographic fluctuation concerning the /o/ vowel in צ(ו)רף (spelled *plene* in 10:14 but defectively in 51:17) and יעק(ו)ב (spelled defectively in 10:16 but *plene* in 51:19). The differences in the Greek versions of both sections are discussed below.

35 See, e.g., Parke-Taylor 2000: esp. 177–180. In my opinion, no single solution can be offered for all such duplicates, and the matter should be dealt with discriminatively; cf. Rofé 2009.

36 See, e.g., Crüsemann 1969: 111–114; Rudman 1998: 63–73; Lundbom 1999–2004: 1.596–600. Note especially the nuanced approach of Ben-Dov 2000, who accepts the common view that vv. 12–16 represent an independent unit but identifies signs for its literary complexity. For him, vv. 12–13 are the kernel of the hymnic layer of the prophecy as a whole (with vv. 6–7 and 10 as later expansions). In his view, the hymnic layer is related to doxologies added to prophetic literature as part of its redactional history (cf. already Tov 1981: 154, n. 27), as exemplified especially by the Book of Amos (cf. Crenshaw 1969 and 1971: esp. 75–114). Thematically, the doxologies concentrate on the motif of God the Creator, who also takes care of the regular maintenance of his world. Stylistically, they make extensive use of participles. Furthermore, they link to the employment of the formula, "YHWH of Hosts is his name" (יהוה צבאות שמו), which indeed occurs in v. 16. In my opinion, however, these characteristics do not apply equally to all the hymnic passages of Jer 10:1–16. None of them matches vv. 6–7, and the name formula depends exclusively on v. 16, which (according to Ben-Dov himself) was not originally connected to the hymnic passage of vv. 12–13. This example provides further indication that it is better to refrain from considering all the hymnic passages of Jer 10:1–16 as belonging to the same stratum. In any case, their resemblance to the Amos doxologies does not appear to me to bear satisfactory explanatory potential.

in them exactly the same two literary strands that run through the prophetic unit as a whole: a satirical presentation of idolatry on the one hand (vv. 14–15; cf. vv. 2–5, 8–9) and a hymnic praise of YHWH on the other (vv. 12–13; cf. vv. 6–7, 10). The thematic and stylistic differentiation makes little sense within vv. 12–16 on their own; it becomes understandable only within the broader context of Jer 10:1–16. Moreover, the satirical passages, including vv. 14–15, integrate into a continuous, narrative-like description, thus suggesting that they all stem from a single literary source. Finally, vv. 12–16 do not display greater textual stability than other segments of the prophecy; like all other passages, this section too evinces significant differences between 𝔐 and 𝔊, including shorter readings in 𝔊 for vv. 13 and 16. The inescapable conclusion is that Jer 10:12–16 cannot be considered as a self-standing unit that had existed separately of the other parts of the prophecy in Jer 10:1–16. On the contrary, it is manifestly nothing but a section abruptly cut out from its original context and secondarily interpolated into Chapter 51.

Examination of the parallel section in Jer 51:15–19 leads to a complementary conclusion. First, this section does not interact in any way with its immediate context. Jer 51:15–19 is embedded within a collection of prophecies against Babylon (Jer 50–51), but vv. 15–19 contain no reference or even hint to Babylon, which is the conspicuous theme of all the prophecies surrounding it. Second, the section contains a condemnation of idol worship (vv. 17–18 ‖ 10:14–15) that has neither antecedent nor continuation in the prophecies against Babylon contained in Chapters 50–51. To be sure, these prophecies do occasionally predict destruction for idols (Jer 51:47, 52; cf. 50:38),[37] but these oracles do so only by explicitly identifying such idols as the *Babylonian* gods, so that their destruction functions as a symbol for the pending loss of Babylonia at large. By contrast, the polemic of vv. 17–18 is directed against idolatry as such, without making any geographical or ethnic identification. Third, vv. 15–19 also differ from their context in some formal respects, such as their discursive situation: in the prophetic units that precede this section (Jer 51:11–14, especially vv. 13–14) and follow it (Jer 51:20–24), God speaks in the first person, whereas our section begins with a description of God in the third person (in vv. 15–16 ‖ Jer 10:12–13), thereby interrupting the sequence of divine speeches in the first person. These facts converge in indicating that vv.

---

37 Note Qimḥi's attempt to utilize this fact in explaining why the section from Chapter 10 was integrated into Chapter 51: האלילים שהיו בוטחים בהם בני בבל והיו חושבים כי בעבודתם היתה הצלחה ושנה הפרשה הנה לעניין (Cohen 2012: 254), "He reiterated the passage here because of the issue of the idols, in which the Babylonians were trusting and thinking that their worship ensures their success." But this explanation lacks conviction as it ignores the fact that the Babylonian idols are not mentioned in the immediate context of our section; namely, in the preceding and following units within Chapter 51.

15–19 are alien to their present context in Chapter 51. Their presence there surely results from a secondary interpolation, while their source is to be identified in Chapter 10.

The evidence furnished by both Chapters 10 and 51 indicates that the parallel in Jer 51:15–19 may well be valuable for text-critical purposes, but it cannot testify to older stages in the compositional history of the text contained therein. Its presence in Chapter 51 can only point to the later *reception* of the prophecy included in Chapter 10.[38] This state of affairs obviously prompts the question: Why was this section inserted into Chapter 51? A perceptive comment of the medieval Jewish commentator Menaḥem of Posquières suggests a possible answer for this query:[39]

עשה: הטעם בעבור שהזכיר למעלה נשבע ה' צבאות הגיד הכתוב שיש לו כח לקיים שבועתו
כי הוא היה עושה ארץ בכוח וכל אלה הפליאות שמגידה זאת הפרשה

"Who makes [the earth by his power, etc.]" [Jer 51:15]: The motivation [for citing this paragraph here] is that since it is mentioned above that "YHWH of Hosts *has sworn*" [v. 14], the passage explicates that He indeed has the power to fulfil his oath, for he was "the maker of the land by his power" [v. 12] and all the other miraculous deeds that this paragraph tells about.

According to this proposition, the divine oath that Babylon will suffer a mass invasion (v. 14) is amplified by reminding the (potentially skeptical) audience that God had already committed greater deeds, such as the creation of the world, thus affirming that he indeed possesses the power to bring destruction even to a mighty kingdom such as the Neo-Babylonian empire.[40]

---

38 Another important witness for a later stage in the reception of our prophecy is the apocryphal work *Epistle of Jeremiah*, which is appended to Jeremiah, Baruch, and Lamentations in 𝕲 (see most recently Adams 2014). Since analysis of this work entails many complications due to its peculiar literary features, the following discussion addresses this work only in as much as it bears on elucidating textual points of Jer 10:1–16.

39 See Cohen 2012: 255. A similar view was also expressed in modern scholarship, cf. Hill 1999: 174–176.

40 Menaḥem does not adduce comparable instances in which a divine oath is accompanied by a demonstration of God's sovereignty over the universe, but he may have had in mind cases such as Am 8:7–9, in which a divine oath to take revenge of oppressors of poor people (v. 7: "The Lord has sworn [נשבע יהוה] by the pride of Jacob: Surely I will never forget any of their deeds") is immediately followed by a depiction of a cosmic uproar (v. 8: "Shall not the land tremble on this account, and everyone mourn who lives in it, and all of it rise like the Nile, and be tossed about and sink again, like the Nile of Egypt? On that day, says the Lord God, I will make the sun go down at noon, and darken the earth in broad daylight," etc.).

If this exegetical insight has any merit, it suggests a sort of an internal, utilitarian intertextuality within the book of Jeremiah: a passage from an early part of the book was reused in order to serve a rhetorical function at a later point. For such a hypothesis to become fully convincing, it must be tested against other cases of doublets in Jeremiah, but this task is beyond the confines of the present discussion. Suffice it to note that regardless of one's preferred solution for the possible motivation of duplicating Jer 10:12–16 in 51:15–19, the latter passage is secondarily excerpted from its original context in the prophecy now contained in Chapter 10.

NB. 𝕲 Jer 51(28):15–19 differs in several details from the parallel section of 𝕲 Jer 10:12–16, and a certain textual trajectory is discernible in some of these differences. As is well known, 𝕲 breaks into two parts – or translation units – known as Jer-α and Jer-β. Jer-α represents the Old Greek version of the book. The nature of Jer-β is debated, but I concur with the opinion that it reflects an ancient, pre-Hexaplaric revision.[41] The point of transition between them is usually identified between the end of Chapter 28 (𝔐 51) and the beginning of Chapter 29 (𝔐 47).[42] However, 𝕲 Jer 51(28):15–19 approximates 𝔐 more closely and more consistently than 𝕲 Jer 10:12–16.[43] This state of affairs suggests that Jer-β, or at least some traces of it, may actually be found already *within* Chapter 28 (𝔐 51). If so, the text-critical value of 𝕲 Jer 51(28):15–19 is somewhat inferior to that of 𝕲 Jer 10:12–16, because the former may have been submitted to secondary reworking that distanced it from the deviant Hebrew *Vorlage* underlying 𝕲.

§4.4 Parallels in Deutero-Isaiah

A final element complicating the discussion of Jer 10:1–16 is the remarkable similarities between this prophecy and Deutero-Isaiah's polemic against idolatry. Admittedly, the Book of Jeremiah has its share of anti-idolatry statements (e.g., Jer 2:26–28; 3:6–10), but it contains no comparable case of detailed, satirical depictions of the idols and their manufacture as those found in Jer 10:1–16. On the other hand, these precise features are characteristic of Deutero-Isaiah.[44]

Relatedly, the form of cult images native to Judah – as can be recovered from the formulaic descriptions of Jeremiah and his contemporaries – was relatively modest and presumably made of easily obtainable materials such as wood and

---

41 Tov 1976. For a different view, see Soderlund 1985. Cf. Michael 2006.
42 Tov 1976: 105–106.
43 For examples, see Chapter 2, §4 (p. 79, n. 15; p. 83, n. 33) and §6 (p. 93, n. 53).
44 See especially Isa 40:19–20; 41:6–7, 21–29; 42:17; 44:9–20; 46:1–7.

stone. By contrast, Deutero-Isaiah and Jer 10:1–16 depict idols made of much more expensive materials – including gold, silver, and precious fabrics – suggesting that the cultural background of these descriptions should be sought in another environment; namely, the Mesopotamian civilization.

Since Deutero-Isaiah flourished in Babylonia in the mid-sixth century BCE, the natural conclusion seems to be that the prophecy of Jer 10:1–16 similarly should be regarded as a product of the exilic age. According to this line of reasoning, the prophecy reflects an attempt by an exilic community to cope with the spiritual challenges posed by the overwhelming encounter with Mesopotamian culture at its heyday, during the Neo-Babylonian period.

This argument, however, suffers from several weaknesses. First, even if one grants the thematic, theological, and verbal resemblance between Jer 10:1–16 and Deutero-Isaiah, the issue of literary relation – and all the more so, literary dependence – remains unsettled. Originally, scholars tended to assume that Jer 10:1–16 forms an interpolation made by either Deutero-Isaiah himself or by a later, anonymous author who was deeply influenced by Deutero-Isaiah.[45] Later, scholars proposed an opposite model of literary dependence, arguing that it is Deutero-Isaiah who was influenced by Jeremiah.[46] The scholarship also suggested the intermediate possibilities that both prophets drew from a common source[47] or that they both reflect the same genre.[48] Finally, it has been argued that Deutero-Isaiah's polemic against idolatry is restricted to secondary insertions that form a relatively later stratum (or even a conglomerate of late expansions).[49] Thus, the nature and direction of the interdependence between Jer 10:1–16 and Deutero-Isaiah is far from being self-evident.

In my opinion, some of the presuppositions underlying this entire discussion deserve critical reassessment, because at least some of the verbal contacts between Jer 10:1–16 and Deutero-Isaiah are text-critically suspicious. For instance, the word מַעֲצָד "adze" is famously shared by only Jer 10:3 and Isa 44:12, two passages that describe the artisans involved in producing the idols, and this fact is universally adduced as a proof for the tight dependence between the two texts.[50]

---

45 Movers 1837: 43–44.
46 Cassuto 1973: 143–160 (originally published in 1911–13). For the notion of Jeremiah's influence over Deutero-Isaiah, cf. Paul 1969; Sommer 1998: 32–72, 217–238.
47 Hurowitz 2012: 263, n. 18.
48 Roth 1975. Cf. Preuss 1971: esp. 166–170.
49 Kratz 1991: esp. 192–205; Ammann 2015: esp. 18–106.
50 Note, however, that the match between the two passages might be less striking than it appears upon first glance, because Jer 10:3 refers to the מעצד as a tool for cutting wood, whereas Isa 44:12 gives the impression that it is a tool used by blacksmiths (notwithstanding the excuse supplied by Koller 2013: 182).

However, the occurrence of this technical term in Jer 10:3 is not represented by
𝕲, which makes no mention of any cutting tool, thus limiting the verbal contact
with Deutero-Isaiah to 𝔐. If 𝕲 indeed testifies to an older formation of the text,
then one must consider the possibility that the pervasive resemblance to Deutero-
Isaiah – or at least to some of its manifestations – is not necessarily an original
feature of Jer 10:1–16 but rather a product of later development, i.e., secondary
harmonization with Deutero-Isaiah's depictions, which took place along the
textual transmission of prophetic literature.[51]

More crucial, however, is the breaching of the methodological principle that
analysis of potential intertextual relations is to be conducted as an independent
stage of the literary investigation, and it should not be intermingled with the
internal analysis of each individual text. Thus, the evidence of Jer 10:1–16 must
be considered and weighed in and of itself, prior to any comparison with other
texts; otherwise, one runs the risk of projecting alien elements into the text
under scrutiny. And indeed, if one attempts to read Jer 10:1–16 independently of
Deutero-Isaiah, new and significant patterns emerge, which are bound to change
our understanding of the text and its history.

§5 Overview of this study

In light of the aforementioned considerations, the present study systematically
explores the prophecy of Jer 10:1–16 along the analytical distinctions between
the satirical and hymnic strands. The Aramaic passage (v. 11) is separated from
the satirical strand to which it was annexed relatively late in its history, and the
hymnic passages – which do not join to a single, continuous document – similarly
are treated independently of one another, as distinct reflections of different eras
in the history of Hebrew religious poetry. The discussion of each such element
relies on detailed scrutiny of the literary, textual, and linguistic evidence, in an
attempt to map as accurately as possible the complex paths of compositional
development that every text underwent, to the extent that it can be recovered on
the basis of the evidence at our disposal. The order of chapters follows the reconstructed sequence of the various compositional stages, from the earliest recoverable formation to the latest supplementation.

Chapter 1 is devoted to the satirical passages, which form the backbone of the
prophecy as a whole: vv. 2–5, 8–9, 14–15 (in consideration also of the framework
represented by vv. 1, 16). While acknowledging the compositional unity of this

---

51 For a fuller discussion see below, Chapter 1.

strand, I nevertheless argue that two literary strata may be identified within it. I submit that at the heart of the satirical presentation of idolatry lies a quotation from a lost literary source that described with some detail the manufacturing of cult images. This quotation was extracted and reframed by polemical statements, aiming at ridiculing its descriptions and exposing the falsehood of idolatry. While in some intriguing respects the cultic source is akin to biblical priestly literature, the framing statements are couched in the style and phraseology that typify the rest of the Book of Jeremiah. The linguistic profile of this strand also allows for the possibility that the prophecy – in this early formation – should not be divorced from the corpus of material attributed to Jeremiah in other parts of the book (especially the relatively early strata of this material).

Chapter 2 turns to vv. 12–13, which comprise the oldest hymnic passage integrated into the prophecy – as indicated by the fact that it is the only passage of its kind witnessed by 𝔊. Although evidently this hymnic passage was incorporated into the prophetic unit as a single block, I argue that a close reading uncovers signs of its being the product of combining two different – and originally independent – ingredients: a sapiential saying, which takes its roots in wisdom literature, and a psalmic description of the benevolent deity. The combination of two such disparate traditions motivated several rounds of textual reshuffling, but traces of the various stages are still discernible in both direct textual witnesses and indirect testimonies, embedded in a number of biblical and apocryphal sources. Neither the passage nor its constituents exhibit linguistic markers of a late date, so that they may well belong to relatively early material contained in Jeremiah. The insertion of vv. 12–13 into the specific context of the polemical prophecy may have happened at a later stage, but there are some grounds for thinking that this stage too belongs to an early phase in the formation of the unit.

Chapter 3 focuses on v. 11. While its content and polemical tone connect this passage to the satirical strand, its Aramaic language and several other peculiar features indicate that it originates in a different source. I argue that this passage was cut and pasted from a piece of imperial Achaemenid propaganda, which can be dated to the mid-fifth century BCE. As the passage predicts destruction to all gods that lack the power of creation, a Judean scribe appropriated this passage in order to amplify the anti-idolatry message of the prophecy. Detached from its original context, however, the passage implicitly questions the divine nature of the idols, so that its incorporation into the prophecy contributed to the gradual transformation of its polemical rhetoric into a statement of (proto-)monotheistic belief. Moreover, tracing the subsequent development of v. 11 in the Aramaic versions reveals the growing importance of the ethnic component in the communal identity reflected in and promoted by the prophecy.

Chapter 4 moves to the hymnic passage of v. 10. Although it comprises a very short textual sample, its language nevertheless suggests that, in its present form, it stems from the early exilic period. Some clues suggest that the text of the passage underwent a significant, theologically-motivated change, which transformed it from a hymn glorifying God's sovereignty over nature into a praise of his political control of the nations. This change enhances the sensitivity to the ethnic component in the identity of the community that fostered the transmission of the prophecy, thus betraying something of the spiritual challenges it had to face when the passage was supplemented into the text.

Chapter 5 deals with the hymnic passage of vv. 6–7. Its language suggests that it is the latest text supplemented to the prophecy, deep into the exilic period. It appears to constitute a complete poem, which draws from a theological and literary tradition that underscores God's incomparability. A comparative study of other manifestations of this tradition confirms that vv. 6–7 represent a relatively late stage and stylistically sophisticated crystallization of this tradition. At the same time, it brings to a climax the process by which the prophecy has turned into an expression of monotheism.

The discussion in each chapter builds upon analysis of evidence culled from various sources. Particularly intricate matters that required a more technical mode of discussion are presented as *nota bene* (NB) digressions from the main text. Indeed, much of my argumentation relies on linguistic considerations. However, contrary to what one might have expected, I deliberately refrained from relegating the linguistic discussion to separate compartments in each chapter. Rather, I integrated such observations into the fabric of the literary-historical analysis, in order to demonstrate my contention that linguistic examination forms an inseparable part of the philological toolkit, and it should be used in close conjunction with all the other perspectives available to critical scholars – primarily textual criticism and literary-historical analysis.[52]

---

52 Readers will notice that my chronological evaluation of certain linguistic matters differs from that of Hornkohl 2014, who considers the language of Jeremiah to reflect consistently the transitional stage in the history of Biblical Hebrew, effectively datable to the sixth century BCE. Since Hornkohl's work is the most detailed, systematic, and solid study of the language of Jeremiah, and comprises a firm basis for any further exploration of this topic, an explicit comment is in place concerning our difference of opinion. This is partly because of the different scope of our projects. Hornkohl deals with the Book of Jeremiah as a whole, so that his analysis naturally opts for diachronic generalizations that can capture as many linguistic details in his corpus as possible. By contrast, the present study is a sort of 'micro-analysis' that focuses on a single prophetic unit, thus allowing for higher resolution when examining specific and isolated cases, which may be exceptional vis-à-vis the book as a whole. In addition, our approaches also differ on a more basic methodological ground, since I grant greater weight to the literary complexity of the book, which, to my mind, cannot be reduced to the differences between 𝔐 and 𝔊 and cannot

§6 Caveat

A word of caution is required before embarking to the voyage of tracing and reconstructing the compositional history of the prophecy in Jer 10:1–16. By its nature, this is a sort of a time travel – an attempt to delve back into earlier phases of the text, against the unidirectional current of diachronic progression. A range of philological tools is employed to uncover (sometimes very faint) traces of past developments, trying to overcome the obliterating effect of subsequent changes that have blurred such traces. As one proceeds further back in time, such traces become less and less clear; the outline of early developments gradually becomes increasingly hypothetical, or even speculative. Ideally, the reconstruction of every link in the chain is based on some evidence; but at a certain point – which changes from one case to another – the endeavor to reconstruct the full sequence of events becomes crucially dependent upon conjectures. Such a point marks the final frontier; from this point on, our evidence no longer allows even an informed guess. This is an unavoidable consequence of the partial nature of the evidence and of the methodological limitations of the philological method.

Every scholar who went along this path knows how thorny it might be and how tempting it is to surrender to hypotheses when the actual evidence becomes too slender to fully rely upon.[53] I have no delusion that I escaped all such entrapments, but I have tried to refrain from imposing any *unnecessary* hypotheses on the data. I can only hope that I did not err too often in my investigation. My prime objective was to respect as fully and as honestly as possible the available and recoverable evidence, and I have made my best attempt to grant due consideration to every relevant detail. If I have learned anything from years of conducting text-critical and historical-linguistic studies, it is this: small details, which may easily be dismissed as mere minutia, are sometimes revealed to preserve precious clues about the past. Their testimony deserves to be heard, even if it takes greater patience to make their sound audible. Finding the proper place for each such detail in the jigsaw puzzle is a frustrating task, since so many of its parts have been lost forever. Nevertheless, even small details have the potential to merge ultimately into a comprehensive new story, many aspects of which have not been told before.

---

be compressed into any single century. By the same token, I find implausible the proposition of Fischer 2005, who suggests that Jeremiah as a whole should be dated to the late Persian period, in the fourth century BCE (a hypothesis that is also improbabale from a linguistic point of view).

53 One needs not adhere to all strictures of the psychoanalyitical method in order to agree with Freud that "no probability, however seductive, can protect us from error; even if all parts of a problem seem to fit together like pieces of a jigsaw puzzle, one has to remember that the probable need not necessarily be the truth and the truth not always probable" (Freud 1939: 29–30).

Chapter 1

From cult to polemic

(Jer 10:2–5, 8–9, 14–16)

2 כֹּה ׀ אָמַר יְהֹוָה אֶל־דֶּרֶךְ הַגּוֹיִם אַל־תִּלְמָדוּ וּמֵאֹתוֹת הַשָּׁמַיִם אַל־תֵּחָתּוּ
כִּי־יֵחַתּוּ הַגּוֹיִם מֵהֵמָּה: 3 כִּי־חֻקּוֹת הָעַמִּים הֶבֶל הוּא כִּי־עֵץ מִיַּעַר כְּרָתוֹ מַעֲשֵׂה
יְדֵי־חָרָשׁ בַּמַּעֲצָד: 4 בְּכֶסֶף וּבְזָהָב יְיַפֵּהוּ בְּמַסְמְרוֹת וּבְמַקָּבוֹת יְחַזְּקוּם וְלוֹא יָפִיק:
5 כְּתֹמֶר מִקְשָׁה הֵמָּה וְלֹא יְדַבֵּרוּ נָשׂוֹא יִנָּשׂוּא כִּי לֹא יִצְעָדוּ אַל־תִּירְאוּ מֵהֶם
כִּי־לֹא יָרֵעוּ וְגַם־הֵיטֵיב אֵין אוֹתָם: [...] 8 וּבְאַחַת יִבְעֲרוּ וְיִכְסָלוּ מוּסַר הֲבָלִים
עֵץ הוּא: 9 כֶּסֶף מְרֻקָּע מִתַּרְשִׁישׁ יוּבָא וְזָהָב מֵאוּפָז מַעֲשֵׂה חָרָשׁ וִידֵי צוֹרֵף
תְּכֵלֶת וְאַרְגָּמָן לְבוּשָׁם מַעֲשֵׂה חֲכָמִים כֻּלָּם: [...] 14 נִבְעַר כָּל־אָדָם מִדַּעַת הֹבִישׁ
כָּל־צוֹרֵף מִפָּסֶל כִּי שֶׁקֶר נִסְכּוֹ וְלֹא־רוּחַ בָּם 15 הֶבֶל הֵמָּה מַעֲשֵׂה תַּעְתֻּעִים בְּעֵת
פְּקֻדָּתָם יֹאבֵדוּ: 16 לֹא־כְאֵלֶּה חֵלֶק יַעֲקֹב כִּי־יוֹצֵר הַכֹּל הוּא וְיִשְׂרָאֵל שֵׁבֶט נַחֲלָתוֹ
יְהֹוָה צְבָאוֹת שְׁמוֹ:

[2] Thus says the LORD: Do not learn the way of the nations, or be dismayed at the signs of the heavens; for the nations are dismayed at them. [3] For the customs of the peoples are false: a tree from the forest is cut down, and worked with an ax by the hands of an artisan; [4] people deck it with silver and gold; they fasten it with hammer and nails so that it cannot move. [5] Their idols are like a wrought palm tree, and they cannot speak; they have to be carried, for they cannot walk. Do not be afraid of them, for they cannot do evil, nor is it in them to do good. [...] [8] They are both stupid and foolish; the instruction given by idols is no better than wood! [9] Beaten silver is brought from Tarshish, and gold from Uphaz. They are the work of the artisan and of the hands of the goldsmith; their clothing is blue and purple; they are all the product of skilled workers. [...] [14] Everyone is stupid and without knowledge; goldsmiths are all put to shame by their idols; for their images are false, and there is no breath in them. [15] They are worthless, a work of delusion; at the time of their punishment they shall perish. [16] Not like these is the LORD, the portion of Jacob, for he is the one who formed all things, and Israel is the tribe of his inheritance; the LORD of hosts is his name (NRSV, slightly modified in v. 5).

DOI 10.1515/9783110530162-002

§1 Prolusion

Three passages that mock idolatry – vv. 2–5, 8–9, 14–16 – comprise the principle literary strand of the prophecy contained in Jer 10:1–16. Quantitatively, these passages encompass more than half of the material contained in the prophetic unit. Qualitatively, they grant the entire prophecy its anti-idolatrous character, which extends to other literary strands even though they do not necessarily express the same ideological trend on their own. Thus, the harsh, satirical presentation of the idols as human-made objects easily absorbs the Aramaic passage (v. 11), which predicts destruction for "gods that did not make the heavens and the earth." The hymnic passages, which praise YHWH as the creator (vv. 12–13) and universal sovereign (vv. 6–7, 10), are likewise easily integrated into the fabric of the prophecy as presenting a counterbalance for the idols' impotency to do anything at all.

From a compositional point of view, each of the strands now intertwined in the prophecy can be separated analytically from the others, thus revealing their original independence as textual segments. However, only the satirical passages form a coherent sequence of their own, exhibiting a narrative-like logic that guides its sequence. The hymnic passages do not converge; they are best regarded as either complete or fragmentary poems supplemented to the prophecy at different stages in its compositional history.[1] In many respects, the Aramaic passage is a *sui generis* fragment in prophetic literature at large.[2] The satirical passages, by contrast, are so tightly interconnected in their language, literary form, subject matter, and ideology that they must be regarded as stemming from the same original document, which was only secondarily divided into distinct paragraphs.

𝕲 furnishes partial confirmation for the original continuity between the satirical passages; there, two hymnic passages (vv. 6–7, 10) are entirely absent, and the satirical passages separated by them are closely combined (albeit with some important textual variation, discussed below). Nevertheless, 𝕲 does not fully preserve the original form of the prophetic unit because there too, hymnic (vv. 12–13) and Aramaic (v. 11) passages interfere between the satirical passages (vv. 2–5a + 9 + 5b on the one hand and vv. 14–16 on the other). Apparently, 𝕲 already evinces the marks of a relatively late reworking and supplementation.[3]

---

1 See below, Chapters 2, 4, and 5.
2 See below, Chapter 3.
3 The methodological necessity to distinguish between the concrete form of 𝕲 and the abstract notion of the *Urtext* of the prophecy is corroborated by some text-critical evidence suggesting that textual corruptions have occurred in the Hebrew text underlying 𝕲. Interestingly enough, some such corruptions are shared by 𝔐, while the original readings are witnessed by other versions (for an instructive example see below, at the end of §2.1).

Study of the satirical passages should also take into account another aspect of the literary evidence. While these passages appear to stem from an original, continuous document, this reconstructed text does not necessarily form an unanalyzable literary unity. On the contrary, the starting point for this chapter is the recognition that a close reading of the satirical passages exposes internal tensions suggesting that this strand of material should be viewed as a literary composite comprising of two sub-strands.

On the one hand, the satirical passages contain a series of clauses that depict in great detail the process of manufacturing statues of gods (vv. 3b–5a, 9). These clauses emphasize the high value of the precious materials utilized for making the cult images: silver and gold imported from distant lands, and blue and purple garments that typify royal and divine clothing. These clauses also highlight the skilled craftsmanship of the artisans entrusted with the production of the cult images: carpenters, metal smiths, and tailors.[4] Tellingly, none of these clauses explicitly condemns idolatry. Rather, they form neutral descriptions of the cult images. In other words, such clauses depict the statues without expressing a value judgment of their worship.

On the other hand, the satirical passages also contain clauses of a very different nature that aggressively ridicule idolatry, denying any divine property from such cult images (vv. 2–3a, 5b, 8, 14–16). Some of these clauses are formulated as prohibitions, reiterating the negative particle אַל "do not..." (vv. 2, 5b), thus emphasizing the beliefs and customs that the addressees are required to abstain from. These admonitory clauses grant the satirical passages their polemical character. Yet, as a matter of fact, the fierce attack on idolatry is alien to the descriptive clauses; it is restricted to the polemical clauses only.

The contrast between the two types of clauses – the descriptive vs. the polemical ones – is also evident with respect to their varying degrees of integration into the context. The descriptive clauses can be extracted easily from their present context and can be read as consecutive parts of a coherent, continuous depiction. They join into a rich and detailed piece of narrative-like sequence, which accurately portrays the process of production of cult images (§2.3). In contradistinction, the polemical passages cannot be separated from their context; when taken by themselves, they do not form a coherent textual sequence.[5]

Furthermore, the polemical clauses frame the descriptive ones and refer to them directly (§2.1–2). One who has no knowledge of the description of the idols

---

4 For the technical terminology employed in these clauses, see Schroer 1987: 197–210; cf. King 1996.

5 For instance, one cannot easily move from v. 3a (כִּי חֻקּוֹת הָעַמִּים הֶבֶל הוּא, "for the customs of the peoples are false") to v. 5b (אַל תִּירְאוּ מֵהֶם, "do not be afraid of them"), because of the grammatical incongruence in gender between the feminine subject of v. 3a (חֻקּוֹת) and the masculine pronominal suffix in v. 5b (מהם).

as being made of wood chopped especially for this purpose (v. 3b: "a tree [עֵץ] from the forest is cut down") would not comprehend the wordplay employed in v. 8 (בער as denoting both inflammation on the one hand and stupidity on the other).[6] Nor would such a reader understand why the latter passage mentions wood at all ("the instruction given by idols is no better than wood [עֵץ]"). By the same token, a reader ignorant of the specification of the metallic overlay of the statue (v. 4a: "they beautify it with silver and gold"; v. 9a: "beaten silver is brought from Tarshish, and gold from Uphaz; they are the work of the artisan and of the hands of the goldsmith [צוֹרֵף]") would find it difficult to understand why v. 14 suddenly turns to the goldsmith ("every goldsmith [צוֹרֵף] is put to shame by their idols").

The thematic, rhetorical and stylistic differences between the two types of clauses, as well as their varying relation to their context, all prompt the hypothesis that the satirical passages comprise of two literary sub-strands (§3). At its basis lies an independent, coherent, and continuous description of the production of cult images, which approaches such statues in a neutral way (vv. 3b–5a + 9; hereafter the "descriptive passages"). This text was then reframed by polemical statements, which target specific details of the basic description and construe them as nonsense (vv. 2–3a, 5b, 14–16; the "polemical passages").[7] As such, these passages function as a redactional framework, characterized by its rhetorical devices and theological tendentiousness (§4).[8] If this analysis is correct, particular attention should be granted to the descriptive passages, which testify to a lost literary source of a cultic nature (§5) – traces of which might still be found in another biblical text (§6).

§2 Layout of structural constituents

The descriptive passages in 𝔐 form two fragments (vv. 3b–5a and v. 9), each of which is framed by polemical passages (vv. 2–3a and 5b; vv. 8 and 14–15). The literary relation between the opening and closing clauses of the polemical frame of each fragment manifests itself in patterns of semantic or lexical repetition of certain keywords.

---

6 Numerous commentators recognized this wordplay, e.g., Holladay 1986–89: 1.332.

7 The final passage of v. 16 appears to form the original conclusion of the prophetic unit; see below, §7.

8 This conclusion is diametrically opposed to the view of Duhm 1901: 98–103, who considers vv. 3b–5a as a later insertion into the prophecy. For him, v. 9 is an even later hodgepodge of glosses for vv. 4a and 3b.

§2.1 The first passage

The first descriptive passage of vv. 3b–5a is enveloped by vv. 2–3a and v. 5b. The tight link between the framing polemical passages is evident in their repeated employment of a prohibitory formulation, in both the opening statement (v. 2: אל תלמדו... אל תחתו, "do not learn... do not be dismayed") and the closing one (v. 5b: אל תיראו, "do not be afraid"):

Polemical frame:	2 כה אמר יהוה אל דרך הגוים אל תלמדו ומאתות השמים אל תחתו כי יחתו הגוים מהמה 3 כי חֻקות העמים הבל הוא
	² Thus says the LORD: Do not learn the way of the nations, or be dismayed at the signs of the heavens; for the nations are dismayed at them. ³ For the customs of the peoples are false:
Descriptive fragment:	כי עץ מיער כרתו מעשה ידי חרש במעצד 4 בכסף ובזהב ייפהו במסמרות ובמקבות יחזקום ולא יפיק 5 כְּתֹמֶר מקשה המה ולא ידברו נשוא יָנָּשׂוא כי לא יצעדו
	A tree from the forest is cut down, and worked with an ax by the hands of an artisan; ⁴ people deck it with silver and gold; they fasten it with hammer and nails so that it cannot move. ⁵ Their idols are like a wrought palm tree, and they cannot speak; they have to be carried, for they cannot walk.
Polemical frame:	אל תיראו מהם כי לא ירעו וגם היטיב אין אותם
	Do not be afraid of them, for they cannot do evil, nor is it in them to do good.

The opening and closing statements also complement each other semantically. In Biblical Hebrew, the political and religious notion of worshipping can be denoted by the verb ירא, which is indeed employed in the closing statement. The opening, however, employs in its stead the verb חתת (v. 2). This distribution suggests that ירא actually is used in its concrete sense of "to fear, to be afraid'" (in which case ירא is an intransitive verb), rather than in the abstract sense of "to worship" (in which case it would have been used transitively).⁹ It follows that the opening passage restricts, in advance, the semantic scope of the verb employed in the

---

9 This usage may also explain the repetitive use of the preposition מן "from" (v. 2: ומאתות השמים; אל תחתו כי יחתו הגוים מהמה; v. 5b: אל תיראו מהם), which also makes clear that ירא, in the closing passage, is used intransitively. Therefore, ירא is to be rendered as "to be afraid" (so, correctly, the NRSV).

closing passage, thereby expressing the theological argument that there is no reason to fear the idols, thus also implying that it is also pointless to worship them.[10]

The move from the polemical framework to the descriptive content is marked by the word כי that opens v. 3b. Syntactically, this particle marks the logical relation between the generalization asserted in the polemical opening (cf. v. 3a: *"for the customs[11] of the peoples are false"*) and the detailed description that follows (vv. 3b–5a). Put differently, this construction justifies the prohibitions contained in the polemical frame. Yet in Biblical Hebrew, the particle כי may also fulfill a discursive function in organizing the structure of the text (beyond the inter-clausal level), by marking a shift between two levels of speech, such as the narrator's words and the quoted speech of other characters.[12] In other words, כי may mark the beginning of a citation, as a particular application of the usage known as "כי

---

10 ⑤ apparently attempted to capture the close relationship between חתת and ירא by rendering the former with φοβέω, which is the stereotypical equivalent of ירא. Similarly, ⵚ renders the pertinent forms with the verb ܕ݂ܚ݂ܠ, and not with ܬ݂ܒ݂ܪ, which is the usual equivalent of חתת (cf. ℭ). Saley (2010) did not realize this aspect of the translator's lexical choice, and reconstructed a variant reading in v. 2 (אל תיראו כי יֵרַאוּ, as against 𝔐 אל תחתו כי יחתו). However, this is a superfluous reconstruction (cf. below, nn. 64 and 102). Another example of unnecessary complications caused by such a mechanistic approach is provided by Saley's treatment of v. 3, in which he retroverts ⑤ τὰ νόμιμα τῶν ἐθνῶν as חֻקּוֹת הגוים for 𝔐 חֻקּוֹת העמים. Indeed, the Greek translator of Jeremiah normally employs ἔθνος for rendering גוי, whereas עם is normally rendered with λαός. However, the Greek version of the Minor Prophets – which is possibly the work of the same translator as that of Jeremiah (or at least of Jer-α)–occasionally utilizes ἔθνος for עַם (Joel 2:17; Zech 12:3; Mal 2:9), and this equivalent is found elsewhere in the Septuagint. Thus, no need exists to assume a divergent *Vorlage* in Jer 10:3 as well.

11 The term חֻקּוֹת (derived from חקק "engrave, inscribe") is probably used in this context with a double entendre. On the one hand, it refers to the idolatrous *customs* of the nations, thus paralleling דרך הגוים "the way of the nations" (v. 2; cf. חקות הגוי/הגוים in Lev 20:23; 2 Kgs 17:8). See, e.g., Ehrlich 1901: 195. On the other hand, the phrase חֻקּוֹת העמים may also denote the cultic images themselves, which are wooden, *engraved* objects (cf. Ezek 43:11; see also 1 Kgs 6:35; Ezek 8:10; 23:14). Compare the semantic ambiguity of the equivalent Akkadian term *parṣu* (Cohen and Hurowitz 1999: 277–287). At any rate, there is no need for the conjectural emendation of חקות to חתת or חתות, as proposed by BHK (following Giesebrecht 1894: 62); cf. Ehrlich 1912: 269; Tur-Sinai 1967: 182–183; Holladay 1986–89: 1.322 n. 3a.

12 The discursive use of כי is not easily translatable into other languages. This may be the reason why ⑤ lacks a rendition for the כי of v. 3b – in contrast to the כי of v. 3a, which has a syntactic, inter-clausal function – and it is appropriately rendered by ὅτι, used in ⑤ mainly for expressing a causative relation. Nevertheless, the absence of a Greek equivalent for כי in v. 3b is still puzzling, because ὅτι can actually introduce quotations and citations (LSJ *ad loc.*, §II). Moreover, under this capacity, ὅτι is often employed in ⑤ for marking citations within citations. See Aejmelaeus 1990 (=1993: 37–48).

recitativum."[13] Its occurrence here can also be interpreted as a formal marker of the shift from prophetic admonition to a quotation from a different source.

NB. The first descriptive passage contains an additional point of text-critical interest. In v. 4, 𝔐 reads בכסף ובזהב ייפהו, "*they shall beautify it* with silver and gold," and 𝔊 reads ἀργυρίῳ καὶ χρυσίῳ κεκαλλωπισμένα ἐστίν, "*they have been beautified* with silver and gold." Notwithstanding the grammatical difference between the active and passive voice, both versions clearly stem from a verbal form derived from יפה "beautiful." By contrast, 𝔗's מחפי ליה and 𝔖's ܡܨܒܬܐ testify to a variant reading ויצפהו, "and they shall deck it."[14] Aramaic חפי normally renders Hebrew כסי, and sometimes also Hebrew צפי (in the D stem: Exod 36:38; 38:28; 1 Kgs 6:32, 35).[15] In all these occurrences, 𝔖 employs the verb ܨܒܬ. Analysis of the equivalents thus makes it difficult to argue that 𝔗 exhibits here an *ad hoc* translation or a contextually-motivated rendition, e.g., because a statute is beautified by overlaying it with silver and gold.[16]

At the same time, one cannot easily deny another alternative explanation; namely, that 𝔗 might result from harmonization to Isa 40:19, וצרף בזהב ירקענו, "and a goldsmith overlays it with gold," which 𝔗 translates literally as וקינאה בדהב מחפי ליה.[17] The verbal form מחפי does not correspond lexically to anything in Jer 10:4, whereas it perfectly fits the context in Isa 40:19. According to this line of reasoning, 𝔗 does not testify to a variant Hebrew reading in Jer 10:4 but derives from an exegetical harmonization with a thematically similar passage – a phenomenon that is indeed a typical feature of 𝔗.[18] However, this reasoning does not explain 𝔖, which generally reveals no similar tendency towards harmonization between different prophetic books. Since the agreement between 𝔗 and 𝔖 does not involve their lexis but rather the semantic

---

13 BDB, 471a–472a, s.v. כי §1b. For a different opinion, see Miller 1996: 103–116. A comparable use of כי for marking a citation from another literary source whose theological argument is under rhetorical attack by the reframing passages is presented by the Song of Hannah (1 Sam 2:3); see Segal 2002: esp. 89–92.
14 Cf. Ehrlich 1912: 269. Although the passive participle employed by 𝔖 is superficially similar to the construction found in 𝔊, the two versions differ lexically from each other.
15 This lexical replacement is also characteristic of late Biblical Hebrew, probably under Aramaic influence. Compare the descriptions of Solomon's temple: ויצפהו זהב סגור, "he *decked* it with pure gold" (1 Kgs 6:20) vs. ויחפהו זהב טוב, "he *overlaid* it with fine gold" (2 Chr 3:8).
16 As suggested by Komlosh 1973: 411.
17 Churgin 1927: 52–77, esp. 75; Hayward 1987: 79 n. 2. 𝔖 renders Isa 40:19 again with ܨܒܬ.
18 Churgin (1927: 74 and n. 4) records a reverse case in which Isa 44:12 is harmonized to Jer 10:4. Note, in passing, that v. 9, in which 𝔗 translates כסף מרקע with כספא דמחפן, may further corroborate the notion of an inner-Targumic harmonization.

content of their readings, it stands to reason that they independently testify to the same Hebrew reading, shared by their *Vorlagen* but different from the one reflected in 𝔐 and 𝔊.

The scribal phenomenon responsible for this variant is confusion between the graphically similar letters צ/י in the Old Hebrew script.[19] This fact suggests that the variant developed at an early stage of the textual transmission. Moreover, the originality of the reading ויצפהו is confirmed by another – patently independent – description of cult images: וטמאתם את צפוי פסילי ואת כסף ואת אפדת מסכת זהב, "Then you will defile your silver-*covered* idols and your gold-plated images" (Isa 30:22).[20]

The conclusion that 𝔊 contains a textual corruption of this sort supports the contention – reached on independent, literary grounds – that its text is already somewhat remote from the *Urtext* of the prophetic unit (cf. above, §1).

§2.2 The second passage

The second descriptive fragment consists of v. 9, which is enveloped by v. 8 and vv. 14–15.[21] However, subsequent literary development disturbed the original layout. The Aramaic passage (v. 11) and some hymnic passages (vv. 10, 12–13) were interpolated just preceding vv. 14–15, thus distancing the closing polemical statement from its place.[22] Still, the original link between the framing statements is evident in their common employment of the verb בער (vv. 8, 14):

Polemical frame:	8 ובאחת יבערו ויכסלו מוסר הבלים עץ הוא
	[8] They are both stupid and foolish; the instruction given by idols is no better than wood!
Descriptive fragment:	9 כסף מרקע מתרשיש יובא וזהב מאופז מעשה חרש וידי צורף תכלת וארגמן לבושם מעשה חכמים כלם [...]
	[9] Beaten silver is brought from Tarshish, and gold from Uphaz. They are the work of the artisan and of the hands of the goldsmith; their clothing is blue and purple; they are all the product of skilled workers. [...]

---

19 For this type of textual corruption, see Talmon 1985 (=2010: esp. 159–170).
20 Perles 1906: 388.
21 Notably, vv. 14–15 are duplicated in Jer 51:17–18, but with no significant difference between the two versions, neither in 𝔐 nor in 𝔊.
22 For the possible reasons for the interpolation of these passages in their present place, see the following chapters that discuss each passage respectively.

Polemical *frame:*	14 נבער כל אדם מדעת הביש כל צורף מפסל כי שקר נסכו ולא רוח בם 15 הבל המה מעשה תעתעים בעת פקדתם יאבדו [14] Everyone is stupid and without knowledge; goldsmiths are all put to shame by their idols; for their images are false, and there is no breath in them. [15] They are worthless, a work of delusion; at the time of their punishment they shall perish.

Here, too, the opening and closing passages complement each other semantically. The keyword that connects both polemical statements is semantically ambiguous, since the verb בער may be interpreted in either a concrete sense ("to flame, burn") or an abstract sense ("to be stupid, brutish").[23] Yet the direction of the semantic complementation between the two statements is opposed to the one exhibited by the first passage. In the latter, the semantic scope of ירא was *narrowed* to the concrete sense, already in the opening statement. In the present case, however, the semantic scope of בער is *broadened* to include also its abstract sense. Moreover, this broadening takes place only in the closing statement, while the opening one (v. 8) plays on the semantic ambiguity of the verb: the conjoining of the words יבערו ויכסלו directs the reader to the abstract sense, while the continuation עץ הוא hints to the concrete one.

This contrast in rhetorical strategy between the two passages is not incidental. Arguably, it relates to a textual difference between v. 8 and the other polemical passages; namely, the fact that v. 8 is absent from 𝔊 (unlike vv. 2–3a, 5b and 14–15, which are all represented therein). The convergence of two types of evidence – the textual and the semantic – suggests that v. 8 is not an original part of the redactional layer represented by the other polemical passages but was added to it somewhat later. Whoever interpolated v. 8 did his best to integrate it, as smoothly as possible, into the structure and rhetorical texture of the prophetic unit. Still, the peculiar treatment of the keyword, as well as the absence of v. 8 from 𝔊, betray v. 8 as being a patch sewn into its present place at a relatively late stage.

Attention to another difference between the textual witnesses may help illuminate the purpose of this addition. In 𝔊, v. 9 does not stand by its own (as it does in 𝔐) but directly continues v. 5a. Thus the need to separate v. 9 by placing v. 8 preceding it does not exist in the shorter text of 𝔊. Such a redactional need exists

---

23 Some lexica surmise that these two senses should be divided between historically distinct verbs, i.e., בער₁ "to burn" (< *b-ġ-r) and בער₂ "to graze" (< *b-ʕ-r, denominative from בְּעִיר "livestock, cattle"), on the basis of an Arabic verb بَغَرَ "to have an unquenchable thirst" (Barth 1902: 6–7; cf. HALOT, 145–146; Ges18 1.164–165). However, the existence of *b-ʕ-r "to burn" is confirmed by Ugaritic (del Olmo Lete and Sanmartín 2004: 1.212), even though its phonological inventory still preserves the historical consonant *ġ. Hence, we should refrain from distinguishing between two homonymic lexemes and maintain בער as a single, polysemic verb.

only in the longer text of 𝔐, in which v. 9 forms a fragment of its own, independent of vv. 3b–5a. If 𝔊 reflects here an older form of the text (as advocated below), the addition of v. 8 should be explained as part of the separation of v. 9 from vv. 3b–5a. Originally, there was only *one* descriptive passage (vv. 3b–5a + 9), surrounded by a single rhetorical frame with vv. 2–3a functioning as its opening and v. 5b + 14–15 as its closure. The fact that v. 5b and vv. 14–15 originally belonged together is reflected in their similar syntax, since both passages make use of a causal construction marked by כי.[24] Only after the descriptive passage was divided into *two* fragments was each of them embedded into its own polemical framework. At this later stage, v. 5b was employed as the closing statement of the first fragment (with vv. 2–3a becoming the opening statement of the first fragment alone), while v. 8 was interpolated in order to supply an opening statement for the second fragment (for which vv. 14–15 alone have now become the closing statement).[25]

§2.3 Internal logic of the descriptive passages

As it turns out, the textual witnesses present two formations of the descriptive passages: they are found as a single block in 𝔊, and in two separate fragments in 𝔐. Thematically, these passages unfold the full chain of production of manufacturing cult images, stage by stage. It begins with the selection of a suitable tree, which is then chopped with an appropriate cutting tool (v. 3b).[26] The narrator then moves to describe how the wooden core is overlaid with precious metals (v. 4a) and how its disparate parts are connected together, again by using specific tools (v. 4b). The finished statue – by now considered

---

24 In v. 5b, this construction is employed for explaining the admonition not to fear the idols (אל תיראו מהם כי לא ירעו, "Do not be afraid of them, *for* they cannot do evil" etc.). In v. 14, the same construction explains why people should feel ashamed and stupid for worshipping lifeless objects (נבער כל אדם מדעת הביש כל צורף מפסל כי שקר נסכו ולא רוח בם, "Everyone is stupid and without knowledge, goldsmiths are all put to shame by their idols, *for* their images are false, and there is no breath in them"). Thus, both passages share the same rhetorical matrix, which independently suggests that they belong together.

25 Note, in passing, that the redactional reshuffling resulted in an incidental, internal parallel between the two groups of passages in terms of the order of reference to the materials used for constructing cultic images, beginning with wood and followed by silver and gold: "A *tree* from the forest is cut down, and worked with an ax by the hands of an artisan; people deck it with *silver and gold*" (vv. 3b–4a), "the instruction given by idols is no better than *wood!* Beaten *silver* is brought from Tarshish, and *gold* from Uphaz" (vv. 8b–9a).

26 For identification of מעצד as an adze see Koller 2012: 61–70; 2013 (but note the critique of Williamson 2015: 682).

a single piece of workmanship (מקשה) – is then carried away, i.e., outside of the artisans' workshop.

At this point, a problem surfaces in the narrative-like sequence according to 𝔐. It presents a regression to a previous stage in the chain of production, by having v. 9 describing the lavish garments with which the statues are adorned: jewelry made of precious metals imported from distant lands (v. 9a) and royal clothing made of blue and purple fabrics (v. 9b). Based on the narrative logic of the description, one would have expected this depiction to be located *after* the description of the overlaying of the body of the statue (v. 4) and joining its limbs together (v. 5a), but *before* the stage in which the finished statue is carried away (v. 5b). In other words, one would expect v. 9 to be placed exactly where it is indeed found according to 𝔊; i.e., following v. 5a:[27]

³ ὅτι τὰ νόμιμα τῶν ἐθνῶν μάταια· ξύλον ἐστὶν ἐκ τοῦ δρυμοῦ ἐκκεκομμένον, ἔργον τέκτονος καὶ χώνευμα· ⁴ ἀργυρίῳ καὶ χρυσίῳ κεκαλλωπισμένα ἐστίν· ἐν σφύραις καὶ ἥλοις ἐστερέωσαν αὐτά, καὶ οὐ κινηθήσονται· ⁵ᵃ ἀργύριον τορευτόν ἐστιν, οὐ πορεύσονται· ⁹ *ἀργύριον προσβλητὸν ἀπὸ Θαρσις ἥξει, χρυσίον Μωφας καὶ χεὶρ χρυσοχόων, ἔργα τεχνιτῶν πάντα· ὑάκινθον καὶ πορφύραν ἐνδύσουσιν αὐτά·* ⁵ᵇ αἰρόμενα ἀρθήσονται, ὅτι οὐκ ἐπιβήσονται. μὴ φοβηθῆτε αὐτά, ὅτι οὐ μὴ κακοποιήσωσι, καὶ ἀγαθὸν οὐκ ἔστιν ἐν αὐτοῖς.

³ Because the precepts of the nations are vain: there is a tree from the forest, cut down, a work of a craftsman, and a molten image. ⁴ They have been beautified with silver and gold; they fastened them with hammers and nails, and they shall not be moved. ⁵ᵃ Wrought silver it is – they will not walk. ⁹ *Beaten silver will come from Tharsis, gold of Mophas,*[28] *and a hand of goldsmiths – works of craftsmen all; they will clothe them in blue and purple.* ⁵ᵇ Raised they will be carried, because they will not walk. Do not be afraid of them, because they shall not do evil, and there is no good in them.

---

27 I see no justification for the arbitrary determination of some commentators that the correct place of v. 9 is within v. 4 (e.g., Rudolph 1958: 64, 67; Bright 1965: 76, 79–80).

28 𝔊's reading Μωφας is evidently a transcription, but it is difficult to know to what extent the *Vorlage* differed from 𝔐. Does the transcription reflect an approximate pronunciation of מאופז (with phonetic elision of the glottal stop)? Or does it reflect a divergent consonantal text (cf. מופז in 1 Kgs 10:18)? Or does it interpret the word as a place name, i.e., Mofaz (as implied by Ziegler 1976: 200, who printed Μωφας)? In either case, the variant reading מאופיר, "from Ophir," witnessed by 𝔖 and 𝔗 (and possibly also Theodotion) may well be the preferred reading at this point. For the text-critical problem, cf. Barthélemy 1986: 544; Gregor 1988. For Jerome's comment *ad loc.*, see Graves 2007: 124–125.

This state of affairs confirms the originality of the textual sequence witnessed by 𝔊 and supports the contention that its formation of the satirical passages is earlier than the one reflected in 𝔐.

> NB. The older age of the text underlying 𝔊 may be discerned in yet another detail, which also bears important implications for evaluating the literary relation between the idol parodies of Deutero-Isaiah and the polemical passages of Jer 10:1–16.

As mentioned above, v. 3b refers to a cutting tool denoted by the term מעצד. This term is one of the most conspicuous points of contact between the prophecy of Jer 10:1–16 and Deutero-Isaiah, since its distribution in Biblical Hebrew is restricted to Jer 10:3b and Isa 44:12. However, in contrast to Isa 44:12, where מעצד is aptly rendered by 𝔊 with σκέπαρνον, in Jer 10:3b the term is attested to only according to 𝔐. 𝔊 testifies to a different, shorter text: ἔργον τέκτονος καὶ χώνευμα, "a work of a craftsman and a molten image," which may be retroverted as מעשה חרש ומסכה. Moreover, 𝔊's reading is supported by an independent description of idol production: ויעשו להם מסכה מכספם כתבונם עצבים מעשה חרשים כלה, "they made for themselves *a molten image* (𝔊 χώνευμα) made of their silver, according to their understanding, idols all of which are the *work of craftsmen* (𝔊 ἔργα τεκτόνων)" (Hos 13:2).

𝔐's מעשה ידי חרש evidently represents an expansion of the original reading מעשה חרש (witnessed by 𝔊),[29] possibly under the liturgical influence of the covenantal curses listed in Deut 27:15,[30] which reads:

ארור האיש אשר יעשה **פסל ומסכה**	Cursed be anyone who makes *an idol or a molten image*,
תועבת יהוה **מעשה ידי חרש**	anything abhorrent to the LORD, *the work of a craftsman*,
ושם בסתר	and sets it up in secret.

If this hypothesis is correct, 𝔐's reading may reflect a Deuteronomistic-like element. At any rate, the difference between 𝔊 and 𝔐 at this point is better credited to a deliberate reworking rather than to textual corruption.[31]

---

29 Cf. below, §3.

30 As suggested by Janzen 1973: 38.

31 Contrary to Streane (1896: 123), who thinks that במעצד developed from ומצק, since מצק in 1 Kgs 7:16 is rendered there in 𝔊 by χωνευτός. Cf. Rabin, Talmon and Tov 1997: נג, n. 4 for v. 3.

§2.4 Fragmentation

Both literary-historical and text-critical considerations indicate that the descriptive passages originally comprised a single, continuous quotation from an unknown literary source, which is preserved relatively intact in 𝕲. At a later stage, represented by 𝔐, the citation was broken into two fragments – each of which was then embedded within its own rhetorical framework.

What was the ideological motivation of this redactional process of fragmentation? Its main element appears to be the moving of v. 5b from its original place – following the descriptive citation, i.e., after v. 9 (as in 𝕲) – to an alternative location following v. 5a (as in 𝔐).[32] If so, any solution to the problem should begin with analysis of the content and style of v. 5b.

In its original context, v. 5b had joined v. 2–3a as the corresponding parts of the rhetorical framework. Indeed, v. 2 and v. 5b are the only passages in our prophecy that directly address the audience in the second person plural, and both are formulated as prohibitions that encourage the addressees not to fear the gods of the nations:

v. 2:   ומאתות השמים אל תחתו   Do not be afraid of the signs of the heavens.
v. 5b: אל תיראו מהם   Do not fear them.

At the same time, a clause contained in v. 5b is similar in form to the negative clauses contained in the descriptive v. 5a:[33]

v. 5b: כי לא ידעו   ...for they cannot do evil.
v. 5a: ולא ידברו [...] כי לא יצעדו   ...and they cannot speak... for they cannot walk.

The relocation of v. 5b so that it would immediately follow v. 5a apparently relies on – and amplifies – the latter similarity of formulation. The older formation of the prophecy contained, in the descriptive passages, an explicit admittance that the idols lack the power to move independently as humans. The redactor responsible for moving the polemical v. 5b to a point following v. 5a wished to underscore this argument even further: not only are the idols unable to move on their own, they have no power whatsoever to influence human lives, as they can cause humans neither good nor harm. In other words, placing v. 5b as a direct sequel of vv. 4b–5a radicalizes the polemical interpretation of the descriptive passages.

---

32 This is in contrast to the view of most commentators, who believe that the main difference between 𝕲 and 𝔐, in this respect, pertains to the location of v. 9. For instance, McKane (1986–89: 1.220) argues that the different locations of v. 9 suggest that it is a secondary insertion (on p. 224, he hesitantly suggests an additional hypothesis; namely, that the placement of v. 9 depends on that of v. 8a).

33 In my view, the negative clauses of v. 5a indeed comprise part and parcel of the descriptive passages; see the detailed discussion below, §5.1.

Therefore, a theological and rhetorical continuation exists between the two redactional stages identified above:

(a) Originally, a single quotation was reframed with an opening and concluding statements that target those descriptive elements that admit the idols' weakest points: their material nature, the human proficiency of the artisans preparing them, and the explicit declaration that the images cannot move by themselves. The rhetorical framework deduced, from these points, that as human-made artifacts, the idols are inherently impotent.

(b) Later, special attention was paid to the last point; the polemical conclusion deduced from it was enhanced by moving v. 5b so that it would follow v. 5a, thereby breaking the descriptive quotation into two fragments. Tellingly, the redactor sought to repair the damaged rhetorical framework by adding a new opening statement to the second fragment (v. 8). This procedure suggests that the redactor was still aware of the original nature of the descriptive passages as forming a quotation from another source and was determined to maintain the literary strategy of reframing them with polemical statements.

The redactor's awareness of the original nature of the descriptive passages, matched by the close stylistic similarity between v. 8 and the other polemical passages, suggest the possibility (that cannot be proven definitively) that the time-span separating between the two redactional stages was not very great and that both stages originate in the same scribal and ideological circle.

§3 Stylistic profiles

The descriptive and polemical passages differ from each other not only in their content but also in their style and phraseology. The descriptive nature of the former group results primarily from nominal clauses, which imply a given state of affairs:

v. 5a: כתמר מקשה המה They are like a wrought palm tree.
v. 9: תכלת וארגמן לבושם Their clothing is blue and purple.
מעשה חכמים כלם They are all the product of skilled workers.

The descriptive passages, however, also include verbal clauses, in which the verb takes a *yiqtol* form, which occupies a clause-final position:

v. 4: בכסף ובזהב ייפהו They beautify it with silver and gold.
במסמרות ובמקבות יחזקום They fasten it with hammer and nails.
v. 9: כסף מרֻקע מתרשיש יובא Beaten silver is brought from Tarshis.

The grammatical form and constituent-order both point that, in these clauses, the verb encodes non-volitive modality, which is commonly attached to the progressive or habitual present (that can also extend into the future).[34] Put differently, all these clauses depict the normal state of affairs, whose duration is not chronologically delimited. As such, their syntactic texture is diametrically opposed to the polemical passages, which seek to demonstrate that the idols are temporary and perishable objects, whose destruction is pending.

Thematically, the descriptive passages betray intimate knowledge of cult images and the process of their manufacturing – knowledge that can hardly be imagined without some sort of contact with the cultic context in which such images were present and functional. It stands to reason, therefore, that the descriptive passages originate from a literary source that described cultic images and related ritual practices (I thus designate it hereafter as the "cultic source").

Confirmation for the hypothesis that the thematic and stylistic differences between the two types of passages result from the imposition of a redactional stratum on an older, cultic source comes from inspection of the distinct phraseologies of the polemical and descriptive passages.

(a) In the descriptive passages, one finds construct phrases whose *nomen regens* is מעשה, "work, workmanship," while the *nomen rectum* refers to the artisan:[35]

v. 3b: מעשה ידי חרש   work by the hands of a craftsman
v. 9:   מעשה חרש וידי צורף   work of a craftsman, by the hands of a goldsmith
          מעשה חכמים   work of skilled men

These expressions are unparalleled within the book of Jeremiah, nor in the idol parodies of Deutero-Isaiah. By contrast, they resemble the typical phraseology

---

34 In contradistinction, when a *yiqtol* form takes a clause-initial position, it encodes a volitive modality; i.e., it functions as a jussive (even if the grammatical form is formally ambiguous). Joosten (2011) demonstrates the different syntactic constructions by contrasting the following two passages: ישמעו העברים, "Let the Hebrews hear!" (1 Sam 13:3; volitive modality) vs. וכל העם ישמעו, "All the people will hear" (Deut 17:13; non-volitive modality). Cf. Joosten 2012: esp. 261–267, 333–340.

35 Note, in passing, that this type of phrase furnishes yet another example of the way in which the polemical passages directly address and mock the descriptive ones. The polemical redaction takes up the pattern of מעשה חרש and satirically modulates it as a מעשה תעתעים, "work of mockery" (v. 15). It is not impossible that the latter expression is also intended as a wordplay on a specific technical term such as מעשה צעצעים (2 Chr 3:10, used in reference to the cherubim). The term צעצעים seems to denote a casting (see the lexica *ad loc.*), even though contextually it appears to refer to wooden objects only plated with gold. Hence, thematically, the allegation implicit in the wordplay might resonate with the earlier mention of כֶּתֶם/כְּתֹמֶר מקשה (v. 5a; cf. below, §5.1 [2]).

of Pentateuchal, Priestly literature (P) – especially the detailed instructions concerning the establishment of the Tabernacle and the manufacturing of its cultic paraphernalia.[36] Indeed, P overflows with comparable – albeit not identical – phrases:

- מעשה חָרָשׁ, "work of an artisan"[37]
- מעשה חֹשֵׁב, "work of a cloth-worker"[38]
- מעשה רֹקֵם, "work of an embroider"[39]
- מעשה אֹרֵג, "work of a weaver"[40]
- מעשה רֹקֵח, "work of a perfumer"[41]

The descriptive passages also employ other words and phrases that distinguish them from the rest of the book of Jeremiah:

(b) The word כסף refers to the metal utilized by goldsmiths (vv. 4, 9),[42] rather than denoting the silver ingots used in economic transactions.[43]

(c) The collocation תכלת וארגמן "blue and purple" (v. 9) is found in no other passage of Jeremiah; however, it is very common in P's cultic instructions as well as in Ezekiel's prophecies, which may also be viewed as an extension of priestly literature.[44]

(d) The technical term מקשה "wrought metal, hammered work" (v. 5a) is attested in the Hebrew Bible only here and in P.[45]

---

36 To be sure, such expressions are not unique to Priestly sources. The phrase מעשה חרשים, "work of craftsmen," is also found in a non-Priestly source such as Hos 13:2 (though note that it is employed there in describing cult images); and the phrase מעשה אֹפֶה, "work of a baker," is used in Gen 40:17 for denoting pastries brought to Pharaoh's table. Nonetheless, the distribution of phrases of this type, as well as their semantic structure (i.e., their care to explicitly name the artisan responsible for the product), are characteristic of cultic specifications like the technical instructions embedded in Priestly literature.
37 Exod 28:11.
38 Exod 26:1, 31; 28:6, 15; 36:8, 35; 39:3, 8.
39 Exod 26:36; 27:16; 28:39; 36:37; 38:18; 39:29.
40 Exod 28:32; 39:22, 27.
41 Exod 30:35; 37:29.
42 Compare Ezek 16:13, 17; 22:18, 20, 22, etc.
43 So Jer 32:9, 10, 25, 44; cf. Ezek 7:19, etc.
44 Exod 25:4; 26:1, 31, 36; 27:16; 28:5, 6, 8, 15, 33; 35:6, 23, 25, 35; 36:8, 35, 37; 38:18, 23; 39:1, 2, 3, 5, 8, 24, 29; Ezek 27:7. Compare the descriptions of the temple in 2 Chr 2:13; 3:14, which are apparently influenced by the Priestly depictions of the Tabernacle.
45 See below, n. 94.

By contrast, the polemical passages exhibit a number of terms and expressions that typify the Book of Jeremiah as a whole:[46]

(e) The noun הבל, a keyword recurring time and again in vv. 3a, 8, 15 and highlighting the null nature of the idols, is a typical item of Jeremiah's diction, especially in reference to idols.[47]

(f) The admonitory address אל תחתו "do not be afraid" (v. 2) is a common formula in Jeremiah.[48] It is also reminiscent of a Deuteronomistic phrase attested in the Books of Deuteronomy and Joshua.[49]

(g) The temporal designation בעת פקדתם, "at the time of their visitation" (v. 15), is an item unique to Jeremiah's phraseology.[50]

(h) The compound, contrastive clause לא ירעו וגם היטיב אין אותם, "they cannot do evil, nor is it in them to do good" (v. 5b), also resembles the formulation of other passages in this book.[51]

As is common in Jeremiah, it is difficult to determine regarding items (e)–(h) whether they are anchored in the original wording of the prophet or rather should be assigned to later – especially Deuteronomistic – redactors.[52] Still, it is safe to conclude that the style and phraseology of the polemical passages are essentially characteristics of other parts of the Book of Jeremiah. Such passages sharply differ from the conspicuous stylistic profile of the descriptive passages. This fact

---

46 Obviously, scholars have already sensed the stylistic affinity between such passages and the diction characteristic of Jeremiah, but they did not distinguish between the polemical and the descriptive passages, considering both to comprise a single literary layer. See, e.g., Holladay 1986–89: 1.329.

47 Jer 2:5; 8:19; 14:22; 16:19; cf. Deut 32:21; 1 Kgs 16:13, 26; 2 Kgs 17:15. Cohen and Hurowitz (1999: 287–290) call attention to the comparable employment of Akkadian *zaqīqu* in a literary work that ridicules a heterodox cult that Nabonidus practiced only a few decades after the life-course of Jeremiah.

48 Jer 1:17; 17:18; 30:10; 46:27; cf. Ezek 2:6; Isa 51:7.

49 Deut 1:21; Josh 1:9; 8:1; 10:25.

50 Jer 8:12; cf. 46:21; 50:27; 51:18. Compare the similar phrase בשנת פקדתם "at the year of their visitation" in Jer 11:23; 23:12; 48:44. In Jer 10:15, 4QJer[b] reads a finite verb, בעת פקדתם "at the time that I visit them" (rather than the verbal noun פְּקֻדָּה, as found in 𝔐), but this formula too is found in other passages of the book. See Jer 6:15; cf. 49:8; 50:31.

51 Cf. Jer 4:22, חכמים המה להרע ולהיטיב לא ידעו, "They are skilled in doing evil, but do not know how to do good"; 13:23, גם אתם תוכלו להיטיב לְמֻדֵי הרע, "Then also you can do good who are accustomed to do evil". However, while this feature may be typical of Jeremiah, it cannot be considered unique to this book, for it is also found in other biblical sources, e.g., Isa 41:23, אף תיטיבו ותרעו, "do good, or do harm"; cf. Lev 5:4; Josh 24:20; Zeph 1:12.

52 Note, for instance, the hesitance regarding הבל exhibited by Thiel 1973: 81.

lends further corroboration to the basic distinction between the two types of passages within the satirical passages.

This conclusion casts some doubt on the common – albeit not universal – critical contention that Jer 10:1–16 as a whole has no connection with prophecies attributable to Jeremiah, due primarily to its conspicuous similarities with the idol parodies found in Deutero-Isaiah. This point does not depend on the intriguing question of whether Deutero-Isaiah's idol parodies indeed stem from the anonymous prophet of the mid-sixth century BCE, or whether they should be viewed as later additions.[53] The crucial point for the present discussion is only the fact that the similarities of Jer 10:1–16 to Deutero-Isaiah are actually limited in scope, as far as the formation witnessed by 𝕲 is concerned. They become more pronounced mostly in the reworked version of 𝔐. This situation, in addition to the fact that the polemical passages comprising the prophetic redaction of the cultic source actually exhibit stylistic traits that are characteristic of the Book of Jeremiah, supports the possibility that at least the satirical passages – which form the core of the prophecy in Jer 10:1–16 – indeed belong to the corpus of prophecies authored by Jeremiah or at least attributed to him at a very early stage of the compositional history of the book.

§4 Subsequent development

Scrutiny of the text-critical evidence suggests that the redactional activity that reshaped the cultic source was neither the product of a single scribal act nor a one-time manipulation of the underlying text. Rather, it was a continuous process, during which the distinctive stylistic features of the cultic source were gradually eroding, being adapted, step-by-step, to the typical diction of the Book of Jeremiah.

This process may be illustrated with phrases of the type מעשה חרש, "work of a craftsman." In such cases, 𝕲 reflects readings that match simple construct phrases, while 𝔐 expands them by integrating a reference to the artisans' hands:

– v. 3b: 𝕲 ἔργον τέκτονος = מעשה חרש, "work of a craftsman"

   vs. 𝔐 מעשה ידי חרש, "work *by the hands* of a craftsman"

---

53 See the Introduction, §4.4.

- v. 9: 𝕲 καὶ χεὶρ χρυσοχόων ἔργα τεχνιτῶν = יד צורף מעשה חרש, "and a hand of a goldsmiths, works of craftsmen"[54]
vs. 𝔐 מעשה חרש וידי צורף, "work of a craftsman *and by the hands* of a goldsmith"[55]

𝕲's readings are consistent with the pattern "work of a craftsman," which is common in Priestly cultic instructions, whereas 𝔐's expanded phrases follow the alternative pattern of "work *by the hands* of a craftsman." The latter is recorded in various passages throughout the Hebrew Bible, especially in polemical descriptions of human-made idols;[56] but it is particularly characteristic to the book of Jeremiah,[57] and more generally to Deuteronomic and Deuteronomistic literature.[58]

It is difficult to assume a process of adaptation that progresses in the opposite direction – from 𝔐 to 𝕲. Why would anyone take the trouble of blurring stylistic traits that are common in Jeremiah and changing them into distinctive features alien to their present context? It is much more reasonable that the stylistic traits of the cultic source were originally exceptional vis-à-vis Jeremiah at large, and they were leveled out by scribes and copyists in order to adapt them to the thematic and contextual framework imposed by the polemical redaction and in accordance with the lexis and phraseology typical of Jeremiah.

---

54 Note the difference in grammatical number between 𝕲 and 𝔐 with respect to the *nomina recta*: plural in 𝕲 ("and a hand of *goldsmiths*, works of *craftsmen*") vs. singular in 𝔐 ("a work of a *craftsman* and by the hand of a *goldsmith*"). This grammatical difference, however, need not be credited to the Hebrew *Vorlage* of the Greek translator. Although the double marking of the plural in construct phrases is not uncommon in the Book of Jeremiah (Hornkohl 2014: 273–282, §7.11), the terms חרש and צורף in 𝔐 are meant as collective singulars, so that their rendition by Greek plural forms is reasonable.

55 The goldsmiths' hands are also mentioned in 𝕲, but this version reflects a different syntax compared to 𝔐. In 𝕲, the "hands of goldsmiths" and "works of craftsmen" comprise two independent construct phrases, whereas in 𝔐 they are integrated into a single, complex construct phrase: "a work of a craftsman and by the hand of a goldsmith." Hence, the relation between the two versions is not exhausted by simple transposition between the phrases מעשה חרש and ידי צורף.

56 This pattern is common in biblical poetry, including prophetic literature (e.g., Isa 2:8; 17:8; Hos 14:4; Mic 5:12, etc.) and psalmic literature (e.g., Ps 115:4; 135:15, etc.). Thus, 𝔐's readings again reflect the trend of adapting the text to common stylistic standards that are alien to their original formulation.

57 Jer 1:16; 25:6, 7, 14; 32:30; 44:8.

58 See especially Deut 4:28; 27:15; 2 Kgs 19:18 ‖ Isa 37:19; cf. Deut 2:7; 14:29; 16:15; 24:19; 28:12; 30:9; 31:29; 1 Kgs 16:7; 2 Kgs 22:17. See Kratz 1991: 201 and cf. below, end of §2.3. Note that the phrase מעשה־ידי-X never occurs in Priestly literature, nor in the other narrative sources embedded in the Pentateuch and the Former Prophets. For the ideological background of this phrase, cf. Dick 1999: 34–41.

The process of stylistic adaptation also involved an ideological implication. To some extent, the mentioning of the artisan's hands diverts the focus of the prophetic polemic by shifting the attention from the cultic object (the idol) to its manufacturer (the human artisan). This ideological recalibration transpires from additional differences between the two versions:

1. V. 3 describes the chopping of the wood for the purpose of making an idol. 𝕲 reads ξύλον ἐστὶν ἐκ τοῦ δρυμοῦ ἐκκεκομμένον, "there is a tree from the forest, cut down," employing a passive participle modifying "tree." 𝔐, however, reads עֵץ מִיַּעַר כְּרָתוֹ, employing instead a finite verb whose subject is the human carpenter.[59]

2. V. 4 describes the overlaying of the statue with precious metals. 𝕲 reads ἀργυρίῳ καὶ χρυσίῳ κεκαλλωπισμένα ἐστίν, "*they have been beautified with silver and gold*," employing a participle referring to the cult images.[60] 𝔐 reads בכסף ובזהב ייפהו, "*he beautifies* it with silver and gold," again with a finite verb whose subject is the human artisan.

3. V. 9 lists various people involved in producing the cult images. 𝕲 mentions only two such artisans, καὶ χεὶρ χρυσοχόων ἔργα τεχνιτῶν πάντα, "and a hand of *goldsmiths* – works of *craftsmen* all." 𝔐, however, mentions three: מעשה חרש וידי צורף [...] מעשה חכמים כֻּלָּם, "They are the work of the *artisan* and of the hands of the *goldsmith* [...] they are all the product of *skilled workers*."[61] It follows that 𝔐 assigns a greater role to the humans engaged in manufacturing the statues. Furthermore, the hypothesis that 𝔐's מעשה חכמים כלם is a later interpolation explains the slight grammatical difference between the

---

59 More commonly, however, this variant is credited to a textual corruption, e.g., metathesis (e.g., Streane 1896: 122; Saley 2010: 34). Elsewhere, the participial form ἐκκεκομμένον renders כֻּרָת (Judg 6:28), which is an internal passive of the G stem. But usually, this grammatical category is spelled defectively in Biblical Hebrew. If one seeks to maintain the *waw* found in כרתו, it is perhaps better to reconstruct 𝕲's *Vorlage* at this point as כָּרוּת, which is a pattern commonly spelled *plene* in Biblical Hebrew.

60 It is unclear which Hebrew form may be underlying the participial phrase κεκαλλωπισμένα ἐστίν: should the phrase be retroverted as מְיֻפִּים (Streane 1896: 123) or יֻפּוּ (Workman 1889: 303)? The passive form cannot easily be projected back to the Hebrew *Vorlage*, but lexically it must have been a derivative of יפה (cf. above, §2.1).

61 The term חכמים is employed here as a technical designation of "skilled workers" (as correctly rendered by the NRSV), and in its present context it may refer specifically to the tailors responsible for preparing the lavish garments of the cult images; cf., e.g., Exod 28:3; 35:25. In my opinion, the term does not allude to the notion of wisdom (which is evoked only in v. 12), and it has no essential relation to sapiential literature. For a different view, see Ammann 2015: 131–133.

plural form employed in this clause (חכמים) and the collective singulars attested earlier in the passage (חרש... צורף).[62]

4. V. 14 relates the shame that the artisans are supposed to feel at the false outcome of their craftsmanship. 𝕲 employs a passive construction: κατῃσχύνθη πᾶς χρυσοχόος ἐπὶ τοῖς γλυπτοῖς αὐτοῦ, "every goldsmith was put to shame at his carved images."[63] 𝔐, however, adopts an active construction, which again places the emphasis on the human agent: הביש כל צורף מפסל, "every goldsmith is ashamed by the idol."

Against these four instances, in which 𝔐 passes harsh judgment on the human craftsmen while 𝕲 reserves its criticism to the idols, there are only two opposite instances in which the two versions reflect reverse preferences:

5. V. 9 reports that the cultic statues were dressed with garments made of valuable fabrics. 𝔐 reads תכלת וארגמן לבושם, "*their clothing* is blue and purple," referring to the statues. 𝕲, however, reads ὑάκινθον καὶ πορφύραν ἐνδύσουσιν αὐτά, "*they will clothe them* in blue and purple," with an active, finite verb referring to the tailors who produced the garments.[64]

6. V. 14 refers to the statue as a molten image. 𝔐 reads כי שקר נסכו, "for *his molten image* is false," employing the noun נֶסֶךְ, which denotes the statue (cf. Isa 48:5) as a product of casting metal (cf. Isa 30:1; 40:19; 44:10). 𝕲, however, reads ὅτι ψευδῆ ἐχώνευσαν, "because *they cast* lies," with a finite verb, whose subject is the human craftsmen. 𝕲's reading is further supported by 𝔖 (ܢܣܟܘ) and 𝔗 (אתיכונון), all of which apparently presuppose the variant reading נָסְכוּ.[65]

It appears, therefore, that both 𝔐 and 𝕲 oscillate between two options regarding the precise target of the polemic: the idols or their makers. Still, 𝕲 favors the former option, while 𝔐 favors the latter. The different preferences may result from 𝕲's translation technique rather than from its Hebrew *Vorlage* (especially in cases that involve passive constructions, whose Hebrew basis cannot be

---

62 Note further the semantic similarity between the Hebrew phrase מעשה חכמים and its Akkadian equivalent *šipir ummâni* (*CAD* Š/3, 83, §6b), which suggests the possibility of a calque that betrays a late date (I thank Dr. Uri Gabbay for this observation).

63 The same syntax is found in the parallel passage of Jer 51(28):17, with only a slight variation in the preposition: κατῃσχύνθη πᾶς χρυσοχόος ἀπὸ τῶν γλυπτῶν αὐτοῦ, "every goldsmith was put to shame *by* his carved images."

64 Saley (2010: 9–10) believes that 𝕲 presupposes לבשום, which relates to 𝔐's לבושם by way of metathesis. However, the verb ἐνδύω has a causative meaning here (cf. LSJ s.v., §II), which cannot be easily retrovert as a verb in the G stem (or the D stem, which is not otherwise recorded for לבש). A verb in the H stem would have been more natural here (cf. Gen 3:21; Lev 8:13).

65 Cf., e.g., Streane 1896: 125.

easily retroverted), but this exegetical problem delves deep into the fabric of the prophecy. The shift in emphasis may well be the result of an internal development within the Greek transmission, i.e., it reflects the translator's reception of the prophecy. Put differently, 𝔊 is not only a witness to an older Hebrew formation of the text, but also a witness of its later interpretation.

* * *

An interim conclusion is in order at this point in the discussion. Philological analysis reveals several stages in the compositional history of the satirical passages that mock idolatry and comprise the main literary strand of the prophecy in Jer 10:1–16. Underlying them is a description quoted from a cultic source, which depicted the manufacturing of divine statues that serve as cult images. This description was submitted to a theologically-tendentious redaction, which polemicizes the underlying source in an attempt to present its descriptive statements as proof of the idols' impotence and, more generally, of the erroneous nature of idolatry.

The rhetorical device of citing an existing source and presenting an opposite argument based on statements detached from their original context is a common trope in Jeremiah's prophecies and in prophetic literature in general.[66] Indeed, the phraseology that typifies the polemical passages – which comprise the redactional framework – is characteristic of the general diction and style of the Book of Jeremiah at large. Such processes of literary reworking and theological reshuffling – which intend to deny the divinity of the gods of the nations by degrading them to the level of inanimate idols – are quite common in biblical literature in general and in prophecy in particular. They were operative for a long period, beginning with the very initial stages of oral prophetic speeches and extending through the latest stages of their textual transmission.[67] Indeed, comparison of the textual witnesses suggests that the redactional process was a continual one. Nonetheless, one may entertain the possibility that the satirical passages (at least in the stage of formation represented by 𝔊), which form the core of the prophetic unit, belong to one of the earliest strata in the Book of Jeremiah and theoretically may stem from the prophet's oeuvre.

§5 The cultic source

Is it possible to learn some more details about the original features of the cultic source underlying the satirical passages? An answer to this query depends, to some extent, on the textual formation of the prophecy that is submitted to scrutiny. If the starting point is 𝔐, then the quotation is broken into two fragments

---

66 See, e.g., Rom-Shiloni 2010: 58–131.
67 See, e.g., Goldstein 2005a.

(vv. 3b–5a, 9), separated not only by the framing polemical passages (vv. 5b, 8), but also by hymnic (vv. 6–7, 10) and even Aramaic (v. 11) passages, all stemming from different sources altogether. Moreover, interfering segments are also present in 𝕲. Nonetheless, 𝕲 (supported by 4QJer[b]) still testifies to an alternative literary formation, according to which at least the descriptive passages assignable to the cultic source indeed comprise part of a single block of text (vv. 3b–5a + 9), while the polemical passages do not invade into the quotation but rather frame its external margins (vv. 2–3a preceding the citation and v. 5b following it). As concluded above, 𝕲 appears to represent an older literary stage compared to the discontinuous formation represented by 𝔐.

§5.1 The negative clauses

The formation represented by 𝕲 presents a comprehensible narrative flow. However, even there, the descriptive sequence is thrice interrupted by short negative clauses that assert that cult images cannot perform vital actions:

v. 4:	ולוא יפיק[68]	καὶ οὐ κινηθήσονται	"And they[69] shall not be moved."
v. 5a:	ולא ידברו	οὐ πορεύσονται	"They will not walk."
	כי לא יצעדו	ὅτι οὐκ ἐπιβήσονται	"Because they will not walk."[70]

On first sight, these cases resemble the negative clauses characteristic of the polemical passages:

v. 5b:	כי לא ידעו	ὅτι οὐ μὴ κακοποιήσωσιν	"for they cannot do evil
	וגם היטיב אין אותם	καὶ ἀγαθὸν οὐκ ἔστιν ἐν αὐτοῖς	nor is it in them to do good"
v. 14:	ולא רוח בם	οὐκ ἔστι πνεῦμα ἐν αὐτοῖς	"and there is no breath in them"

---

68 The orthography of the negative particle fluctuates in 𝔐: the first occurrence is spelled *plene* (לוא), while the following two tokens are spelled defectively (לא, as usual in Biblical Hebrew). It might be tempting to consider the *plene* spelling as a marker of a late date, since it is very common in Qumran Hebrew. However, it is virtually absent from biblical books whose late date is indisputable. Moreover, it is attested sporadically in classical prose (Gen 31:35; Lev 5:1; 1 Sam 2:24; 2 Kgs 5:17; 6:12), as well as in books that represent the transitional period between classical and late Biblical Hebrew (Isa 55:2; 65:1; Ezek 16:56; 24:16; Lam 1:12), including Jeremiah (2:25; 3:3; 5:10, 12; 6:8; 7:26; 8:6, 20; 15:11; 29:23; 48:27). See Hornkohl 2011: 77–79, §4.2.2.3 (this section was omitted from Hornkohl 2014). The orthographic evidence thus supports a dating of the satirical passages to the late monarchic period.

69 For the grammatical difference between singular (in 𝔐) and plural (in 𝕲), cf. below, n. 88.

70 The Greek verb is perhaps better translated as "tread" rather than "walk," since it is employed in the LXX as an equivalent of the Hebrew רכב and דרך (indeed, it translates as צעד only here).

The latter clauses too predicate that the idols are merely inanimate objects; they are unable to affect people for either better or worse (v. 5b) and are lifeless in general (v. 14). This similarity prompts the possibility that the negative clauses of vv. 4–5a stem from the polemical redaction and represent secondary interpolations into the descriptive passages.

However, the similarity between the negative clauses of vv. 4–5a and vv. 5b + 14 is only superficial, as the two groups of clauses differ in their function within their respective contexts. In the polemical passages, the clauses of vv. 5b + 14 justify the sweeping repudiation of the divinity allegedly inherent in the cult images, and they argue that such idols are useless. The negative clauses כי לא ידעו וגם היטיב אין אותם supply the reason for the categorical demand אל תיראו מהם, "do not fear them" (v. 5b). Similarly, the assertion ולא רוח בם directly continues the harsh reproach of the shamed artisans: הביש כל צורף מפסל כי שקר נסכו, "every goldsmith is put to shame by the idols; for his molten image is false" (v. 14). By contrast, it is not necessary to extract a comparable meaning from the negative clauses of vv. 4–5a, which are embedded within the descriptive passages. These clauses can be read as objective propositions about the cult images. Obviously, this is not how they were read by the prophetic redactor, who targeted these clauses precisely because he had interpreted them as the pagans' admittance of the falsehood of their own cult. It may well be that the very inclusion of these negative clauses within this section of the cultic source was the key factor in motivating its quotation in the first place. However, when read within their immediate context, these clauses do not imply the same contempt as their equivalents in the polemical passages. Therefore, it is worthwhile to explore the alternative possibility that the three negative clauses of vv. 4–5a indeed comprise an original part of the cultic source.

A piece of indirect evidence supporting this line of inquiry may be culled from a Mesopotamian cultic work, the ritual known as *mīs pî pīt pî*, "Mouth washing, mouth opening," which concerns the induction of cult images.[71] This ritual was performed during a two-day ceremony and included prayers and incantations recited at various points.[72] One of these incantations supplies a highly instructive parallel for the negative clauses of vv. 4–5a.

---

71 For the relation between this text and prophetic idol parodies, see especially Berlejung 1998: 315–413, esp. 369–411; Dick 1999; Lundberg 2007. For a critical edition of this work, see Walker and Dick 2001 (a revised version is available in https://sites.google.com/a/siena.edu/mis-pi/). Cf. Walker and Dick 1999; Hurowitz 2003; Borger 2005.

72 Such liturgical texts are referred to in the ritual by quoting their incipit; but they were copied independently, sometimes in conjunction with other rituals that made use of the same incantations. The editors of the *mīs pî* ritual compiled these incantations from a variety of sources, but we still lack the full text of some incantations required by the ritual. On the other hand, the edition also includes some prayers that were probably performed during the ritual, even though they were not explicitly mentioned there.

This liturgical text has a strategic placement within the ritual, as explicated in both its versions.[73] It is uttered shortly before the conclusion of a series of prayers chanted during the second day of the ritual, and before performing a cultic act that forms a ritual climax; namely, the washing and opening of the statue's mouth, after which another prayer is chanted and the priest performs a ritual of purification and whispering into the statue's ear. In other words, the relevant incantation is integrated into the ritual just a moment before the induction of the cult image and its transformation into a living symbol of the deity's numen.[74] At this crucial moment, we have an incantation called, by its incipit, "When the god was fashioned."[75]

The incantation includes, among other things, a bipartite declaration. It begins by requisition of human artisans' responsibility for creating the statue, asserting that the cult image is actually the product of the gods themselves (line 69: "this statue that Ninkura, Ninagal, Kusibanda, Ninildu, Ninzadim have made...").[76] It then moves to an explicit admittance that without performing the ritual mouth-opening act, the statue still cannot demonstrate any vital signs (lines 70–71):[77]

ṣalam[78] annû	This statue –
ina lā pīt pî	without the opening of the mouth (ceremony) –
qutrinna ul iṣṣin	*it cannot smell incense,*
akala ul ikkal	*it cannot eat food,*
mê ul išatti	*it cannot drink water.*

Therefore, we have a series of three short negative clauses, which objectively demonstrate the inanimate nature of the cult image. In its context, this series prepares the ground for the cultic act that immediately follows: the statue cannot yet do anything on its own, but this situation is about the change when its mouth

---

73 Nineveh Ritual, lines 159–161 (Walker and Dick 2001: 49, 64–65) || Babylonian Ritual, lines 46–47 (Walker and Dick 2001: 72, 76, 80).

74 Gabbay 2015: 186–188, 211–214.

75 Walker and Dick 2001: 140–141, 151 (Incantation Tablet III, B 49–96). It is extent in two versions, Sumerian and Akkadian. The ritual most likely entailed the recitation of the Sumerian text only; but for our comparative purpose, the Akkadian version better illustrates the similarity between the pertinent sources.

76 Walker and Dick 2001: 140.

77 Walker and Dick 2001: 141.

78 One might have expected this word to take the form ṣalmu, but ṣa-lam is the explicit reading of MS H. Other copies are fragmentary at this point, and the editors restored them with the sumerogram MIN.

is washed and opened, thus activating the still object and turning it into a living representation of the deity.

In drawing a comparison to the *mīs pî* ritual, I do not seek to argue that there is a literary dependence of any sort between this ritual and the cultic source that underlies our prophecy. In contrast to other biblical passages that may indeed betray knowledge of a ritual like the *mīs pî*,[79] the texts under scrutiny differ substantially from each other, referring to two different timespans. The cited fragment of the cultic source describes the production of the cult images, and only at its end does it allude to their carrying away from the workshop. The Mesopotamian ritual begins where the former ends; i.e., after the statue was taken away ceremonially from the craftsmen's workshop (*bīt mārē ummâni*),[80] but before it is placed in the location assigned for it within the temple. The main concern of the ritual is to supply detailed instructions regarding where and how to induce the cult image in a sacred garden, located by the river bank.

Other differences are derived from this basic dissimilarity. On the one hand, the cultic source contains a colorful depiction of the statue and the materials utilized for its production, but such matters are only incidentally touched upon in the *mīs pî* ritual and the accompanying incantations. On the other hand, the Mesopotamian work devotes much attention to purification ceremonies, culminating in the washing of the statue's mouth with the river water, but such matters are not even hinted at in the cultic source, or at least in the fragment embedded in our prophecy. Therefore, there seems to be no reason to assume that the latter depends on either direct or indirect knowledge of the Mesopotamian ritual.

Nevertheless, "When the god was fashioned" can indeed supply a highly instructive phenomenological parallel for the content and formulation of Jer 10:4–5. After all, this incantation fulfills an essential function in justifying the cultic activity surrounding a cult image, and it does so by openly admitting that the god's statue has no sensory capabilities – at least prior to its ritual activation. Moreover, this admittance takes the form of a series of three negative clauses, which refer to basic aspects of life. Arguably, the comparable series of three negative clauses included in the Hebrew text similarly was part and parcel of the cultic source underlying the prophecy.

---

79 Cf. below, the discussion of Deut 4:28.
80 Nineveh Ritual, line 55 || Babylonian Ritual, line 5 (Walker and Dick 2001: 41, 70, respectively).

There is no need, therefore, to suspect its originality or attribute it to the polemical redaction.

NB. In my opinion, the similarity between the Mesopotamian incantation "When the god was fashioned" and the cultic source quoted in Jer 10:3b–5a + 9 is phenomenological in nature. However, another biblical passage may well betray a more direct literary dependence upon the Mesopotamian text. Both content and form of Deut 4:28 closely correspond to the ritual declaration contained in the above quoted passage of the incantation:

ועבדתם שם אלהים	A	There you will serve gods
מעשה ידי אדם		made by human hands,
עץ ואבן		objects of wood and stone
אשר לא יראון	B	that neither see,
ולא ישמעון		nor hear,
ולא יאכלון		nor eat,
ולא יריחן		nor smell.

Part A, which asserts that the cult images are human-made products, is formulated in a typical Deuteronomic diction (cf. Deut 28:36, 64). At the same time, it clearly stands in direct opposition to the insistence of the Mesopotamian incantation that the cult images are divinely produced. Part B exhibits an even greater similarity to the incantation, in providing an atypical series of negative clauses that demonstrate the inanimate nature of such statues. This part parallels so closely the passage from "When the god was fashioned" that the possibility of literary dependence may be entertained.[81]

Many scholars assume that Deut 4:28 (as part of Deut 4:25–31) belongs to an exilic or post-exilic stratum within D. Be that as it may, knowledge of the Mesopotamian source could be assumed also for the pre-exilic period. A copy of Incantation Tablet III, which includes precisely the pertinent lines containing "When the god was fashioned," was found in the Syrian city of Hama, dating to the ninth or eighth century BCE. This text was thus known, in

---

81 An inner-biblical parallel for Deut 4:28 found in Ps 115:4–6 || 135:15–17 is discussed in greater detail below, §6.

the Neo-Assyrian period, also in the Levant.[82] This situation lends credence to the contention that the historical background for biblical anti-idolatry polemics, especially the prophetic idol parodies, is the Neo-Assyrian and Neo-Babylonian periods, which witnessed a particularly intense production of cult images and the renovation of damaged ones.[83]

Some additional differences between the Mesopotamian ritual and the Hebrew cultic source are noteworthy as well, since they may reveal further clues concerning the nature of the latter text. As indicated above, the cultic source employs phrases of the type "work of an artisan" (vv. 3b, 9), which resemble expressions that characterize Priestly literature. The Mesopotamian ritual, however, makes no use of comparable phrases.[84] This phraseological difference confirms the impression that attempting to locate the provenance of the cultic source within the Mesopotamian sphere is pointless. On the contrary, the phraseology suggests that the cultic source is well rooted in a tradition that is akin – but not identical – to Hebrew Priestly literature.

Another, thematic difference between the two texts lies in the specific actions that are negated. "When the god was fashioned" asserts that the statue cannot smell, eat, or drink, because these actions correspond to the three types of offerings brought to the gods in their temples: incense, food-offerings, and libations. The incantation makes no mention of the statue's inability to move, because this capacity is immaterial for its function as a carrier of the divine numen. Even after its cultic activation, the statue remains firmly set in its place in the shrine, without leading to any questioning of its divine nature. The Hebrew cultic source, however, lists three other

---

82 Walker and Dick 2001: 28 with n. 100.
83 Hurowitz 1995: 347, n. 35; cf. Cohen and Hurowitz 1999: 290, n. 33.
84 Only one passage of the ritual – contained in the same Incantation Tablet III that also includes the prayer discussed above – comes close to such a formulation. This passage concerns the speaker's declaration that the statue has the shape of gods and humans alike (ṣalam [bun]nanê ša ilī u awīlī). At this point, MS F adds a supplementary statement that the statue is binût ilī epšet amēlūti, "the creation of gods, the product of humankind" (Walker and Dick 2001: 139, 150; cf. Hurowitz 2012: 265). Note, however, that the theologoumenon implied by this passage is again that the statue is not an exclusively human-made product, but rather owes its existence to the active involvement of the gods. Thus, it is diametrically opposed to the argument inherent in the terms of the type מעשה חרש. Another text from Assyria (TuL 27) (that is intimately related to the mīs pî ritual, although it is not a copy of the work) employs several times the similar term šipir ili, "product of the god," for denoting a statue that serves as a cult image, or for the act of renovating a damaged image of this sort (lines 19, 21, 23, 28; Walker and Dick 2001: 233–234). Cf. Farber 2003: 209–210.

actions; yet their exact nature requires close study of some linguistic and text-critical details:

(1) Moving or breaking?

In v. 4b, 𝔐 reads: במסמרות ובמקבות יחזקום ולוא יפיק, "They fasten it with hammer and nails so that it cannot move."[85] The "fastening" apparently alludes to the joining of disparate parts of the statue, produced independently of each other, into a single, full-blown body (cf. Isa 41:7). More specifically, the "fastening" may denote the joining of the limbs, especially the hands, to the torso of the statue.[86]

The verb in the negative clause ולוא יפיק is a notorious *crux interpretum*. The context suggests that פוק is a motion verb,[87] and the entire clause should mean something like "so that it cannot move."[88] In other words, the various parts of the statue were fastened tightly to each other, so that the full image looks like a

---

85 𝔊 reflects a reverse order of the working tools: ἐν σφύραις καὶ ἥλοις ἐστερέωσαν αὐτά, "they fastened them with hammers and nails." The reading is supported by 4QJer[b], although it is only partially preserved: במקבות [ובמסמרות]. The same order is reflected in the parallel description of Deutero-Isaiah: ויחזק חרש את צרף מחליק פטיש את הולם פעם אמר לדבק טוב הוא ויחזקהו במסמרים לא ימוט, "The artisan encourages the goldsmith, and the one who smooths with the *hammer* encourages the one who strikes the anvil, saying of the soldering, 'It is good'; and they fasten it with *nails* so that it cannot be moved" (Isa 41:7; note also the employment of the verb חזק). Streane (1896: 123) thinks that the metathesis occurred in 𝔊, motivated by harmonization to Isa 41:7. But this explanation does not grant adequate weight to the fact that both readings are meaningful in their context in Jer 10:4. 𝔊's reading makes sense as part of the narrative-like description, because nails are used to fasten together a wooden construction (whereas hammers are only used for fixing the nails into place). 𝔐's reading reflects the theologically-motivated polemic that fits the idol parody by creating a satirical picture, in which the statue is "strengthened" by hammer blows. It stands to reason, therefore, that 𝔊's reading is the original, whereas 𝔐 is the result of further redactional reworking.
86 The verb חזק (in the D stem) is commonly employed in association with hands or arms: Judg 9:24; 1 Sam 23:16; Isa 35:3; Jer 23:14; Ezek 13:22; Job 4:3; Ezra 6:22; Neh 2:18; 6:9; cf. Ezek 30:24; Hos 7:15.
87 The etymological cognates of this verb range widely in their meanings, but the semantic component of motion or spatial position is shared by some of them, e.g., Arabic فوق "to be above, superior" and Akkadian *piāqu, pâqu*, which seems to denote "to make narrow, tight." Lexicographers often connect the Hebrew פוק with the Aramaic נפק "to leave, go out," which is also a motion verb (e.g., BDB, 807, s.v. II פוק), but I doubt the validity of such a connection. In several proverbs, פוק apparently parallels מצא "to find" (Prov 3:13; 8:35; 18:22), but this usage does not help clarifying our passage.
88 Compare 𝔊, even though it employs a passive form: καὶ οὐ κινηθήσονται, "and they shall not be moved." The exact same Greek formulation is employed in Isa 41:7 for לא ימוט, while the Greek rendition of Num 14:44 and Prov 17:13 suggest the alternative retroversion ולא ימיש(ו). In either case, the change to plural forms in order to achieve grammatical agreement is probably to be credited to the translators.

single, immovable piece. Jewish medieval commentators suggest that פוק means "to shake, tremble," based on linking it to the expression פִּק בִּרְכַים, which occurs between "melting heart" and "all loins quake" (Nah 2:11; cf. Dan 5:6).[89]

All such interpretations are based on *hapax legomena* and depend heavily on contextual considerations. Therefore, one may also consider an alternative, text-critical solution: the form יפיק may be a corruption of יפרק, due to an interchange between the graphically similar letters ק/ר.[90] If so, the clause ולא יפרק should be rende-red as "and it will not break, come apart."[91] This reading may, in fact, be witnessed by ܘܠܐ ܡܬܦܫܚ S.[92] The verb פרק is attested elsewhere in Biblical Hebrew in this sense (1 Kgs 19:11). The verb פרק "to break" is again used in the context of manufacturing a cult image in the story about the golden calf (Exod 32:2–3, 24), although it is employed there for denoting a different stage of the process; namely, the collection of jewels to be crushed in order to supply the gold required for producing the calf.[93] The Aramaic Targums employ פרק for translating Hebrew מוט (Isa 24:19; 54:10), and the parallel description of Deutero-Isaiah indeed reads at this point ולא ימוט (Isa 41:7; cf. 40:20).

(2) Talking or walking?

In v. 5a, 𝔐 reads: כתֹמֶר מִקשָׁה המה ולא ידברו. The first words are intelligible, but their combination is perplexing. The term מקשה (often rendered as "wrought") is normally applied to metallic objects.[94] It seems to imply that such objects are

---

89 See, e.g., Rashi, Qimḥi, Isaiah di Trani, and Menaḥem of Posquières (Cohen 2012: 68–69). Note also Am 2:13, הנה אנכי מעיק תחתיכם כאשר תעיק העגלה המלאה לה עמיר, "So, I will press you down in your place, just as a cart *presses down* when it is full of sheaves," which 𝔗 translates האנא מיתי עליכון עקא ומעיק לכון באתרכון כמא דפָיָקָא (נ"א: דעייקא) עגלתא דטעינא עמירא (נ"א: עיבורא) "Behold I will bring *distress* (var. *shaking, tottering*) upon you, and I will impede you in your place just as a cart is impeded when it is laden with sheaves" (Cathcart and Gordon 1989: 80). 𝔗 thus presents a picture of a cart that cannot bear the weight of the sheaves, so it shakes and gives the impression that it is about to break.

90 This is not a very common interchange, but it is recorded nevertheless. For another instance, see Mizrahi 2016: 52–53.

91 The verb can be vocalized either in the G (יִפְרֹק) or Du (יְפֹרַק) stems.

92 Assuming that ܦܫܚ is to be interpreted not as "save" (in the G and Gt stems), but rather as "break" (in the D and Dt stems); cf. S 1 Kgs 19:11; see also S Jer 4:24 (for a different opinion, see Rabin, Talmon, and Tov 1997: נו, n. 4 *ad* v. 4). 𝔗 translates our clause as ודלא יצטלי, just as it did with לא ימוט in Isa 40:20; 41:7.

93 Hurowitz (2012: 290 and n. 56) noted the technical use of this verb.

94 The cherubim (Exod 25:18; 37:7), the golden lampstand (Exod 25:31, 36; 37:17, 22; Num 8:4), and the silver trumpets (Num 10:2). The Masoretic vocalization distinguishes between the metal-lurgical term מקשָׁה and מקשָׁה (Isa 3:24; the context suggests that this term refers to a coiffure).

made of a single cast and not composed of different parts. But if so, why is it asso-
ciated with תֹּמֶר, "palm tree"?

𝔊 reads "silver" (ἀργύριον) rather than "palm tree," but its *Vorlage* hardly
read כסף. It is better reconstructed as employing the lexeme כֶּתֶם "gold," which
is peculiar to biblical poetic diction.[95] The phrase כתם מקשה is equivalent to the
phrase מקשה זהב (which occurs in the Priestly description of the lampstand in
Num 8:4), and it intends to emphasize that although the core of the cult images is
made of wood and only covered with gold, they nevertheless look as if they were
fully cast of pure gold.

𝔐's reading כתמר underlies the rest of the ancient versions, which take it
in its literal sense as referring to the date palm. Commentators and lexicographers debate about the meaning of this image and offer a range of interpretations that sometimes verge on the bizarre.[96] However, this reading clearly
refocuses the theological polemic, since the image of the palm tree supplies
an element that is otherwise missing from the cultic source; namely, the
shape of the cult images. The cult images were usually automatically assumed
to be anthropomorphic, but actually, nowhere in the text is this feature
explicated, and 𝔐 might reflect an alternative, non-anthropomorphic
interpretation. Its assertion that the cult images were shaped like palm trees
connects the cultic source to a well-known iconographic motif – a stylized
representation of the date palm that was common in the Levant in the first

---

95 So, e.g., Holladay 1986–89: 1.322, n. 5c–c; Carrol 1986: 253. A similar rendition is found in 𝔊
for Lam 4:1, איכה יועם זהב יִשְׁנָא הכתם הטוב, "How the *gold* has grown dim, how the *pure gold* is changed!", which 𝔊 translates πῶς ἀμαυρωθήσεται χρυσίον, ἀλλοιωθήσεται τὸ ἀργύριον τὸ ἀγαθόν,
"How *gold* will grow dim; the *good silver* will be altered" (cf. Rabin, Talmon and Tov 1997: נג, n. 1
for v. 5). I suggest, however, that scholars err in thinking that the *word* כתם "gold" is rendered by
ἀργύριον "silver." It is more likely that in both passages (Jer 10:5; Lam 4:1), the rare word-*pair* זהב
כתם // (cf. Prov 25:12; Job 31:24) was replaced by the more common word-pair זהב // כסף (e.g., Isa
30:22; Ezek 7:19; Prov 17:3, etc.).
96 For a survey of such solutions, see HALOT, 1757, s.v. II תמר; cf. Eichler 2017. Eichler reverts
back to an old idea that the image refers to a metallic model of a tree, adding to it the twist that
this tree is to be identified with an image of the sacred tree of Assyrian iconography. A particularly influential direction in the history of interpretation was marked by v. 69 of the *Epistle
of Jeremiah*: ὥσπερ γὰρ ἐν σικυηράτῳ προβασκάνιον οὐδὲν φυλάσσον οὕτως οἱ θεοὶ αὐτῶν εἰσι
ξύλινοι καὶ περίχρυσοι καὶ περιάργυροι, commonly rendered "*Like a scarecrow in a cucumber bed*
(KJV: *in a garden of cucumbers*), which guards nothing, so are their gods of wood, overlaid with
gold and silver" (cf. Adams 2014: 173, 201). The testimony of this passage, however, has been
adduced repeatedly without being properly interpreted in its own right, and in my opinion it
sheds no light whatsoever on the original sense of Jer 10:5a.

millennium BCE.[97] The simile כתמר can be interpreted, therefore, against the background of the religious iconography of the late monarchic period (including, theoretically, Jeremiah's own life time).

Notably, a potential connotation of the palm tree may be relevant, related to its material properties. No direct knowledge exists regarding such customs in the Levant, but Mesopotamian sources inform us that formal cultic images – i.e., statues of gods designed for temples – were made from very specific kinds of wood. Only trees of particular durability were considered worthy to serve as the "flesh of gods" (cf. Isa 44:14).[98] The popular date palm, by contrast, generally was not considered as one of the precious or prestigious sources of wood for such a purpose.[99] According to this line of thought, asserting that the idols are "like a palm tree" implies scorn, as it suggests that the idols were made of cheap and easily obtainable material. Moreover, the wood produced of the date palm is highly fibrous, and when dry its fibers crumble very easily. Comparing such a material to a cast of metal is contradictory in terms, and apt for a satirical description. Hence, 𝔐's reading is surely secondary, as it introduces the satire into the wording of the cultic source itself.

Whatever meaning one extracts from the simile in the first part of the sentence, how does it relate to the following, negative clause ולא ידברו? The latter is usually interpreted as referring to the idols' inability to talk (cf. 𝔗 ולא ממללין,

---

97 A famous example of this motif is drawn on pithos A from Kuntillet 'Ajrud; see Ornan 2012 (cf. Beck 1982: 13–15 = Meshel et al. 2012: 153–155; the relation between this image and the Assyrian sacred tree – discussed by Eichler 2017 – requires further study). Biblical Hebrew may refer to three-dimensional representations of this motif by the term אֲשֵׁרִים, as the verbs referring to destruction of such cultic objects (גדע "to chop," שרף "to burn") suggest that they were made of wood. If so, it is noteworthy that another prophecy in Jeremiah explicitly condemns the people for worshipping such objects (Jer 17:1–14). Cf. the parallelism between אשרים and פְּסָלִים "statues" in Deut 7:5; 12:3.
98 Hurowitz 2006; cf. Hurowitz 2012: 280–292. Mesopotamian sources identify the typical kind of wood utilized for this purpose as originating in the *mēsu*-tree. As Eph'al 1986–89 demonstrated, the related Sumerian term *musukkannu*, referring to *mēsu*-trees from the land of Magan (modern Oman), occurs in the idol parodies of Deutero-Isaiah: המסכן תרומה עץ לא ירקב, "As a gift one chooses the *musukkannu* – wood that will not rot" (Isa 40:19). Various kinds of trees used for supplying the wood for producing "the flesh of the gods" are also implied by mystical descriptions of divine bodies (Livingstone 1986: 92–112). The date palm is mentioned there as well (I VAT 8917 obv. 11), but only for the sake of illustrating the tallness of the god, not the material its body is made of.
99 We may also deduce that the wooden core of formal cult images did not ordinarily originate in palm trees from a sapiential work – a fictional dialogue between a date palm and a tamarisk, in which the tamarisk (*bīnu*) boasts of being used as the "flesh of the gods," while the date palm (*gišimmaru*) is forced to contend with saying that the "flesh" (i.e., wooden core) is invisible, because it is coated with silver. See Cohen 2013: 177–198, esp. 182–185, 194.

and so also 𝕊), but such an interpretation makes little sense. I propose instead to consider דבר as a motion verb, in a sense that is amply documented in Aramaic (also in the D stem).[100] Indeed, the Targums often employ דבר for rendering the Hebrew הלך "to walk."[101] Apparently, this is also how the verb was perceived by 𝕲, which properly renders it with οὐ πορεύσονται, "they will not *walk*." This rendition is often perceived as deriving from an etymological exegesis under the influence of Aramaic, i.e., as reflecting a mistaken interpretation of the passage.[102] Contextually, however, it appears that in this instance 𝕲 actually reflects a correct and literal interpretation of its *Vorlage*, which, at this point, was identical to 𝕸.

(3) Walking or marching?

In v. 5a, 𝕸 continues: נָשׂוֹא יִנָּשֵׂוּא כִּי לֹא יִצְעָדוּ, "They have to be carried, for they cannot walk." Unlike the previous cases, the literal interpretation of this sentence poses no special difficulty. However, the phraseology it employs deserves attention, because the verb צעד is not a common lexeme in Biblical Hebrew. It is normally restricted to biblical poetic diction,[103] and its sole occurrence in prose refers to marching in a cultic parade (2 Sam 6:13):

ויהי כי צעדו נשאי ארון יהוה ששה צעדים	When those who bore the ark of the Lord had *gone* six paces,
ויזבח שור ומריא	he (i.e., David) sacrificed an ox and a fatling.

This description of the ceremonial bringing of the Ark to Jerusalem is also the only other biblical passage that juxtaposes צעד with נשא. It stands to reason, therefore, that these terms connote a ceremonial procession of cultic paraphernalia.

---

100 For the semantic relation between speech and motion senses, see BDB, 180, s.v. דבר. There is no need to impose on the text forced etymologies or conjectural emendations, as suggested in HALOT, 209, s.v. דבר. Cf. Barr 1968 (1987): 324, nos. 81–84.
101 This rendition is found particularly in the formula יהוה ההלך לפניכם/עמכם, "YHWH who *walks* before/with you" and similar variations. See Targum Onkelos for Exod 13:21a; 14:19; Num 14:14; Deut 1:30, 33; 20:4; 31:6, 8; Targum Jonathan for Isa 52:12. Cf. Targum Jonathan for Jer 31:2; Zech 9:14.
102 Cf. BHK and BHS *ad loc.* (though their emendation of the vocalization is unnecessary); Rabin, Talmon, and Tov 1997: נג, n. 3 for v. 5. Thus, the proposal to retrovert 𝕲 as ולא ילכו (Saley 2010: 9) is superfluous.
103 Most occurrences of צעד are limited to archaic poetry (Gen 49:22; Judg 5:4; Hab 3:12; Ps 68:8), but they are sporadically found in other poetic texts as well (Prov 7:8; Job 18:14). The noun צַעַד is also confined mostly to poetic diction (2 Sam 22:37 ‖ Ps 18:37; Jer 10:23; Job 14:16; 18:7; 31:4, 37; 34:21; Prov 4:12; 5:5; 16:9; 30:29; Lam 4:18).

NB. The grammatical form of the verb יֵשֹׁוא is also noteworthy for chronological reasons. It follows the pattern of III-*y* verbs (cf., e.g., יֵצֵא in Exod 21:22), as opposed to the pattern of strong verbs (e.g., יִנָּשֵׂא in Ezek 1:19–20). This formation is attested elsewhere in Jeremiah (e.g., Jer 9:17, וְתִשֶּׂנָה עָלֵינוּ נהי , "let them raise a dirge over us"), and it appears to typify the transitional period in the history of Biblical Hebrew.[104] Hence, this comprises yet another piece of linguistic evidence that sets the satirical passages within a chronological timeframe fitting of Jeremiah's own prophecies.

★ ★ ★

The above discussion of the three negative clauses suggests that the last two clauses concern the statues' inability to move, whereas the first (somewhat enigmatic) clause can at least be interpreted likewise. The repeated assertion that the idols are motionless is sharply different from the threefold declaration of the Mesopotamian incantation that the statues cannot smell, eat, or drink.

As explained above, the latter reality plays a role in the course of the induction of the cult image: until the mouth of the statue is washed and opened, it cannot exhibit any vital sign; but following its ritual activation, the statue is considered as a living body capable of accepting the offerings of incense, food, and libations. But what could be the function, within the Hebrew cultic source, of a reiterated declaration that the cult images cannot move? Which element of such sacred objects is served by highlighting this feature? Such an emphasis points towards a religious tradition that differs substantially from the one that finds expression in the *mīs pî* ritual. By the same token, the language of the cultic source betrays no sign of Akkadian influence.[105] Comprehension of the repeated emphasis of the immovability of the cult images can only be achieved by way of analyzing internal evidence, culled from the cultic source itself. Does such evidence supply any hint about the original nature and possible provenance of the cultic source?

---

104 Hornkohl 2014: 103–107, §3.9 (concerning the verb רפא). Cf. Hornkohl 2011: 82–83, §5.1 (1). In any case, the form ינשׂוא is not the result of textual confusion by way of metathesis from ינשׂאו (e.g., Holladay 1986–89: 1.323, n. 5c–c; cf. already Qimhi *ad loc.*).
105 Contrast the language of Deutero-Isaiah's idol parodies, which contains technical terminology borrowed from Mesopotamian culture (e.g., above, n. 98), as could be expected from prophetic sources written in an exilic context. See further below (n. 114), concerning Hab 2:18.

§5.2 Origin and provenance of the cultic source

The quotation from the cultic source comprises only a short segment of the text, which is not enough for establishing its origin and provenance with certainty. Every attempt to elucidate such aspects based on internal evidence is bound to remain speculative, to a greater or lesser extent. Nevertheless, some clues may be recovered, although their interpretation will likely remain controversial.

The first issue to be discussed is that of genre. The default assumption so far has been that the cultic source was a ritual, designed as part of a particular cultic practice, either dictating its course or supposed to be recited during it. Indeed, prophetic idol parodies were compared to Mesopotamian cultic works such as the *mīs pî* ritual[106] or liturgies.[107]

Still, it is worthwhile to recall that descriptions of cult images and their production are also contained in texts of other genres, especially ones that exhibit a propagandistic *Tendenz*. An instructive example is furnished by a royal inscription of Esarhaddon (AsBbA), in which the Assyrian king boasts of repairing the cult images of the gods of Babylon that had been taken – or even demolished – by his father Sennacherib. Esarhaddon narrates how he initiated the project and oversaw the entire process: the gathering of various artisans at the workshop; ensuring the supply of gold, precious gems and other materials by importing them from the distant mountains; and producing the divine crown, pedestal, shining statues, etc. Finally, he made sure that the statues were carried to their proper place and set within their shrines.[108] The text of this inscription embeds citations from patently cultic sources.[109]

In light of this parallel, one cannot be entirely certain whether vv. 3b–5a + 9 were drawn directly from a cultic source (in the strict sense of the term) or possibly from an intermediate, possibly a propagandistic narrative, which made secondary use of cultic texts or alluded to cultic practices. The latter option introduces a theoretical complication into the reconstructed trajectory of the compositional history of the prophecy, but it should be noted nevertheless.

Next, there is the issue of provenance. The language of the cultic source contains several elements that distinguish it from standard Biblical Hebrew, such as the

---

106 Cf. above, n. 71.
107 Hoffman 1999: 199.
108 Leichty 2011: 103–109, Inscription 48.
109 Baruchi-Unna 2012 and 2017.

use of דבר as a motion (rather than a speech) verb,[110] and perhaps also the occurrence of the verb פוק (if one accepts 𝔐's reading, which may be textually suspicious). The cultic source also contains technical terminology whose Hebraic nature is undeniable (e.g., the juxtaposition of צעד and נשא), including terms and phrases of the sort that typify Priestly literature (e.g., the technical term מקשה, or phrases of the type מעשה חרש). The combined force of all these indications points at a native, Hebrew religious tradition, but one that is non-normative from a biblical point of view.[111]

The cultic reality reflected in the source under consideration may be anchored in a relatively restricted social circle, such as the clan or small towns, which were probably populated by families of mostly common descent.[112] Local cults of this sort are condemned harshly in another prophecy of Jeremiah (2:26–28):

> As a thief is shamed when caught, so the house of Israel shall be shamed – they, their kings, their officials, their priests, and their prophets, who say to a tree, "You are my father," and to a stone, "You gave me birth." For they have turned their backs to me, and not their faces. But in the time of their trouble they say, "Come and save us!" But where are your gods that you made for yourself? Let them come, if they can save you, in your time of trouble; for you have as many gods as you have towns, O Judah.[113]

---

110 This particular verb supplies an additional argument against the possibility of an Akkadian influence and in favor of the alternative possibility of a native, Hebrew tradition. The normal form of the Akkadian cognate is *duppuru* "to move away, withdraw, stay away," while the form *dubburu* is practically restricted to Peripheral Akkadian of the El-Amarna tablets (*CAD*, D, 186b–188b, esp. 188a, §2a2′). To be sure, this distinction depends on the orthographical habits of the Canaanite scribes (Rainey 1996: 1.14). But if it holds, *dubburu* confirms that דבר as a motion verb is a native Hebrew lexeme that was inherited from Canaanite.

111 This thesis may be compared to a similar proposal that Goldstein (2010–11) suggested concerning the Song of Moses. According to him, Deut 32 embeds passages (vv. 8–9, 43) quoted from an ancient Hebrew psalm that was similar, in its literary characteristics, to Babylonian hymns exalting Ištar. Goldstein considers this ancient psalm – only fragments of which survive – to have originally expressed a henotheistic theology, which was rejected and covered up by later redactional reworking.

112 Notably, the deities worshiped in such contexts are not necessarily "foreign," and the cultic objects may well have been utilized (also) for the worship of YHWH. Compare the narrative in Judg 17–18, which describes a cult for YHWH as taking place in a local context and with the aid of "an idol of cast metal" (פסל ומסכה) produced by a silversmith (צורף; Judg 17:4). Micah even recruits a Levite to minister in his local shrine (Judg 17:7–13). While the plot of this narrative is situated in the time of the Judges, the religious reality it reflects applies to later periods as well, especially in the (late) monarchic era.

113 𝔊 reads a longer version of v. 28, adding to it "and according to the number of Jerusalem's streets, they were sacrificing to Baal." The same passage is found in the conclusion of another short prophecy, which also testifies to the worship of idols in local towns (Jer 11:11–13). According to 𝔐, however, the explicit identification with the Baal cult is restricted to Jer 11:11–13, and it is absent from 2:26–28.

This allegation establishes that the cult of images made of "wood and stone" was a popular phenomenon throughout Judah (v. 28b).[114] The direct address to the idols as parental figures (v. 27a) suggests that these objects represented eponymous persons in the history of the family or settlement. Allegedly, moreover, the worship of such cult images was taking place in parallel to the official cult of YHWH, to whom people addressed at times of countrywide needs (v. 27b).[115] Such a worship of the forefathers requires that the cult images at their focus be maintained. After all, it is their permanent presence that ensures the safety of the settlement and the protection of its inhabitants. If this speculation has any merit, it may supply the missing motivation for underscoring that the cult images are immovable. The point is not that they *cannot* move, but rather that they *should not be* moved once they were brought into their local shrine.

There might be another, more practical motivation for emphasizing that such cult images do not walk on their own. Due to the precious material coating these objects – and the powers of fertility and protection attributed to them – they must have been likely targets for burglary.[116] A ritual induction of such cult images may

---

114 Indeed, Jer 2:26–28 mention idols made of wood and stone, presumably common in the Levant, while Jer 10:3b–5a + 9 speak about idols plated with silver and gold, allegedly typical of Mesopotamia. In reality, however, all these materials were used for producing statues of various sorts throughout the ancient Near East. Mesopotamian cult images were also made of wood and only overlain with precious metals. Cf. Hab 2:19, הוי אמר לעץ הקיצה עורי לאבן דומם הוא יורה הנה הוא תפוש זהב וכסף וכל רוח אין בקרבו, "Alas for you who say to the wood, 'Wake up!' to silent stone, 'Rouse yourself!' Can it teach? See, it is gold and silver plated, and there is no breath in it at all." The Babylonian background of this passage is revealed by its peculiar use of the verb תפש, which is not employed here in the usual sense of "seize," bur rather denotes "plating, overlaying." This is a calque of Akkadian *uḫḫuzu* (cognate of Hebrew אחז "to seize, grasp"), which is employed in technical terminology to denote the coating and decorating of objects with precious materials. See *CAD*, A/1, 179–180, s.v. *aḫāzu*, §8; cf. the adjective *uḫḫuzu(m)* in *CAD*, U/W, 44.

115 Holladay (1986–89: 1.103–105) offers an alternative explanation for the mention of wood and stone, arguing that v. 27 serves as a literary allusion to Deut 32:18, "You were unmindful of the Rock that bore you; you forgot the God who gave you birth." But even if one accepts the (questionable) assumption that this prophecy depends here on the Song of Moses, it may still faithfully depict a certain cultic reality of Judah in the late monarchic period.

116 Compare the cases of stealing the Teraphim, which are also cultic images clearly linked to the familial sphere (still in circulation in the late monarchic period, as suggested by 2 Kgs 23:24). Tellingly, they are sometimes explicitly designated as "gods" (אלהים; cf. Gen 31:30, 32; Judg 17:5; 18:17, 24). For the religious customs within the sphere of the family home, see Bodel and Olyan 2008 (especially the contribution of Albertz and Olyan, *ibid.*, 89–112, 113–126, respectively). For the integration of such customs into the construction of social identity, the regulating mechanisms of inheritance, and distribution of economic assets, see van der Toorn 1995. For a survey of opinions on the nature of biblical Teraphim, see, e.g., Flynn 2012.

well have included an explicit incantation designed to magically set them firm in their place, so that they will not be moved away from there. Such a need may also lie behind the repetition that the statues do not move.[117]

Finally, the hypothesis that the objects portrayed in the cultic source were worshipped in familial or local contexts may also explain how the prophet had access to such a literary source. The popularity of local cults throughout Judah in the late monarchic period suggests that literary depictions of such cult images – and perhaps also the ritual of their induction – were relatively well known, at least among priests residing in peripheral towns. Jeremiah himself is reported to have come from such a priestly family (Jer 1:1). The idea that Jeremiah quotes from a literary source that was circulating in his social milieu and geographical context is, at least, conceivable.

Notably, the proposed considerations regarding the nature, origin, and provenance of the cultic source are bound to remain highly hypothetical, and they have only little effect on the literary analysis of the text of the prophecy as presented above. The most crucial aspect in regard to the present discussion is the acknowledgement that the work from which the descriptive passages are drawn reflects a theological and cultic worldview that generally is comparable to the one underlying Mesopotamian sources, as well as their phenomenological parallels from other civilizations of the ancient Near East.[118] Since no such work was unearthed in the land of Israel thus far,[119] the discovery of a putative fragment of this kind supplies us with a rare opportunity to learn something about the religiosity of those who are so vigorously condemned by the prophecy.

§6 Another echo of the cultic source

Biblical polemics with idolatry are not confined to prophecy, but extend to psalmic literature. Two psalms in particular are often discussed in conjunction with Jer 10:1–16 and other idol parodies: Ps 115 and Ps 135. Indeed, their comparative analysis supplies an additional piece of evidence in support of the identification of the cultic source that underlies the satirical passages.

---

117 A different understanding of the negative clauses – which had a decisive influence on the history of interpretation – transpires from the *Epistle of Jeremiah*, which considers them as reflecting a picture of a cultic procession that takes place in Babylon (vv. 3–5, cf. v. 26), probably under the influence of the Deutero-Isaiah (Isa 46:6–7; cf. 45:20).
118 Note especially the Egyptian ritual of Mouth Opening, which took place mostly within the artisans' workshop (Lorton 1999: 147–179).
119 Cf. Lewis 2005: 90–91.

Both psalms are composite works, but their constituent parts can be isolated relatively easily. The sections relevant for our concern are the first part of Ps 115 and the last part of Ps 135:[120]

Ps 115	**Ps 135**
A ׃לֹא לָנוּ יְהוָה לֹא לָנוּ כִּי־לְשִׁמְךָ תֵּן כָּבוֹד 1 עַל־חַסְדְּךָ עַל־אֲמִתֶּךָ׃ 2 לָמָּה יֹאמְרוּ הַגּוֹיִם אַיֵּה־נָא אֱלֹהֵיהֶם׃ 3 וֵאלֹהֵינוּ בַשָּׁמָיִם כֹּל אֲשֶׁר־חָפֵץ עָשָׂה׃	[...] 13 יְהוָה שִׁמְךָ לְעוֹלָם יְהוָה זִכְרְךָ לְדֹר־וָדֹר׃ 14 כִּי־יָדִין יְהוָה עַמּוֹ וְעַל־עֲבָדָיו יִתְנֶחָם׃
[1] Not to us, O LORD, not to us, but to your name give glory, for the sake of your steadfast love and your faithfulness. [2] Why should the nations say, "Where is their God?" [3] Our God is in the heavens; he does whatever he pleases.	[13] Your name, O LORD, endures forever, your renown, O LORD, throughout all ages. [14] For the LORD will vindicate his people, and have compassion on his servants.
B עֲצַבֵּיהֶם כֶּסֶף וְזָהָב מַעֲשֵׂה יְדֵי אָדָם׃ 5 פֶּה־ לָהֶם וְלֹא יְדַבֵּרוּ עֵינַיִם לָהֶם וְלֹא יִרְאוּ׃ 6 אָזְנַיִם לָהֶם וְלֹא יִשְׁמָעוּ אַף לָהֶם וְלֹא יְרִיחוּן׃ 7 יְדֵיהֶם וְלֹא יְמִישׁוּן רַגְלֵיהֶם וְלֹא יְהַלֵּכוּ לֹא־יֶהְגּוּ בִּגְרוֹנָם׃ 8 כְּמוֹהֶם יִהְיוּ עֹשֵׂיהֶם כֹּל אֲשֶׁר־בֹּטֵחַ בָּהֶם׃	15 עֲצַבֵּי הַגּוֹיִם כֶּסֶף וְזָהָב מַעֲשֵׂה יְדֵי אָדָם׃ 16 פֶּה־לָהֶם וְלֹא יְדַבֵּרוּ עֵינַיִם לָהֶם וְלֹא יִרְאוּ׃ 17 אָזְנַיִם לָהֶם וְלֹא יַאֲזִינוּ אַף אֵין־יֶשׁ־רוּחַ בְּפִיהֶם׃ 18 כְּמוֹהֶם יִהְיוּ עֹשֵׂיהֶם כֹּל אֲשֶׁר־בֹּטֵחַ בָּהֶם׃
[4] Their idols are silver and gold, the work of human hands. [5] They have mouths, but do not speak; eyes, but do not see. [6] They have ears, but do not hear; noses, but do not smell. [7] They have hands, but do not feel; feet, but do not walk; they make no sound in their throats. [8] Those who make them are like them; so are all who trust in them.	[15] The idols of the nations are silver and gold, the work of human hands. [16] They have mouths, but they do not speak; they have eyes, but they do not see; [17] they have ears, but they do not hear, and there is no breath in their mouths. [18] Those who make them and all who trust them shall become like them.
C יִשְׂרָאֵל בְּטַח בַּיהוָה עֶזְרָם וּמָגִנָּם הוּא׃ 9 בֵּית אַהֲרֹן בִּטְחוּ בַיהוָה עֶזְרָם וּמָגִנָּם הוּא׃ 10 יִרְאֵי יְהוָה בִּטְחוּ בַיהוָה עֶזְרָם וּמָגִנָּם הוּא׃ 11 יְהוָה זְכָרָנוּ יְבָרֵךְ יְבָרֵךְ אֶת־בֵּית יִשְׂרָאֵל 12 יְבָרֵךְ אֶת־בֵּית אַהֲרֹן׃ 13 יְבָרֵךְ יִרְאֵי יְהוָה הַקְּטַנִּים עִם־הַגְּדֹלִים׃ [...]	19 בֵּית יִשְׂרָאֵל בָּרְכוּ אֶת־יְהוָה בֵּית אַהֲרֹן בָּרְכוּ אֶת־יְהוָה׃ 20 בֵּית הַלֵּוִי בָּרְכוּ אֶת־יְהוָה יִרְאֵי יְהוָה בָּרְכוּ אֶת־יְהוָה׃ 21 בָּרוּךְ יְהוָה מִצִּיּוֹן שֹׁכֵן יְרוּשָׁלָ͏ִם הַלְלוּ־יָהּ׃

---

120 In addition to the studies mentioned above (n. 71), see further Zenger 2001; Levtow 2008: 72–75; Ammann 2015: 137–147.

⁹ O Israel, trust in the LORD! He is their help and their shield. ¹⁰ O house of Aaron, trust in the LORD! He is their help and their shield. ¹¹ You who fear the LORD, trust in the LORD! He is their help and their shield. ¹² The LORD has been mindful of us; he will bless us; he will bless the house of Israel; he will bless the house of Aaron; ¹³ he will bless those who fear the LORD, both small and great.

¹⁹ O house of Israel, bless the LORD! O house of Aaron, bless the LORD! ²⁰ O house of Levi, bless the LORD! You that fear the LORD, bless the LORD! ²¹ Blessed be the LORD from Zion, he who resides in Jerusalem. Praise the LORD!

While full critical analysis of both psalms lies beyond the scope of this study, clearly they are closely related to each other, either by way of direct literary dependence on one another or by drawing from a common source. The intertextual relationship is particularly evident in the case of Section B, in which the two psalms are identical almost to the word. It is also patent in Section C, which concerns the exchange of blessings between YHWH and his people, described as comprising different groups (Israelites, God fearers, Levities, and Aaronite priests) that stand in varying degrees of proximity to the deity. The two psalms appear quite distinct in Section A, but there too they share several motifs, such as the exaltation of YHWH's name and the underscoring of his sovereignty over the world.

Section B, which is repeated almost verbatim in both psalms, comprises a stand-alone literary unit that directly polemicizes with idolatry. Comparison of the parallel versions reveals a coherent internal structure of this section:

	Ps 115	Ps 135
Opening:	4 עצביהם כסף וזהב	15 עצבי הגוים כסף וזהב
	מעשה ידי אדם	מעשה ידי אדם
Body:	5 פה להם ולא ידברו	16 פה להם ולא ידברו
	עינים להם ולא יראו	עינים להם ולא יראו
	6 אזנים להם ולא ישמעו	17 אזנים להם ולא יאזינו
	אף להם ולא יריחון	אף אין יש רוח בפיהם
	7 ידיהם ולא ימישון	
	רגליהם ולא יהלכו	
	לא יהגו בגרונם	
Conclusion:	8 כמוהם יהיו עשיהם	18 כמוהם יהיו עשיהם
	כל אשר בטח בהם	כל אשר בֹּטח בהם

The literary framework of this section consists of an opening (Ps 115:4 ‖ 135:15) and closing (Ps 115:8 ‖ 135:18) passages. The main element of the opening is the assertion that the idols are the product of human industry, "the work of human hands" (Ps 115:4a ‖ 135:15a), which is concluded from specifying their material constituents: "The idols of the nations are silver and gold" (Ps 135:15b; Ps 115:4b slightly differs, in reading "their idols" for "the idols of the nations"). Similarly, in their conclusion, both psalms move from the idols to their makers: "Those who make them are like them; so are all who trust in them" (Ps 115:8 ‖ 135:18).[121]

In their body, however, the similarity between the two psalms is limited. Both psalms list the qualities – or rather defects – of the idols. The first three items are almost identical (Ps 115:5–6a ‖ Ps 135:16–17a), but the fourth item is defined and formulated differently (Ps 115:6b; 135:17b). Moreover, the two lists differ in length, with Ps 115 including seven items, whereas Ps 135 has only four.[122] How should one account for these differences?

The answer to the question lies in an observation regarding another parallel for the passages under scrutiny; namely, Deut 4:28, which may itself be alluding to the Mesopotamian incantation "When the god was fashioned" (cf. above, §5.1):

ועבדתם שם אלהים מעשה ידי אדם עץ ואבן   There you will serve gods made by human hands, objects of wood and stone

אשר לא יראון ולא ישמעון ולא יאכלון ולא יריחן   that neither see, nor hear, nor eat, nor smell.

The first part of the Deuteronomic passage parallels the opening of the psalmic section (Ps 115:4 ‖ 135:15), though with transposition of the latter's components. The idols are defined as "work by the hands of a human," and their material composition is given in some detail ("wood and stone" in the Deuteronomic section, "silver and gold" in the psalmic one). The main difference between the sources is that in Deut 4:28, the idols are identified as the deities (אלהים) that the Israelites will worship in their exile, whereas in the psalmic passages, the idols are identified as belonging to the nations (Ps 115:4a ‖ 135:15a).

The second part of the Deuteronomic passage enumerates four sensory capabilities that the idols do not possess.[123] Tellingly, the series overlaps only those items that are shared by both psalmic passages:

---

121 As noted above (§4), a similar shift of focus typifies 𝔐's version of the satirical passages, whereas 𝔊 retains a focus on the idols themselves.
122 This rule applies for 𝔐, while 𝔊 testifies to a longer version of Ps 135, which includes a verbatim parallel for Ps 115:6–7. However, the latter is clearly a secondary expansion meant to harmonize the two psalms.
123 If this series of four negative clauses indeed derives from a cultic source such as one of the incantations accompanying the Mesopotamian *mīs pî* ritual, then it is instructive to see how Deut 4:28 slightly expands the shorter, three-item series found there. The psalmic passages continue the expansionist trajectory by both detailing each item (explicating which body part is concerned) and adding new items.

Deut 4:28	Ps 115:4–4 ‖ 135:15–17
(a) לא יראון	עינים להם ולא יראו (Ps 115:5b ‖ 135:16b)
They do not see.	They have eyes, but do not see.
(b) ולא ישמעון	אזנים להם ולא ישמעו/יאזינו (Ps 115:6a ‖ 135:17a)
They do not hear.	They have ears, but do not hear.[124]
(c) ולא יריחָן	אף להם ולא יריחון (Ps 115:6b)
They do not smell.	They have noses, but do not smell.
	Cf. אף אין יש רוח בפיהם (Ps 135:17b)[125]
	There is no breath in their mouths.
(d) ולא יאכלון	Cf. פה להם ולא ידברו (Ps 115:5a ‖ 135:16a)[126]
They do not eat.	They have mouths, but do not speak.

Up to this point, Deut 4:28 closely resembles the psalms (especially Ps 115).[127] Here, however, the two psalms depart from each other: Ps 135 moves directly to the conclusion of the section, whereas Ps 115 adds another three negative clauses:

---

124 The wording of Ps 115:6a (ולא ישמעו) is closer to Deut 4:28 (ולא ישמעון), while Ps 135:17a (ולא יאזינו) replaces the verb with a synonymous term. The verbs שמע and האזין form a standard word-pair in Biblical Hebrew in general (e.g., Exod 15:26; Deut 1:45) and in poetic diction in particular (e.g., Gen 4:23; Num 23:18; Deut 32:1; Judg 5:3; Isa 1:2, 10). The lexical replacement, though, has two noteworthy effects. First, it enhances the stylistic coherence of the passage in Ps 135, by linking more clearly between the body part concerned (אזנים, "ears") and the related action (יאזינו). Second, the replacement offers a semantic sharpening of the polemical argument: שמע usually denotes the physical ability to hear, so its standard object is קול "voice," while האזין may refer to the mental capacity to listen, so that its object is usually a term referring to a verbal utterance (often derived from אמר "to say"; cf. Gen 4:23; Isa 32:9). Therefore, the Deuteronomic passage – followed by Ps 115 – deny of the idols the physical ability to *hear*, whereas Ps 135 goes one step further and argues that they cannot *listen*. In so doing, Ps 135 underscores that it is pointless to address the idols, because they are unable to perceive the prayers of their worshippers.
125 In this item too, Deut 4:28 and Ps 115 resemble one another more closely (extending even to the grammatical form of the verb, which exhibits the *nun paragogicum*), while Ps 135 apparently reflects a more progressed stage in the reworking of the tradition. Ps 135 probably highlights the action of breathing because its absence marks the complete lack of the spirit of life. For its wording cf. Job 27:3, כי כל עוד נשמתי בי ורוח אלוה באפי, "as long as my breath is in me and the spirit of God is in my nostrils."
126 In this item, no literal parallel exists between Deut 4:28 and Ps 115:5a ‖ 135:16a, but both texts at least relate to the same body part; namely, the mouth.
127 Hurowitz (2012: 265–266) indeed suggested that Ps 115 directly polemicizes with Mesopotamian sources such as the *mīs pî* ritual, but in my opinion, the literary relation between the texts is more complicated and indirect in nature (cf. above, n. 123).

(e) ידיהם ולֹא ימישון, "They have hands, but do not feel."
(f) רגליהם ולא יהלכו, "They have feet, but do not walk."
(g) לא יהגו בגרונם, "They make no sound in their throats."[128]

Clauses (e)–(g) also differ syntactically from clauses (a)–(d) in their protasis. In the first four items, the possessive relation is expressed by way of an independent prepositional phrase (פה להם... עינים להם... אזנים להם... אף להם). In the next three items, the same syntactic relation is expressed with a pronominal suffix (ידיהם... רגליהם... גרונם).[129] Admittedly, the difference is slight and purely grammatical in nature, but it is peculiar nevertheless. If one author composed all items, why did he suddenly change their wording? And why did the change take place where it did?

All these questions are settled by the hypothesis that the two groups of clauses, (a)–(d) and (e)–(g), stem from two distinct sources. Despite some difference of content and form, items (a)–(d) closely parallel Deut 4:28, whereas items (e)–(g) were probably imported from a different tradition. Tellingly, items (e) and (f) concern the idols' inability to move their limbs (Ps 115:7) – a motif that cannot but remind us the picture that transpires from the cultic source embedded in Jer 10:3b–5a + 9.[130] The two texts exhibit a remarkable thematic resemblance, but – apart from using the syntactic construction of negation – there is no similarity in their wording. This fact suggests that neither text directly depends on the other; rather, both texts appear to draw from a shared tradition.

To conclude, Ps 115 appears to rely on two sources in formulating its polemic with idolatry and highlighting the defects of cult images. In a section that is repeated almost verbatim in Ps 135, it embeds a tradition that lists the sensory capabilities that idols do not exhibit. This is an elaboration of a tradition represented, in a more condensed form, by Deut 4:28, which possibly draws from a cultic source such as the incantation accompanying the Mesopotamian *mīs pî* ritual. Following this, however, is another section that has no parallel in Ps 135, in which Ps 115 shifts to highlighting a different kind of a physiological profile; namely, the idols' inability to move independently. This tradition finds a parallel in the cultic source presumably quoted in the satirical passages of our prophecy (Jer 10:3b–5a + 9). Both traditions were fused together in the combined list of

---

128 Note that the final item differs from the previous two in its inversion of constituents: the body part is mentioned in the apodosis, whereas the negative clause moves to the protasis. This structural distinction serves a discursive function; namely, to mark the item as the closure of the series. Its thematic echo of the first item (since both refer to speech) similarly functions as a poetic means of closure.
129 For the syntax of such utterances, see Kogut 1993.
130 Interestingly, item (g) may derive from a misinterpretation of the clause ולא ידברו (Jer 10:5a) as "they do not *talk*" rather than "they do not *walk*."

Ps 115, but their distinct origins can still be traced thanks to the different wording of the statements drawn from each source. Furthermore, the latter tradition is missing from the parallel text of Ps 135, thus affording an independent piece of text-critical evidence for the discrete origin of both components. Comparison of both psalms and analysis of the subtle linguistic differences between the literary components they integrate enables an untangling of the complexity of literary strands and a reconstruction of the process of their composition. This analysis supports the identification and reconstruction of a cultic source as an independent literary document underlying the satirical passages of Jer 10:1–16.

§7 The concluding passage (v. 16)

There are some grounds for thinking that v. 16 served as the original conclusion of the prophecy in its initial stage; i.e., when it was still comprised of the satirical passages only. At first glance, v. 16 exhibits none of the distinctive traits of the phraseology typical of Jeremiah. Thematically, however, it addresses directly the equation between idolatry and the nations made in the polemical passages, asserting that "not like *these* [i.e., the idols] is the LORD, the portion of *Jacob* [i.e., as against the nations]." While the idols are human-made products, "a work of delusion" (v. 15: מעשה תעתעים), YHWH is presented as "the creator of everything" (v. 16: יוצר הכל).[131] Moreover, while the idols remain anonymous throughout the satirical passages, v. 16 concludes with the solemn declaration that God's name is YHWH.[132]

---

131 The lexical choice in the participial form of יצר is noteworthy. On the one hand, it is very typical of Deutero-Isaiah's diction (Isa 43:1; 44:2, 9, 24; 45:7, 9, 11, 18; 49:5; cf. 64:7; Hab 2:18). On the other hand, elsewhere in Jeremiah, the term is used in a concrete sense to designate a potter (Jer 18:1–11; cf. Isa 45:9; 64:7). In the context of the satirical passages, then, the employment of יוצר (in v. 16) might connote a contrast between the divine potter, who has the unique ability to create life, and the human artisans, who should be ashamed for producing inanimate objects (vv. 14–15; cf. Isa 44:9). At any rate, the proclamation that God is "the creator of everything" introduces into the satirical strand the notion of creation. Quite likely, moreover, in turn this isolated usage motivated the interpolation of the oldest hymnic passage (vv. 12–13), which was supplemented as an expansion of this motif (see below, Chapter 2, §8).

132 Note the textual difference at this point between 𝕲 (κύριος ὄνομα αὐτῷ = יהוה שמו, "YHWH is his name") and 𝔐 (שמו) יהוה צבאות שמו, "YHWH of Hosts is his name"). While the absence of צבאות in 𝕲 at this point, as in other places in Jeremiah, may be due to a secondary abbreviation (as proposed by Rofé 1991), I consider it more probable that in this particular case, the term צבאות is a late insertion. The formula יהוה שמו is found elsewhere for describing God as the creator (Jer 33:2; Am 9:6), while the alternative formula יהוה צבאות שמו typifies redactional additions in both Jeremiah and Deutero-Isaiah, as indicated by its lack of grammatical agreement with the context (e.g., Isa 51:15; Jer 46:18) or by the fact that the term breaks the parallelism structure (e.g., Isa 48:2; 54:5).

The nature of the connection between YHWH and Israel was apparently a matter that invited scribal intervention, since it is the focus of some textual variation. While 𝔐's description extends to two cola (כי יוצר הכל הוא / וישראל שבט נחלתו, "for he is the creator of everything, and Israel is the tribe of his inheritance"), 𝔊 has only a single colon that makes no mention of the name "Israel" (ὅτι ὁ πλάσας τὰ πάντα αὐτὸς [ἐστι] κληρονομία αὐτοῦ = כי יוצר הכל הוא נחלתו, "for the creator of everything is his inheritance").[133] 𝔊's reading closely parallels a formulaic description of the Levites:

> The levitical priests, the whole tribe of Levi, shall have no allotment or inheritance within Israel. They may eat the sacrifices that are the LORD's portion, but they shall have no inheritance (חלק ונחלה) among the other members of the community; the Lord is their inheritance (יהוה הוא נחלתו), as he promised them (Deut 18:1–2).[134]

This formula explains why the tribe of Levi is not allotted any portion of the Promised Land: as God's servants, the Levites are not supposed to possess any real estate of their own; they have no independent source of income – a provision with far-reaching economic implications. In Jer 10:16, however, the same formula is applied differently. First, its scope extends from a specific tribe (Levi) to the entire people (Jacob). Second, and more crucially, the proposition shifts from the realm of agrarian assets to the sphere of theology: the issue is no longer the *territories* (not) assigned to certain tribes but rather the *deities* worshiped by different nations. 𝔐's reading intensifies the notion of ethnic exclusivity by introducing the name of Israel into the context and by treating Israel as a "tribe," i.e., a distinct and ethnically identifiable group (cf. Ps 74:2).

The Deuteronomic wording, the language of "portion" (חלק) and "inheritance" (נחלה) as applied to Jacob, the oscillation between territorial and theological notions, and the redactional insertion of "Israel" for rendering explicit the notion of ethnic exclusivity all suggest that Jer 10:16 closely relates to Deut 32:8–9, a passage now embedded in the Song of Moses:

| בהנחל עליון גוים | When the Most High apportioned the nations, |
| בהפרידו בני אדם | when he divided humankind, |

---

[133] Intriguingly, 𝔐 in the parallel section of Jer 51:19, כי יוצר הכל הוא ושבט נחלתו, "for he is the creator of everything and the tribe of his inheritance," makes no sense on its own: What does it mean that God is "the tribe of his inheritance"? (Tellingly, NRSV was urged to correct the text of Jer 51:19, rendering it: "for he is the one who formed all things, and *Israel* is the tribe of his inheritance.") This reading is comprehensible only as an intermediate stage between 𝔐's and 𝔊's readings in Jer 10:16 (cf. Loewenstamm 1992: 340 and n. 34).

[134] The formula is Deuteronomic (cf. Deut 10:9; Josh 13:14, 33), but the idea also occurs in Priestly passages (cf. Num 18:20; Josh 18:7).

יצב גבלת עמים	he fixed the boundaries of the peoples
למספר בני [...]	according to the number of X,
כי חלק יהוה עמו	for YHWH's own portion was his people
יעקב חבל נחלתו	Jacob his allotted share.

As is well known, the textual witnesses differ greatly with respect to a crucial detail in v. 8: the identity of those whose number serves as the model for dividing the world into distinct lands. According to the alarmingly polytheistic reading of 4QDeut^j, they are "the gods" (בני אלוהים). 𝕲 softens this theologically charged expression by rendering "the angels of god" (ἀγγέλων θεοῦ). And 𝔐 solves the problem altogether through the 'nationalistic' reading, "the sons of Israel" (בני ישראל).[135] The scholarship has discussed this passage of the Song of Moses extensively;[136] its analysis lies beyond the scope of the present discussion. Suffice it to note that it translates the political borders between nations into a picture of the divine assembly, asserting the unique relationship between YHWH and the people designated by the name "Jacob." Tellingly, the concluding statement in v. 9 is somewhat ambiguous: it is commonly interpreted as asserting that *the people of Israel is God's own share*, but it may also be understood as expressing the reverse argument, namely, that *YHWH is Israel's share*. 𝕲's reading of Jer 10:16 and 51:19 follows the latter interpretation, whereas 𝔐's reading of Jer 10:16 apparently amplifies the former understanding of Deut 32:9.[137]

The intimate relation between Deut 32:8–9 and Jer 10:16 may be interpreted as part of a broader phenomenon in Jeremiah. A number of passages in this book exhibit verbal contacts and theological affinity with passages from the Song of Moses.[138] Regardless of whether all or part of these passages may be ascribed to the prophet himself or rather to later redactors, this feature establishes that v. 16 should not be divorced from the rest of the Book of Jeremiah. In this respect, v. 16 has a clear affinity with the polemical passages, and it may be regarded as the original conclusion of the prophecy in its earliest recoverable formation; i.e., when consisting of only the satirical strand.

---

135 To be sure, 𝕲 does introduce Israel; but at a later point, in v. 9: "and his people Jacob became the Lord's portion, *Israel* a measured part of his inheritance." 𝕲 thus expanded the reference to Jacob into the standard word-pair of "Jacob // Israel" (cf., e.g., Ps 78:71).

136 Goldstein 2010–11, with ample references to previous studies. In his view, vv. 8–9 form a fragment from an older, henotheistic work that was embedded and theologically reworked in the Song of Moses.

137 See also Chapter 4, §4, concerning the possible change of שמים to גוים in v. 10, in a manner comparable to what one finds in Deut 32:43 (which, according to Goldstein 2010–11, comprises part of the same ancient psalm as Deut 32:8–9).

138 See, e.g., Holladay 1966: esp. 18–21; 2004: esp. 63–64; cf. Weinfeld 1972 (1992): 361.

§8 Conclusion

The main literary strand of the prophetic unit of Jer 10:1–16 consists of satirical passages (vv. 2–5, 8–9, 14–16), which belong to the genre of idol parodies. However, a variety of considerations lead to the conclusion that these passages as well are not a literary unity but rather a composite text. Two literary strata can be identified within the unit, and they differ from each other in their language, style, and theological outlook.

Underlying the satirical passages is a quotation from a cultic source that depicts the manufacturing of cult images. It is preserved almost intact in 𝕲, but it was broken into two fragments and further reworked in 𝔐. Due to the limited extent of this text, it is difficult to conclude decisively regarding the exact nature of the original document from which the quotation was drawn, but it might have concerned cult images employed in local cultic contexts. At any rate, the text does not seem to be the result of an external – specifically Babylonian – influence. Rather, this literary-historical analysis discloses the remains of an ancient work that supplies us, for the first time, a Hebrew parallel for a type of cultic works known from other civilizations of the ancient Near East.

Rhetorical statements that polemicize with the citation from the cultic source have reframed it. The framework mocks the assertions contained in the cultic source and considers its subject matter as perishable objects of no use and the result of foreign influence. The phraseology of this redactional frame is essentially identical to what one finds throughout the book of Jeremiah, suggesting that the satirical passages – in their composite form – is essentially similar to the corpus of other prophecies attributable to Jeremiah, which were compiled and redacted in the book bearing his name. Linguistically as well, the satirical passages – in their composite form – fit neatly into the language of the late monarchic period.

Text-critical evidence suggests that the text of the prophecy was subject to extended processes of literary reworking that continued to amplify the theological polemic; their impact is evident on both its literary composition and its textual development and stylistic adaptation. These processes also slightly diverted the focus of the polemic, shifting it from the idols to their makers. They blurred the original profile of the cultic source and gradually eroded its distinctive language by conforming it to the stylistic norms that govern the rest of the book of Jeremiah. But while 𝔐 represents a relatively progressed stage of this later development, 𝕲 enables access to an older formation of the literary material, which was not yet submitted to as much intervention by later scribes.

Chapter 2

From wisdom to hymn

(Jer 10:12–13)

12 עֹשֵׂה אֶרֶץ בְּכֹחוֹ מֵכִין תֵּבֵל בְּחָכְמָתוֹ וּבִתְבוּנָתוֹ נָטָה שָׁמָיִם: 13 לְקוֹל תִּתּוֹ הֲמוֹן מַיִם בַּשָּׁמַיִם וַיַּעֲלֶה נְשִׂאִים מִקְצֵה ארץ (הָאָרֶץ) בְּרָקִים לַמָּטָר עָשָׂה וַיּוֹצֵא רוּחַ מֵאֹצְרֹתָיו:

[12] It is he who made the earth by his power, who established the world by his wisdom, and by his understanding stretched out the heavens. [13] When he utters his voice, there is a tumult of waters in the heavens, and he makes the mist rise from the ends of the earth. He makes lightnings for the rain, and he brings out the wind from his storehouses (NRSV).

§1 Prolusion

Of the three hymnic passages incorporated in Jer 10:1–16, only one (vv. 12–13) is shared by both the long text represented by 𝔐 (as well as 4QJer[a] and 4QJer[c]) and the shorter text represented by 𝔊 (and 4QJer[b]). The other two passages, vv. 6–7 and v. 10, are absent from the short text and remain confined to the long text (which is also reflected in 𝔙, 𝔖 and 𝔗). This state of affairs indicates that the material contained in vv. 12–13 is older than that of the other hymnic passages. Likewise, its insertion into the prophetic unit took place at a relatively early stage of the compositional history of the unit as a whole, in any case earlier than the integration of vv. 6–7 and v. 10.[1]

Vv. 12–13 are often treated as a literary unity, usually as part of the larger segment of vv. 12–16. In contradistinction, in this chapter I argue that several types of evidence indicate that vv. 12–13 form a literary composite. This unit comprises of two originally independent segments, each stemming from its own distinct tradition and has its particular literary background, which can still be recovered to some extent. Furthermore, the short text of 𝔊 again

---

1 Some scholars have surmised that vv. 12–13 originally formed a direct continuation of v. 10; i.e., that these two passages stem from the same source, but to my mind this is untenable (cf. below, Chapter 4, §1).

DOI 10.1515/9783110530162-003

reveals an earlier form of the passage. Close attention to details of the textual evidence affords us with valuable data enabling a novel reconstruction of the compositional history of vv. 12–13 and a new understanding of the formation of Jer 10:1–16.

The philological analysis is somewhat complicated by the necessity to take into consideration also the parallel section of Jer 51. For this reason, the following discussion begins with a general presentation of the textual evidence, including also the relation between vv. 12–13 and the parallel text of Jer 51(𝕲 28):15–16 (§2). This is followed by a detailed account of the reasons for suspecting that v. 12 and v. 13 should be separated from one another, albeit not too mechanically (§3). The two passages thus distinguished are then discussed independently: v. 12 is placed against the background of wisdom literature (§4), while v. 13 is set in the context of psalmody (§5). The discussion proceeds to address why and in which context the two passages were fused together (§6). Analysis up to this point is based on internal evidence – culled from the literary, linguistic and text-critical realms – but some external corroboration can be adduced from literary parallels in both biblical and apocryphal literature (§7). Attention is then given to the possible reasons for absorbing vv. 12–13 into the polemical texture of the prophetic unit (§8). The converging lines of evidence are summarized in the concluding section (§9).

§2 Textual evidence

Since some significant differences exist between 𝔐 and 𝕲 in vv. 12–13, it is useful to begin exploration of the passage with a panoramic view of their form in the two text forms:

עשה ארץ בכחו	12	κύριος ὁ ποιήσας τὴν γῆν ἐν τῇ ἰσχύι αὐτοῦ, It is the Lord who made the earth by his strength,
מכין תבל בחכמתו		ὁ ἀνορθώσας τὴν οἰκουμένην ἐν τῇ σοφίᾳ αὐτοῦ who set upright the world by his wisdom,
ובתבונתו נטה שמים		καὶ τῇ φρονήσει αὐτοῦ ἐξέτεινε τὸν οὐρανὸν and by his prudence he stretched out the sky,
לקול תתו המון מים בשמים	13	καὶ πλῆθος ὕδατος ἐν οὐρανῷ and a quantity of water was in the sky,
ויעלה נשׂאים מקצה (ה)ארץ		καὶ ἀνήγαγε νεφέλας ἐξ ἐσχάτου τῆς γῆς, and he brought up clouds from the end of the earth.

ברקים למטר עשה	ἀστραπὰς εἰς ὑετὸν ἐποίησε
	Lightnings he made into rain,
ויוצא רוח מאצרתיו	καὶ ἐξήγαγε φῶς ἐκ θησαυρῶν αὐτοῦ.
	and he brought out light from his storehouses.

NB. Two points of philological interest should be noted regarding the text of v. 13. First, while Jer 10:13 reads ויעלה (a reading supported by 4QJer[c]), the parallel section of 51:16 reads ויעל. The latter reading is seemingly preferable from a grammatical point of view, because the preterite or *wayyiqtol* form is morphologically based on the short form of the prefix conjugation (i.e., the one formally identical with the jussive). Still, the interchange between the long and short verbal forms in this category is common in weak verbs of the III-*y* type. One might have expected that the long preterite would be a marker of late Biblical Hebrew, but its distribution does not typify late books.[2] Most occurrences of the long form are found in Kings, Jeremiah, and Ezekiel, whereas this form is completely absent from the Pentateuch and is only seldom and sporadically attested in the indisputably late books.[3] These data suggest that the long preterite is characteristic of the transitional stage between classical and late Biblical Hebrew, i.e., the late monarchic through early exilic period. From a text-critical point of view, since it is impossible to prefer one form over the other, the passage is hereafter cited with the two forms side by side as ויעל/ויעלה.

Another issue is the grammatical state of ארץ, as read by the *Kətīb* text (K), while the *Qərê* tradition (Q) reads it as הארץ, i.e., with the definite article. The parallel passage of Jer 51:16 supports the K reading, which has no definite article; this is also the reading attested by 4QJer[b]. The Q reading, with the definite article, is supported by the parallel text of Ps 135:7. As demonstrated below (§7.1), this detail has bearing on our understanding of the chronological relation between the various sources. Furthermore, an inner-Masoretic dispute exists regarding this word: the distinction between an indefinite K (ארץ) and a definite Q (הארץ) is explicitly identified as a "western" (מערבאי, i.e., Palestinian) tradition, while the "eastern" (מדינחאי, i.e., Babylonian) tradition knows only the indefinite form in this particular verse.[4]

---

2 For instance, contrast ותעלה המלחמה in 1 Kgs 22:35 with ותעל המלחמה in the parallel passage of 2 Chr 18:34.

3 Hornkohl 2014: 171–180.

4 See Rabin, Talmon and Tov 1997: נג, apparatus IV.

§3 Untying vv. 12–13

Upon first glance, vv. 12–13 look as if they conjoin into a single, coherent stretch of a hymnic psalm.[5] Formally, a prosodic similarity exists between the triple rhythm of all poetic lines of v. 12 and the two concluding lines of v. 13:

v. 12:	עשה ארץ בכחו	– – –
	מכין תבל בחכמתו	– – –
	ובתבונתו נטה שמים	– – –
v. 13:	…	
	ברקים למטר עשה	– – –
	ויוצא רוח מאצרתיו	– – –

Content-wise, vv. 12–13 both praise God in the third person for his control over nature. In addition, it is tempting to interpret the logical relation between the two verses as that between a general statement and its detailed demonstration.[6] According to this construal, v. 12 generally asserts that God created the world by his wisdom, while v. 13 exemplifies the divine masterplan embedded in the creation by focusing on the weather, whose diverse phenomena are viewed as parts of a coherent system designed for supplying rain (למטר עשה, "he made… *for rain*"),[7] thus implying its ultimate goal of ensuring the universal cycle of fertility and human cultivation of the earth (cf. Ps 104:10–15).

In reality, however, the verses do not correlate perfectly. Wisdom is mentioned in each and every poetic line of v. 12, but it is conspicuously missing from v. 13. Moreover, not all the elements mentioned in v. 12 play a role in v. 13. The only element that is fully shared by both verses is the earth (ארץ). The heavens (שמים) are mentioned in v. 12; but they are not explicitly named in v. 13, although they are

---

5 For the verbal points of contact between vv. 12–13 and biblical psalmody (and Deutero-Isaiah), see Davidson 1973–74: 51.

6 This line of reasoning is already discernible in rabbinic literature, as in *Genesis Rabbah* 13:4, אמר רבי רבי הושעיא: קשה היא גבורות גשמים ששקולה כנגד כל מעשה בראשית [...] רבי אחא מייתי לה מן הכא: "עושה ארץ בכחו, מכין תבל בחכמתו" וגו', "לקול תתו המון מים בשמים" וגו'. ואין "קול" אלא גשמים, היד מה דאת אמר: "תהום אל תהום קורא לקול צנוריך" (ed. Theodor and Albeck 1965: 1:115–116), "R. Hoshaya said: Wonderful is the might of rain, for it is reckoned as equivalent to the whole of creation. [...] R. Aḥa proved it from the following: 'He that hath made the earth by His power,' etc. (Jer. x, 12). 'At the sound of his giving a multitude of waters in the heavens' (ibid., 13). Now 'sound' signifies nought but rain, as you read: 'Deep calleth unto deep at the sound of Thy cataracts' (Ps. xlii, 8)" (tr. Freedman in Freedman and Simon 1939: 1.101). Cf. *Mishnat R. Eliezer* 15 (ed. Enelow 1933: 281–282).

7 Cf. Menaḥem of Posquières: "למטר" – לצורך מטר וטעם (ed. Chohen 2012: 255), "the meaning of למטר is 'for the purpose of rain.'"

at least implied by the reference to atmospheric phenomena (clouds, lightning, and rain). The inhabited world (תבל), by contrast, is named in v. 12, but it is not even hinted at in v. 13.[8] Comparison of the two verses reveals a series of additional differences between them:

- *Poetic form*: The prosodic similarity between the two verses is only partial, because the two lines that open v. 13 do not adhere to the triple rhythm. They do not even resemble each other, as the first line contains five accented words, which naturally break into two uneven feet:

$$- - - / - -$$ לקול תתו / המון מים בשמים

  In contrast, the second line consists of four accented words, which fall into two symmetrical feet of double stress each:

$$- - / - -$$ ויעלה נשׂאים / מקצה (ה)ארץ

  In so doing, they interrupt the prosodic continuation between v. 12 and v. 13b. At the same time, they also prompt the question: What is the relation between the two parts of v. 13?

- *Content*: The two verses are thematically distinct, since v. 12 praises God as a wise creator, whereas v. 13 hails him as the one who controls the natural elements. In principle, these two themes can be easily connected, but the specific praise of each verse takes its respective theme in a different direction: v. 12 focuses on the wisdom that typifies the creation, while v. 13 reflects on the wonders of the weather.

- *Literary background*: The two verses display intertextual links to different literary traditions. The focus on wisdom that characterizes v. 12 finds close parallels in wisdom literature (Prov 3:19; Job 26:12).[9] In contradistinction, v. 13 exhibits no special relation to sapiential sources; even the general notion of divine wisdom plays no role in it. On the other hand, it has some peculiar ties with psalmody.[10]

---

8 The term תבל usually pairs with ארץ, but some of its occurrences (e.g., Isa 26:18; 34:1; Nah 1:5) betray the semantic difference between them: ארץ refers to the dry land in general, while תבל denotes only the fertile or inhabited land (cf. the apt rendition of 𝕲 for our passage, οἰκουμένη); cf. BDB, 385b. For a different view, cf. HALOT, 1682–1683. In either case, תבל is not mentioned in v. 13, nor does this verse indirectly reflect the specific signification of the term.

9 Scholars have briefly noted the similarity between these passages (e.g., Ben-Dov 2000: 126 and n. 84), but its significance was not systematically explored thus far. See the detailed discussion below, §4.

10 The natural phenomena depicted in v. 13 (sounds, clouds, lightning, and winds) correlate with descriptions of theophany, which are mostly found in poetic texts, e.g., Ps 77:17–20; 97:4–5; cf. Judg 5:4; Hab 3:11; Zech 9:14; Ps 18:14–16 ‖ 2 Sam 22:14–16; see, e.g., Preuss 1971: 168–169. However, no concrete similarity exists between the specific descriptions of v. 13 and the images of theophany in such passages. Furthermore, an explicit designation of purpose like "he made the lightning *for rain*" (v. 13) is not to be expected in a theophany, which is interested in divine revelation, not in managing rainfall.

- *Formulation*: The two verses also differ from each other in their language, and especially in their syntax. V. 12 mostly takes the form of a static, descriptive utterance, thereby employing participles (עשׂה...מבין). By contrast, v. 13 is formulated as a narrative of past events, making use of preterite forms (ויעל/ ויעלה...ויוצא). It even pre-poses an infinitival, circumstantial clause in a way typical to biblical prose narratives.[11]

All these differences make it difficult to assume that vv. 12–13 originate from the same literary source. In contrast, they indicate that the two verses were unconnected to each other in the first place, and their present juxtaposition is redactional.

The secondary nature of the connection between vv. 12–13 is indeed evident in its syntactic awkwardness. According to 𝔐's verse division, v. 13 holds two asymmetrical parts: it begins with a long and cumbersome adverbial complement (לקול תתו המן מים בשׁמים) and continues with a series of three short clauses (ויעל/ ויעלה נשׂאים מקצה [ה]ארץ / ברקים למטר עשׂה / ויוצא רוח מאצרתיו). This composition poses a syntactical problem, because in cases of pre-posing an adverbial complement, the verb of the main clause is expected to take the form of either *qatal* (e.g., Jer 11:16) or *yiqtol* (e.g., Ezek 27:28), but not of *wayyiqtol* (ויעל/ויעלה) – which is normally reserved for the clause-initial position, as found here.[12]

Tellingly, this issue is avoided in 𝔊, because the two most problematic words, לקול תתו, are not represented in its version of v. 13.[13] Moreover, their continuation links backwards to v. 12, rather than forward to the rest of v. 13.[14] In my opinion, this form of the text stems from a variant version of v. 12 that differs from 𝔐 in including a fourth poetic line, [ו]המן מים בשׁמים, which adheres to the triple rhythm of all the other lines in this verse. To be sure, this line deviates from the preceding ones in

---

11 Note, though, that despite the employment of preterital forms, the order of actions as unfolded in the passage is not consistent with the expected linguistic texture of a narrative (see further below, §5).
12 The medieval commentator Isaiah di Trani sensed this difficulty, and commented on this verse that "the *waw* is superfluous" (הוי"ו יתירה, ed. Cohen 2012: 255). He apparently refers to the *waw* of (ה)ויעל, indicating that the expected form is (ה)יעל. Compare his comments on Jer 4:1; 6:19, etc.
13 These words might have been absent also from the text of 4QJer[c] (4Q72, frg. 6 = col. V); see Tov 1997: 187. A more doubtful testimony is that of 4QJer[b] (4Q71), which is generally close to the presumed *Vorlage* of 𝔊. Only the left part of a column is preserved, and reconstruction of the missing text requires the assumption that its line length was unusually wide. Consequently, the exact content of the lost text cannot be restored with confidence; indeed, scholars disagree as to whether or not to include the words לקול תתו in the reconstruction. For the inclusion, see Tov 1997: 176; for exclusion, see Saley 2010: 8, 10.
14 According to the verse numeration in the standard editions of the Septuagint (e.g., Tischendorf 1856: 2.338; Swete 1894–96: 3.246; Rahlfs 1935: 2.673 for the entire Septuagint, or Ziegler for 𝔊-Jer), the words καὶ πλῆθος ὕδατος ἐν οὐρανῷ, "and a mass of water in the sky," belong to v. 13. Syntactically, however, it is difficult to construe these words as part of v. 13, whereas their content clearly links them to v. 12.

not mentioning wisdom. However, as demonstrated below (§4), parallels for v. 12 in wisdom literature actually support such a textual constellation, thereby affording confirmation for this reconstruction of the original form of the text.

Seen against this background, the addition of לקול תתו is possibly motivated by the secondary combination of vv. 12–13. As argued in greater detail below (§6), the added words reflect an attempt to polish the coarse transition from one passage to another. If this hypothesis is correct – and much of the following discussion either leads to it or stems from it – it transpires that 𝕲 for vv. 12–13 represent an intermediate compositional stage, in which the two verses were already juxtaposed but not yet fully clamped to each other, whereas 𝔐 reflects a later, more advanced stage in the process of integrating them.[15] The following discussion thus proceeds to analyze each verse in its own right, as a prerequisite for pondering on their combination and eventual integration into the prophetic unit of Jer 10:1–16.

§4 v. 12 and its background

Wisdom is thrice mentioned in the present form of v. 12. The theological argument spelled out by this emphasis is that the entire creation reflects divine sapience – a motif typical of wisdom literature. This ideological affinity is vindicated by a stylistic piece of evidence: of the three synonymous terms for "wisdom" employed in this verse, חכמה and תבונה form a standard word-pair, but all their occurrences in synonymous parallelism are concentrated in wisdom literature.[16] These indications certify that v. 12 is intimately related to wisdom literature.

Indeed, the verse finds specific parallels in sapiential literature, in both its didactic and philosophical branches (Prov 3:19–20 and Job 26:12–13, respectively). While each passage naturally has its distinct content, they all patently follow the

---

15 In contradistinction, 𝕲 for Jer 51(28):15–16 reflects a text that is closer to 𝔐 in representing the words לקול תתו with εἰς φωνὴν ἔθετο ἦχος ὕδατος ἐν τῷ οὐρανῷ, "He set roar of water into a voice in the heaven" (Walser 2012: 113), substituting the awkward infinitive with a finite verb. The Greek rendition of the parallel passage thus approximates 𝔐, suggesting its affiliation with the revisional character of the second part of 𝕲-Jer (cf. the Introduction, end of §4.3 [p. 18]).

16 Job 12:12–13; Prov 2:2; 3:13; 5:1; 8:1; 24:3. By contrast, occurrences of this word-pair in coordinated constructions (i.e., חכמה ותבונה) are not limited to wisdom literature (Exod 36:1; 1 Kgs 5:9; Ezek 28:4), although they are found there as well (Prov 10:23; 21:30). Usually, the pair may be expanded into a triplet by the word דעת (Exod 31:3; 35:31; 1 Kgs 7:14; Prov 2:6; 3:19–20), and seldom with another lexeme such as זמה (Prov 10:23) or עצה (Prov 21:30). In this particular passage, however, the basic word-pair is expanded with כח (lit. "power, force"). This lexical choice is surprising, but it may be explained as reflecting a shift from the semantic domain of power to that of intelligence, witnessed by a number of passages both in wisdom literature (Job 12:13; 26:12) and elsewhere (Isa 11:2; Ps 147:5; Dan 2:20, 23). Compare the ironic usage of the term גבורה (lit. "might, strength") in reference to חכמה in Eccl 9:16 as well as in the proverb quoted in Jer 9:22.

same literary pattern of "three... four" (henceforth "3/4").[17] This pattern ratifies God's wisdom as revealed in the created world (in lines a–c), and concludes with the most decisive demonstration of this principle (in line d):

Jer 10:12(–13a)	Prov 3:19–20	Job 26:12–13	
[יהוה] עֹשֵׂה אֶרֶץ בְּכֹחוֹ	יהוה בְּחָכְמָה יָסַד אָרֶץ	בְּכֹחוֹ רָגַע הַיָּם	a
מֵכִין תֵּבֵל בְּחָכְמָתוֹ	כּוֹנֵן שָׁמַיִם בִּתְבוּנָה	ובתובנתו (וּבִתְבוּנָתוֹ) מָחַץ רָהַב	b
וּבִתְבוּנָתוֹ נָטָה שָׁמָיִם	בְּדַעְתּוֹ תְּהוֹמוֹת נִבְקָעוּ	ברוחו שָׁמַיִם שִׁפְרָה	c
[וַ]הֲמוֹן מַיִם בַּשָּׁמַיִם	וּשְׁחָקִים יִרְעֲפוּ טָל	חֹלְלָה יָדוֹ נָחָשׁ בָּרִחַ	d

a	[The Lord][18] makes the earth by his power;	The Lord, by wisdom, founded the earth;	By his power, he stilled the Sea,
b	he establishes the world by his wisdom,	by understanding, he established the heavens;	and by his understanding, he struck down Rahab;
c	and by his understanding he had stretched out[19] the heavens	by his knowledge, the deeps broke open,	by his wind, the heavens were made fair;[20]
d	[and][21] the multitude of water in the heavens.	and the clouds drop down the dew.	his hand pierced the fleeing serpent.

Of the two parallels, the one closest to our passage is Prov 3:19–20, because it demonstrates the Creation, first and foremost, by the making of the earth and heavens (in this particular order!),[22] whereas Job 26:12–13 is concerned with the

---

17 For the compositional use of this pattern in wisdom literature, see Zakovitch 1979: 1.201–213 and 2.369–372, 478–489.

18 Following 𝔊, see the detailed discussion below.

19 According to this construal, the verb נטה (lit. "to stretch out") governs not only "the heavens" (in line c; cf. Isa 42:5; 44:24; Job 9:8), but also the water contained therein (line d), thus reflecting a semantic extension of the verb from the concrete sense "to stretch out" (related to the image of the sky as a cosmic tent; cf. Ps 104:2) to the abstract notion "to create" (cf. Isa 51:13; Zech 12:1; Job 26:7). In the present context, the verb also may be rendered "to plan, devise in one's thought" (cf. Ps 21:12), thus referring specifically to God's wisdom.

20 This is an approximate translation of 𝔐, whose last word is virtually unintelligible. The text is better emended to שִׁפְרָה/שַׂפְרֹ(ר)ה בְּרוּחוֹ שָׂם יָם שִׁפְרֹה, "and by his wind, he captured the Sea in/with his net," following Tur-Sinai 1957: 383–384. Cf. Greenstein 1982; Goldstein 2005b: 489–490.

21 Again, following 𝔊.

22 The standard word-pair of ארץ // שמים has been expanded in both passages with a third element (תבל in Jer 10:12; תהומות in Prov 3:19) in order to adapt it to the first triad of the "3/4" pattern. The expansion with תבל in Jer 10:12 is explained below. The expansion with תהומות in Prov 3:19 (cf. 1QHᵃ 9:11, 15–16) brings the passage close to Job 26:12–13 in its allusion to the fight between God and the Chaos monsters that are represented by the abyss water – a motif that belongs to the mythological background of the known world's Creation. Yet the mythological connotation is dimmed in Prov 3:19, both because of the employment of the plural form (which suggests that תהום is a common, not a proper noun) and by the context (which treats תהומות as a mere source of water).

myth of God's glorious defeat of the sea monsters.[23] Like v. 12, Prov 3:19–20 refrains from mentioning God's wisdom in the concluding line d (and so also Job 26:12–13);[24]; similarly, moreover, it devotes this line to the bringing of rainfall.[25] These agreements confirm the validity of the reconstruction – prompted by 𝕲 – of an original continuity between v. 12 and the reference to water stored in the heavens in v. 13a.[26] Thus not only the basic pattern of "3/4" but also its conclusion with the motif of rain are common to Jer 10:*12 and Prov 3:19–20.[27]

---

23 Cf. Ayali-Darshan 2014.

24 Line d of Prov 3:19–20 is also distinguished from the preceding lines in its morpho-syntax. Lines a–c employ *qatal* verbs (נבקעו ...כונן... יסד), whereas line d is the only one employing a *yiqtol* form (ירעפו). This difference is related to the different subject matter of these lines. The first three refer to the primeval age of Creation, and accordingly they utilize a verbal form referring to the distant past. The fourth line refers to present reality, thus selecting a verbal form that conveys the notion of iterative action (which also has an imperfective dimension).

25 In Job 26:12–13 as well, the fourth line differs from the former three in making no use of a word meaning "wisdom." However, since this line directly continues the theme of God's triumph over the primeval sea monsters, the shift from the first triad to the fourth line has been blurred to some extent. The thematic fuzziness, however, is compensated by the conspicuous contrast in syntactic structure. Lines a–c place the adverbial complement in a clause-initial position (thus topicalizing the wisdom motif), and the verb is pushed to the second position. Line d restores the normal constituent-order, in which the verb takes the clause-initial position.

26 For this reason, and for the sake of convenience, line d will be treated hereafter as an integral part of v. *12, even though it actually forms part of v. 13a according to 𝔐 and the sources that depend on it. When required, this line will be referred to as v. *12d. Cf. below, n. 39.

27 The idea that the rain demonstrates God's wisdom inherent in the creation apparently motivated a rabbinic homily, which compares between the rain as described in Jer 10:12–13 and the Torah. See, e.g., *Midrash Psalms* 1:18, כך ,"מה המים נתונים מן השמים, שנאמר "לקול תתו המון מים בשמים דברי תורה נתונים מן השמים, שנאמר "אתם ראיתם כי מן השמים דברתי עמכם" (ed. Buber 1891: 17), "Like waters given from heaven, as it is said 'As the sound of His giving a multitude of waters in the heavens' (Jer. 10:13), so were the words of the Torah given from heaven, as it is said 'Ye yourselves have seen that I talked with you from heaven' (Ex. 20:19)" (tr. Braude 1959: 1.24–25). Cf. *Canticles Rabbah* 1:3, נמשלו ד"ת [=דברי תורה] במים... מה מים מן השמים שנא' "לקול תתו המון מים בשמים", כך תורה מן השמים שנאמר "כי מן השמים דברתי עמכם", "The words of the Torah are compared to water... Just as water is from heaven, as it says, 'At the sound of his giving a latitude of waters in the heavens' (Jer. x, 13), so the Torah is from heaven, as it says, 'I have talked with you from heaven' (Ex. xx, 19)" (tr. Simon, in Freedman and Simon 1939: 9.33). Interestingly, a similar homiletic equation underlies Jerome's commentary on our passage, even though he naturally gives it a different turn: "'When he utters his voice there is a tumult of waters in the heavens,' for all of the Lord's teaching flows down from the heavenly realm [...] 'He Makes lightnings for the rain,' for when the rain of doctrine has come and parched human hearts have been satisfied, then you will find flashes and bright lightnings of wisdom" (Graves and Hall 2011: 68). For the original Latin text, see Reiter 1960: 106.

The reconstruction of v. *12 is amplified by yet another detail of Prov 3:19–20;
namely, the employment of the Tetragrammaton at the very beginning of line a.[28]
This reconstruction is prompted by 𝕲 for v. 12, which is supported by 𝕾 (ܪܒܐ ܐܪܥܐ
ܒܚܘܟܡܬܗ ܐܬܩܢ). There is no reason to assume that 𝕾 depends on 𝕲 with respect to any
element of vv. 12–13; thus, its reading may be taken as an independent corroboration.[29]

Alongside the similarities, it is also important to take due note of the dissi-
milarities between these passages. Prov 3:19–20 is integrated into a more general
argument – and a typically sapiential one – that unfolds in the following passage
(vv. 21–23): just as God himself was assisted by wisdom in creating the world, so
should the human addressee act wisely at any time in order to ensure himself a
good and safe life. In the broader context, then, God's wisdom is mentioned not
for the sake of an abstract theological reflection but rather as a rhetorical means
for achieving a concrete, didactic effect; namely, teaching the attentive student a
practical lesson. The lack of this kind of justification in Jer 10:12 suggests that it
was taken out from a broader context, which might have been a similarly didactic
work of wisdom literature.[30]

----

28 Curiously, Tur-Sinai (1967: 184) has similarly reconstructed the word "God" at the beginning
of v. 12, although he did not rely on 𝕲 but rather on a conjectural emendation of the end of v. 11:
ומן תחות שמיא אלה. In his view, the final pronoun is unnecessary, and the Masoretic vocalization
of the word is unwarranted for two reasons. Morphologically, the normal Aramaic demonstrative
is אלין (Dan 2:40, 44; 6:3, 7; 7:17). Syntactically, in the single other occurrence of the form אלה in
Biblical Aramaic (but only according to the K reading), the pronoun precedes the noun rather
than following it: אלה מאניא (אל), "these vessels" (Ezra 5:15). Tur-Sinai therefore transfers the
word אלה from the end of v. 11 to the beginning of v. 12, re-vocalizing it as אֱלָהּ. His arguments,
however, are untenable and incompatible with the linguistic features of Official Aramaic, to
which the Aramaic passages of Jer 10:11 and Ezra also belong. The pronoun אלה is well attested in
Aramaic documents found in Egypt from the Persian period, and the same applies to the peculiar
word-order of such phrases, e.g. מליא אלה "these words" (*TAD* A6.11:3), גבריא אלה "these men"
(*TAD* B4.4:13). See Muraoka and Porten 2003: 56–57; Vogt 2008: 35. Another, similarly forced
conjecture takes 𝕲's κύριος as resulting from dittography of ה (the last letter of אלה), assuming
that it was misinterpreted, by the Greek translator, as an abbreviation of the Tetragrammaton
(Rabin, Talmon and Tov 1997: נח).
29 Note the prosodic implication of this reconstruction. The Tetragrammaton seemingly interrupts the triple rhythm that dominates both Jer 10:12 and Prov 3:19–20; in fact, however, it is
relegated from the rhythmic scheme because of its marked syntactical status as a pre-posed component of the clause, either as a *casus pendens* (Jer 10:12) or as a topicalized element (Prov 3:19).
30 Some ancient readers still had a sense for the original link between v. 12 and sapiential literature. Note, for instance, 𝕾's surprising rendition of תבונה as ܬܪܥܝܬܐ (Greenberg 2002: 52–53).
In 𝕾-Jer, the Syriac term ܬܪܥܝܬܐ usually renders עצה (Jer 18:18; 19:7; 32:19; 49:20; 50:45; cf.
מועצה in 7:24), and occasionally also זמה (Jer 23:20; 30:24; 51:11), but never תבונה. Likewise in
the 𝕾 in general: תבונה occurs over 40 times in the Hebrew Bible, and 𝕾 normally translates

Another difference between these passages is to be found in their language, and more specifically in their verbal syntax. As indicated above, Jer 10:12 prefers participles (עשה ארץ בכחו / מכין תבל בחכמתו [יהוה]), but it also contains use of a *qatal* form in one instance (ובתבונתו נטה שמים). This tendency is not self-evident, because *qatal* does not normally alternate with participles. By contrast, the employment of a *qatal* form is easily explainable against the background of Prov 3:19–20, which employs it throughout (יהוה בחכמה יסד ארץ / כונן שמים בתבונה / בדעתו תהומות נבקעו /. The *qatal* form is indeed the appropriate means for describing the distant, primeval past; i.e., the Dawn of Creation (likewise with the more distant parallel of Job 26:12–13, which consistently employs *qatal* forms). The latter form is thus presumably reflective of the original wording of the pattern; in any case, it perfectly corresponds with the description of the Creation in mythological terms. Seen in this light, the single *qatal* form in v. 12 appears to be a relic of an older formulation of the passage;[31] the participles contained therein result from secondary adjustment for hymnic usage, as the employment of participial epithets for God comprises one of the conspicuous characteristics of biblical hymnody.[32] This trajectory of stylistic development is carried even further in 𝕲, which adds articles that reinforce the nominalization of the participles and expands them into divine epithets: ὁ ποιήσας τὴν γῆν... ὁ ἀνορθώσας τὴν οἰκουμένην.[33] In any case, the diversity of verbal forms in 𝔐 as well as 𝕲 for v. 12 thus testifies to an

---

it by ܥܒܕܐ – which is also the word employed in the parallel passage of Jer 51:15 – but not with ܝܨܘܦܐ (Isa 44:19 notwithstanding). The translator's lexical choice in Jer 10:12 arguably reflects an attempt to convey the sapiential connotation of the Hebrew wording. Compare the list of professional designations of social institutions that is employed in Jer 18:18, ܘܕܒܪ ܡܢܒܝܐ ܥܡ ܥܒܕܐ (ܘܡܠܟܐ) ܡܟܚܡ ܘܥܨܐ ܡܟܢ ܬܘܪܐ ܬܐܒܕ ܠܐ ܟܝ, "for instruction shall not perish from the priest, *nor counsel from the sage*, nor the word from the prophet."

31 This point deserves emphasis because the grammatical form of *qatal* depends, in this case, on the Masoretic vocalization (נָטָה), while the so-called consonantal text could have just as easily be read as a participle (i.e., נֹטֶה, cf. עֹשֶׂה in line a). 𝔐's vocalization is corroborated by 𝕲, which renders נטה with a simple, finite aorist (ἐξέτεινεν), whereas the other verbal forms in the passage (עשה... מכין) are rendered with aorist participles (ποιήσας... ἀνορθώσας).

32 See especially Crüsemann 1969: 81–154. Ben-Dov 2000 also underscored the implications of this feature for understanding Jer 10:12–13, though from a different point of view.

33 Cf. Ps 134(133):3, עשה שמים וארץ, ὁ ποιήσας τὸν οὐρανὸν καὶ τὴν γῆν; Job 9:8, נטה שמים לבדו, ὁ τανύσας τὸν οὐρανὸν μόνος. In contradistinction, 𝕲 Jer 51(28):15 refrains from adding articles, thus approximating more closely 𝔐, which similarly makes no use of the definite article (עשה ארץ... מכין תבל = ποιῶν γῆν... ἑτοιμάζων οἰκουμένην). This difference vis-à-vis 𝕲 for Jer 10:12 reflects a different translation technique (cf. the Introduction, end of §4.3 [p. 18]). Cf. Ziegler 1958: 114, 145–147.

intermediate stage in the process of literary reworking of an originally sapiential passage and its adaptation into a new, psalmic function.[34]

Another detail that possibly resulted from the psalmic adaptation of the passage is the constituent order of lines a–c, regarding especially the position of the adverbial complement. In Job 26:12–13, this constituent always takes a clause-initial position, whereas in Prov 3:19–20 it freely wanders around. Jer 10:*12 seemingly takes a middle course between these two poles: in lines a–b, the adverbial complement takes the clause-final position, while in line c it takes a clause-initial position:

Job 26:12–13	Jer 10:*12	Prov 3:19–20
בכחו רגע הים	[יהוה] עשה ארץ בכחו	יהוה בחכמה יסד ארץ
ובתובנתו (וּבְתָבוּנָתוֹ) מחץ רהב	מכין תבל בחכמתו	כונן שמים בתבונה
ברוחו שמים שפרה	ובתבונתו נטה שמים	בדעתו תהומות נבקעו

This layout grants line c with an appearance of poetic closure.[35] Indeed, this feature may well have motivated the verse division reflected in 𝔐 and the transference of line d to the beginning of v. 13. Arguably, though, this is only a secondary result of placing the passage in a psalm-like context, which entailed its recasting into in a new poetic pattern. The original structure of "3/4" was changed to an alternative arrangement in couplets. The first couplet forms a synonymous parallelism based on the word-pair ארץ // תבל (cf. Isa 18:3; 34:1; Ps 19:5 etc.) and marked by a grammatical rhyme (the 3m.sg pronominal suffix):[36]

[יהוה] עשה ארץ בכחו   YHWH makes the earth by *his* power.
מכין תבל בחכמתו   He establishes the world by *his* wisdom.

The second couplet is a kind of a synthetic parallelism, and it is marked by repetition of the last word:[37]

ובתבונתו נטה שמים   And by his understanding, he stretched out *the heavens*,
[ו]המון מים בשמים   and a multitude of water in *the heavens*.

---

34 Later versions (𝔙, 𝔖 and 𝔗) submitted the verse to grammatical harmonization that unified the verbal forms in one direction or another, thus eliminating the diversity that characterizes the earlier witnesses.

35 Cf. Ben-Dov 2000: 120, "One notes that in v. 12 the first two cola open with a participle, while the third has a finite verb in its middle in order to achieve a closing effect."

36 Cf. the rhyming of Ps 86:8–10 discussed below, Chapter 5, §3.3.

37 Cf. Isa 34:4a; Ps 148:4.

If this analysis is correct, v. *12 was drawn from wisdom literature, but its style was subsequently adapted to hymnic usage. The transition between the two genres or literary modes may be explained against a broader phenomenon in psalmody, which often integrates allusions to the Creation in hymns that praise YHWH. Ps 89 furnishes an instructive example, as its opening with invocation (v. 2)[38] and continuation with a motive clause introduced by כי (v. 3) mark it as a hymn. This is a long and complex psalm, and its analysis exceeds the scope of the present discussion. Suffice it to note that it contains a paragraph that praises God the Creator for his victory over the mythological monsters of Chaos (vv. 10–11) and for the creation of the world (vv. 12–13). Most relevant in the context of the present discussion is v. 12:

לך שמים אף לך ארץ	The heavens are yours, the earth also is yours;
תבל ומלאה אתה יסדתם	the world and all that is in it – you have founded them.

The form and content of this passage are patently close to Jer 10:*12, as both of them list the same three natural elements – the heavens (שמים), the earth (ארץ), and the inhabited world (תבל) – in the context of Creation. Simultaneously, Ps 89:12 differs from Jer 10:*12 in containing no reference to the motif of wisdom – the backbone of the sapiential saying that underlies Jer 10:*12 and its parallels in wisdom literature.

Thus, Jer 10:*12 itself can be seen as an amalgamation of two originally distinct traditions: a sapiential saying patterned like Prov 3:19–20 and a hymnic declaration in the model of Ps 89:12. The two traditions share some common features that facilitated their merger: they both make use of a threefold construction, and they both employ the basic word-pair of "heavens and earth." Jer 10:*12 relies on the sapiential tradition in thrice reiterating the mention of wisdom, while it draws from the hymnic tradition the participial formulation and possibly also the inclusion of תבל when conforming the pair of "heavens and earth" into the triple pattern shared by both traditions. In so doing, the passage blends components from both traditions.

Such a reworking of v. 12 may be explained, at least partly, by its combination with v. 13, assuming that such a redactional move resulted in stylistic adjustment of the two passages, eventually extending to adapting their content and form as well. This stage of their compositional history is discussed at greater length below (§6); first, however, it is necessary to analyze v. 13 in an attempt to illuminate its earlier form and original literary background.

---

38 Admittedly, the invocation is not the usual imperative in the plural but rather consists of self-encouraging volitives (v. 2: חסדי יהוה עולם אשירה // לדר ודר אודיע אמונתך בפי, "*I will sing* of the Lord's steadfast love forever; with my mouth *I will proclaim* your faithfulness to all generations"); yet this comprises a well-known subclass of the hymnic genre; cf., e.g., Exod 15:1; Ps 101; 108.

§5 v. 13 and its background

The original form of v. 13 can hardly by represented by 𝔐, in which the passage falls into two uneven parts that greatly differ in their form and style, the transition between which is syntactically cumbersome (cf. above, §2). The above analysis of v. 12 showed that the first poetic line of v. 13 (in a shorter form, as witnessed by 𝔊) was originally part of v. *12. If so, v. *13 had consisted of only the three clauses that describe – by employing finite verbs – God's maintenance of the global climate.[39] In the first two lines, the two witnesses agree on the phenomena so described, while in the last one they disagree as to which natural element is the focus of the description:

(a) 𝔐 ויעל/ויעלה נשׂאים מקצה (ה)ארץ is precisely equaled by 𝔊, referring to the *clouds* brought from the end of earth: καὶ ἀνήγαγεν νεφέλας ἐξ ἐσχάτου τῆς γῆς.

(b) 𝔐 ברקים למטר עשה is again accurately paralleled by 𝔊 in describing the *lightning* that accompanies the rain: ἀστραπὰς εἰς ὑετὸν ἐποίησεν.

(c) According to 𝔐, it is the *wind* that is stored in God's heavenly storehouses: ויוצא רוח מאצרתיו. But according to 𝔊, it is the *light*: καὶ ἐξήγαγεν **φῶς** ἐκ θησαυρῶν αὐτοῦ.[40]

This situation raises several questions. The most basic problem pertains to the sequence of lines as witnessed by both 𝔊 and 𝔐. As far as content is concerned, all clauses appear to aim at the climax point of rainfall. This thematic focus, however, did not receive the linguistic design one would expect. All three clauses employ finite verbal forms, either *wayyiqtol* (lines a, c) or *qatal* (line b), in accordance with classical Biblical Hebrew norms. However, the sequence of actions does not conform to the natural order of such events. Had the text been describing a narrative sequence culminating in rainfall, it should have mentioned the rain at the *end* of the sequence rather than in its middle (in the seemingly parenthetic formulation of line b).[41]

---

39 This older form of v. 13, i.e., without the initial words לקול תתו המון מים בשמים, is marked hereafter as v. *13 (cf. above, n. 26).

40 Both readings are echoed in the *Epistle of Jeremiah*; see below, §7.3.

41 Kissane 1952 sensed this problem, but he sought to solve it by amending the text from ברקים "lightnings" to בדקים "fissures" (cf. 2 Kgs 12:6–9; 22:5 ‖ 2 Chr 34:10), interpreting the resulting image as referring to the opening of the windows of heaven (cf. Gen 7:11; Ps 42:8). Some commentators assessed this proposal favorably (e.g., McKane 1986–96: 1.226, though he eventually preferred to maintain 𝔐 as it stands). The emendation, however, is linguistically implausible. The grammatical form of בֶּדֶק in BH is a collective singular, so the hypothetical plural בדקים is

This consideration is not purely theoretical. The expected sequence does indeed occur in another passage taken from narrative prose, which depicts the long-desired arrival of rain after an extended drought at the time of Ahab (1 Kgs 18:45):

ויהי עד כה ועד כה	In a little while
והשמים התקדרו עבים ורוח	the heavens grew black with clouds and wind;
ויהי גשם גדול	there was a heavy rain.

This passage mentions first the clouds, then the wind, and only at the end does it address the rain. Such a natural sequencing of events is by no means limited to prose. It is also found in a poetic, hymnic passage (Ps 147:8):

המכסה שמים בעבים	He who covers the heavens with clouds,
המכין לארץ מטר	who prepares rain for the earth,
המצמיח הרים חציר	who makes grass grow on the hills.

It is tempting, therefore, to consider the possibility that the attested sequence of poetic lines in Jer 10:*13 is not their original order. Presumably, they were arranged in a way that better conforms to the natural course of such events (i.e., a-c-b):[42]

a	ויעל/ויעלה נשאים מקצה (ה)ארץ	He made the mist rise from the ends of the earth,
c	ויוצא רוח מאצרתיו	and he brought out the wind from his storehouses;
b	ברקים למטר עשה	Lightnings he made for the rain.

This hypothesis solves another syntactic difficulty caused by the attested order of lines, which scholars tend to overlook. The reconstructed sequence explains the meaning of the change in constituent-order, which took place in line b (ברקים למטר עשה), namely the movement of the verb from a clause-initial to clause-final position. In the recorded sequence (a-b-c), it is difficult to understand why the object and adverbial complement were pre-posed (in terms of the syntactic surface) or topicalized (in terms of the underlying message). But if line b was originally the concluding line, then the divergence from the normal, unmarked constituent

---

questionable. Also, the parallels adduced by Kissane are too partial and distant to substantiate his reconstruction. An alternative emendation of ברקים to פרקים "appointed times" was proposed by Perles 1912: 108, but – as admitted by Perles himself – this word is not otherwise recorded in Hebrew before Mishnaic Hebrew.

42 Indirect corroboration for this reconstruction may be found in the reworking of Jer 10:12–13 in EpJer 59–61 (see below, §7.3). Carmignac 1970 attempted a similar path of inquiry, motivated to think in this direction by another alternative sequence that is recorded in the citation of Jer 10:12–13 in the *Hymn to the Creator*. His approach, however, is fraught with difficulties (see below, n. 78).

order can be easily interpreted as a common discursive technique of marking a discourse boundary; namely, the end of an utterance. The first two lines exhibit an unmarked order, in which the verb takes the clause-initial position, whereas the movement of the verb to a clause-final position marks the delimiting line, thus indicating the conclusion of the entire poetic unit:[43]

a   **ויעל/ויעלה** נשאים מקצה ארץ

c   **ויוצא** רוח מאצרתיו

b   ברקים למטר **עשה**

Moreover, the marked constituent order becomes fully intelligible on the level of the message as well, as it emphasizes that God toils in creating all these climatic effects for a single purpose – the bringing of rain, the practical meaning of which is ensuring the world fertility.[44]

The metathesis between the last two lines (a-c-b > a-b-c) must have taken place at a relatively early stage, since it is reflected in both 𝕲 and 𝔐. It might be related to the interpolation of vv. 12–13 as a whole within its present context in the prophetic unit (cf. below, §8). Line c refers to the wind (רוּחַ) kept by God in his heavenly storehouses. Moving it to its current place, at the end of v. 13, creates a contrast to the following v. 14 – which belongs to the original, polemical core of the prophecy – as the latter passage concludes with asserting that the idols have no spirit of life (רוח).

The reconstructed order of lines has yet another advantage that speaks in its favor, albeit indirectly. Such a sequence is more conveniently linked to the following, polemical passage of vv. 14–15 by presenting a positive counterpart of a sapiential saying that is formulated in the negative (Prov 25:14):

נְשִׂיאִים וְרוּחַ וְגֶשֶׁם אָיִן   Like clouds and wind without rain

אִישׁ מִתְהַלֵּל בְּמַתַּת־שָׁקֶר: is one who boasts of a gift never given.

The fact that these passages contain the only two occurrences in the Hebrew Bible of the term נְשִׂיאִים with the rare sense of "clouds" suggests their intertextual relation. Moreover, closer inspection reveals that the similarity between these texts

---

43 Lunn 2006: 144–150, esp. 148–149.

44 Some support for this reconstruction may be furnished by the comparable formulation of a Deuteronomic blessing, which first alludes to God's heavenly storehouses and then gets to the rain, formulating it as an adverbial complement that marks it as God's purpose: יפתח יהוה לך את אוצרו הטוב את השמים לתת מטר ארצך בעתו, "The Lord will open for you his rich storehouse, the heavens, to give the rain of your land in its season" (Deut 28:12).

is not limited to a single point of verbal contact but rather extends to a striking correspondence in the order of their components:[45]

	Prov 25:14	Jer 10:13–14 || 51:16–17			
i	**נשיאים**	מקצה (ה)ארץ	**נשאים**	ויעל/ויעלה	v. 13
ii	**ורוח**	מאצרתיו	**רוח**	ויוצא	
iii	וגשם אין	עשה	**למטר**	ברקים	
iv	**איש**	מדעת	**אדם**	נבער כל	v. 14
v	**מתהלל**	כל צורף מפסל	**הביש**		
vi	במתת **שקר**	נסכו	**שקר**	כי	
vii		בם	רוח	ולא	

If this observation has some merit, it suggests that the integration of v. *13 into its present place, and especially its linking to v. 14, might also be inspired by wisdom literature, at least to some extent. Notably, however, this relation is not as evident as it is with respect to v. *12, and it does not necessarily explain the original form of v. *13 in itself – only (perhaps) its secondary interpolation.

This point brings us inevitably to the central question: What is the provenance and literary background of v. *13? Unfortunately, due to the paucity of data, no definitive answer can be offered to this query. But a somewhat speculative proposal may nevertheless by made, based on the exceptional interest of this passage in atmospheric phenomena. On the one hand, v. *13 is cast in a poetic form that suggests its affinity with psalmody. On the other hand, its closest thematic parallel is embedded in a narrative telling about a drought in Ahab's days (1 Kgs 18:41–45). Thus, v. *13 might have originated in a psalm of thanksgiving for the termination of a drought, which related – among other things – the favorable change of the climate conditions.[46]

Admittedly, the Hebrew Bible contains no certain example of such a psalm. However, the book of Jeremiah itself includes a petitionary prayer motivated by a drought (Jer 14:1–9; cf. 1 Kgs 8:35–36 \|\| 2 Chr 6:26–27). It stands to reasons that thanksgiving prayers were similarly performed when the cause of distress

---

45 In three cases, the keyword in Prov 25:14 is literally reproduced in Jer 10:13–14 with מטר (i), רוח (ii), שקר (vi). In two cases, synonymous terms are used in place of verbatim repetitions: גשם // מטר (iii), cf. Zech 10:1; Job 37:6; אדם // איש (iv), cf. Prov 30:2; Ps 62:10, etc. In one case, a pair of antonyms is employed: מתהלל // הביש (v), cf. Ps 97:7.

46 Kruger 1993 went as far as to suggest that the entire prophetic unit of Jer 10:1–16 is to be interpreted against a context of drought, arguing further that the theological polemic it expresses is specifically directed against the idea that idols are capable of bringing rain and thus fertility to the land. However, the context of drought can only be anchored in v. 13, and extending it to the entire prophetic unit is forced, as noted by Ben-Dov 2000: 105–106 and n. 22.

ameliorated and the rain had finally arrived. In accordance with the conventions of the psalmic genre of thanksgiving, such a prayer would surely describe in detail both the distress (i.e., the drought) and God's response to the people's cry for help (i.e., the bringing of rain).[47]

In any case, and regardless of the hypothetical identification of the presumed origin of v. *13, the parallels adduced above are helpful for comprehending a textual problem; namely, the relation between the variant readings in line c: "he brought out the *wind* (𝔐) / *light* (𝔊) from his storehouses." Both the prosaic parallel of 1 Kgs 18:45 ("In a little while the heavens grew black with clouds and *wind*; there was a heavy rain") and the sapiential saying of Prov 25:14 ("Like clouds and *wind* without rain is one who boasts of a gift never given") confirm the originality of 𝔐's "wind" as against 𝔊's "light." This situation comprises an intriguing example of an internal, independent development within the textual branch represented by 𝔊. Even though the readings testified by 𝔊 (or its Hebrew *Vorlage*) usually reflect a literary form of the prophecy that is older than the one witnessed by 𝔐, 𝔊 cannot be taken as representing its *Urtext*, and it too reflects a text submitted to some reworking and secondary developments, albeit to a more limited degree compared to 𝔐.

The hypothesis that 𝔊's reading "he brought out the *light* from his storehouses" is secondary has already been proposed in scholarship, but on different grounds. Scholars have debated whether to attribute the reading "light" to the Greek translator or to his Hebrew *Vorlage*, and they disagreed in their identification of its cultural background.[48] Yet I doubt if the word "light" should be credited with too much significance in the present context. More likely, it was inserted at this point in an attempt to solve the problem caused by the reshuffling of lines of v. *13 – especially the transposition of line c to the end of the passage, which

---

47 For the generic characteristics of thanksgiving psalms, see Gunkel and Begrich 1998: 240–247; Mowinckel 1962: 2.26–30; Crüsemann 1969: 155–209. It has been proposed in the scholarship that Ps 85 and Ps 126 are drought psalms, but I am not convinced that this identification is supported by their actual content. See, e.g., Becking 2014: 244–249.

48 Seeligmann (2002: 116–117) leans towards the assumption that the Greek translator introduced the change, reflecting a Hellenistic, proto-Gnostic background. Ben-Dov 2005 prefers to interpret this reading against the background of the development of cosmology in the Second Temple period, without determining if the change took place at the stage of translation or rather beforehand, in the underlying Hebrew *Vorlage*. Streane (1896: 125) proposed a different, text-critical interpretation; under this approach, the word "light" is a mistaken supplementation of the parallelism. Although Streane does not explicate his position, he probably means that the word was paired with "lightnings" (see Hab 3:11; cf. Ps 77:19; 97:4).

seriously interrupts the narrative-like sequence and renders it incompatible with the natural succession of events.[49]

Replacing "wind" with "light" solved this issue in two parallel spheres. Regarding the image of reality, this substitution results in a descriptive sequence that continues the meteorological chain of events beyond the rainfall; it culminates in the parting of clouds and the breaking of sunlight through them. Regarding theological signification, the appearance of light symbolizes the divine salvation that is kept for God's loyal ones.[50] The 𝔊 reading thus supplies a suitable conclusion for the hymnic passage by highlighting, yet again, the contrast between worshippers of YHWH and the heathen idolaters, who are the subject of a detailed description in the following passage (vv. 14–15).

§6 The combination of vv. 12–13

The above analysis suggests that v. *12 and v.*13 originate in distinct literary traditions. The first passage comprises a sapiential proverb, while the latter comprises a fragment of a psalm. The shared theme of rain apparently formed the basis for combining the two passages: v. *12d is the climax of the wisdom saying, but it does not elaborate on the rain as such; v. *13 supplements this lacuna by supplying a detailed depiction of the gradual change of the weather through the much-anticipated moment of rainfall. V. *12 was thus expanded by appending it

---

49 The rabbis found the same issue disturbing, but they obviously did not resort to textual intervention but rather deduced that the given sequence intends to convey a particular lesson; namely, that God is not subject to the same natural laws that apply to humans: ר' אלעזר אמ' ר' חנינא: בוא וראה שלא כמדת הקב"ה מדת בשר ודם. מדת בשר ודם: אדם שופת קדרה, ואחר כך נותן לתוכה מים. אבל הקב"ה נותן מים, ואחר כך שופת הקדרה. שנ' "לקול תתו המון מים בשמים" (*b. Meg.* 15a), "R. Elazar further said in the name of R. Hanina: Come and observe that the way of the Holy One, blessed be He, is not like the way of flesh and blood – The way of flesh and blood is that a man places a pot on the fire and then pours water into it, but God first puts in the water and then sets the pot, to fulfil what is written: 'At the sound of his giving a multitude of waters in the heavens' (Jer. x, 13)" (tr. M. Simon, in Epstein 1935: 5.15a). Compare *Mishnat R. Eliezer* 11 (ed. Enelow 1933: 214).

50 For parallelism between the actual light (φῶς) and the salvation it symbolizes (σωτηρία), cf. Isa 49:6. For the picture of salvation stored in the divine treasures, cf. 𝔊 Isa 33:6, ἐν θησαυροῖς ἡ σωτηρία ἡμῶν, ἐκεῖ σοφία καὶ ἐπιστήμη καὶ εὐσέβεια πρὸς τὸν κύριον· οὗτοί εἰσι θησαυροὶ δικαιοσύνης, "Our salvation is in treasures: wisdom and knowledge and piety toward the Lord are there; these are the treasures of righteousness" vs. 𝔐, והיה אמונת עתיך חסן ישועת חכמת ודעת יראת יהוה היא אוצרו, "He will be the stability of your times, abundance of salvation, wisdom, and knowledge; the fear of the Lord is Zion's treasure" (Seeligmann 1958: 133–134 [=1996: 418] already referred to this passage).

with v. *13, and the unified passage has become an extended demonstration of God's control over the natural elements.

It is, however, in the nature of literary development that by solving one problem, a new one is created at a different point. In the case at hand, juxtaposing the two verses rendered ambiguous the status of the line [ו]המון מים בשמים, in two respects:

(a) Structurally, its function in the immediate context has changed. Formerly, it concluded v. *12, but its re-contextualization caused the assertion that water is stored in the heavenly storehouses to look more like an opening for the narrative-like description of how such stored water is released and turns into rain. All the more so since the secondary linking of this line with v. *13 might have been reinforced by a stylistic factor: v. *12d refers to "the heavens," whereas v. *13a mentions "the earth," so that the two poetic lines could have been roughly construed as a sort of a parallelism based on the very common word-pair of שמים // ארץ.

(b) Exegetically, the word המון that opens v. *12d has been subjected to a renewed interpretation. Originally, in the context of v. *12, the word meant "multitude."[51] The entire line conveyed the idea that God, in his wisdom, ensured the eternal abundance of rain, because the heavens were planned in advance as storehouses for precipitation (cf. Job 38:22). By contrast, within the context of v. *13, the word is better understood in the sense of "sound, roar" (cf. 1 Kgs 18:41), and it was taken as a reference to the pyrotechnic effects that accompany rainfall: thunder and lightning ("There is a tumult of waters in the heavens... He made lightnings for the rain"), clouds and winds ("He brought forth the mist from the ends of the earth... and he brought out the wind from his storehouses").[52]

---

51 To be sure, from the perspective of historical semantics, the original sense of המון was "sound, roar," and it shifted to denote copiousness and abundance only at later stages of the semantic development (cf. BDB, 242, s.v.). However, the relatively late sense of "a large group of people, a big crowd" is already recorded in classical Biblical Hebrew (e.g., Judg 4:7; 2 Sam 6:19; 1 Kgs 20:13, 28). Moreover, the sense of "abundance" is reflected in another context in Jeremiah (Jer 49:32), and it may possibly be evoked with respect to water (Jer 51:42). So no reason exists to deny the possibility of applying this sense to the original form of v. *12, whose language is classical Biblical Hebrew.

52 This understanding assumes that the words לקול תתו refer to the voice of thunder (cf. below, n. 57). Alternative interpretations seem less likely. For instance, the medieval Jewish commentator Joseph Qara was also disturbed by the sequence exhibited by MT between לקול תתו המון מים בשמים and ויעלה נשאים מקצה (ה)ארץ, but he sought to remedy this difficulty with a sophisticated climatological explanation. He describes an elaborate chain of events that begins with God's oral command (his interpretation of the words לקול תתו) to store water in the heavens. The clouds then "drink" the water of the oceans (thus bringing it up to the heavens), after which they are sent from the end of the earth to wherever God wishes in order to pour the rain over the earth. It remains doubtful, however, that such a scientific conceptualization of the weather may be assumed to underlie v. 13.

The Hebrew text tolerates the semantic ambiguity of the noun המון (cf. Isa 17:12). But the ancient versions testify to the exegetical problem it creates, because the translators were forced to decide which of the two possible senses is to be represented in their target language. The unavoidable hesitation in this regard is particularly reflected in 𝔊: it renders the word as πλῆθος "multitude" in Jer 10:13 (cf. Jer 49:32 etc), and as ἦχος "sound, roar" in Jer 51(28):16 (cf. Jer 47:3 etc.).[53]

I propose that the semantic ambiguity of the word המון, and the structural hesitation regarding how to construe v. *12d, both motivated the exegetical addition of the words לקול תתו, as attested by 𝔐 and its dependent versions.[54] Exegetes and critical commentators have debated how to interpret these words, but in my opinion there has been some exaggeration in describing the syntactic difficulty they create. The various conjectural emendations of the text that have been advanced are usually superfluous, and often they create even greater linguistic difficulties than those they strive to solve.[55] Most plausibly, this construction reflects a common stylistic device; namely, an inverted construct phrase, so that לקול תתו equals לתתו קול "when he makes a sound."[56] However, the real significance of

---

[53] This is yet another demonstration of the difference between the distinct characters of the Greek versions of Chapters 10 and 51(28). The interpretation of המון as "multitude" is appropriate for the older form of Jer 10:*12 as it is recorded in 𝔊, whereas "sound, roar" fits better the sense of the word as it was re-contextualized in Jer 10:13 ‖ 51(28):16, in the reworked text represented by 𝔐. In other words, the Greek version of Chapter 51(28):15–16 approximates the proto-Masoretic tradition. This revisional-like feature better corresponds with the second part of 𝔊-Jer. See the Introduction, end of §4.3 (p. 18).

[54] Including 𝔊 Jer 51(28):15–16 (cf. above, n. 53).

[55] Scholarly literature abounds with such futile emendations, surveyed in the various critical commentaries. Cf. Barthélemy 1986: 545–546, and see further below, n. 56. Perhaps the most brilliant conjecture is that of Duhm 1901: 102, who emended the text to לקולו נתך המון מים בשמים, "By his command (lit. at his sound), a multitude of water has poured in the heavens", based on 2 Sam 21:10, עד נתך מים עליהם מן השמים, "until rain *fell* on them from the heavens". Cf. Rudolph 1958: 66; Holladay 1986–89: 1.324 n. 13a. This proposal, however, assumes too many scribal faults (both the ligature of נ+ו for producing a ת, and the change of כ/ך into ו), and it is further complicated by the fact that the following prepositional phrase is introduced by a ב־ ("*in* the heavens") rather than by מן ("*from* the heavens"), as one would have expected. G.R. Driver 1938: 106 took a different approach; he conjectured that the noun הֲמוֹן was graphically mutilated from the verb יֶהֱמָיֶן.

[56] Althann 1989. For the stylistic phenomenon of inverted construct phrases, cf. Avishur 1993. There is no need, therefore, to emend the text by transposing the words into לְתִתּוֹ קוֹל as suggested by BHK and BHS, following Giesebrecht 1907: 65 (note, however, that Rudolph, who edited Jeremiah for both BHK and BHS, preferred to adopt Duhm's emendation in his own commentary on Jeremiah). At any rate, 𝔐's wording is maintained in 4QJer[a], which is not only the oldest textual witness of Jeremiah but also one of the three most ancient scrolls found in Qumran (cf. above, p. 10, n. 23).

this addition has escaped the attention of scholars thus far: they respond to the exegetical questions raised by the juxtaposition of vv. 12–13. Structurally, they detach the words המון מים בשמים from v. 12 and link it to v. 13. Semantically, they explicate that the sense of המון refers to the sound (קול) of rainfall, which may also include the voice of thunder.[57]

Other critical commentators consider the beginning of v. 13 as a curtailed text, since they find it difficult to understand the function of the words לקול תתו in their present context.[58] Actually, though, these words supply a decided response to the exegetical queries prompted by the juxtaposition of vv. 12–13. At the same time, they also push the text of 𝔐 away from the original form and meaning of the passage – both of which are more faithfully reflected in 𝔊, which structurally treats v. *12d as a direct continuation of v. 12, and which correctly renders the word המון as "multitude." These indications suggest that the words לקול תתו were added not only after vv. 12–13 were combined, but also after the unified passage was interpolated into the prophetic unit of Jer 10:1–16. Their addition, therefore, is to be regarded as one of the internal developments that have taken place within the long textual tradition, which is characterized by intensive reworking and a plethora of expansions compared to the more conservative, shorter tradition represented by 𝔊.

The hypothetical intermediate stage, in which vv. 12–13 were already juxtaposed but the words לקול תתו were not yet added, may be indirectly witnessed by the *Hymn to the Creator* (see below, §7.2). Nevertheless, this stage is more difficult to pin down. Theoretically, the two verses could have been juxtaposed only as part of the prophetic unit, assuming that they were drawn from their distinct sources and added independently (or simultaneously) to the prophetic unit. Alternately,

---

57 Compare to 1 Sam 12:17–18, אקרא אל יהוה ויתן קלות ומטר... ויתן יהוה קלת ומטר ביום ההוא, "I will call upon the Lord, that he may send thunder and rain... and the LORD sent thunder and rain that day" (cf. Exod 9:23, 33–34; Ps 77:18). Note that in rabbinic literature, this particular passage is even considered to be a piece of evidence supporting the cosmological perception that thunder sounds in fact are produced by the water poured from one cloud to another (*b. Ber.* 59a, when discussing the words ועל הרעמים, "concerning the thunders", of *m. Ber.* 9:2). By evoking this interpretation – which is akin to the literal sense of the scriptural proof-text – the Babylonian rabbis may imply a polemic with another, more midrashic treatment of the passage, such as the one included in the Palestinian *Genesis Rabbah* 5:4 (ed. Theodor and Albeck 1965: 1.34–35; tr. Freedman, in Freedman and Simon 1939: 1.36), which interprets the word קול as a cry (בכי, alluding to Jer 31:15), going as far as to claim that the sound uttered by the water at the time of Creation – and separation of the upper waters from the lower ones (according to Gen 1:6–7) – was also the sound of a cry (alluding to Job 28:11).

58 See, e.g., Bright 1965: 77 n. *e–e*. Cf. Reimer 1988, who reconstructs קול תתו *בערפל**, based on the Ugaritic myth of Baal: *wtn qlh bʕrpt // šrh lảrṣ brqm* (*CTA* 1.4 V 8–9), "And may he give his voice in the clouds / May he flash to the earth lightning" (tr. M.S. Smith in Parker 1997: 129). The resulting syntax of the reconstructed text of the passage, however, is ungrammatical in Hebrew.

they might have been combined at a previous stage and interpolated into the prophetic unit as a single passage. No conclusive evidence exists in support of either one option over the other, but the latter scenario is a bit more appealing. As suggested above, v. *12 was supplemented by v. *13, expanding the line [ו]המון מים בשמים, thus elaborating the depiction of rainfall and highlighting the theologoumenon that YHWH is responsible for bringing rain. This idea is not echoed in any other passage of the prophetic unit of Jer 10:1–16, thus confirming that vv. 12–13 as a whole are alien to their present context and quoted from a different context.

The most reasonable setting for such a combination is psalmody, which by its very nature comprises a modular mode of literary production; it tends to recycle existing material and integrate given passages and standard formulae into new combinations. Furthermore, Hebrew psalmody also includes wisdom psalms, which belong to sapiential literature in terms of their content and ideology but take the poetic form of psalms and hymns. An unknown psalm of this sort might have been the locus where a sapiential saying in the form of v. *12 (itself reflecting some influence from hymnody) was combined together with a psalmic fragment such as v. *13 in order to produce a hymnic description of God's greatness, as expressed by his control over nature.[59]

These considerations can be amplified by paying attention to the theological outlook of the synthetic passage of vv. 12–13. The detailed account of God's dominion in nature actually encodes the idea that he has full ownership of his world. The expression of this notion indeed typifies psalmody. For instance, a passage already alluded to above (Ps 89:12) contains an explicit declaration of ownership:

לך שמים אף לך ארץ   The heavens are yours, the earth also is yours;
תבל ומלאה אתה יסדתם   the world and all that is in it – you have founded them.

The Creation of all levels of the universe – the heavens, the earth, and the inhabited world – and controlling them – and whatever takes place within them – advertise God's ownership of what he had brought into being.

---

59 According to this line of reasoning, the weight of the sapiential dimension was subject to constant change throughout the compositional history of the text under review. It was inherent to v. *12, but it has become of relatively minor importance in vv. 12–13, at least on the compositional level. While v. *12 underscores God's wisdom, this motif was pushed aside by the addition of v. *13, whose emphasis is more on God's responsibility for the proper maintenance of the natural order and especially for brining rain. Interestingly, though, the wisdom motif regained the center stage when vv. 12–13 were integrated – as a unified hymnic passage – into the prophetic unit. This new context yields a contrast between God's wisdom as asserted by v. 12 and human stupidity as lamented over in v. 14 (נבער כל אדם מדעת, "Everyone is stupid and without knowledge"). For a different opinion, see von Rad 1972: 177–185; Ammann 2015: 121–123.

Similarly, biblical psalmody affords some examples for expressing this theologoumenon by explicitly connecting it to the notion of wisdom:

- Ps 104:24, מה רבו מעשיך יהוה / כֻּלָּם בחכמה עשית / מלאה הארץ קנינך, "O LORD, how manifold are your works! *In wisdom* you have made them all; the earth is full of your creatures."
- Ps 136:3–5, הודו לאדֹנֵי האדֹנים... לעֹשה השמים בתבונה, "O give thanks to the Lord of lords... who *by understanding* made the heavens."

Seen in this light, the combination of vv. 12–13 is best explained as having occurred in a psalmic context, possibly within a wisdom psalm, although the specific source in which this combination took place was not preserved independently as a stand-alone text.

Another consideration should be noted in this discussion. The subject matter of vv. 12–13 as a psalmic fragment – which, in itself, is not directly related to the polemic against idolatry – may be echoed in another prophecy in the book of Jeremiah, in which God complains, in the first person, about Israel's treachery (Jer 5:20ff.). The divine speaker wonders how it is possible that the Israelites do not fear the one who had tamed the primordial chaotic forces, thus establishing the exiting world (v. 22: "'Do you not fear me?' says the LORD; 'Do you not tremble before me? I placed the sand as a boundary for the sea, a perpetual barrier that it cannot pass; though the waves toss, they cannot prevail, though they roar, they cannot pass over it.'"). This assertion is then attached poignantly to the notion that God is also the one who brings rain on time (v. 24: "They do not say in their hearts, 'Let us fear the LORD our God, who gives the rain in its season, the autumn rain and the spring rain, and keeps for us the weeks appointed for the harvest.'"). The logic of this argument is very close to the one transpiring vv. 12–13, in their combined form. The technique of citing psalms and psalm fragments typifies the book of Jeremiah as a whole; indeed, this tendency is characteristic of Jeremiah's authentic prophecies already (as far as they can be identified). Potentially, therefore, the psalmic fragment represented in vv. 12–13 was absorbed into the corpus of Jeremiah's prophecies at a very early – perhaps even primary – phase, as suggested by its echo in Chapter 5, but it was placed in its present context at a later compositional stage. This conclusion stands in line with the linguistic profile of the fragment, which is compatible with a late monarchic date.[60]

---

60 See above, §2 (concerning the grammatical form of וַיַּעֲלֶה); below, n. 69.

§7 Parallel sources

The discussion thus far focused on exposing internal clues for the gradual literary growth of vv. 12–13 from their distinct sources. Admittedly, both the general trajectory and specific turns of the literary and textual development are by and large hypothetical. Nevertheless, some aspects and even reconstructed stages may be witnessed indirectly by literary sources that contain parallels to the passages under scrutiny.

§7.1 Ps 135:7

Ps 135 has an eclectic character, comprising an assortment of fragments of diverse nature.[61] Between a passage of praise that serves as a hymnic introit (vv. 1–6) and a historical survey of the Exodus and conquest of the land of Canaan that serves as the body of the hymn (vv. 8–12), one finds v. 7, which praises God for His control over the natural elements.[62] The secondary status of v. 7 in Ps 135 is signaled, first and foremost, by the way it interrupts the continuity between the hymnic introit (vv. 1–6) and the body of the hymn (vv. 8–12). This status is further indicated by a linguistic difference between this passage and the rest of the psalm: this is the only passage that makes use of participles, whereas all the other verbs recorded in Ps 135 are finite forms, either of the *qatal* type in the words of praise (vv. 4–6) and in the historical survey (vv. 8–12), or of the *yiqtol* type in a paragraph that polemicizes with idolatry (vv. 13–18). The reason for interpolating v. 7 into its present place is also quite evident: it expands v. 6 ("Whatever the LORD pleases he does, in heaven and on earth, in the seas and all deeps"), demonstrating the rule that God is an exclusive sovereign of His world (v. 6) by controlling the weather (v. 7), whose particular phenomena connect between the heavens and earth (mentioned in both verses).

Ps 135:7 closely parallels v. *13 in lacking the long adverbial complement that opens v. 13 according to 𝔐:

a	מעלה נשאים מקצה הארץ	He makes the clouds rise at the end of the earth.
b	ברקים למטר עשה	Lightnings he made for the rain.
c	מוצא רוח מאוצרותיו	He brings out the wind from his storehouses.

---

61 Cf. above, Chapter 1, §6.

62 Critical commentators of the Psalter usually prefer considering vs. 7 as part of a broader thematic unit (vv. 5–7). See, e.g., Kraus 1988–89: 2.490–494, esp. 493; Hossfeld and Zenger 2005–11: 3.492–501, esp. 493, 497–498. Enough indications exist, however, that this is a composite psalm, and that v. 7 in particular was imported from a different context, as explained presently.

It is tempting, therefore, to interpret Ps 135:7 as witnessing the independent existence of our v. *13. Still, some subtle indications exist that this parallel text does not necessarily reflect the original – or even an independent – form of the hymnic passage but rather a later reworking that already assumes the form of the passage as part of Jer 10:1–16.[63]

First and foremost, the sequence of poetic lines in Ps 135:7 differs from the reconstructed order of the original form of this passage; it is, in fact, identical to the presumably secondary order witnessed by both 𝔊 and 𝔐 for Jer 10:13 || 51(28):16. Had this sequence been produced as part of the integration of vv. 12–13 into the broader context of Jer 10:1–16, Ps 135:7 would depend – either directly or indirectly – on some form of this particular prophecy.

Second, two of the three poetic lines include participles (lines a, c), but one of them also employs a *qatal* form (line b), which is not a normal alternative of participles; therefore, its presence is unexpected. On the other hand, the presence of a *qatal* form is predictable in the equivalent line b of Jer 10:13, because there it functions as the regular, automatic alternative of the *wayyiqtol* forms that are used in the other lines (a, c):[64]

	Ps 135:7		**Jer 10:13 || 51:15**
a	מעלה נשאים מקצה הארץ (participle), vs.		ויעל/ויעלה נשאים מקצה (ה)ארץ (*wayyiqtol*)
b	ברקים למטר עשה (*qatal*)		ברקים למטר עשה (*qatal*)
c	מוצא רוח מאוצרותיו (participle), vs.		ויוצא רוח מאצרתיו (*wayyiqtol*)

Thus, the *qatal* form in line b is best understood as a relic from an earlier form of the text that was either identical or closely similar to that of Jer 10:13. The change of *wayyiqtol* forms into participles is nothing but a direct continuation of the trend to adapt the passage to a hymnic function,[65] in a manner similar to the process Jer 10:12 underwent vis-à-vis its parallels in the wisdom literature (above, §4).

---

63 Ps 135 contains a number of parallels for various parts of Jer 10:1–16, but so as to avoid the risk of circular reasoning, as well as any potentially false deductions, the following discussion focuses on analyzing only the internal evidence supplied by v. 7 – the direct parallel for the passage under discussion (while considering parallels for other parts of the prophetic unit external to our present concern).

64 Notwithstanding some exceptions, the syntactic rule in classical Biblical Hebrew is that *wayyiqtol* normally occupies a clause-initial position. Marked variants of this order are generated by pre-posing another constituent (e.g., for the purpose of topicalization); the verb is then pushed to a clause-medial or clause-final position, and it does not retain the form of *wayyiqtol* but rather transforms into *qatal*. So also in our line b: ברקים למטר עשה.

65 For a different opinion, see Ben-Dov 2000: 120.

Another noteworthy linguistic difference between the sources relates to the definite article. In 𝔐, the mythological term ארץ "Earth" is read in Jer 10:13 (K) ‖ 51:16 without the definite article, whereas Ps 135:7 reads the word with an article (and hence also the Q reading in Jer 10:13, הָאָרֶץ). The definite article is known to be a linguistic innovation in Canaanite; Hebrew had inherited it, but its distribution in biblical poetry – which is generally characterized by linguistic conservatism – is largely restricted compared to narrative prose.[66] Tellingly, though, it significantly expands in poetry composed in late Biblical Hebrew.[67] Its appearance in Ps 135:7, therefore, is suggestive of a late linguistic recasting of the passage. Needless to say, this feature cannot prove such a dating by itself, but the chronological suspicion is further corroborated by other linguistic details that betray a late, post-exilic date.[68] In contradistinction, hardly any trace of late Biblical Hebrew can be found in Jer 10:12–13 ‖ 51:15–16, and this passage is consistently compatible with classical Biblical Hebrew.[69]

Thus, Ps 135:7 appears to be based on an already reworked version of v. 13; the psalmist has taken the text another step forward in terms of adapting it to hymnic, stylistic standards and to the linguistic norms of late Biblical Hebrew. Ps 135:7 may be directly dependent upon Jer 10:13.[70] But one cannot exclude the possibility that both Jer 10:13 and Ps 135:7 draw from a common tradition, which was preserved relatively faithfully in Jer 10:13 and reworked more freely in Ps 135:7. In this case, the latter source indirectly supports the proposed contention that this passage had its own history prior to being integrated into the prophetic unit of Jer 10:1–16.

§7.2 Hymn to the creator

Another parallel for Jer 10:12–13 is embedded in a short psalm that came to light with the publication of 11QPs[a] (col. 26, line 9ff.). From a compositional perspective, it is a patchwork of citations from a variety of sources, some of which

---

66 But note Waltke and O'Connor 1990: 250, §13.7; Barr 1989: 310–312.
67 Cf. Hurvitz 1985.
68 Hurvitz 1972: 174; Hurvitz 1982.
69 Compare the observation made by Hornkohl 2014: 60, that v. 12 employs several synonyms for expressing the notion of "wisdom," but it does not employ the lexeme מדע, an Aramaic loanword that typifies late Biblical Hebrew. Generally speaking, vv. 12–13 hardly reflect any Aramaic influence, either direct or indirect. In this, they differ markedly from another hymnic passage integrated into Jer 10:1–16; namely, vv. 6–7 (see below, Chapter 5).
70 See, e.g., Ammann 2015: 137, 143–144.

are biblical. Among other quotations, it also includes the following passage (line 13–15):[71]

ברוך עושה ארץ בכוחו	Blessed be the one who makes the earth by his power,
מכין תבל בחכמתו	who establishes the world by his wisdom.
בתבונתו נטה שמים	By his understanding, he had stretched out the heavens,
ויוצא [רו]חֹ מאֹוֹ[צרותיו	and he brought out [the win]d from his sto[rehouses.
ברקים למט[ר עשה	Lightnings] he made [for the rai]n,
ויעל נשיא[ים מ[קצֹה [ארץ]	and he made the cloud[s] rise [from] the ends of [the earth.]

The *Hymn* intriguingly differs from the Jeremiah passage in several respects, but evaluating its testimony should take into account its peculiar treatment of the sources it quotes or alludes to.

A. Shorter text of v. 13. Like Ps 135, the *Hymn* seemingly lacks the entire adverbial complement that opens v. 13 (לקול תתו המון מים בשמים). Unlike the situation regarding Ps 135:7, however, this finding cannot be taken as evidence for an older form of vv. 12–13, because the missing segment includes the words that had formerly constituted v. *12d (המון מים בשמים), and whose originality – as part of v. *12 – is not in doubt.[72] The absence of the first part of v. 13, then, is more likely due to secondary omission.

Contributing to this suspicion is the fact that some of the missing words actually reverberate in another passage of the *Hymn*, which describes God's royal entourage:

לפניו הדר ילך	Honor goes before him,[73]
ואחריו המון מים רבים	and a multitude of much water is after him.

The words המון מים רבים seem to allude to the missing poetic line of המון מים בשמים.[74] Moreover, the employment of the adjective רבים ("much, many") seems to reflect

---

71 Cf. Sanders 1965: 47, 89–91; cf. Sanders 1967: 84–85, 129–131.

72 A similarly short text is reflected in Eusebius of Caesarea's *Preparation for the Gospel* (*Praeparatio evangelica*) VII.11, where Jer 10:12–13 is extensively quoted (without the first part of v. 13) as a proof for the principle that God the Creator continues to manage his world in the present as well – a principle that is further demonstrated with the help of other biblical passages, mostly from Deutero-Isaiah. Eusebius' testimony, however, should be carefully weighed in accordance with his method of citation in this apologetic composition. See Inowlocki 2006: esp. 83–86, 90, 100–103 (she does not explicitly refer to our case, but notes that the biblical citations in book VII of the *Preparation* constitute a special group that must be studied on its own).

73 Cf. Ps 96:6 ‖ 1 Chr 16:27, הוד והדר לפניו, "Honor and majesty are before him".

74 These words are usually understood as alluding to Ezekiel, especially 1:24; 43:2 (both making use of the phrase כקול מים רבים, "like the sound of much water"). See, e.g., Weinfeld 1976: 18; Chazon 2003: 90–94, at 92. However, unlike המון מים, the phrase מים רבים is not unique to Ezekiel but rather found about 30 times throughout the Hebrew Bible. The argument that an intertextual

an attempt to disambiguate the sense of המון by interpreting it as "multitude"
rather than "sound."[75] This finding suggests that the form of vv. 12–13 underlying
the *Hymn* did not lack the entire first part of v. 13. Yet no other line of the *Hymn*
(at least in its surviving parts) hints in any way to the words לקול תתו.[76] Hence,
indeed, the *Hymn* may be quoting from a somewhat earlier form of vv. 12–13 compared to 𝔐; namely, a stage at which this exegetically motivated addition was not
yet interpolated into the text.[77]

    B. Sequence. Another issue that calls for attention is the peculiar order of
poetic lines exhibited by the *Hymn*:

	Hymn to the Creator	**Jer 10:13**	
c	ויצא [רו]חֹ מאֹו[צרותיו	ויעל/ויעלה נשאים מקצה (ה)(ארץ	a
b	ברקים למט[ר עשה	ברקים למטר עשה	b
a	ויעל נשיא[ים מ[קֹצֹה [ארץ]	ויוצא רוח מאצרתיו	c

A change of sequence is in line with the hypothesis that the original form of the
passage had a different line order. However, the specific order attested in the

---

relation exists between this line of the *Hymn* and Ezekiel is not suggested by the evidence but
rather emanates from the contestable presupposition that the *Hymn* is somehow related to the
Qedushah liturgy; cf. Chazon 2000: 101–102 and n. 21. Thus, the alternative interpretation offered above is more compelling: the phrase המון מים is shared uniquely by Jer 10:13 ‖ 51:16 and the
Hymn, constituting a transparent allusion to our verse, and the adjective רבים is nothing but an
exegetical gloss to the ambiguous word המון.

75 Cf. 𝔙, which semantically harmonizes the two occurrences in the first direction: "ad vocem
suam dat *multitudinem* aquarum in caelo" (Jer 10:13), "dante eo vocem *multiplicantur* aquae
in caelo" (Jer 51:16). By contrast, 𝔖 exhibits a harmonization in the other direction: ܡܚ ܒܩܠ
ܪܓܫܐ ܘܕܠܬ ܟܢܫܐ ܕܡܝܐ (cf. 𝔖 Exod 9:23; 1 Sam 12:17–18). The phrase ܩܠ ܪܓܫܐ(ܐ)ܓ renders in
𝔖 the Hebrew expressions קול המון (1 Kgs 18:41; Isa 13:4a) and קול שאון (Isa 13:4b), and the word
ܪܓܫܐ ܓ(ܐ) by itself translates as both המון (Joel 4:14) and שאון (Jer 25:13). 𝔗 is ambiguous as it
employs a rare Aramaic term whose meaning is unclear and debated by lexicographers.

76 Note that the *Hymn* highlights the sense of sight, as in lines 11–12: מבדיל אור מאפלה... אז ראו כול
מלאכיו וירננו כי הראם את אשר לוא ידעו, "who distinguishes light from darkness... then all his angels
saw and sang praises, for he has shown them what they had not known" (a citation of Jub 2:2–3; cf.
Kister 2007: 244 n. 49); however, it makes no reference to anything related to the sense of hearing.

77 Thus, the text underlying the *Hymn* may have been fairly close to the presumed *Vorlage* of 𝔊.
Still, the two texts were not identical, as suggested by variance between "wind" in 𝔐 and "light"
in 𝔊 for v. 13. The *Hymn*'s reading at this point is uncertain because of a lacuna in the scroll, but
the single trace of letter that survives is more compatible with *ḥet* than *reš*. If this decipherment
is correct, the *Hymn* had read רוח, like 𝔐 (which, in my opinion, preserves here the original reading). This piece of evidence also supports the conclusion that the change of "wind" to "light" is
an internal development, particular to the textual tradition 𝔊 represents.

Hymn does not conform to the reconstruction suggested above.[78] In fact, it makes no logical sense of its own, since the lightning and rain (line b) normally follow the gathering of clouds (line a), rather than the other way round.

The simplest explanation appears to be that the *Hymn* cites a version of v. 13 whose order of lines was identical to the (secondary) sequence found in Jer 10:13, according to all the textual witnesses at our disposal (as well as the parallel of Ps 135:7). The author, however, switched the places of the first and last lines in maintaining a well-known stylistic device, namely, as a discursive marker of quotation from another source:[79]

Jer 10:13		*Hymn to the Creator*	
a	ויעל/ויעלה נשאים מקצה (ה)ארץ	ויוצא [רו]ח מאֹו[ֹ]צרותיו	c
b	ברקים למטר עשה	ברקים למט[ר עשה	b
c	ויוצא רוח מאצרתיו	ויעל נשיא[ים מ[קצֹה [ארץ]	a

The literary character of the psalm as a whole corroborates this observation. As indicated above, a close reading of the *Hymn* reveals that it consists of reworked citations drawn from a variety of sources. No wonder, therefore, that the device of inverting the order of cited components recurs elsewhere in this psalm (lines 10–11), with respect to another biblical passage:

Hymn to the Creator		Ps 89:15	
b	חסד ואמת סביב פניו	צדק ומשפט מכון כסאך	a
a	אמת ומשפט וצדק מכון כסאו	חסד ואמת יקדמו פניך	b

C. *Opening formula*. Finally, one should account for the blessing formula at the very beginning of v. 12 according to the *Hymn*: ברוך עושה ארץ בכוחו, *"Blessed be*

---

78 Carmignac 1970 proposed that the original sequence was c-a-b, and it was corrupted in differing directions in Jer 10:13 and the *Hymn* (cf. above, n. 42). Line c – whose position as the opening line is witnessed by the *Hymn* – was dropped by homoioteleuton (due to the graphic similarity between ויוצא and ויעלה). It was then restored from a marginal gloss but inserted in the wrong place in Jer 10:13. This complicated hypothesis, however, is untenable. No real graphic similarity that could explain the alleged homoioteleuton exists, and Carmignac offers no explanation for the fact that line b appears as the second line also in the *Hymn*, although according to his reconstruction it should have been placed in the third place.

79 This device is known in Hebrew scholarship as Seidel's Law after Seidel 1978: *1–*108. While not all of his examples are equally persuasive, the phenomenon he had discovered is well anchored in the evidence. This stylistic device in not limited to biblical literature; it is also found in Second Temple literature and beyond; see Beentjes 1982.

the one who makes the earth by his power," etc. This is probably an addition, or possibly a substitute for the Tetragrammaton, which had originally taken this spot in v. *12, as witnessed by 𝕲.

The secondary nature of this reading is suggested by lack of concord between the resulting formulation and the regular blessing formulae employed by biblical prayers, in which ברוך is usually followed by the divine name. Still, it may echo some liturgical passages that accompany God's name with an extended epithet that revolves around a participle:

Ps 72:18   ברוך יהוה אלהים אלהי ישראל עשה נפלאות לבדו
Blessed be the Lord, the God of Israel, who alone does wondrous things.
Ps 135:21   ברוך יהוה מציון שכן ירושלם
Blessed be the Lord from Zion, he who resides in Jerusalem.

The *Hymn* may also be compared, in this regard, to the conspicuously liturgical adaptation of Ps 145 in the very same scroll (11QPsᵃ, col. 17), which adds the refrain ברוך יהוה וברוך שמו לעולם ועד, "Blessed is the Lord and blessed is his name for ever and ever," after every verse of the alphabetic acrostic.

This feature of the *Hymn*, therefore, does not testify to an on older or original form of Jer 10:12; however, it does demonstrate the vital role that vv. 12–13 continued to play in the living liturgical tradition of Second Temple psalmody.[80] Yet note that opening a psalm with ברוך typifies thanksgiving psalms,[81] so nonetheless its occurrence here may comprise a distant echo of the original context of v. *13.

§7.3 Epistle of Jeremiah 59–62

The *Epistle of Jeremiah* is an apocryphal work preserved in 𝕲 as an appendix to the complex of books of Jeremiah, Baruch and Lamentations. It is based, to a large extent, on rewriting the prophetic unit of Jer 10:1–16 while embedding it in an epistolary framework that is inspired by Jer 29. Our concern here is with vv. 59–62, which rework Jer 10:13 and possibly reflect a variant form of this passage:[82]

⁵⁹ **ἥλιος** μὲν γὰρ καὶ **σελήνη** καὶ **ἄστρα** ὄντα λαμπρὰ καὶ ἀποστελλόμενα ἐπὶ χρείας εὐήκοά εἰσιν· ⁶⁰ ὡσαύτως καὶ **ἀστραπή**, ὅταν ἐπιφανῇ, εὔοπτός ἐστιν·

---

80 Ben-Dov 2000: 116 especially emphasized this point.
81 Gunkel and Begrich 1998: 242.
82 For the Greek version, see Ziegler 1976: 502–503. This English translation is taken from NETS (B.G. Wright); cf. Adams 2014: 172–173.

τὸ δ' αὐτὸ καὶ **πνεῦμα** ἐν πάσῃ χώρᾳ πνεῖ· ⁶¹ καὶ **νεφέλαις** ὅταν ἐπιταγῇ ὑπὸ τοῦ θεοῦ ἐπιπορεύεσθαι ἐφ' ὅλην τὴν οἰκουμένην, συντελοῦσι τὸ ταχθέν· ⁶² τό τε **πῦρ** ἐξαποσταλὲν ἄνωθεν ἐξαναλῶσαι ὄρη καὶ δρυμοὺς ποιεῖ τὸ συνταχθέν.

⁵⁹ For *sun* and *moon* and *stars* are bright, and when they are sent for a service, they are obedient. ⁶⁰ So also *lightnings*, when it flashes, is conspicuous. And the same *wind* also blows in every country. ⁶¹ And as for *clouds*, when ordered by God to traverse the entire inhabited world, they accomplish what is ordained. ⁶² And the *fire* sent out from above to destroy utterly mountains and woods will do what is prescribed...

As with the *Hymn to the Creator*, analysis of the indirect evidence furnished by the *Epistle* must consider its technique of rewriting the underlying scriptural passages. An obvious link exists between the celestial agents mentioned in vv. 60–61 (lightning, wind, and clouds) and those referred to in Jer 10:13, but each such element was elaborated on to a great extent.[83] Nevertheless, a few points of interest transpire from the text of the *Epistle*.

A. The beginning of v. 13. The heavenly luminaries are listed in v. 59: "sun and moon and stars." This elaboration seems to be exegetically anchored in the word המון interpreted as "multitude," i.e., as referring to the heavenly host that consists of the various luminaries.[84] The *Epistle* further stresses that all the luminaries "are obedient," and this description seems again reflective of an exegesis of a Hebrew expression; namely, the word לקול, which was interpreted as denoting the notion of obedience.[85] If this is indeed the case, then the *Epistle* testifies to an extended text of v. 13 that closely resembles 𝔐. In other words, at this particular point, the Hebrew text underlying the *Epistle* appears to be closer to 𝔐 than to 𝔊 for v. 13.

B. The reading of line c. Line c of v. 13 exhibits a lexical difference between 𝔐 ("wind") and 𝔊 ("light"), but interestingly enough, both readings are reflected in the *Epistle*:
- "And the same *wind* (πνεῦμα) also blows in every country" (v. 60b) is clearly based on 𝔐's reading as "wind" (רוח).
- "The *fire* (πῦρ) sent out from above to destroy utterly mountains and woods" (v. 62) is most probably based on a Hebrew *Vorlage* that is related to 𝔊's reading as "light" (φῶς); however, the consonantal text אור was vocalized as אוּר "fire" rather than אוֹר "light."[86]

---

83 These verses of the *Epistle* do not directly allude to the notion of rain (expressed in Jer 10:13 by the words מים and מטר), but the notion is reflected in another passage of the work as part of its condemnation of the idols: οὔτε ὑετὸν ἀνθρώποις οὐ μὴ δῶσιν, "nor will they give rain to the people" (v. 52).
84 For the use of המון in the sense of "host," see Judg 4:7; Isa 13:4; cf. Isa 29:7–8; 31:4.
85 Compare the common Hebrew phrase שמע לקול פלוני, lit. "to hear the voice (of a person)", which idiomatically means "to obey (this person)." See, e.g., Gen 3:17; 16:2; Exod 3:18; 15:26; 18:24; Judg 2:20; 1 Sam 2:25; Ps 81:12.
86 But note that the detailed description of the fire in this passage also integrates allusions to

If this interpretation is correct, it follows that the *Epistle* is aware not only of a text like 𝔐 but also of a version that is closer to 𝔊.[87] Moreover, the deviant vocalization of the Hebrew word אוֹר suggests that the *Epistle* is not directly based on 𝔊; rather, it is knowledgeable of its Hebrew *Vorlage*, or at the very least of an alternative Greek version of this unit.[88]

C. *Sequence*. No discernible relation exists between the given order of poetic lines in v. 13 (a-b-c) and that of the *Epistle* (b-c-a). However, comparing the *Epistle* in this regard with the original sequence as reconstructed above (a-c-b; see §5) clearly reveals that these texts display a chiastic relation:

Jer 10:*13		**EpJer 60–61**	
a	He made the *clouds* rise from the ends of the earth,	b	So also *lightnings*, when it flashes, is conspicuous.
c	and he brought out the *wind* from his storehouses;	c	And the same *wind* also blows in every country.
b	*Lightnings* he made for the rain.	a	And as for *clouds*, when ordered by God to traverse the entire inhabited world

Arguably, this is not an incidental finding but rather another example of Seidel's Law. The *Epistle* inverts the order of the first and last components of the underlying text so as to alert the reader that the text so treated is a citation from another

---

other scriptural passages. Depicting the fire as aiming to utterly destroy "mountains and woods" evidently draws from Ps 83:15, כאש תבער יער // וכלהבה תלהט הרים, "As fire consumes the forest, as the flame sets the mountains ablaze." The underlying reading of Jer 10:13, ויוצא *אוּר* מאצרתיו, "he brings out fire from his storehouses," was perhaps influenced by Jer 50:25, פתח יהוה את אוצרו ויוצא את כלי זעמו, "The Lord has opened his armory [lit. storehouse], and brought out the weapons of his wrath."

87 Scholars of the *Epistle* are divided regarding which version of Jeremiah underlies it, whether the short version of 𝔊 or the long version of 𝔐. See especially the detailed analyses of Kratz 1995 and Thomas 2008. The evidence discussed above suggests a different solution to the problem, at least as far as vv. 12–13 are concerned. The *Epistle* apparently alludes to – and creatively interprets – particular readings of both versions. The author, therefore, may have had access to at least two versions of Jeremiah at the same time, conflating readings drawn from both (or all) sources.

88 Such a version could have been a revision that approximated a proto-Masoretic text, such as the pre-Hexaplaric revision contained in the second part of 𝔊-Jer. It is not, however, one of the 'Three' (i.e., Aquila, Symmachus and Theodotion), which read here the word ἄνεμος ("wind"); see Field 1871–75: 2.599.

source. If this is indeed the case, then the *Epistle* may be indirectly testifying to the existence of a Hebrew witness of Jer 10:13 whose sequence of poetic lines was still the original one, as reconstructed above on other, independent grounds.

§8 The integration of vv. 12–13 into Jer 10:1–16

Thus far, the discussion focused on exposing the literary prehistory of vv. 12–13 in and of themselves and independently of the prophetic unit of Jer 10:1–16. Each of the two verses originates in its own literary tradition, and even their combination was presumably undertaken prior to their integration – as a single passage – into the book of Jeremiah. However, we know of this passage as part of the prophecy wherein it is embedded presently, so why was it interpolated into its present context?

First and foremost, it stands to reason that the interpolation of our specific passage into the given polemical prophecy of Jer 10:1–16 rests upon a known rhetorical usage of comparable traditions and motifs as part of an anti-idolatry discourse. Indeed, this assumption is strengthened by another passage of Jeremiah that similarly utilizes the motif of rain for advancing a polemical agenda (Jer 14:22):

הֲיֵשׁ בְּהַבְלֵי הַגּוֹיִם מַגְשִׁמִים	Can any idols of the nations bring rain?
וְאִם הַשָּׁמַיִם יִתְּנוּ רְבִבִים	Or can the heavens give showers?
הֲלֹא אַתָּה הוּא יהוה אֱלֹהֵינוּ	Is it not you, O LORD our God?
וּנְקַוֶּה לָּךְ	We set our hope on you,
כִּי אַתָּה עָשִׂיתָ אֶת כָּל אֵלֶּה	for it is you who do all this.

This passage similarly expresses the theological argument that bringing rain is beyond the competence of pagan wizards but does fall within the scope of YHWH's deeds. No direct literary dependence exists between Jer 14:22 and 10:12–13; the two passages share no concrete formulation of vocabulary, but they do employ the same motifs and organize them in the same rhetorical logic and for the same polemical purpose. In so doing, Jer 14:22 supplies a general rhetorical background for the inclusion of the hymnic passage of Jer 10:12–13 within the anti-idolatry prophecy of Jer 10:1–16.

However, this background only comprises part of the picture. Another, more specific factor that was apparently operative in drawing vv. 12–13 into the orbit of Jer 10:1–16 is the actual wording of this passage and its potential bearing on the stylistic design of the polemical discourse. Another potential motivation for adding v. 12–13, beyond the polemical matrix demonstrated by Jer 14:22, might have been the desire to supplement the original conclusion of the prophetic unit, which very briefly asserts that YHWH is unlike the idols "for he is the creator of everything" (v. 16: כי יוצר הכל הוא). In the original formation of the prophecy, this attribute remains unspecified, since all other segments of the satirical passages are devoted to either description of the idols or their condemnation. By supplementing the prophecy with vv. 12–13, substance was added into the embryonic reference to God's power of creation.

The placing of vv. 12–13 between v. 5b and v. 14 serves well both framing passages. By following v. 5b, vv. 12–13 provide a contrast between the impotent idols, who "cannot do evil, nor is it in them to do good," and the all-mighty YHWH, who created the world and continues to manage it on a daily basis. And by preceding v. 14, vv. 12–13 amplify the rebuke of the human artisans for their stupidity; after describing YHWH's full control of the natural elements, truly "everyone is stupid and without knowledge" and "goldsmiths are all put to shame by their idols," if they do not realize that "their images are false, and there is no breath in them."[89]

This discussion will not be complete without briefly noting a subsequent development of the text of vv. 12–13. The next stage in the compositional history of the prophetic unit is marked by further expansion with the supplementation of the Aramaic v. 11, which asserts that "the gods who did not make the *heavens* and the *earth* shall perish from the *earth* and from under the *heavens*."[90] It stands to reason that v. 11 was integrated into its place precisely because it neatly corresponds to the mentioning of the earth and the heavens in vv. 12–13, which present a symmetrically opposed image of YHWH as the creator "who makes the *earth*... who stretched the *heavens*" (v. 12), and who continues to control the natural elements contained in these realms: "When he utters his voice, there is a tumult of waters in the *heavens*, and he makes the clouds rise from the ends of the *earth*" (v. 13).[91] On a compositional level, then, the condemnation of idolatry

---

89 Ehrlich 1901: 197 (this comment was not precisely reproduced in his German *Randglossen*, see Ehrlich 1912: 270–271).

90 See below, Chapter 3.

91 Compare Joseph Qara's comment: ובלשון שמגנה בעבודה זרה, דכתיב "שמיא וארקא לא עבדו", בו בלשון מקלס להקדוש ברוך הוא בצידו: "עושה ארץ בכחו, מכין תבל בחכמתו, ובתבונתו נטה שמים" (ed. Cohen 2012: 69), "The language used for condemning idolatry, 'they did not make the heavens and the earth', is the same one used to praise the Holy One, blessed be He, in the immediately following passage: 'he makes the earth by his power, he establishes the world by his wisdom, and by his understanding he stretched out the heavens'" (cf. already the earlier commentary of Judah ibn Balaam, ed. Perez 2002: 57). In this observation, Qara follows a rabbinic insight expressed most explicitly in *Exodus Rabbah* 16:2 (see the Introduction, §3 [p. 7, n. 15]). Cf. already the *Mekhilta of R. Shimon Bar Yoḥai*: כל מקום שמזכיר גניאה שלעב' זר', שם הוא הוא מזכיר שבחו שלמק' (ed. Epstein and Melammed 1955: 15–16), "Any instance that recalls the shame of idolatry, [also] recalls the praise of God" (tr. Nelson 2006: 26) – a hermeneutical principle whose scriptural demonstration begins there with examples drawn from Jer 10.

that is found in v. 11 provides a counter-weight for the preceding, hymnic praise of vv. 12–13, thus resuming the polemical tone interrupted by the insertion of vv. 12–13.[92]

The interrelationship between v. 11 on the one hand and vv. 12–13 on the other was amplified in some of the ancient versions. For instance, vv. 12–13 employ several verbs for denoting the act of creation, including Aramaic עבד in v. 11 and Hebrew עשׂה in v. 12. The latter, however, translates into Aramaic also as עבד. The resulting formulation of 𝕊 thus underscores the symmetrical contrast between the powerless idols of v. 11 and the potent God of v. 12:

v. 11: ܐܠܗܐ ܕܫܡܝܐ ܘܐܪܥܐ ܠܐ ܥܒܕܘ

the gods who *did not create* the heavens and the earth

vs. v. 12: ܡܪܝܐ ܥܒܕ ܐܪܥܐ

The Lord *created* the earth...

Further enhancement of this trend characterizes 𝕿, which embeds v. 11ff. within a new discursive framework, similar to the epistolary framing of the *Epistle of Jeremiah*. 𝕿 sets these passages as parts of a potential dialogue between the Judean exiles in Babylonia and the nations that surround them, which might attempt to impose idolatry on the Judeans. Accordingly, each of the passages is introduced by an explication of its place and function within the dialogue. Tellingly enough, the introductory words of v.11 and v. 12 employ parallel phraseology. This symmetrical construction applies to both the added discursive frame and the expanded, direct speech:[93]

	v. 11a	v. 11b	v. 12
Discursive frame:	דאם יימרון לכון עממיא דאתון ביניהון	כדין תתיבון וכדין תימרון להון	כדנן תימרון להון
	If the nations among whom you are *should say to you...*	Thus you shall answer and *thus shall you say to them...*	*Thus you shall say to them...*
Direct speech:	פלחו לטעותא בית ישראל	טעון די אתון פלחין להון – טעון דלית בהון צרוך אנין	אנחנא פלחין לדעבד ארעא בחיליה
	[The nations' address:] *Worship the idols, O house of Israel!*	[The Judeans' response:] *The idols which you worship* are idols in which there is no profit...	*We worship him* who made the earth by his might

---

92 Cf. the analysis of the hymnic fragment preserved in Jer 10:10 (below, Chapter 4).
93 The English translation is quoted from Hayward 1987: 79–80.

All this material obviously reflects an exegetically derived expansion stemming from the translators without reflecting any deviant Hebrew *Vorlage*. Still, in rendering explicit the comparable features of vv. 11 vis-à-vis vv. 12–13, this version captures – and enhances – an essential aspect of the theological *Tendenz* inherent in the biblical text itself, at least in the form witnessed by 𝔐. The trajectory of textual development, which is discernible already within 𝔊 and 𝔐, thus finds direct continuation in the 𝔖 and 𝔗.

§9 Conclusion

The analysis in this chapter demonstrates that vv. 12–13 do not comprise an original literary unity. Rather, they are drawn from separate traditions, each with its own distinct literary background. V. 12 – together with an additional poetic line that is now embedded in the first part of v. 13 – is a sapiential saying that originates in wisdom literature. V. 13 (minus its first part) is a psalmic fragment detached from its original context; therefore, it is more difficult to identify v. 13's source, but the verse may have been quoted from a thanksgiving psalm that was celebrating the termination of a drought.

The text contained in vv. 12–13 reveals, to the discerning eye, the signs of complex processes of literary growth. At first, v. *12 was expanded by attaching it to v. *13. The final, emphatic, poetic line of v. *12 focuses on rain – the cosmic element that brings life to all creatures. As the driving force of nature and human life, rain is perceived as a prime example of the divine wisdom inherent throughout creation. This motif was expanded by a psalmic assertion of God's control of the weather, dramatically depicting the accumulation of atmospheric signs for the pending rainfall. This stage of the compositional history of the passage probably took place in a hymnic framework, which did not survive as an independent psalm. Only at a later stage were vv. 12–13 interpolated into the prophetic unit of Jer 10:1–16, and later still v. 11 was added following them, in order to balance the latter's negative presentation of the idols with a hymnic praise of YHWH – a theological trend that continued to be operative in later versions such as 𝔖 and 𝔗.

More limited additional reworking continued to take place in vv. 12–13. Some of it took place at early stages, hence affecting the text of the prophecy that is shared by both 𝔊 and 𝔐 (e.g., the transposition of poetic lines in v. 13). Further developments, however, are restricted to individual textual branches and witnesses, thus demonstrating the dynamic nature of the transmission. In 𝔊, the predicative participles in v. 12 have become nominalized epithets, thus bringing into fruition the transition from a sapiential saying into a hymnic description. In addition, the poetic line dealing with the wind has changed focus to the light that symbolizes divine salvation. In 𝔐, an entire poetic line has shifted place to v. 13, and the phrase המן מים was reinterpreted as "a multitude of waters" (perhaps influenced by the context of drought). Both of these developments were explicated by the addition of the words לקול תתו. This process clamped the connection between vv. 12–13 and amplified the motif of divine sovereignty over the heavens and the earth, thus presenting YHWH as a theologically preferable alternative to the idols of the nations, which the polemical prophecy condemns wholeheartedly.

Chapter 3
Language and identity

(Jer 10:11)

כִּדְנָה תֵּאמְרוּן לְהוֹם אֱלָהַיָּא דִּי־שְׁמַיָּא וְאַרְקָא לָא עֲבַדוּ יֵאבַדוּ מֵאַרְעָא וּמִן־תְּחוֹת
שְׁמַיָּא אֵלֶּה:

Thus shall you say to them: The gods who did not make the heavens and
the earth shall perish from the earth and from under the heavens. (NRSV)

§1 Prolusion

The various threads interwoven into the fabric of the prophecy of Jer 10:1–16 differ
from each other in their thematic content, literary genre, and stylistic mode,
although it takes closer inspection to realize that they may also be distinguished
from one another by way of theological outlook and linguistic profile. However,
v. 11 stands out from afar in its language, since it is the only passage in the prophecy – and, indeed, in prophetic literature at large – that is fully phrased in
Aramaic.[1] The Masoretic paragraphing system also indicates the unique nature of
this passage; according to this system, v. 11 comprises an independent section –
the only paragraph within the literary unit of Jer 10:1–16 that consists of a single
verse.[2]

---

[1] The language shift was deemed exegetically significant in rabbinic literature, which takes it as
an indication for the special status of Aramaic vis-à-vis other foreign tongues, given its employment in all three wings of Scriptures: the Pentateuch (alluding to Gen 31:47), Prophets (Jer 10:11),
and Writings (Dan 2:4ff.). See y. Soṭah 7:2 21c (col. 933; tr. Neusner 1984: 179); Genesis Rabbah 74:14
(ed. Theodor and Albeck 1965: 2.871; tr. Freedman, in Freedman and Simon 1939: 2.685–686).

[2] According to 𝔐, Jer 10:1–16 consists of four paragraphs: vv. 1–5, 6–10, 11, 12–16. This division is
otherwise independent of literary or stylistic distinctions, as demonstrated by the fact that the
second and fourth paragraphs (vv. 6–10, 12–16) each contain both satirical and hymnic passages. Apparently, the Aramaic language of v. 11 motivated its treatment as a self-standing paragraph. The Masoretic paragraphing is basically confirmed by 4QJerᵃ, though the two witnesses
differ in the type of blank interval they employ: 𝔐 separates v. 11 from v. 12ff by a short interval
(פרשה סתומה, "closed section"), whereas 4QJerᵃ has done so by leaving the rest of the line blank
(corresponding to a Masoretic פרשה פתוחה, "open section") followed by an additional blank
line, which is unusual in the scriptural scrolls from Qumran (Tov 1997: 158). As for 4QJerᵇ, its

DOI 10.1515/9783110530162-004

Several literary and stylistic features of v. 11 indeed demonstrate that this passage comprises a self-standing unit, which was originally independent of the prophecy contained in Jer 10:1–16 (§2). Furthermore, a number of indications hint that the origin of v. 11 should be sought for in a scribal circle that is culturally remote from those that produced the satirical passages, on the one hand, or the hymnic passages on the other (§3). The issue of origin and provenance is discussed herein in light of the functions the passage fulfills in the various formations of the prophecy (§4). Finally, the integration of an Aramaic utterance into a Hebrew composition must be carefully decoded in terms of its potential sociolinguistic message for the audience of the prophecy; this aspect is illuminated when taking into consideration the unique challenge v. 11 posed for later generations of tradents, whose first language was no longer Hebrew but rather Aramaic. An investigation of the Aramaic versions of the prophecy demonstrate that essential aspects of the text indeed had to be manipulated and transformed in order to adapt it to a new cultural context (§5). The textual and literary history of Jer 10:11 thus illustrates that the life of the text transcends the usual categories of composition, transmission, and reception.

§2 Literary structure

Jer 10:11 breaks down into two unequal parts. The first part (כדנה תאמרון להום, "thus you will say to them") consists of a predictive clause.[3] It asserts that a certain group of people (addressed in the 2m.pl) will deliver a message to a second group of people (referred to by the 3m.pl), without explicitly identifying any of them. The second part of v. 11 comprises the bi-clausal message to be delivered:

אלהיא די שמיא וארקע לא עבדו   The gods who did not make the heavens and the earth –

---

paragraphing system cannot be securely established, due to the exceptionally wide line-length of the reconstructed column, only the left-hand part of which is preserved. According to Tov (1997: 175–176), a short interval (of about 4 letter-spaces) may be reconstructed between v. 11 and v. 12, but none between v. 10 and v. 11. Saley (2010) proposed an alternative reconstruction absent any discussion of the issue of paragraphing (although he excluded from his calculation the interval reconstructed by Tov).

3 The verbal form תאמרון is in the indicative mood. The speaker does not will the action of saying but simply indicates that it is bound to happen in an appropriate context in the future, hence the NRSV, "thus *shall* you say to them," is better corrected to "thus *will* you say to them."

יאבדו מארעא ומן תחות שמיא אלה   they[4] shall[5] perish from the earth and from under the heavens

Several features indicate that v. 11 is not an original part of the prophecy but rather a later supplementation, though it was incorporated into the prophecy at a relatively early date, as suggested by the fact that it is already recorded in the shorter text represented by both 4QJer[b] and 𝕾, which usually represent an older stage of the prophetic unit compared to 𝔐.[6] The most obvious sign of the original distinctiveness of v. 11 is, of course, its Aramaic language, as the language of all other components of the prophecy is Hebrew. Yet this feature was interpreted in several ways, and some scholars indeed argued that it can be explained as a stylistic device employed as part of the original, prophetic composition.[7]

A more telling feature is the literary structuring of the passage. As many scholars acknowledge, the message contained in v. 11b comprises a self-standing

---

4 The demonstrative אלה is placed at the end of the clause, a position that motivated most commentators and translators to take it as a modifier of שמיא (so already 𝕾: καὶ ὑποκάτωθεν τοῦ οὐρανοῦ τούτου, "and from under *this* sky"). However, as Hornkohl (2014: 57, n. 5) recognized, 𝔐 places a disjunctive accent (*ṭipḥā*) under שמיא, suggesting that אלה is actually the subject of the second clause: "*these* (gods) shall be destroyed from the earth and under the heavens." The movement of the subject to this odd, clause-final position is apparently conditioned by a literary restriction; namely, the chiastic design of the entire utterance (see further below). A few commentators have already proposed such an interpretation, though without mentioning the cantillation tradition (e.g., Keil 1873–74: 1.200; Holladay 1986–89: 1.335).

5 The verbal form יאבדו is a jussive (e.g., Bauer and Leander 1927: 89, §26d). Hence, the message is a willed statement, most probably intended as a curse. Therefore, we must reject the views of commentators such as Holladay (1986–89: 1.328, 334), who states that the grammatical form of יאבדו is ambiguous and can be interpreted either as an indicative or as a volitive, or Lundbom (1999–2004: 1.594), who prefers to consider יאבדו as an indicative form for thematic reasons. Such commentators were probably mislead by Margaliot (1980: 303), who argued that in Biblical Aramaic, the jussive form can also be employed as an indicative one on the basis of comparison to Biblical Hebrew, without noticing that the two languages are by no means identical with respect to their verbal syntax.

6 Note, however, that 4QJer[b] and 𝕾 should not be mistaken to indicate that v. 11 comprises an *original* part of the prophecy, as is sometimes suggested in the scholarship (e.g., Reid 2006; Adcock 2017). These texts comprise only a random selection from the full spectrum of textual witnesses of Jeremiah that circulated in Antiquity. In establishing the compositional status of any literary component, we cannot rely solely on the recorded text-critical evidence; rather, we should also take into consideration literary-historical analysis. Indeed, even among those who argue for the literary unity of Jer 10:1–16 as a whole – sometimes insisting on Jeremiah's own authorship of it – there are some scholars who admit that v. 11 must be a late insertion (e.g., Ackroyd 1963; Labuschagne 1966: 68, n. 2).

7 So, e.g., Margaliot 1980: 301–302. But note Ehrlich's sarcastic comment: "Even one who is not used to critical inquiry should easily recognize that these words, formulated in Aramaic, are not Jeremiah's words" (Ehrlich 1901: 196, my translation from the Hebrew); interestingly, his wording in the German edition of the *Randglossen* is less polemical (Ehrlich 1912: 270).

literary unit, set apart by its perfect chiastic pattern. It amplifies the bi-clausal construction of the message, presenting an exact equivalent, in the second clause, for every element of the first clause:

A		אלהיא
	B	די שמיא
	C	וארקא
	D	לא עבדו
	D′	יאבדו
	C′	מארעא
	B′	ומן תחות שמיא
A′		אלה

Chiastic structures normally aim at calling attention to the innermost element, which is the ideological core of the text thus constructed. In the present case, an additional stylistic device – namely, the wordplay between עבד "to do, make, create" and אבד "to perish" – further emphasizes the centrality of element D-D′. Both devices stress the causative relation between the two clauses: "the gods" do not hold the power of creation; hence, they are perishable and doomed for destruction.

NB. The wordplay between עבד/אבד enables the evaluation of a neglected variant reading implied by a homily embedded in a relatively late rabbinic Midrash (*Tanḥuma, Šofṭim*, 12):

ד"א: "כי הגוים האלה אשר אתה יורש אותם אל מעוננים ואל קוסמים ישמעו" – אמר ירמיה הנביא "כדנא תימרון להון" וג'.

Another thing: "For these nations that you are about to dispossess do give heed to soothsayers and diviners" (Deut 18:14) – Jeremiah the Prophet said "Thus you will say to them" etc. (Jer 10:11).

א"ר אליעזר: "כדנא תימרון" – אם יאמרו לכם או"ה לעבוד ע"ג, אמרו להם: אם יכולה היא להעביר השמים והארץ, נעבדנה. ואם לאו, "יאבדו מארעא".

R. Eliezer said: "Thus you will say" – if the nations say to you to worship idols, say to them, 'If it can remove the heavens and the earth, we shall worship it; but if not – "they shall perish from the earth".'

ר' יהושע אמר: אמרו להם: אם יכולין לעשות שמים וארץ, נעבדנה. ואם לא, "יאבדו מארעא".

R. Joshua said: Say to them, 'If they can make the heavens and the earth, we shall worship it; but if not – "they shall perish from the earth".'

ר' עקיבא אומר: אמרו להם: אם יכולים
להעביר את השמים ואת הארץ ולעשות
אחרים מצבע אחר, נעבדנה. ואם לאו,
"יאבדו מארעא"

R. Akiva says: 'Say to them, 'If they can remove the heavens and the earth, and make alternative ones with a different color, we shall worship it; but if not – "they shall perish from the earth".'

The homily rests on the graphic similarity of the letters ר/ד, which produced an interchange between לא עבדו and לא עברו.[8] The words of R. Joshua are based on the reading לא עבדו (recorded in all available witnesses), whereas R. Eliezer apparently presupposes the variant reading לא עברו (hitherto unrecorded in other sources), and R. Akiva's formulation mediates between the two readings. Arguably, the reading לא עברו may comprise a hermeneutic illusion, created by an אל תקרי type of Midrash. But even if it is indeed presupposed by this homily, לא עברו is probably a secondary development, because the wordplay between עבד/אבד is essential for the literary structure of v. 11b, as indicated above.

It turns out that v. 11b comprises a compact literary unit. This unit takes the form of an independent, almost proverbial saying, which makes effective use of rhetorical means to convey its message as efficiently as possible.[9] Its distinctive rhetorical features are nowhere to be found in any of the other components of Jer 10:1–16.[10] It is legitimate to conclude, therefore, that the Aramaic v. 11 comprises

---

8 Compare Jer 15:14, in which 𝔐 reads והעברתי את אויביך, while 𝔗's rendition וישתעבדון לבעלי דבבכן presupposes והעבדתי rather than והעברתי. Scholars, however, debate whether 𝔗 indeed reflects, in this case, a variant reading or merely a Midrashic exegesis (Tomes 1997: 241–242).

9 This rhetorical character apparently motivated Duhm (1901: 101–102) to propose that v. 11 is a magical utterance, an incantation or a spell meant as protection from the "heavenly signs" (v. 2). While this hypothesis aptly highlights the literary independence of the passage, Duhm offered no parallel from magical literature as support for his proposal. Nonetheless, some later commentators accepted his speculation (e.g., Carrol 1986: 256–257), while others hesitated between considering v. 11 as an exorcist spell ("Bannspruch") or a polemical slogan ("Shlagwort") that was popular among Jews in their contacts with gentiles (e.g., Volz 1928: 122). In my opinion, though, the entire magical reasoning is unwarranted; ancient magicians normally did not pretend to destroy gods or malicious superhuman entities, but rather focused their efforts on directing the harmful activity of such forces away from the human sphere.

10 Attempts to find these features in other passages are forced and untenable. For instance, Lundbom (1997: 87) compares the wordplay of לא עבדו / יאבדו with the juxtaposed verbs in passages such as גם ממצרים תבושי / כאשר בשת מאשור, "You shall be put to shame by Egypt, as you were put to shame by Assyria" (Jer 2:36b), or נערו כגורי אריות / יחדו ככפרים ישאגו, "Like lions they shall roar together; they shall growl like lions' whelps" (Jer 51:38). In the first case, however, we simply have the same verb in two different conjugations, while the second case makes use of verbs that are semantically close but phonetically distinct. None of these cases resembles the wordplay between לא עבדו and יאבדו of Jer 10:11. Similarly, I see no point in comparing the explicit chiastic structure of Jer 10:11, which is based on concrete, verbal repetition, with the looser thematic "antithetic structure" (Krašovec 1984: 76–85) that some scholars find in Jer 10:1–16 as a whole (e.g., Clendenen 1987: esp. 404).

a self-standing unit, originally unrelated to the rest of Jer 10:1–16 or any of its discrete constituents.[11]

§3 Provenance and original function

No direct evidence exists for the employment of the Aramaic text of v. 11 outside the confines of the prophecy contained in Jer 10:1–16. Still, its present form betrays several clues for the original provenance of the passage, while also suggesting that it is chronologically later than the main stratum of the prophecy – which presumably constituted, at least in its initial stage, only the satirical passages.

§3.1 Language shift

From the perspective of ancient Hebrew readers, the very shift from Hebrew to Aramaic marks the text as stemming from a foreign source. Indeed, it is a stylistic norm in classical biblical literature to employ selectively Aramaic lexemes, grammatical forms, or syntactic constructions in order to mark certain figures, events, or scenes as foreign in character.[12] In the exilic period, when Hebrew speakers gradually became bilinguals, Hebrew itself absorbed an ever-growing number of Aramaic loanwords, as well as grammatical and syntactic interferences. Naturally, in such a situation of intense contact between the languages, the classical convention could not have been effective any longer. Still, it was not completely abandoned, but rather occasionally replaced with more emphatic means; namely, the pronounced shift from Hebrew to Aramaic.

To be sure, this device too is rooted in classical literature. For instance, to demonstrate the ethnic difference between the Israelite forefather Jacob and Laban the Aramaean, the two eponyms give different names for the heap of stones symbolizing the political border between Israel and Aram (Gen 31:47): Laban pronounces

---

11 Seemingly, an additional argument in favor of this conclusion may be adduced from Ammann's analysis of the links between the anti-idolatry prophecy and the world of wisdom (Ammann 2015, following von Rad 1972: 177–185). According to her findings, v. 11 exhibits no sign of sapiential terminology or worldview, unlike the other components of the prophecy (Ammann 2015: 129). But the scope and weight of wisdom in the prophecy appear to me to be much more limited than they are in Ammann's view. In my opinion, sapiential residues can be traced only in the hymnic passage of vv. 12–13, which does not comprise an organic part of the original prophecy. If so, such a line of inquiry is not necessarily helpful for establishing the original independence of v. 11.
12 See especially Rendsburg 1995 and 2015, with previous literature adduced there.

the Aramaic phrase יגר שהדותא, "the heap of witnessing" (cf. ⑤ βουνὸς τῆς μαρτυρίας), while Jacob simultaneously refers to it by the Hebrew phrase גל עד, "the witnessing heap" (cf. ⑤ βουνὸς μάρτυς). Similarly, the prophecy against the nations in Isa 21:11–12 illustrates the foreign idiom of the land of Dumah by coloring the speech of the local watchmen with Aramaic words and forms, even though their true language was certainly not Aramaic but rather an Arabian dialect.[13]

This stylistic device was utilized further in late, post-exilic literature.[14] Thus, the Aramaic material in Ezra mostly comprises of official letters cited therein, and the move from the narrator's words to the quoted letter supplies the literary justification for the language shift in Ezra 4:8:

וכתב הנשתון כתוב ארמית ומתרגם ארמית	the letter was written in Aramaic and translated into Aramaic:
רחום בעל טעם ושמשי ספרא	*Rehum the royal deputy and Shimshai the scribe*
כְּתַבוּ אגרה חדה על ירושלים	*wrote a letter against Jerusalem...*

By the same token, Dan 2:4 departs from the narrator's Hebrew only to quote the Aramaic speech of the Chaldean magicians:

וידברו הכשדים למלך ארמית	The Chaldeans said to the king in Aramaic:
מלכא לעלמין חיי	*O king, live forever! ...*

It is immaterial, for our purposes, whether these shifts comprise an original part of the narratives or rather should be explained as a redactional solution for the problem caused by integrating preexisting documents, originally written in different languages. The crucial point is that as far as the literary conventions of biblical literature are concerned, the shift from Hebrew to Aramaic in Jer 10:11 was enough to indicate to ancient readership that the passage stems from a foreign source, regardless of the question of whether this marking reflects its genuine provenance or not.[15]

---

13 Both examples are adduced by Tur-Sinai 1950: 594.
14 The wordplay between עבד and אבד is sometimes thought to be peculiar to Aramaic (e.g., Lundbom 1999–2004: 1.593, who suggests that the pun explains why the originally independent passage was left untranslated into Hebrew), but the two verbs are played within Hebrew passages as well (even though the verb עבד is naturally employed there in a different sense), for instance: כי הגוי והממלכה אשר לא יעבדוך – יאבדו, "For the nation and kingdom that will not *serve* you shall *perish*" (Isa 60:12; cf. Ps 119:176; 143:12; see further Deut 8:19; 12:2; Josh 23:16; 2 Kgs 10:19).
15 Cf. Snell 1980.

§3.2 Non-Yahwistic theology

If v. 11 is isolated from its context and read on its own, one can detect in it no trace of the belief in and worship of YHWH, the God of Israel – either in Judah or elsewhere. To be sure, the polemical argument embedded therein refers negatively to "the gods who did not create the heavens and the earth"; however, it does not make the complementary, positive argument that YHWH is the creator.[16] The passage makes no mention of YHWH at all; nor does it contain any other element that might indicate that it was written by a Judean scribe, or even a scribe of Judean descent.

> NB. A possible exception to this rule may be culled from the linguistic realm, in the assimilated form of the preposition in מארעא. The preposition מן does not normally assimilate to the following consonant in Old and Official Aramaic, and it is usually written as a separate word in these chronolects.[17] Only in a relatively small number of cases do we find in the ancient dialects an assimilated מן; most such cases are attested in Jewish Aramaic, and they probably reflect a Hebrew interference, since the latter language exhibits the opposite trend of having the preposition assimilated.[18] Hence, the spelling מארעא seemingly indicates that a Judean scribe penned the passage. However, this is only 𝔐's reading, whereas 4QJer^b – which preserves a shorter text very close to 𝔊 – reads at this point מן ארעא. Since the unassimilated form is what one would expect in such a specimen of Official Aramaic (cf. below, §3.4), and it occurs in an ancient witness whose text is demonstrably older than that of 𝔐, this reading may be taken as the original one. 𝔐's reading מארעא does not bear testimony to the original text, but rather betrays the background of the witness.[19]

---

16 In this regard, the theological argument expressed in Jer 10:11 stands in dire contrast to Deutero-Isaiah's polemic with idolatry, e.g., "I am the Lord, and there is no other; besides me there is no god. I arm you, though you do not know me, so that they may know, from the rising of the sun and from the west, that there is no one besides me; I am the LORD, and there is no other. I form light and create darkness, I make weal and create woe; I the LORD do all these things" (Isa 45:5–7), etc.

17 All the more so since Aramaic exhibits a clear phonological preference for dissimilation, which extends to its tendency to resolve consonantal gemination with the help of sonorant consonants, especially /n/ (e.g., מַנְדַּע < מַדַּע* in Dan 2:21; 5:12; *TAD* C1.1:53 etc.). See Bauer and Leander 1927: 50, §13*d–f*; Muraoka and Porten 2003: 13–16, §3*c–d*.

18 Muraoka 2011: 7, §3.a.1 (note, however, the more reserved approach of Stadel 2008: 109–111).

19 An unassimilated form of the preposition also occurs in 𝔖 (ܐܪܥܐ ܡܢ ܗܘ ܕܝܢ ܐ); however, this is in keeping with standard Syriac grammar, so no conclusion may be based on this fact.

§3.3 Political implications

The main message of v. 11 is not exhausted by a theoretical argument concerning other gods, but rather extends to a concrete expectation for their total annihilation. This line of reasoning transcends the theological realm, strictly speaking, and it better fits a political threat. It is no coincidence that the partial parallels one finds in the Bible for the curse formula יאבדו מארעא ומן תחות שמיא always refer to human individuals and peoples, and never to divine beings.[20] Indeed, scholars have already demonstrated that the biblical polemic against idolatry was common in the ancient Near East as a symbolic expression of power-relations between kingdoms and political groups.[21] More specifically, a concrete threat in demolishing divine statues – which is equivalent to killing the gods – served as both a rhetorical and practical weapon in the hands of various conquerors in the ancient Near East.[22]

A telling parallel is furnished by the intertextual relationship between the Babylonian myth of creation, *Enūma Eliš*, and another Babylonian work known as the *Esagila Chronicle*, which concerns Marduk, the divine patron of Babylon.[23] The rise of Marduk to the top of the Babylonian pantheon was expressed by depicting his figure as the creator in *Enūma Eliš*, Tablet VI.[24] Consequently, the *Esagila Chronicle* refers to Marduk as *šar kišš[at šam]ê u erṣet[i]*, "the king of all heavens and earth" (line 39). Marduk's supremacy over other gods, the patrons of kings who are aggressive towards Babylon – including gods designated as *ilānū* (*rabûtu*) *ša šamê u erṣeti*, "the (great) gods of the heavens and earth" (lines 34a, 39) – is expressed by the assertion that Marduk is able to destroy them completely: the gods (i.e., their statues) are tied, dressed in filthy cloths, and chopped into wooden chips (line 36). The speaker also contends that the light of the star

---

20 For אבד מארעא, "to perish from the earth," compare אָבֹד תֹּאבֵדוּן מַהֵר מֵעַל הָאָרֶץ, "you will soon utterly *perish from the land*" (Deut 4:26; cf. Deut 11:17; Josh 23:16; Jer 9:11; Ezek 25:7; Mic 7:2; Ps 10:16; 21:11; Job 18:17). For אבד מן תחות שמיא, "to perish from under the heavens," compare וְהַאֲבַדְתָּ אֶת שְׁמָם מִתַּחַת הַשָּׁמָיִם, "you shall *blot out* their name from *under the heavens*" (Deut 7:24).
21 Levtow 2008. Cf. the recent proposal of Adcock (2017: 74–87) that v. 11 is a war taunt, although I am not persuaded by the specific details of his proposal, namely, that this is "a divine call for a war taunt from an imagined 'Foe from the North' besieging army" (ibid., 84), which is an original and integral part of the prophecy.
22 Schaudig 2012.
23 Margaliot (1980: 303–304) already noted the connection between Jer 10:11 and descriptions of Marduk in Babylonian literature, although, like most commentators, he presupposed that the prophetic passage necessarily refers to YHWH.
24 For an English translation of this work, see Glassner 2004: 263–269.

representing such a defeated god will no longer stand at the heaven (alluding to *Enūma Eliš* IV 23), and his site (i.e., temple) will become the dwelling place of demons only (line 37b).[25] In other words, not only will the cult image be demolished, but also the divine presence that resides within it will be destroyed, because this god has sinned "against the god of this city" (line 37a: *ilu ša ana ili āli šâšu ugallalu*); namely, Marduk of Babylon.[26]

Evidently, the *Esagila Chronicle* is not a theoretical treatise of theology but rather a politically-derived work that promotes Babylonian domination in the Mesopotamian sphere. By the same token, the Aramaic message contained in v. 11 originates in a politically-oriented source. It may be viewed as a slogan, or a product of imperial propaganda, which was formulated in theological terms but also communicated a political message. Further scrutiny may disclose additional clues as to the historical context of this propagandistic source.

§3.4 Linguistic traits

The language of v. 11 is Official Aramaic, and its grammatical hallmarks match the language recorded in documents of the Persian period.[27] So, for instance, is the differentiated usage of verbal forms for expressing the indicative (תאמרון) and volitive (יאבדו) moods.[28] In Egyptian Aramaic, the volitive forms are still used throughout, but the first signs of collapse of the morphological system encoding verbal modality are already detected.[29] In later periods, the morphological

---

25 Schaudig 2012: 130–134; cf. Glassner 2004: 264–267.

26 The tight relation between Marduk's opposite powers to destroy (*abātu*, the etymological cognate of Hebrew אבד) and to create (*banû*, cognate of Hebrew בנה "to build, construct") is highlighted in *Enūma Eliš*: Marduk is the one "who destroyed Tiāmat's gods, and made peoples from part of them" (VII 90: *ābit ilānī ša Tiāmat ēpiš nišī ina mimmišun*), and the gods address him by saying, "command and bring annihilation and re-creation" (IV 22: *abātu u banû qibi liktūnu*). For the text and translation see Lambert 2013: 128–129, 86–87, respectively (cf. Talon 2005: 73, 51).

27 Some scholars have argued that the Aramaic language of Jer 10:11 needs not testify to its lateness because Aramaic was the *lingua franca* throughout the ancient Near East already by the Assyrian period (e.g., Lundbom 1999–2004: 1.593, following Overholt 1965: 5). However, the language of our passage is not Common Aramaic but rather a particular chronolect, as already recognized by Driver (1906: 354), who correctly observed that the linguistic markers best fit the fifth century BCE. Similarly, I see no need for the superfluous hypothesis that the passage is based on an Old Aramaic text whose orthography was later updated by later scribes (Tur-Sinai 1960: 112; 1967: 184).

28 In 4QJerᵃ, the verbal form contained in v. 11a was originally a jussive-like form (תאמרו), but it was later corrected to an indicative form by adding a supralinear *nun*.

29 Muraoka and Porten 2003: 198–201, §53.

distinction between indicative and volitive forms tends to blur, leading eventually to neutralization, so that the indicative forms encroach on the realm of the volitives.[30] Syntactic features of the passage are also typical of Official Aramaic, such as the constituent order of the subordinated clause די שמיא וארקא לא עבדו, "which did not make the heavens and the earth," in which the direct object takes a preverbal position.[31]

Other linguistic traits of the passage enable us to narrow down the possible timespan by setting it within the fifth century BCE. The 3m.pl pronominal suffix (להום) still concludes with an /m/, which is usual in Official Aramaic (cf. Ezra 5:3–4, לְהֹם), rather than with /n/, as is found in the Hellenistic period (cf. Dan 3:14, לְהֹון).[32] Another telling datum is the orthographic interchange between ארקא (a spelling typical of Old Aramaic) and ארעא (the common spelling of Middle

---

30 Admittedly, volitive forms are still attested in Qumran Aramaic, suggesting that the modal system survived, at least in Palestine, through the Greco-Roman period (Muraoka 2011: 170–171, §53).

31 It is more complicate to assess the syntax of the main clause, אלהיא... יאבדו מארעא ומן תחות שמיא אלה, because of the doubt concerning the syntactic function of the demonstrative אלה (cf. above, n. 4). If this word modifies שמיא, as commonly thought, then its constituent-order is in line with what one finds in Biblical Aramaic: the subject takes the first position, followed by the verb, in an object-less clause (Rosenthal 2006: 60, §183). But if אלה is in fact co-referential with the subject אלהיא, it comprises a *casus pendens* construction with an exceptional constituent-order. Normally in such cases, the anaphoric pronoun takes a pre-verbal position (cf. Muraoka and Porten 2003: 313–314, §79a); yet the word-order in this case is patently conditioned by the chiastic literary structure of the passage as a whole. The paucity of literary – especially poetic – texts in Official Aramaic renders difficult the attempt to properly evaluate the degree of uniqueness of this syntactic construal.

32 The (*plene*) spelling הון is dominant in Daniel, whereas in Ezra it is employed alongside the (defective) spelling הֹם. This distribution suggests that Ezra's Aramaic represents a transitional stage between the Official Aramaic of the Persian period and the Literary Aramaic of the Hellenistic period. This chronological distinction is confirmed by Aramaic documents found in Egypt, in which the spelling הון is recorded only in late texts of the third century BCE and on (Muraoka and Porten 2003: 54, §12k). The *plene* spelling יהום (rather than הם, as found in Ezra) is not attested elsewhere in the Bible, but it typifies Aramaic documents from Egypt dated to the fifth century BCE, e.g., בהום (*TAD* A4.7:17 ‖ 8:16; cf. *TAD* A4.7:13, 24; 8:8). The *plene* spelling also occurs – next to the defective one – in the Aramaic version of the Bisitun inscription: נכסיהום ובתיהם (*TAD* C2.1 II 2). Notably, though, while 𝔐 reads להום, 4QJerᵃ witnesses the defective spelling: [כד]ה תאמרון להם. This is not only the oldest surviving manuscript of Jeremiah, but also one of the three oldest scrolls found in Qumran (cf. above, p. 10, n. 23). It stands to reason that the defective spelling recorded in this scroll is closer to the original orthography of the passage. But even if this is not the case, the grammatical form of the pronoun is enough to suggest a dating in the Persian rather than the Hellenistic period.

Aramaic dialects).[33] As recognized long ago, this interchange typically occurs within the same document in Official Aramaic texts of the fifth century BCE – such as in a legal document from Miḇṭaḥiah's archive concerning the ownership of some real estate, signed in 464 BCE (*TAD* B2.2:15–16):[34]

וארקא זך אפם זילך	...and moreover that *land* is yours,
ואנת רחיק מן כל דין	and you are withdrawn from any suit
זי יקבלון עליך	(in) which they shall complain against you
עלדבר ארעא זך	on account of that *land*.

§3.5 Theological terminology

The content of v. 11 echoes a specific theology, which highlights the creation of the heavens and the earth as the distinct quality of divine potency. This emphasis correlates with one of the most typical divine attributes of the Persian period: אלהי השמים, "the God of heavens,"[35] which is a calque of the

---

33 So according to 𝔐. These words are not preserved in 4QJer[a], while in 4QJer[b] only the second occurrence survives and it spells ארעא, as in 𝔐. Most of the ancient versions obviously did not distinguish between the two different spellings but rather represented them by employing the same lexeme in their target-languages. Compare the explicit distinction made by the medieval Karaite commentator, Japhet ben Ali: when *transcribing* the passage in Arabic script, he was careful to distinguish between وارقا and ميارعا; but in his Arabic *translation,* he employed the same word for both occurrences, والارض ... من الارض (Sabih 2009: 191). Nonetheless, the orthographic interchange recorded in 𝔐 is confirmed by Aquila, which offers a different rendering for each spelling: the form ארעא is rendered by γῆ (as usual in 𝔊, also for the Hebrew cognate ארץ), whereas ארקא is represented by ἔδαφος (which is rarely employed in 𝔊 for ארץ; see Ezek 41:16, 20; cf. Isa 25:12; 26:5).
34 Porten and Yardeni 1986–99: 2.20–21. The first to recognize the chronological significance of this interchange seems to be Driver 1906: 354 ("The Aramaic is that of a particular dialect [...] ארקא and ארעא occur side by side in some Aramaic inscriptions, of the 5th cent. B.C."), although this insight is usually credited to Baumgartner 1927: 100–101. For a fuller picture of the Aramaic evidence, cf. Folmer 1995: 63–70, esp. 67–68. For the phonetic nature of the historical consonant marked first by ק and later by ע, see Al-Jallad 2016, and the previous studies adduced there.
35 Jon 1:9; Ezra 1:2 ǁ 2 Chr 36:23; Neh 1:4–5; 2:4, 20; cf. Gen 24:7. For the expression אלהי השמים in Cyrus' Edict (Ezra 1:2 ǁ 2 Chr 36:23), see Bickerman 1946: 256–257. It is conceivable that the explicit identification with YHWH reflects a local attempt, made in Yehud (or by Judeans), whereas the more general epithet אלהי השמים belongs to the underlying, unspecified template of an official edict distributed among various ethnic communities throughout the Persian Empire.

Aramaic phrase אלה שמיא[36] – an abbreviation of the fuller epithet אלה שמיא
וארעא.[37]

Moreover, the focus of Jer 10:11 on the motif of creation of heavens and earth, which is also manifested in the Aramaic epithet of אלה שמיא וארעא, possibly echoes an emphasis sometimes made at the introductory clauses of Achaemenid royal inscriptions, written in Old Persian. Such clauses solemnly declare that Ahuramazda had created, among other things, the earth and the heavens. Especially relevant in this regard are the inscriptions of Darius I, who ruled in 522–486 BCE; for instance:

> A Great god is Ahuramazda, who created this earth, who created yonder sky (*hya : imām : būmim : adā : hya : avam : asmānam : adā*), who created man, who created happiness for man, who made Darius king, one king of many, one lord of many.[38]

⋆ ⋆ ⋆

The last two considerations (§3.4–5) lead to an interim conclusion: Jer 10:11 – or, at least, the chiastically-structured message contained in v. 11b – stems from the imperial propaganda of the Persian period. In its original context, the passage aimed at confirming the supremacy of the imperial power vis-à-vis the subjugated countries and ethnic groups by highlighting the feebleness of their gods, compared to the senior divinity representing the imperial center. This intention was expressed by the theological argument that the power of creation is reserved for the highest god, whereas the other gods are like mortals compared to him.

This conclusion should not come as a surprise. Deutero-Isaiah already, as early as the mid-sixth century BCE, reflects the direct influence of Persian imperial propaganda, which manifests itself, among other things, in the dramatically increasing importance of the motif of God the creator, which occupies a rather marginal place in the prophetic literature of the preceding age.[39]

---

36 Ezra 5:12; 6:9–10; 7:12, 21, 23; Dan 2:18, 19, 37, 44. So also in the Elephantine papyri, not only in the internal documents of the Jewish community (*TAD* A4.3:[2], 3, 5; A3.6:1), but also in letters addressed to Persian officials (A4.7:2 ‖ 8:2). All these documents are dated to the fifth century BCE.

37 Ezra 5:11; cf. Gen 24:3. Cf. Andrews 1964. Gen 24 may also be a product of the same period (Rofé 1990; for a different opinion, see Rendsburg 2002: 24–35; Rendsburg 2015).

38 Kent 1953: 137–138, Inscription DNa, lines 1–8. The same formula recurs in the aforementioned inscription of his son, Xerxes I (XPh; cf. below, n. 43). It is also found sporadically in inscriptions of their successors during the fifth and early fourth centuries BCE.

39 Smith 1963.

At any rate, the aforementioned conclusion of the literary analysis of Jer 10:11 may be corroborated by general, historical considerations, which independently point to the fifth century BCE.

§3.6 Echoes of religious reform?

The literary model of praising the chief deity as the creator of heavens and earth is rooted in ancient Mesopotamian tradition. In Babylonia, this deity was identified as Marduk, but in the Persian period, the Zoroastrian Creator Ahuramazda took the center stage. The adoption of Babylonian models of propaganda by the Achaemenid kings comprises a well-known phenomenon, recorded as early as the mid-fifth century BCE with the Cyrus Cylinder, which commemorates the triumphant entry of the Persian king into Babylon.[40] This is basically a building inscription, composed as a first-person account of the king himself. It ascribes Cyrus' victory to the Babylonian god Marduk, describing Cyrus' outstanding efforts to restore the former glory and lawful place of the cult images of the Babylonian gods – statues that had been brought to Babylon after being forcefully taken from their original cities by the command of Nabonidus, the last Chaldean king – to the satisfaction of Marduk, the King of all gods. In both content and style, this document adapts literary and cultural models of Mesopotamian royal propaganda.[41]

By contrast, in the propagandistic source of Jer 10:11, which is presumably later by a century or so compared to the Cyrus Cylinder, the relation between the chief deity and the other gods is again formulated in the polemical manner of the *Esagila Chronicle*: the senior god has the power to destroy the other gods, and he demonstrates no interest in restoring their previous glory. Arguably, this change of heart is related to a fundamental shift that Achaemenid kings demonstrated in their approach to Babylonia. The early years of Xerxes I (Ḫašayarša I, ruled in 486–465 BCE) witnessed rebellions in Babylonia; as part of his retaliation campaign, the Persian king ruined Babylon and captured Marduk's statue.[42] Moreover, in one of his royal inscriptions, Xerxes I boasts of having demolished a temple of the false

---

40 For an English translation, see Cogan in Hallo 1997–2002: 2.314–316. For the historical background, see Tadmor 2011.

41 Kuhrt 1983. The Persians' adoption of Mesopotamian traditions is visible in other modes of propaganda as well, such as royal inscriptions and iconography (e.g., Sancisi-Weerdenburg 1993).

42 See, e.g., Herodotus 1:183. Briant (2002: 515–568, at 543–549) expresses a more skeptical view of Xerxes' approach to Babylonia (and Egypt).

gods (referred to as *daivā*, "demons"), establishing in their place the worship of Ahuramazda:

> And among these countries there was (a place) where previously false gods were worshipped. Afterwards, by the favor of Ahuramazda, I destroyed that sanctuary of the demons (*daivadāna*), and I made proclamation, "The demons shall not be worshipped (*daivā : mā : yadiyaiša*)!" Where previously the demons were worshipped, there I worshipped Ahuramazda and Arta reverent(ly).[43]

During a later period, however, Greek sources testify to a significant change that took place in the official manifestations of the Persian religion. According to Herodotus, the Persians initially employed no figurative representation of their deities, nor did they construct temples for them.[44] But according to Berossos, cult images were introduced as part of the public worship in the temples of central cities throughout the empire by the fourth century BCE.[45] According to these testimonies, the Persian religion became explicitly iconic only at a relatively late period, while in earlier times (during the sixth and fifth centuries BCE) it was characterized by aniconism, famously comparable to – and a possible a source of influence on – the theology of Deutero-Isaiah, which flourished in the mid-sixth century BCE. This basic theological match would have facilitated the quotation of the message, now contained in Jer 10:11, from a propagandistic source that reflects the imperial policy and official theology of the Achaemenid Empire prior to the fourth century BCE.

* * *

---

43 Kent 1953: 150–152, Inscription XPh, lines 35–41. Briant 2002: 550–554 may have gone too far in blurring this change in religious policy. Its echo may still be heard in the literary development of Xerxes' biblical image, i.e., the character of Ahasuerus in the book of Esther. Note especially Esth 3:8, although the justification given there for the persecution of the Jews is more legal than religious: "their laws are different from those of every other people, and they do not keep the king's laws, so that it is not appropriate for the king to tolerate them."
44 Herodotus 1:131.
45 FGrHist (BNJ) 680 F 11, ed. G. de Breucker. This passage of Berossos survived in a somewhat distorted citation embedded in the writings of Clemens of Alexandria (cf. Verbrugghe and Wickersham 2000: 62 [F12] and n. 50). Scholars agree that the text as it stands reflects some historical confusion in attributing the cultic reform to Artaxerxes Ochus, the son of Darius. As a matter of fact, Artaxerxes Ochus (=Artaxerxes III, ruled in 359–338 BCE) was the son of Artaxerxes Mnemon (=Artaxerxes II, ruled in 405–359 BCE), whereas the latter was the son of a Darius (Darius II Nothos, ruled in 423–405 BCE). It seems likely, therefore, that Berossos actually refers to Artaxerxes II. In either case, the cultic reform apparently took place during the fourth century BCE.

Both philological and historical considerations converge in pointing to the fifth century BCE – and perhaps more specifically to the reign of Xerxes I in the first half of this century – as a plausible context for the composition of the hypothetical propagandistic source, a citation of which is embedded in Jer 10:11.[46] Without doubt, much of the evidence is circumstantial, and the exact historical identification is not entirely crucial for the literary analysis. Put differently, one may accept or reject the historical identification regardless of one's view of the strength – or weakness – of the literary conclusion concerning the foreign source of the passage, which, in any case, is likely to be sought in the Achaemenid imperial propaganda.

§4 Function within the prophetic unit

As proposed above, v. 11 originates in a propagandistic source that linked between the imperial authority and divine supremacy of the Creator. This motif is expressed by underscoring the inherent inferiority of other gods – who presumably represent other countries and peoples – that lack the power of creation. Detached from its original context, however, v. 11 can be read as implying a more radical theological assertion, which undermines the very assumption that such "gods" should be recognized at all as divine beings. This potential reading may well comprise the key factor that has drawn the redactor's attention to the propagandistic source in the first place.

By extracting this particular passage and embedding it in a new rhetorical context that condemns the very notion of idolatry, the redactor amplified the theological argument of the prophetic unit. The polemical proclamation that the idols are perishable objects that possess no power whatsoever – neither to do good nor to commit evil – was augmented by the additional assertion that such gods are indeed doomed for destruction and are, in any case, incomparable to the Creator. The presence of such a statement anchored in the imperial propaganda has only served to affirm its authority: from the redactor's point of view, it is nothing but the idolaters' self-incrimination. Their explicit admittance of the gloomy fate awaiting their gods became a highly valuable asset for the polemical redactor, who was happy to quote it in order to magnify the original argument of

---

46 Cf. Halévy (1885: 69–72), who rightly observed the interpolative nature of v. 11, and correctly observed that its language is older than that of Daniel and akin to that of Ezra. Moreover, he was sensitive to the political overtones of the passage, even if his own hypothesis – that Jer 10:11 originates in Darius' letter, as cited in Ezra 6:12 – is not particularly convincing.

the satirical passages.[47] While continuing and amplifying the satirical passages, v. 11 was integrated after vv. 12–13, which supply a diametrically opposed description, namely, a hymnic praise of YWHW as the creator of the heavens and the earth.[48]

This basic function of v. 11 within Jer 10:1–16 is valid for all its textual constellations. However, the passage also serves a more specific function within its immediate context. Since v. 11 was taken out of its original context, readers depend on its new surroundings for disambiguating the mysterious identity of the addressees hinted by the 3m.pl pronominal suffix contained in v. 11a (להום, "to them"). However, this identity transformed in accordance with the changes in the immediate context, which are partly revealed in the textual witnesses.

(a) Originally, v. 11 was incorporated before vv. 12–13, and its content and mode resume the polemical mode of the immediately preceding v. 5b:

| אל תיראו מהם כי לא ירעו | Do not be afraid of *them*, for *they* cannot do evil, |
| וגם היטיב אין אותם | nor is it in *them* to do good. |

In this context, the pronoun contained in v. 11a (כדנה תאמרון להום, "Thus you will say to *them*") is read as a reference to the cult images prepared by the artisans.[49] Readers of this sequence of passages are prone to conclude that the prophet – or God, who speaks through the prophet – commands the Israelites to address the idols directly and publicly announce that the latter are about to vanish from the world.[50] The 3m.pl verbs contained in the Aramaic message of v. 11b thus function as a rhetorical means of expressing a derogatory approach to the idols: despite the formal occasion of speaking to these idols, the verbs suggest that it is pointless to address them in the second person, for they are lifeless objects that cannot perceive any speech.

(b) At later stages, v. 5b was further distanced from v. 11 due to redactional changes that took place in the satirical passages[51] and the gradual incorporation of the hymnic passages of v. 10 as well as vv. 6–7 (in this order),[52] leading

---

47 In this respect, v. 11 resembles the composition of the satirical passages, which similarly contain an originally independent literary source stemming from a different religious milieu (above, Chapter 1), and it differs from the other additions to the prophecy, which are all hymnic in nature (vv. 6–7, 10, 12–13). The thematic and rhetorical nature of v. 11 thus corroborates the hypothesis that this passage was meant to supplement the satirical passages.

48 Cf. above, Chapter 2, §8.

49 For the link between v. 11 and v. 5b see, from a different angle, Stipp 2016: 109–110 (against Vonach 2009: 215, who attempts to maintain 𝔐's originality).

50 Cf. Jerome's interpretation: "This [i.e., v. 11] should be said to false gods that have been put together by craftsmanship" (Graves and Hall 2011: 68; for the original Latin text, see Reiter 1960: 105).

51 See above, Chapter 1.

52 See below, Chapters 4 and 5, respectively.

eventually to a situation in which v. 11 was preceded by the hymnic v. 10. While this basic formation is reflected in 𝔐, some grounds exist for suspecting that the text of v. 10 was originally different from what we find in this witness,[53] ending with a parallelism as follows:

מקצפו תרעש הארץ   At his wrath the *earth* quakes,
ולא יכלו *שמים* זעמו   and the *heavens* cannot endure his indignation.

If this hypothesis is correct, then readers of v. 11 would have interpreted the pro-nominal להום as referring to the cosmological entities of Earth and Heavens, in accordance with a common rhetorical mode of summoning cosmic witnesses when conveying a message of divine rebuking of the people of Israel (e.g., Deut 32:1; Isa 1:2).

(c) Later still, the text of v. 10 was changed – possibly due to a deliberate, theological correction – to read (with 𝔐):

מקצפו תרעש הארץ   At his wrath the earth quakes,
ולא יכלו גוים זעמו   and the *nations* cannot endure his indignation.

When reading v. 11 after this version of v. 10, readers are lead to interpret להום as referring to the "nations," which is the last mentioned item that grammatically agrees with the 3m.pl pronominal suffix.

This new context shifts the identity of the implied addresses of v. 11: "them" are no longer to be identified with the idols, nor with the natural elements that witness the breach of the divine covenant with Israel; rather, "them" refers to the *Israelites* who worship the idols. Thematically, then, the prophecy shifts its focus from an abstract discussion of different perceptions of the divinity to a concrete and exclusionist definition of collective identity, which takes the form of esta-blishing clearer social boundaries between "them" (the nations) and "us" (the "house of Israel").[54] The version of the text represented by 𝔐 thus transformed the theological polemic into an ethnic argument.

---

53 See below, Chapter 4.

54 𝔐's version of Jer 10:1–16 should thus take its place among other texts composed in the early Second Temple period – specifically in pre-Hellenistic times – that foreshadow the rab-binic notion of the גוי, which epitomizes the strict distinction between Jews and gentiles. The genealogy of this notion is the subject of a recent series of studies: Rosen-Zvi and Ophir 2011 and 2015; Rosen-Zvi 2016. For other aspects of the struggle over identity construction that are reflected in Jeremiah, see Rom-Shiloni 2013: 198–225.

§5 The language shift and the Aramaic versions

The integration of an Aramaic utterance within a Hebrew work and the subsequent changes in the immediate context of this implanted segment all affected v. 11 in terms of understanding the language shift it introduces into the text. Language is one of the central means of crystallizing and expressing collective identity, because the use of a distinctive variety (a language, dialect, or sociolect) allows speakers to define their internal coherence on the one hand and to mark their distinction vis-à-vis other speech communities (or individual foreigners) on the other. Multilingual communities, in particular, often demonstrate a delicate balance of power between the various languages spoken by community members – an equilibrium related to the assignment of distinct social values to each of the languages or varieties within the overall cultural system.[55]

The direction, scope, and types of reciprocal influences that languages in contact may exert on each other are not exhausted by inner-linguistic factors; rather, they result from social, cultural, and political pressures that are encoded in the speakers' decision to speak one language over the other or to code-switch between different languages in specific contexts. Such switches and shifts are not incidental, but rather reflect concrete power relations between speech communities; all the more so in the case of ethno-political minorities, which invest much social energy and symbolic capital in constructing their collective identity vis-à-vis their surroundings.

The shift from Hebrew to Aramaic as a cultural code that signifies moving from an 'in-group' communication to an 'out-group' negotiation posed a difficult challenge to the ancient translators of Jeremiah into other languages. All translators of Jer 10:1–16 obviously had to wrestle with the vexing question of how – if at all – they should represent v. 11's shift from Hebrew to Aramaic in their respective target-languages. For translators into Aramaic, however, the task of converting the prophetic words from Hebrew to Aramaic was not exhausted by this technical difficulty; rather, they were forced to cope with the sociolinguistic implication of such a language shift: the emphatic presentation of a contrast between two different worlds of discourse, defined in terms of their idiom (Hebrew vs. Aramaic), ethnic affiliation (the 'house of Israel' vs. 'the nations'), theology (YHWH worshippers vs. idolaters),

---

[55] For previous discussions of the sociolinguistic aspects of the contact between Hebrew and Aramaic, as evident in biblical literature, see especially Polak 2013; Schniedewind 2013. Elsewhere, I have attempted to demonstrate the implications of this situation for the understanding of Jer 10:1–16; see Mizrahi 2014. The present discussion does not replicate my previous treatment of the topic, but rather attempts to harness its conclusions for a better understanding of the compositional history of the prophecy.

and politics (those who recognize their direct submission to God vs. those who are governed by human kings and remain unaware of the true, divine sovereign).

Scrutiny of the evidence indicates that the *Vorlage* of both Aramaic versions, Targum Jonathan and the Peshitta, was a proto-Masoretic text, which was very close – albeit not identical – to the text-form represented by 𝕸. Hence, the translators were well aware that the language shift contained in their *Vorlage* implied a series of fundamental tensions, whose underscoring became the focus of the literary unit in its Masoretic-like formation. For the translators into Aramaic, however, the balance of power between these oppositions was reshuffled, as Aramaic turned into the first language of their audience (the prophecy's prospective readers), whereas Hebrew was rendered to be the non-native language, whose knowledge was not necessarily shared by the broader public and the ability to master it fully increasingly became reserved to limited circles of individuals.

How did the Aramaic translators cope with this delicate challenge, and which strategies did they adopt in representing the shift from one language to another, which is so essential and entrenched in their source-text? As demonstrated below, this question motivated peculiar trajectories of literary development discernible in the Aramaic versions; these trajectories continued the compositional processes underlying the textual development that bridges between 𝕲 and 𝕸.

Two such versions have survived from Antiquity: the Jewish Targum Jonathan[56] and the Christian Peshitta.[57] Both versions resemble each other linguistically, having adapted v. 11 to their respective dialects of Aramaic rather than reproducing its original, Official Aramaic form. They differ markedly from each other, however, in their literary treatment of this passage. Comparing their different, even opposing approaches to this problem enables one to trace the different trajectories of literary and theological development that the prophecy underwent in the various faith communities that had inherited Jeremiah as part of their Scriptures. As we shall see, the intricate processes of textual transmission of this text, its literary growth, exegetical reception, and ideological crystallization as an

---

56 I was unable to locate any remains of other Jewish Targums or alternative Targumic traditions for Jer 10: neither "embedded Targums" (שקיעי תרגום, see Goshen-Gottstein and Kasher 1983–89; Houtman and Sysling 2009) nor "Targumic additions" (תוספתות תרגום, see Kasher 1996) that are scattered in rabbinic and medieval sources.

57 Paul of Tella produced an additional Syriac version of Jeremiah, in the form of the Syro-Hexapla, in the seventh century CE (Ceriani 1876–81: 1.116r–138v, with Chapter 10 in fol. 120v); however, it is an indirect version made from 𝕲. Another Aramaic version of Jeremiah, preserved only fragmentarily, is the Syro-Palestinian one composed in the Christian Palestinian Aramaic of the Byzantine period, but virtually nothing survives from Jer 10:1–16 (see Goshen-Gottstein and Shirun 1973: 84–90; Müller-Kessler and Sokoloff 1997: 149–182).

essential element in the construction of group-identity, are all intimately inter-linked and are better viewed holistically.

§5.1 Targum Jonathan

Targum Jonathan of the Prophets appears to be rooted in the Second Temple period, but it crystallized only in the first centuries CE.[58] Its language is Jewish Standard Literary Aramaic, which, albeit not identical to the vernacular dialects of Middle Aramaic, nevertheless betrays telling isoglosses with the dialects of the Roman period (Palmyrene, Nabbataean, and Qumran Aramaic), while clearly antedating the language of the so-called Palestinian Targums of the Byzantine period.[59] The Targum for the Latter Prophets apparently continued to absorb additions and modification for a relatively long period; thus, its language differs from that of the Targum for the Former Prophets in terms of its linguistic homogeneity, or rather heterogeneity.[60] Yet distinguishing between interpretive expansions that are original to the Targum and others that have been incrementally added to it along its transmission is a challenging task, and the identification of different literary strata within the Targum is not always feasible. Targum Jeremiah (𝕮) comprises an inseparable part of Targum Jonathan of the Latter Prophets.[61]

A useful starting point for the present discussion is recognizing the internal difference in the translation technique employed by 𝕮 in the literary unit of Jer 10:1–16. In the prophecy as a whole, 𝕮 reflects a very literal translation technique, as demonstrated, for instance, in vv. 10 and 12; in v. 11, however, it shifts to an expansive and much freer mode of translation:

---

58 For an updated survey of the state of the art, see Flesher and Chilton 2011: 167–264 (in my opinion, their attempt to distinguish between Tannaitic and Amoraic strata in Targum Jonathan should be viewed with great caution). Cf. Churgin 1927; Smolar and Aberbach 1983 (the former was reprinted in the same volume as the latter). The Second Temple roots of the Targum are suggested, among other things, by certain passages in the Dead Sea Scrolls that seem to presuppose an Aramaic version of the Prophets that approximates the classical Targums (though this tradition may not have been committed to writing yet). See, e.g., Bar-Asher 2000; Hacham 2005.
59 Tal 1975.
60 Tal 1975: בב–כב, 191–203.
61 For an English translation and a comprehensive discussion of 𝕮, see Hayward 1987. His translation is based on the critical edition of Sperber 1959: 133–263 (Chapter 10 is on pp. 159–162). Cf. Flesher and Chilton 2011: 207–213. Wolfsohn 1902 prepared an earlier edition of Jer 1–12 as part of his dissertation. The later edition of Ribera Florit 1992 aspires to present the Babylonian text of 𝕮, although, unavoidably, most its witnesses are actually Yemenite (cf. Ribera Florit 1989). For the sake of a clear presentation of the text, and to avoid unnecessary complications in the typesetting, 𝕮 is quoted hereafter according to the text contained in the Rabbinic Bible edition of Cohen 2012: 68–74; its text of 𝕮 is based on Yemenite manuscripts, but it converts the Babylonian vocalization signs into Tiberian ones. Notable variant readings are discussed wherever necessary.

Tab. A: Synoptic comparison of 𝔐 and 𝔗 for Jer 10:10–13.

	𝔐	NRSV	𝔗	Hayward 1987: 79–80
10	וַיהוָה אֱלֹהִים אֱמֶת הוּא־אֱלֹהִים חַיִּים וּמֶלֶךְ עוֹלָם מִקִּצְפּוֹ תִּרְעַשׁ הָאָרֶץ וְלֹא־יָכִלוּ גוֹיִם זַעְמוֹ׃	But the Lord is the true God; he is the living God and the everlasting King. At his wrath the earth quakes, and the nations cannot endure his indignation.	וַיְיָ אֱלֹהִים קְשׁוֹט הוּא אֱלֹהִים קַיָּם וּמַלְכֵיהּ עָלְמִין מֵרוּגְזֵהּ זָיְעָא אַרְעָא וְלָא יִסְתַּבְּלוּן עַמְמַיָּא זַעְמֵיהּ׃ דְּנָא פַּרְשֶׁגֶן אִגַּרְתָּא דִּשְׁלַח יִרְמְיָה נְבִיָּא לְוָת שְׁאָר סָבֵי גָלוּתָא דִּי בְבָבֶל אֲרֵי אִם יֵימְרוּן לְכוֹן עַמְמַיָּא דִּי אַתּוּן בֵינֵיהוֹן פְּלַחוּ לְטַעֲוָתָא בֵּית יִשְׂרָאֵל כְּדֵין תָּתִיבוּן וּכְדֵין תֵּימְרוּן לְהוֹן	But the Lord God is truth. He is the Living God and King of the Ages. At his anger the earth trembles and the nations are not able to endure his wrath. This is a copy of the letter which Jeremiah the prophet sent to the remnant of the elders of the Exile who were in Babylon. "If the nations among whom you are should say to you, Worship the idols, O house of Israel: thus you shall answer and thus shall you say to them:
11	כִּדְנָה תֵּאמְרוּן לְהוֹם אֱלָהַיָּא דִּי־שְׁמַיָּא וְאַרְקָא לָא עֲבַדוּ יֵאבַדוּ מֵאַרְעָא וּמִן־תְּחוֹת שְׁמַיָּא אֵלֶּה׃	Thus shall you say to them: The gods who did not make the heavens and the earth shall perish from the earth and from under the heavens.	טַעֲוָתָא דִּי אַתּוּן פָּלְחִין לְהֵן טַעֲוָן דְּלֵית בְּהֵן צְרוֹךְ אִנּוּן מִן שְׁמַיָּא לָא יָכְלִין לְאַחָתָא מִטְרָא וּמִן אַרְעָא לָא יָכְלִין לְאַצְמָחָא אִנּוּן וְדִי פָלְחִין לְהוֹן יֵאבַדוּן מֵאַרְעָא וְיִשְׁתֵּיצוּן מִן תְּחוֹת שְׁמַיָּא אִלֵּין׃	'The idols which you worship are idols in which there is no profit.[1] They cannot bring down rain from heaven, and they cannot make fruits sprout forth from the earth. They and those who worship them shall perish from the earth, and shall be destroyed from under these heavens.'

Tab. A (continued)

	𝔐	NRSV	𝔗	Hayward 1987: 79–80
12	עֹשֵׂה אֶרֶץ בְּכֹחוֹ	It is he who made the earth by his power,	דְּכֵן תֵּימְרוּן לְהוֹן אֲנַחְנָא פָלְחִין	Thus you shall say to them: 'We worship
	מֵכִין תֵּבֵל בְּחָכְמָתוֹ	who established the world by his wisdom,	לְעָבֵד אַרְעָא בְּחֵילֵיהּ	him who made the earth by his might, 12
	וּבִתְבוּנָתוֹ נָטָה שָׁמָיִם:	and by his understanding stretched out the heavens.	אַתְקֵין תֵּבֵל בְּחָכְמְתֵיהּ	completed the world by his wisdom,
			וּבְסָכְלְתָנוּתֵיהּ מְתַח שְׁמַיָּא	and by his understanding suspended the heavens.
13	לְקוֹל תִּתּוֹ הֲמוֹן מַיִם בַּשָּׁמַיִם	When he utters his voice, there is a tumult of waters in the heavens,	לְקָל יָהֵיב רִגְשַׁת מַיָּא בִּשְׁמַיָּא	At the sound of his voice, there is a 13 heap of water in the heavens,
	וַיַּעַל נְשִׂאִים מִקְצֵה (הָאָרֶץ)	and he makes the mist rise from the ends of the earth.	וְאַסֵּיק עֲנָנִין מִסְּיָפֵי אַרְעָא	And he brings up clouds from the end of the earth:
	בְּרָקִים לַמָּטָר עָשָׂה	He makes lightnings for the rain,	בַּרְקִין לְמִטְרָא עָבֵד	he makes lightnings at the time of rain,
	וַיּוֹצֵא רוּחַ מֵאֹצְרֹתָיו:	and he brings out the wind from his storehouses.	וּמַפֵּיק רוּחָא מֵאוֹצְרוֹהִי:	and brings forth winds from his treasure-houses.

1 The text of this clause raises a problem of grammatical agreement. The plural form מַעֲשֵׂה is in the feminine, whereas the corresponding אֱלָהַיָּא of the source-text – as well as Hebrew אֱלֹהִים – are in the masculine. For this reason, 𝔗 witnesses an interchange between pronouns in the 3m.pl (בְּהוֹן ...לְהוֹן) and 3f.pl (אִנִּין), and even more so in readings contained in the various manuscripts of 𝔗. For instance, in MS BL Or. 1473 (a very good Yemenite manuscript, whose readings were quoted by Sperber under the siglum 1), the two occurrences of the independent pronoun for 3f.pl (אִנִּין) were replaced with the form for 3m.pl (אִנּוּן; see Ribera-Florit 1992: 96), and so also in other witnesses (cf. the apparatus of Sperber 1959: 160). By contrast, a Genizah fragment with Babylonian vocalization (Eb 133) preserves the feminine אִנִּין, but changes the corresponding pronominal suffix (בְּהוֹן) to the feminine (בְּהֵין; see Ribera-Florit 1992: 98).

Upon first glance, the conspicuous discrepancy between the different translation techniques employed in vv. 10–13 may call for a diachronic explanation. Could potentially the major expansion integrated into v. 11 have been interpolated into 𝕮 at a relatively late stage of its formation?[62] In my opinion, the answer is negative. It is very difficult to separate v. 11 from its surroundings in 𝕮, and it is virtually impossible to extract from the expansive rendition of v. 11 an older kernel of a literal translation that was allegedly expanded at a secondary stage. More probably, the expansive rendition is original to 𝕮, and the change in translation technique embeds a solution for the unique exegetical problems posed by v. 11 – most notably the need to justify the language shift from Hebrew to Aramaic (and back), which is not explicitly explained in the source-text.[63]

The Aramaic text of v. 11 was systematically rewritten in 𝕮. The typical traits of Official Aramaic were replaced with the corresponding distinctive features of Jewish Literary Aramaic.[64] Yet 𝕮's treatment is not exhausted by updating the language of v. 11, but rather extends to reshaping its content as well. According to 𝔐, the passage condemns the gods of the nations that lack the power of creation; although it expects their ultimate annihilation, it still recognizes their present existence and even admits their superhuman nature by explicitly referring to them as "gods" (אלהיא). In contradistinction, 𝕮 no longer refers to the idols as "gods" but rather employs the derogatory designation טעון (literally, "errors"), which is an idiomatic rendition that denotes "idols" in Targumic

---

62 Churgin 1927: 134–135 indeed took such a position. He noted that in Codex Reuchlinianus, the expansive rendition follows a verbal reproduction of the original Aramaic passage, and speculated that the original text of 𝕮 did not include any translation of v. 11 but rather incorporated the source-text of this passage as-is. Subsequent scholars accepted this proposal, in one way or another; unfortunately, however, it is baseless. Even a superficial glance over Codex Reuchlinianus will demonstrate that this manuscript – like many other witnesses of the Aramaic Targums – is written in the method of 'interdigitating' the source-text with its Targum, verse by verse. Put differently, *every single verse of Jeremiah* is immediately followed by its Aramaic rendition, and obviously the very same procedure was applied for v. 11 as well. See the facsimile edition of Sperber 1956: 499.

63 Cf. Komlosh 1973: 415.

64 Orthography and phonology: the historical spellings of תאמרון and יאבדו are changed to the phonetic spellings of תימרון and ייבדו; the obsolete spelling ארקא is replaced with the standard ארעא; and the final nasal consonant of the pronominal suffix for 3m.pl is /n/ rather than /m/ (להון > להום). Morphology: the old demonstratives כדנה and אלה are substituted with כדין (and כדנן; cf. below, n. 70) and אלין, respectively. At the same time, 𝕮 exhibits some degree of linguistic conservatism in keeping the volitive form ייבדו rather than replacing it with the indicative ייבדון. This is a very rare occurrence of the jussive form in the classical Targums (not mentioned in the comprehensive grammar of Dalman 1905: 272, 300).

literature.[65] Moreover, the polemical argument is refocused. The center of gravity in 𝔐 lies in the idols' incompetence to create, whereas 𝕮 emphasizes their inability to manage the world on a regular basis, especially with respect to agricultural fertility as manifested by bringing rainfall and enabling crops to grow.[66] Finally, 𝕮 broadens the scope of the pending destruction: it will encompass not only the idols but also their worshippers: אנון ופלחיהון ייבדו מארעא, "they and those who worship them shall perish from the earth."[67]

All these differences reflect a change of heart concerning idolatry. 𝕮 does not shares 𝔐's degree of anxiety from divine statues. By representing the term "gods" (אלהיא) with the phrase "the errors (or: idols) that you worship" (טען דאתון פלחין להון), 𝕮 reflects the assumption that the true threat no longer stems from the idols themselves – as independent, active deities – but rather from the human practice of their worship. 𝕮 thus takes for granted that the religious identity of its audience had crystallized as a monotheistic set of beliefs to a degree that enables it to shift the focus of the polemics. 𝕮 erases any trace of the mythological conceptualization implied by the original formulation of the Aramaic message of v. 11, rephrasing it in economic terms. The idols are dismissed as mere "errors,"

---

65 For the Targumic method to distinguish between different usages of the Hebrew term אלהים by employing distinct Aramaic equivalents, see Churgin 1927: 111–113. For 𝕮's approach to idolatry, see Smoler and Abrebach 1983: 140–156.

66 𝕮 may be resorting to the agricultural aspect to demonstrate the idols' incompetence by way of a Midrashic interpretation of the phrase עבד + ארעא in the source-text (שמיא וארקא לא עבדו, "[those who] did not make the heavens and the earth") as referring to the cultivation of the land. Compare the Hebrew phrase עבד אדמה, which is normally rendered by פלח בארעא (e.g., Targum Onkelos for Gen 2:5; 3:23; Targum Jonathan for Zech 13:5, etc.). The *Epistle of Jeremiah* resembles 𝕮 in its interpretation of the mentioning of the heavens, but it explains differently the mentioning of the earth as a reference to political reality: "Therefore, to whom is it known that they are not gods? For they can surely not establish a king of the country, nor can they surely give rain to people" (vv. 51–52). Jer 10:11 possibly resurfaces towards the end of the *Epistle*: "Therefore, knowing that they are not gods, do not fear them. For they can neither curse nor bless kings, and they surely do not show signs in heaven for the nations" etc. (vv. 64–66; the motif of "the signs of heavens" alludes to Jer 10:2, and the reference to the opening of the prophecy functions as a means of literary closure).

67 The expansive technique employed at this point is noteworthy for demonstrating the Targumist's literary sensitivity. The source-text, ייאבדו מארעא ומן תחות שמיא אלה, contains the word-pair "heavens" and "earth," but both terms function as the direct object of the single verb ייאבדו. Contrariwise, in 𝕮, the word-pair properly breaks between the two cola of a synonymous parallelism: אנון ופלחיהון ייבדו מארעא // וישתיצון מן תחות שמיא אלין, introducing the verb שיצי so as to complement אבד to a word-pair (cf. Targum Jonathan for Isa 1:9; Hos 11:8). The Aramaic word-pair שיצי // אבד is normally used in the classical Targums for rendering the Hebrew word-pair אבד // שמד (e.g., Targum Onkelos for Deut 4:26 etc.).

and its main argument is no longer theological but rather utilitarian: there is no point in worshipping the idols because they are useless (טעון דלית בהון צרוך אנין, "idols in which there is no profit"),[68] for they can neither bring rain nor yield crops.

The systematic rewriting of the passage extends beyond merely expressing a different view of idolatry. This undertaking also fulfills a literary function in filling in the crucial interpretive gaps between v. 11 and its immediate context. 𝕿 sought to smooth over the somewhat abrupt moves from the hymnic v. 10 to the admonitory v. 11, and from the latter to the (again) hymnic vv. 12–13, by stitching together the differing passages and tightening their internal links.

For instance, the clause אנין ופלחיהון ייבדו מארעא, "they and those who worship them shall perish from *the earth*," echoes the concluding part of v. 10, which, according to 𝔐, predicts a destruction for the idolatrous nations, as well as a global earthquake: מרגזיה תזוע ארעא ולא יכלון עממיא לסוברא רגזיה, "At his anger, *the earth* trembles and the nations are not able to endure his warth."[69] The nations (עממיא) mentioned in v. 10 are again referred to within the long expansion inserted into the beginning of v. 11 (עממיא דאתון ביניהון, "*the nations* among whom you are"); they are also hinted to in the expansion attached to the conclusion of this passage (כדנן תימרון להון, "thus you will say to *them*"). And the latter clause is nothing but a *Wiederaufnahme*, which connects to the expanded instruction at the beginning of the passage (כדין תתיבון וכדין תימרון להון, "thus you shall answer and thus shall you say to *them*").[70] In addition, the expansion within v. 11, and especially the emphasis on

---

68 This formula is sometimes employed in Targumic literature for rendering various epithets that denote idols, especially the negative phrase לֹא־אֵל/אֱלֹהַּ/אֱלֹהִים; cf. Targum Onkelos for Deut 32:17; Targum Jonathan for 1 Kgs 18:21, 24; Jer 2:11; 14:22; Ezek 28:2, 9; Hos 8:6; Hab 2:18.

69 The Hebrew verb יָכִלוּ is represented, in this rendition, by the phrase יכלון... לסוברא, as if the Targumist read his *Vorlage* as יָכְלוּ (לשאת) (cf. Targum Onkelos for Gen 36:7; Num 11:14), or possibly יכלכלו (cf. Targum Jonathan for 1 Kgs 8:27). But the complex expression יכל לסוברא sometimes renders הכיל (cf. Targum Jonathan for Jer 6:11; Am 7:10); hence, no variant reading must be assumed at this point (cf. below, p. 160, n. 29).

70 Note the slight linguistic difference between the two occurrences of the addressing formula: at the beginning of v. 11, one finds the demonstrative כדין (replacing the original כדנה, which typifies Official Aramaic), whereas at the end of the passage, the allomorphic demonstrative כדנן is employed. Both forms are found in Onkelos and Jonathan, but their distribution varies greatly. The formula כדנן + אמר is attested some 460 times, while כדין + אמר is found only in about 30 instances. In other words, אמר + כדנן is the neutral, unmarked form of the phrase, whereas כדין + אמר is its marked counterpart in Targumic Aramaic. It stands to reason that the latter was employed to underscore the shift between two discursive levels, which, in 𝕿, take the literary form of a narrative-like framing of a cited letter. The rare כדין + אמר marks the shift from the narrative to the citation of the letter, which is a formal document couched in a conservative style, whereas the more common כדנן marks the return to the narrative. For the narrative framework added in 𝕿, see further below.

the fact that the idols cannot prompt rainfall, tie the passage closely to the hymnic passage that follows – particularly to v. 13 that describes how YHWH brings rain.

But the most radical and effective means for bridging the gap between v. 11 and its surroundings is 𝕮's overall replacement of the discursive situation of the passage, which manifests itself in the long expansions added both before v. 11 and following it. 𝕮 provides a new narrative framework, which explains the peculiar features of v. 11 – which implies that it has a different audience compared to vv. 10, 12–13 – in its being a discursive unit of its own: it is a copy of a letter (פרשגן אגרתא) sent by Jeremiah to the Judean elders exiled in Babylonia. The purpose of this letter is to instruct its audience in what to tell to the nations among whom they live, should the latter attempt to impose idol worship over the Israelites.[71]

This motif is patently taken from another place within the book of Jeremiah; namely, from Chapter 29, which tells of a letter sent by Jeremiah to the Judean elders at the Babylonian exile, after the exiling of Jehoiachin:[72]

> [1] These are the words of the letter that the prophet Jeremiah sent from Jerusalem to the remaining elders among the exiles, and to the priests, the prophets, and all the people, whom Nebuchadnezzar had taken into exile from Jerusalem to Babylon.[2] This was after King Jeconiah, and the queen mother, the court officials, the leaders of Judah and Jerusalem, the artisans, and the smiths had departed from Jerusalem.[3] The letter was sent by the hand of Elasah son of Shaphan and Gemariah son of Hilkiah, whom King Zedekiah of Judah sent to Babylon to King Nebuchadnezzar of Babylon. It said:
>> [4] Thus says the LORD of hosts, the God of Israel, to all the exiles whom I have sent into exile from Jerusalem to Babylon:[5] Build houses and live in them; plant gardens and eat what they produce.[6] Take wives and have sons and daughters; take wives for your sons, and give your daughters in marriage, that they may bear sons and daughters; multiply there, and do not decrease.[7] But seek the welfare of the city where I have sent you into exile, and pray to the LORD on its behalf, for in its welfare you will find your welfare. [...]
> [10] For thus says the LORD: Only when Babylon's seventy years are completed will I visit you, and I will fulfill to you my promise and bring you back to this place.

---

71 This line of interpretation was favored among Jewish commentators of the Middle Ages, including those of the *Peshat* school, who considered it to be a reasonable solution for problematic shift from the Hebrew context to the Aramaic v. 11. So, e.g., Qimḥi *ad loc.*: זה המאמר שלחהו ירמיהו לבבל לבני הגולה שיענו זה לכשדים [...] וכתב להם המאמר הזה בלשון ארמי שיאמרו אותם לכשדים בלשונם, "Jeremiah sent this text to Babylonia, to the exiles, so that they respond accordingly to the Chaldeans [...] and he wrote to them this text in the Aramaic language, so that they can say it to the Chaldeans in their own language"; cf. Rashi, Isaiah di Trani, and Menaḥem of Posquiè- res (Cohen 2012: 70–71). Such an interpretation even resonates in the critical scholarship, e.g., Kaufmann 1937–63: 3/2.462–466, esp. 464.

72 In this respect, 𝕮 reflects an exegetical tradition that is shared by the apocryphal work *Epistle of Jeremiah*, appended to the books of Jeremiah and Baruch in the LXX; see Kratz 1995; cf. Doe- ring 2005 and 2012. The oldest witness for this tradition may be an *Apocryphon of Jeremiah*, found among the Dead Sea Scrolls, if one of its fragments (4Q389, frg. 1) indeed suggests that Jeremiah sent a letter to Babylon from his captivity in Egypt (Dimant 2001: 220–223; cf. Dimant 2013: esp. 457–461).

The prophetic letter reported in Jer 29 notifies the Judean exiles that they should rebuild their lives in Babylonia, because their exile is bound to last for seventy years. The internalized understanding that exile comprises a long-term state of affairs supplies a new background for the polemic against idolatry, which is now presented as an inherent spiritual challenge for anyone who lives in Babylonia (rather than Judah). Interestingly, although this view is expressed formally in extensive additions added to the biblical text in its Targumic rendering, 𝕿 may be seen as developing here an ideological trajectory inherent to its *Vorlage* (which is more-or-less identical to 𝔐, in this regard); namely, the conspicuous socio-cultural tendency to dissimilate and to underscore the social boundaries between the 'we'-group – those that hold on to monotheism and are identified as an ethnic minority (שאר סבי גלותא דבבבל, "the remnant of the elders of the Exile who were in Babylon") – and the 'they'-group of idol worshippers identified with the surrounding nations (עממיא דאתון ביניהון, "the nations among whom you are").[73]

The new discursive situation also transpires from the expansion that bridges between v. 11 and v. 12ff, which defines another turn of speech within the cited letter. According to this frame, v. 11 includes a first potential response of the Judean elders to the nations' demand that they assimilate idolatry; this is a negative response, which dismisses and condemns the idols and their worshippers. It is followed by a second, consecutive response in vv. 12–13, which is positive in nature, as it praises YHWH as the deity that is able to carry out what the idols cannot. From this point on, 𝕿 resorts back to the literal translation technique that characterizes its rendering of the rest of the prophecy. Indeed, vv. 12–13 are translated word-for-word, without any noteworthy expansion excluding the one connecting them to v. 11:

כדנן תימרון להון: אנחנא פלחין   *Thus you shall say to them: We worship*

לדעבד ארעא בחיליה   *him who made the earth by his might...*

---

[73] Note the contrastive relation, in 𝕿, between the nations' addressing the Judean elders: פלחו לטעותא בית ישראל, "Worship the idols, *O house of Israel!*" and God's addressing the people at the beginning of the prophecy: קבילו ית פתגמא דמליל יי עליכון בית ישראל, "Heed the word which the Lord has spoken against you, *O house of Israel*" (rendering v. 1: שמעו את הדבר אשר דבר יהוה עליכם בית ישראל). The Hebrew expression שמע את הדבר, as well as its Aramaic equivalent קבילו ית פתגמא, connote a requirement of obedience (cf. Josh 1:18; Jer 11:2–3, 6, 10, etc.).

The focal element in this Targumic expansion is the independent pronoun אנחנא, which emphatically underscores the difference between the nations and Israel: *they* are idolaters, whereas *we* worship the only true God, the Creator. In so doing, 𝕮 supplies a literary justification for the sharp shift from the polemical passage of v. 11 to the hymnic passage of vv. 12–13, while integrating the latter into its new narrative framework of Chapter 10 by way of harmonizing it with another prophecy of Jeremiah (in Chapter 29), i.e., by interpreting the scriptural text by aid of Scripture itself.

Finally, 𝕮's comprehensive rewriting of v. 11 portrays a historical period and cultural horizon that fundamentally differ from those reflected in its source-text. This is evident in two respects.

The first issue is that of the respective audiences of the prophetic message. In the source-text, v. 11 stands out since it is a quotation from an alien source, integrated only secondarily into its present context. In 𝔐, this feature has a sociolinguistic implication as marking a functional shift from the messages addressed to the in-group, formulated in Hebrew, to the one addressed to the out-group, which is phrased in Aramaic.

Contrarily, 𝕮 attempts to fully integrate v. 11 within the Jewish context, thereby assuming a communicative model that is simultaneously more complex in terms of the number of participants and simpler in terms of its directionality. 𝕮 explicitly asserts that v. 11 belongs to the prophet's words (a point not explicated in 𝔐), and insists that its group of addressees comprises the Judean elders in Babylonia (i.e., neither the nations nor their idols). But within this general missive, yet another message appears like a note in a bottle; it is only this note that may be conveyed to the out-group (the nations), and even this step can only be taken in case of an emergency involving religious conflicts that threatens the entire community of exiles. It follows that 𝕮 not only affirms the prophetic authority of the Aramaic segment of the literary unit but also integrates it into the internal Jewish discourse, bluntly attempting to keep it as far away as possible from the highly-charged negotiation with outsiders.

The second issue involves the medium of communication employed for conveying the prophetic message. According to the source-text, the Aramaic message is to be delivered *orally* (כדנה תאמרון להום, "thus will you *say* to them"). In the Targumic rendering, however, the act of saying is reserved for the secondary message, the one (potentially) addressed to the nations. The primary message, which is designated for the Judean elders in Babylonia, is conveyed in a *written* form, namely, as a copy of a letter (פרשגן אגרתא).[74] This presentation reflects a profound transformation in the conceptualization of the source of religious authority – a change than can be described as the textualization of prophecy. The prophetic message must be committed to writing in order to fulfill its role as a guide for future generations of the people of Israel. The divine word can no longer be heard by way of a living speech; rather, it should be transmitted as a formal document.

In conclusion, 𝕮 does not directly represents the language shift that occurs in its source-text between v. 11 and its surrounding. Nevertheless, readers of 𝕮 are acutely aware of a fundamental change in the discursive situation of v. 11 vis-à-vis its context, which takes the form of a move from a narrative framework to the citation of a written document. Formally, 𝕮 expands the biblical text and constructs on top of it a new structure of rhetorical, exegetical, and literary complexity. On a deeper level, though, 𝕮 can be viewed as directly continuing and forcefully amplifying an essential feature of 𝕸; namely, the ideological trajectory of cultural dissimilation, thereby enhancing the ethnic and theological tensions between Israel and the nations that were already underscored in the compositional formation of its source-text. In both respects, 𝕮 may be considered another link in the continuous chain of literary growth of the prophecy contained in Jer 10:1–16, which is also the unceasing history of its reception: a constant adaptation of the text to the ever-changing spiritual needs of new generations of readers, who took this text to represent the divine word as mediated by the prophet.

§5.2 Peshitta

The complicated and dynamic relation between content and form revealed when comparing 𝕸 with 𝕮 is further illuminated when examined from a different vantage point, by comparing 𝕮 to the treatment of the prophecy in the Syriac version of Jeremiah (𝕾). The Peshitta has been the Scriptures of the Syriac speaking Christianity, which once extended throughout most of the Middle East and

---

74 This term is borrowed from the technical, scribal terminology of the imperial administration of the Persian period, which is also documented in the formal letters cited in the Book of Ezra (4:11; 5:6; cf. 4:23; 7:11). Jewish authors of the Second Temple period adopted the phrase as a stylistic marker of formal authority, as demonstrated by the opening of the *Vision of Amram*: פרשגן [כתב מלי חזות עמרם בר [קהת בר לוי, "A *copy* of the document of words of the vision of Amram, son of [Kohath, son of Levi]" (4Q543 1a-c 1 ‖ 4Q545 1ai 1). The word פרשגן is also employed in Targumic literature, denoting "text" or "copy," e.g., ויכתוב ליה ית פרשגן אוריתא הדא על ספרא (Targum Onkelos for Deut 17:18, וכתב לו את משנה התורה הזאת על ספר, "he shall have a *copy* of this law written for him on a scroll"), וכתב תמן על אבניא ית פרשגן אוריתא דמשה דכתב קדם בני ישראל (Targum Jonathan for Josh 8:32, ויכתוב שם על האבנים את משנה תורת משה אשר כתב לפני בני ישראל, "And there, in the presence of the Israelites, Joshua wrote on the stones a *copy* of the law of Moses, which he had written").

beyond it,[75] but the socio-religious context in which this project of translation was initiated was mysterious already to the Syriac Church Fathers. Although Christian communities received and transmitted the Syriac version of the Old Testament, it stands to reason that the translation actually began its way among Jews or Judeo-Christians.[76] The time at which Jeremiah was translated into Syriac is also unknown, but like most of the other Old Testament books, it should probably be sought in the first centuries CE, possibly in the second century.[77]

The translation technique of 𝕾 is generally literal; it closely follows the Hebrew source-text, which was evidently of the proto-Masoretic type. Still, close inspection shows that the translator did not hesitate to sacrifice the principle of literal translation – especially in small details – for the purpose of exegetical needs and stylistic considerations.[78] This flexible combination between a general policy of literal translation and the practical willingness to adapt it to local interpretive challenges underlies the most conspicuous feature of 𝕾 for Jer 10:1–16; namely, the fact that readers of this version remain completely unaware of any change in language or discursive situation with regard to v. 11.

This feature stems from two sources. First, like 𝕮, 𝕾 does not preserve the linguistic hallmarks of Official Aramaic, which typify the original, Achaemenid text. Rather, it adapts the language of the passage to the norms of Classical Syriac, which is essentially a dialect of the Roman period.[79] Unlike 𝕮, however, 𝕾 consistently avoids betraying any sign that the source-text originally exhibited a language shift. In the Syriac version, therefore, no difference is discerned in language between v. 11 and its surrounding:

---

75 For a general survey, see Dirksen 1988 (supplemented by the bibliography compiled by Dirksen 1989). For the place of the Peshitta among other Syriac versions of the Bible, see ter Haar Romeny 2005a. For a comprehensive introduction, see Weitzman 1999.

76 See especially Weitzman 1999: 206–262; ter Haar Romeny 2005b: esp. 25–32.

77 The book of Jeremiah was not yet published in the critical edition of the Peshitta Institute of Leiden University, but an extended selection of variant readings collated from the major manuscripts is included in Walter 2006. For an English translation, see Greenberg et al. 2013. In the following discussion, the text of 𝕾 is quoted from MS 7a1 (based on the facsimile edition of Ceriani 1876–81: fol. 329), which also serves as the basic text of the Leiden edition.

78 Greenberg 2002. Note also the critical comments of Williams 2003 (a review of Greenberg's book).

79 Orthography and phonology: the historical spelling ארקא is changed to ܐܪܥܐ, as common in Middle Aramaic dialects; the relative particle is attached to the following word, reflecting its proclitic pronunciation (די שמיא > ܕܫܡܝܐ); the final nasal consonant of the pronominal suffix for 3m.pl is changed from /m/ to /n/ (להום > ܠܗܘܢ). Morphology and morpho-syntax: the inherited demonstratives כדנה and אלה are replaced with the typically Syriac innovations of ܗܟܢܐ and ܗܠܝܢ, respectively; the jussive form of יאבדו lost its place for the indicative ܢܐܒܕܘܢ (and this form also demonstrates the replacement of the inherited prefix y-, marking the third person, with an innovated n-); the old ending marking determined plural in nominals was changed to the regular form typical of Eastern Aramaic (אלהיא > ܐܠܗܐ); and even the vocalic pattern of the preposition "under" was updated (תחות > ܬܚܝܬ).

Tab. B: Synoptic comparison between 𝔐 and ܣ for Jer 10:10–13.

	𝔐	NRSV	ܣ	Greenberg et al. 2013: 65–68	
10	וַיהוָה אֱלֹהִים אֱמֶת	But the Lord is the true God;	ܘܡܪܝܐ ܐܠܗܐ ܫܪܝܪܐ	But the Lord is the God of truth,	10
	הוּא־אֱלֹהִים חַיִּים וּמֶלֶךְ עוֹלָם	he is the living God and the everlasting King.	ܗܘܝܘ ܐܠܗܐ ܚܝܐ ܘܡܠܟܐ ܕܥܠܡܐ	he is the very God of life, king of the ages;	
	מִקִּצְפּוֹ תִּרְעַשׁ הָאָרֶץ	At his wrath the earth quakes,	ܡܢ ܪܘܓܙܗ ܙܐܥܐ ܐܪܥܐ	the earth is shaken by his anger,	
	וְלֹא־יָכִלוּ גוֹיִם זַעְמוֹ׃	and the nations cannot endure his indignation.	ܘܠܐ ܡܣܝܒܪܝܢ ܥܡܡܐ ܠܪܘܓܙܗ	the nations cannot hold out against his anger.	
11	כִּדְנָה תֵּאמְרוּן לְהוֹם	Thus shall you say to them:	ܗܟܢܐ ܐܡܪܘ ܠܗܘܢ	Speak thus to them:	11
	אֱלָהַיָּא דִּי־שְׁמַיָּא וְאַרְקָא לָא עֲבַדוּ	The gods who did not make the heavens and the earth	ܐܠܗܐ ܕܫܡܝܐ ܘܐܪܥܐ ܠܐ ܥܒܕܘ	The gods who did not make the heavens and the earth	
	יֵאבַדוּ מֵאַרְעָא וּמִן־תְּחוֹת שְׁמַיָּא אֵלֶּה׃	shall perish from the earth and from under the heavens.	ܢܐܒܕܘܢ ܡܢ ܐܪܥܐ ܘܡܢ ܬܚܝܬ ܫܡܝܐ ܗܠܝܢ	will perish from the earth and from beneath these heavens.	
12	עֹשֵׂה אֶרֶץ בְּכֹחוֹ	It is he who made the earth by his power,	ܥܒܕ ܐܪܥܐ ܒܚܝܠܗ	The Lord² made the earth with his strength,	12
	מֵכִין תֵּבֵל בְּחָכְמָתוֹ	who established the world by his wisdom,	ܘܡܬܩܢ ܬܒܝܠ ܒܚܟܡܬܗ	established the world with his wisdom,	
	וּבִתְבוּנָתוֹ נָטָה שָׁמָיִם׃	and by his understanding stretched out the heavens.	ܘܒܣܘܟܠܗ ܡܬܚ ܫܡܝܐ	spread out the heavens with his intelligence.	
13	לְקוֹל תִּתּוֹ הֲמוֹן מַיִם בַּשָּׁמַיִם	When he utters his voice, there is a tumult of waters in the heavens,	ܡܢ ܩܠܐ ܕܝܗܒ ܗܡܝܘ ܡܝܐ ܒܫܡܝܐ	He sets (lit. "gives") the sound of the tumult of waters in the heavens,	13

Tab. B (continued)

𝔐	NRSV	𝔖	Greenberg et al. 2013: 65–68
(יָּאֶרֶץ) וּמַעֲלֶה נְשִׂאִים מִקְצֵה הָאָרֶץ	and he makes the mist rise from the ends of the earth.	ܡܣܩ ܥܢܢܐ ܡܢ ܣܘܦܝܗ̇ ܕܐܪܥܐ	brings up the clouds from the ends of the earth,
בְּרָקִים לַמָּטָר עָשָׂה	He makes lightnings for the rain,	ܡܬܝܩ̈ܐ ܠܡܛܪܐ ܥܒܕ	made the lightning (pl.) for the rain,
וַיּוֹצֵא רוּחַ מֵאֹצְרוֹתָיו:	and he brings out the wind from his storehouses.	ܘܡܦܩ ܪ̈ܘܚܐ ܡܢ ܐܘܨܪ̈ܘܗܝ	brings forth the winds from his storehouses.

2 Greenberg 2002: 37 considers this word an exegetical addition on the part of the translator, who intended to clarify the contrast between the condemnation of idols of v. 11 and the praise of the Lord in v. 12. More probably, however, 𝔖 faithfully reflects here a variant reading contained in its *Vorlage*, because the Tetragrammaton is also represented at this point in 𝔊 (which otherwise does not appear to have exerted any influence on 𝔖 in this prophetic unit). For the significance of this reading, see the detailed discussion below, Chapter 4, §4.

Obviously, this translation technique does not eliminate the full range of thematic contrasts expressed in the prophecy, some of which are highlighted by other rhetorical means. Nonetheless, the obliteration of the language shift greatly diminishes the ethnic tension embedded in the source-text. In 𝔐, the strain between the Hebrew-speaking "House of Israel" and the Aramaic-speaking nations is on the same par as the theological tension between YHWH followers and idols worshippers. In 𝔖, however, the ethno-linguistic strain is much attenuated, and the theological tension takes the forefront. Put differently, the linguistic adaptation of v. 11 to Syriac grammar is only the surface expression of a deeper transformation of the balance of power between the divine word as delivered by the prophet, and its audience, which is no longer identified as a particularistic ethnic group that fights to maintain its distinctiveness. Formally, most of the textual difference between 𝔐 and 𝔖 in v. 11 are grammatical in nature, but they actually signal a much more radical adaptation of the text into a new cultural context, which differs in fundamental parameters from the context of the translator's *Vorlage*.

This reshuffle finds another expression in an additional difference between the two versions: their different readings of the verb contained in v. 11a. 𝔐 addresses a *group* of addressees with a verb of speech formulated in 2m.pl: תאמרון (cf. 𝔊 ἐρεῖτε), whereas 𝔖 addresses a *single* addressee by the verb ܐܡܪ.[80] 𝔖 thus differs from 𝔐 in its identification of the subject of the clause. Taken on its own, the verbal form in 𝔐 is exegetically ambiguous, as it may refer either to the "House of Israel" (like the 2m.pl form in vv. 1, 5) or to the "nations" mentioned shortly beforehand (v. 10); however, the broader context points to the former option: the *Israelites* are to address the nations and announce to them that their false gods are about to vanish from the face of the earth. In contradistinction, 𝔖 presents a different discursive situation, because the subject of a verb in the singular (by any

---

80 In addition, the verbal form employed in 𝔐 is in the prefix-conjugation ("you [pl.] will say"), whereas 𝔖 employs a different grammatical form. Unfortunately, its exact interpretation depends on the vocalization, on which the manuscripts disagree. In MS 9a1, there is an upper diacritical dot (ܐܡܪ), indicating that this is a participle ("he says, is saying"). In MS 7a1, one finds a lower diacritical dot (ܐܡܪ), which may be interpreted as either an imperative ("say!") or as a suffix-conjugation ("he said"). In the Mosul edition (1887–88: 2.337), which reflects an eastern reading tradition of the Peshitta, the word was vocalized as ܐܡܪ. However, this vocalization does not solve the exegetical enigma; although the Eastern tradition usually maintains a phonological distinction between the suffix-conjugation and the imperative in I-ʔ verbs, the two categories converge in the verb ܐܡܪ "to say" (Nöldeke 1904: 116, §174A). Be that as it may, Greenberg et al. 2013: 66–67 rendered the verb into English as an imperative ("Speak thus to them").

conceivable vocalization) must be identified with the *prophet*.[81] This difference converges with the general tendency discernible in **ܣ**. The prophecy of destruction is no longer delivered as part of the loaded discourse between ethnic groups (Israel vs. the nations) but rather conducted on the plain of theological argument (the Lord's prophet against the idolaters).

> NB. A different question is to what extent the reading ܐܡܪ goes back to the *Urtext* of **ܣ**, which is a problem that relates to a much broader theoretical issue in Peshitta studies in general. The oldest manuscripts, primarily MS 5b1 of Genesis and Exodus, often witness readings that are closer to **ℳ** compared to what one finds in later manuscripts (which also form the basis of the text of the Peshitta that was made popular in the Modern Age thanks to printed editions). Therefore, Peshitta scholars nowadays tend to assume that the *Urtext* of the Peshitta, in most biblical books, usually had been of a very literal character and closely approximated their proto-Masoretic *Vorlagen*. Such translations, however, were not very idiomatic in Syriac, and they must have included renditions that appeared puzzling to a readership that was no longer versed in Hebrew. Such details were particularly susceptible to correction, and the 'coarse' translation was gradually smoothed by later generations of Syriac scribes. According to this reconstructed trajectory, the text of the Peshitta moved away from **ℳ** over the course of its history of transmission. If so, at least some variant readings witnessed by **ܣ** may actually be the result of inner-Syriac developments rather than true reflections of a deviant *Vorlage*. At the same time, such differences are particularly telling as pieces of evidence for the early reception and interpretation of the Syriac Bible by the hands of its transmitters.

Upon a superficial look, **ܣ** is much closer to **ℳ** than **ℭ**. Essentially, however, **ܣ** reflects an ideological trajectory that sets it apart from both **ℳ** and **ℭ**. The latter two versions underscore the ethnic tension between Israel and the nations in order to construct a clear boundary between the two groups. **ܣ**, in contrast, attempts to attenuate and even to dismiss this very tension, highlighting in its stead

---

81 Note also the difference in verbal modality between the two versions. In **ℳ**, the verb in v. 11a is in the indicative mood, so the clause כדנה תאמרון להום is predictive in nature, while the verb in v. 11b is a jussive (יאבדו), rendering the Aramaic message as a curse. In **ܣ**, by contrast, the verb ܐܡܪ in v. 11a may be an imperative; if so, it renders the clause a command for the prophet to deliver the message, whereas the message contained in v. 11b is simply a prophecy, as the verb contained therein (ܐܒܕܘܢ) is in the future tense.

the spiritual differences between monotheists and pagans. It stands to reason that this tendency accommodates the spiritual needs of the community among – and for – which the Syriac version was created. This community appears to consist of believers who cherished biblical monotheism and prophetic revelation but wished to bridge the gap that separates them from the surrounding ethnic groups, including pagans, by deleting any trace of the language shift that stood out in their source-text.[82]

§6 Conclusion

Analysis of diverse aspects of Jer 10:11 unveils the intricate relation between two components of collective identity encoded in the surviving texts: (a) a religious-theological identity, which promotes a monotheistic credo in contrast to idolatry, and (b) an ethnic-linguistic identity, which contrasts between a minority ('in-group') of Hebrew speakers and the majority ('out-group') of Aramaic speakers. By comparing the different versions of the prophecy, we gain an appreciation of the dynamic and reciprocal relationship between these two aspects, which transformed from one generation to another in accordance with the ever-changing historical conditions and the new spiritual challenges set by every period for the faith-communities among which the text was transmitted. This process can be divided roughly into three schematic stages:

(a) At an early stage, the prophecy consisted mainly of the satirical passages, which condemn idolatry and view it as a pointless worship of inanimate objects (supplemented with the hymnic vv. 12–13, which present the opposite image of YHWH as the almighty Creator). Idolatry was referred to as "the way of the nations" (v. 2), but the core of the argument was a theological polemic. During the Persian period, probably around the mid-fifth century BCE, the addition of a quotation from the Achaemenid imperial propaganda, now embedded in v. 11, enhanced the polemical argument. This citation of an Aramaic source was intended as a demonstration that even the imperial authorities acknowledge the uniqueness of the supreme deity and share the condemnation of false gods.

(b) In this slightly extended formation, the prophecy still placed emphasis on the negative side by sweepingly attacking idolatry. At later stages, however, additonal hymnic passages were integrated gradually into the prophecy, so as

---

82 A similar, Christian *Tendenz* may explain the surprising silence with which Jerome passes over the language shift in his commentary on Jer 10:11 – a silence that perplexed modern scholars and translators of his work (e.g., Meiser 2016: 99).

to present the positive counterpart of YHWH as the living god of Israel and the true sovereign of the universe (vv. 10, 6–7). During this compositional process of incremental supplementation, a new meaning of the Aramaic passage gradually crystallized: it ceased to be a neutral carrier of a theological message and was re-conceptualized as the linguistic expression of an ethnic distinction.

The religious-theological uniqueness was thus amalgamated with the notion of ethno-linguistic distinctiveness, and their combined force in constructing the collective identity of Israel has become the main focus of the prophetic unit as a whole. It is difficult to assess precisely the timespan during which this process took place, but the linguistic profiles of the hymnic passages suggest that it reached fruition in the late Persian period – or at the latest, in the early Hellenistic period. In any case, it cannot be later than the third century BCE, at the end of which the long text of the prophecy is already witnessed by 4QJer^a.

(c) The complex relation between these identity components yielded a spiritual challenge with the destruction of the Second Temple and the emergence of Jewish, Judeo-Christian, and Christian faith-communities in Palestine and the Diaspora. Aramaic versions of Jeremiah reveal some of the different strategies developed in an attempt to cope with this challenge. 𝕿 reflects a process of crystallizing an exclusionist collective identity, defined in ethnic and cultural terms and resulting in deepening the social boundaries between Jews and gentiles. 𝕾 reflects an opposite process of dismantling the notion of ethnic exclusivity, emphasizing theological differentiation, presumably under the belief that identity complex can be resolved by opening one's heart to prophetic revelation.

The treatment of the Aramaic language of v. 11 therefore mirrors crucial cultural changes, which are reflective of diverse historical developments. Originally, this passage was quoted from an external source as an aid for a theological polemic, and its Aramaic language carried no special weight. Later on, however, the Aramaic language of this passage was perceived as a conspicuous marker of identity that no longer corresponds with the self-image of the "House of Israel" as a distinct ethnic group, characterized by Hebrew speech (even though at this time, speakers were probably already bilinguals). This self-image comprised a variety of components – linguistic, ethnic, religious, and political – which were in potential conflict with each other under various cultural and historical conditions. Such conflicts forced different communities to redefine for themselves the mutual relation between the components of their identities – redefinitions that ultimately established these communities' boundaries.

Chapter 4

From nature to history

(Jer 10:10)

וַיהוָה אֱלֹהִים אֱמֶת הוּא־אֱלֹהִים חַיִּים וּמֶלֶךְ עוֹלָם מִקִּצְפּוֹ תִּרְעַשׁ הָאָרֶץ וְלֹא־
יָכִלוּ גוֹיִם זַעְמוֹ:

> But the LORD is the true God; he is the living God and the everlasting
> King. At his wrath the earth quakes, and the nations cannot endure his
> indignation. (NRSV)

§1 Prolusion

Jer 10:10 is one of the two hymnic passages attested to only by the long text
represented by 𝔐 and 4QJerᵃ but missing from the shorter text represented by 𝔊
and 4QJerᵇ. The most basic problem this passage poses involves its relation to
the other hymnic passages contained in the prophetic unit of Jer 10:1–16; i.e.,
vv. 6–7 and 12–13. Does v. 10 have independent standing, or had it originally formed
a unity with any of the other hymnic passages? Some scholars expressed the
opinion that v. 10 joins vv. 6–7 (or that these passages at least belong to the same
literary stratum),[1] whereas others consider vv. 10 and 12–13 as belonging to the same
source.[2] According to both views, v. 10 never existed on its own, but has always been
an integral part of a longer hymn; it was broken into smaller pieces only at a secondary stage, though it remains unclear whether this separation took place while the
hymnic passage was interpolated into the prophetic unit, or whether it was inserted
as part of a larger hymnic text that was fragmented only at later redactional stages.

From a methodological perspective, the two views weigh differently in terms
of their relation to the textual evidence. The first view, which identifies a close
relationship between vv. 10 and 6–7, at least is allowed by the text-critical facts, as

---

1 See, e.g., Ammann 2015: 115. Others were content with noting the similarity between vv. 6–7
and 10, without committing to an essential link between them; e.g., Wambacq 1974: 59.
2 See, e.g., Driver 1906: 60 (note f), 354 (on v. 12); Brettler 1989: 187 n. 43. Compare Menaḥem of
Posquières *ad loc.* Cf. Duhm 1901: 101, who asserts that the passage is actually unnecessary ("Der
Vers ist in der That nicht durchaus notwendig") as it simply summarizes the content of vv. 12–13.

DOI 10.1515/9783110530162-005

both passages are absent from the short text and theoretically can be derived from a single literary source that could have been utilized by the longer text. Contrarily, the view that takes v. 10 to be linked to vv. 12–13 is difficult to sustain, because the short text lacks v. 10 but it does contain vv. 12–13. Therefore, one who argues that these two passages belong together must explain what could have caused the anomalous situation in which one section of the putative source is represented in the short text, while the other section surfaces only in the long one. The only practical solution for this problem is to posit the additional hypothesis that the short text is actually a shortened one; namely, that the long text represents an older textual constellation that was abbreviated or curtailed in a way such that only vv. 12–13 survived in it, while v. 10 was lost.[3] Such reasoning, however, is unnecessarily complicated, and the hypothetical construction seems too forced. The analysis of other segments of the prophetic unit in Jer 10:1–16 demonstrates that 𝕲 indeed emanates from an older stage of the compositional history of the prophecy, while 𝔐 reflects a considerably later stage, characterized by extensive reworking and redactional reshaping.[4] The second view can thus be rejected.

The first view, by contrast, requires more careful reflection. Since the text-critical evidence does not directly contradict it, it must be considered through internal analysis of the literary features of the material. Can vv. 6–7 and 10 be taken as two splinters of the same original literary unit? I posit that the discursive difference between the two passages is enough to rule out such a hypothesis: vv. 6–7 address God in the second person, thus allowing one to define this passage as a prayer, whereas v. 10 speaks about God in the third person, and its expressive mode is hymnic. The two passages thus represent distinct liturgical traditions, and it is difficult to view them as stemming from the same work. Moreover, vv. 6–7 form a complete and independent literary unit demarcated by its *inclusio* structure, with the repeating formula "for there is none like you" at the opening and closure of the prayer.[5] Consequently, there is no point at which v. 10 can connect to vv. 6–7; this fact weighs in strongly against the assumption that both passage had originally formed a literary unity.

It seems, therefore, that v. 10 links up to neither vv. 12–13 nor vv. 6–7, and it must be considered in and of its own. Hence, in what follows I analyze the form (§2) and content (§3) of the passage as a distinct textual segment. I follow this with an attempt to uncover its textual development and compositional history (§4).

---

3 See, e.g., Amara 2015: 143.
4 See above, especially Chapters 1 and 2.
5 For detailed analysis, see Chapter 5.

§2 Form

Both thematically and syntactically, v. 10 falls into two parts, with the breaking point being aptly identified by the cantillation tradition (placing there an *etnaḥtā*). The first part (v. 10a) describes God himself, whereas the second part (v. 10b) depicts the influence of his immense power over the entire universe. The two parts further break into two clauses each, similarly marked by the cantillation tradition (by a *zāqeph*), with every part exhibiting a particular, syntactic type of clauses: v. 10a contains two nominal clauses, whereas v. 10b encompasses two verbal clauses.

v. 10a:	ויהוה אלהים אמת	And the LORD is the true God;
	הוא אלהים חיים ומלך עולם	he is the living God and the everlasting King.
v. 10b:	מקצפו תרעש הארץ	At his wrath the earth quakes,
	ולא יכלו גוים זעמו	and the nations cannot endure his indignation.

This reading produces four clauses that differ from one another in terms of their length and content, so that the whole passage appears to be written in prose. This impression is further strengthened by the absence of patent word-pairs, the building blocks of parallelisms – a structural feature that comprises an essential trait of biblical poetry. For instance, v. 10a makes use of the term אמת, which normally pairs with חסד;[6] however, חסד does not appear at all in v. 10 (nor does the otherwise wide-spread word-pair אמת // חסד appear elsewhere in Jeremiah). In v. 10b, קצף seemingly pairs with זעם, but these two words never function as a word-pair in other synonymous parallelisms in biblical literature, although they may appear in a coordinated construction (Ps 102:11).[7]

A prosaic reading of v. 10 may thus appear to be possible and perhaps even self-evident. Nevertheless, such a construal would be somewhat misguided, since it relies on too sharp and simplistic a distinction between the categories of 'poetry' on the one hand and 'prose' on the other. These are not dichotomous opposites but rather the extreme points of a stylistic and linguistic continuum, along which ancient authors moved in accordance with the literary conventions of their time and place, in correspondence with the specific needs of individual works.[8] Liturgical texts, in particular, are often couched in expressive modes

---

6 Note that in the canonical order of this word-pair, חסד takes the position of the A-word; see, e.g., Isa 16:5; Mic 7:20; Ps 57:11 (the word-pair of חסד // אמת is also very common in coordinated constructions).

7 The normal word-pair in biblical poetic diction is קצף // חמה (Isa 34:2; Ps 38:2; cf. Esth 1:12). In Deuteronomistic phraseology, this pair is expanded into the triad of אף // קצף // חמה (Deut 29:27; Jer 21:5; 32:37; cf. Deut 9:19).

8 Cf. Kugel 1981.

that take an intermediate position between prose and poetry, which is sometimes termed "elevated prose" or the like.[9] Moreover, biblical literature in general and biblical poetry in particular contain the literary output of many generations; hence, it is unreasonable to expect that all poems contained in the Hebrew Bible would adhere to exactly the same set of formal, stylistic, and linguistic conventions. Fundamental changes of poetics must have taken place along the centuries, and biblical poems differ from one another, especially in terms of their use of traditional devices – such as the parallelism structure and the extent to which the phonological material is being submitted to prosodic organization.

Indeed, close inspection of the texture of the passage under scrutiny suggests that it does reflect a poetic dimension by consistently adhering to a particular prosodic scheme. The rhythmic regularity, however, requires a preliminary observation on the division of the passage into poetic lines or colons. Of the four clauses identified above, only one employs a coordinated construction on the constituent level: in the line הוא אלהים חיים ומלך עולם, two divine epithets fill the functional slot of the predicate. This detail suggests that although syntactically this is a single, well-formed clause, it actually comprises of distinct poetic lines and should accordingly be divided to two cola: הוא אלהים חיים / ומלך עולם. Proceeding from this observation, a conspicuous symmetry is revealed in the prosodic organization of the passage, whose cola normally scan as consisting of three stressed words per colon:

Colon	Text	Scansion
(1)	ויהוה אלהים אמת	– – –
(2)	הוא אלהים חיים	– – –
(3)	ומלך עולם	– –
(4)	מקצפו תרעש הארץ	– – –
(5)	ולא יכלו גוים זעמו	– – –

Alternatively, the prosodic structure of the passage can be described as comprising bicloa:

Colon	Text		Scansion
(1–2)	הוא אלהים חיים	ויהוה אלהים אמת	– – – / – – –
(3)		ומלך עולם	– –
(4–5)	ולא יכלו גוים זעמו	מקצפו תרעש הארץ	– – – / – – –

---

9 Cf. below, Chapter 5. This stylistic feature may well be related to the peculiar discursive situation of liturgical utterances, which operate simultaneously on two different levels of communication, each pushing towards its own expressive mode (cf. Mizrahi 2013).

Either way, the feature that stands out is the structural uniqueness of the words ומלך עולם, which comprise a self-standing line.

This analysis requires three clarifications, regarding both the general approach to biblical poetry underlying this kind of analysis and the specific niceties of its implementation. The first clarification pertains to the practical problem of identifying the rhythmic pattern of the colon ולא יכלו גוים זעמו, which consists of four words but scans as having only three stresses. The reason for this mismatch is not the formal observation that according to the cantillation tradition, the word ולא is joined by a *maqqeph* to the following יכלו. After all, in the colon הוא אלהים חיים the word הוא is similarly joined to the following word by a *maqqeph*, but it is nevertheless considered here as carrying an independent stress. In identifying which word is to be (or not to be) counted as a metrically countable stress, one must carefully weigh both syntactic and phonetic factors. Function-words such as particles, especially monosyllabic words (and even more so if they are open syllables, as in our case of the negative particle לא), tend to merge with the words that follow them into a single unit of intonation; i.e., they become proclitics.[10] This feature may apply even if such particles are supplemented by other particles (e.g., the conjunctive *waw*, as we have in the case of ולא), which render their syllabic structure more complex. A close reading of biblical poetry suggests that in such cases, the prosodic status of function-words may adapt to local metrical needs; that is, they may or may not be considered as an independent stress according to specific restrictions that condition the poetic license.

This observation leads to a more general clarification concerning my understanding of the nature of the prosody reflected in biblical poetry. Consensus tends to exist among contemporary scholars that exact metrical systems did not apply to Hebrew poetry until the Middle Ages, during which they developed under the influence of external traditions, especially the quantitative metrical schemes of classical Arabic poetry. Biblical poets surely made no use of precise metrical patterns of the kinds that one finds in Greek and Latin poetry; nevertheless, this fact should not be extended to mean that Hebrew poets had no ear for rhythm.

---

10 Theoretically, independent pronouns (such as the monosyllabic הוא) may also lose their stress and become a proclitic element. However, this possibility does not materialize in the colon הוא אלהים חיים because of a syntactic restriction. The pronoun הוא and the epithet אלהים חיים fulfil two different slots in the syntactic matrix of the clause, with the former functioning as the subject, whereas the latter is the predicate. Thus, an internal, structural pressure exists in favor of preserving their independent stresses. Note, in passing, that some commentators view הוא as belonging to the previous colon, thus punctuating the text (against the cantillation tradition) as ויהוה אלהים אמת הוא, "and the Lord God is truth" (e.g., Cloete 1989: 162–163; Lundbom 1999–2004: 1.590); however, I see no justification for doing so.

Numerous poetic sections in the Hebrew Bible reveal rhythmic regularity and careful, internal balance (often surprisingly systematic), which nowadays reveals itself especially in the number of stressed words per colon.[11] A universal tendency, observable in many languages and diverse poetic traditions, is to construct rhythmic structures on the basis of two or three fundamental units; this tendency is evident also in the prosody of biblical poetry.[12] A typical colon usually comprises of two or three stresses; if it expands to four or five stresses, the latter naturally tend to break into two subunits of two or three stresses each, with the breaking point functioning like a metrical caesura.

The grave theoretical question of whether this kind of regularized rhythm should be considered as a meter, in the strict sense of the term, depends on one's preferred definition for basic notions such as 'rhythm,' 'meter,' 'prosody,' etc. This kind of theorizing, however, is beyond the confines of the present discussion.[13] For our concern, suffice it to acknowledge that at least some poetic units in the Hebrew Bible exhibit patterns of regular (or nearly regular) use of structurers manipulating building blocks of two to three stresses (with a variety of variations on such structures). These patterns are employed for prosodic organization in some poems, and in this sense they serve a function that is, at the very least, comparable to a meter. At the same time, expecting to find this feature in every biblical poem is unrealistic, for the simple reason that biblical poetry, like biblical literature as a whole, is not a uniform body of texts but rather a highly heterogeneous mosaic made of works composed by many authors at different times and in distinct places. Attempting to enforce a single prosodic system over the entire realm

---

11 I should underscore that the rhythmic description of biblical poetry being based on the number of stressed words (or 'heavy accents') does not imply any argument concerning the historical essence of metrical systems in the poetic consciousness of ancient authors. The profound changes that had taken place in Hebrew phonology over the ages allow only a schematic reconstruction of the pronunciation of ancient Hebrew in different phases of its existence and render as speculative any attempt to hypothesize how exactly the sounds of the language were orchestrated within the framework of poetic texts. One can only point to the observable *traces* of a prosodic regularity, as manifest in some poetic works, in their received texts and traditionally given forms. The original principles of this regularity may no longer be recovered, but its trace is revealed in the more-or-less regular number of stressed words per colon, at least in some poetic texts contained in the Hebrew Bible.

12 Harshav 2014: 40–63, esp. 47.

13 Note, nevertheless, that informed exploration of this theoretical issue should also take into account findings from other quarters of ancient Hebrew poetry. Particular attention should be granted to the pre-classical and classical *piyyut*; namely, Hebrew liturgical poetry of Byzantine Palestine. While scholarship generally judged this poetry to reflect no prosodic regularity, some have suggested that it actually reflects a rhythmic system that compares with those observable in biblical poetry. See especially Fleischer 1977.

of biblical poetry is pointless; rather, the scholarly task should be the opposite – namely, to uncover the variety of systems and the wealth of rhythms created by different patterns of joining natural prosodic units, exploring how they come into expressive use in different poems, and trying to comprehend how these varied systems developed and to which poetic needs they responded.

This generalization leads to the final, exegetical clarification, which concerns the interpretation of the rhythmic divergence found in the poetic text under examination. For in Jer 10:10, the words וּמֶלֶךְ עוֹלָם form the only colon exhibiting a double stress, whereas all other cola reflect a triple stress. Syntactically as well, this colon is distinguished from the other cola by not constituting a well-formed clause but rather by being a noun phrase. Structurally, moreover, this colon occupies the central position within v. 10. It stands to reason, therefore, that all these features converge on the rhetorical level, as markers of the special place of this colon as the structural climax and the theological core of the entire passage. The breaking of the prosodic scheme simply serves as another mechanism marking its centrality.

If this conclusion is correct, Jer 10:10 presents a short poetic passage with a transparent structure. To be sure, it is doubtful whether this was originally an independent poem; the absence of opening or closing formula, as well as its beginning with a conjunctive *waw*, both suggest that this is only a fragment cited from a longer poem. However, the passage as it stands presents a complete rhetorical move that unfolds within a coherent internal structure, so one may consider it as a self-standing stanza whose main concern is expressed in the central colon that asserts God's position as a royal sovereign (מלך עולם). Previous cola lead to this assertion through the succession of other divine epithets (הוא אלהים חיים / ויהוה אלהים אמת), while the following cola draw concrete conclusions from God's rule of the world (מקצפו תרעש הארץ / ולא יכלו גוים זעמו). Thematically, the poetic passage is similar to hymns, as it focuses on praising God as a king. To be sure, the passage lacks the form-critical features of biblical hymns,[14]

---

14 The psalmic genre of the hymn begins with an introit, usually formulated as an imperatival clause, which summons the audience to praise God. Then follows the body of the hymn, which serves as a motive clause, explaining the reason for the praise and normally connecting to the preceding part with the subordinator כי. For instance, in Ps 117, v. 1 is the introit (שבחוהו כל האמים // הללו את יהוה כל גוים, "*Praise* the LORD, all you nations! *Extol* him, all you peoples!"), while v. 2a is the body (ואמת יהוה לעולם / כי גבר עלינו חסדו, "*For* great is his steadfast love toward us, and the faithfulness of the LORD endures forever."). In v. 2b, one finds a conclusion that echoes the introit (הללו יה, "Praise the Lord!"). For the hymnic genre and its formal features, see especially Gunkel and Begrich 1998: 22–65; Mowinckel 1962: 1.81–105; Koch 1969: 159–170; Crüsemann 1969 (cf. below, p. 172, n. 18). The native designation of this genre may be תְּהִלָּה "praise" (e.g., Isa 42:10; Ps 40:4; cf. Ps 34:2; 51:17; 100:4 etc.), employed in a generic sense in the superscription of Ps 145, as well as in a description of the musical establishment of the temple (Neh 12:46).

but this absence may be due to the passage's fragmentary nature. In other words, it may have been cut and pasted from a longer hymn, which did exhibit the missing features.[15]

§3 Content

The central place of the colon ומלך עולם has another dimension, which may hold the key for unlocking the thematic unfolding of the entire passage. The text as it stands raises an exegetical question: why and how does the passage move from listing static divine features (v. 10a) to a description of the active influence of God's power over the universe (v. 10b)? I submit that this move is based, first and foremost, on the semantic ambiguity of the word עולם that stands at the very heart of the poetic passage.

The first part of the passage asserts God's immanent qualities – YHWH is declared to be a true God (ויהוה אלהים אמת),[16] a living God (אלהים חיים),[17] and an eternal king (ומלך עולם)[18] – presupposing the classical use of the term עולם as a temporal designation of eternity.[19] By contrast, the second part of the passage demonstrates God's dominion on earth and exemplifies its affect over the nations, thus taking the word עולם in a spatial sense and interpreting the phrase מלך עולם as "king of the world."[20] If so, the colon ומלך עולם also comprises

---

15 This hypothesis may explain the verbal points of contact between v. 10 and the lexis and phraseology of biblical psalms, noted by Davidson 1973–74: 49–50.

16 For this interpretation of the phrase, see the discussion below.

17 In the given context of Jer 10:10, the epithet אלהים חיים implies a polemic with the inanimate idols of the nations, described as ולא רוח בם, "no spirit is in them" (v. 14). However, under the assumption that v. 10 had existed before being incorporated into its present context, one may wonder whether the original sense of אלהים חיים was not somehow linked to the previous epithet אלהים אמת, especially if the two are considered to form a parallelism. Some support for such an interpretation may come from the use of אלהים חיים in Jer 23, which deals with false prophets. This prophecy contrasts between the *falsehood* characteristic of such prophets (vv. 25–26) and the *truth* contained in God's words as delivered by a legitimate prophet (v. 28). The *truthful* words of such a prophet are also tellingly described as דברי אלהים חיים, "the words of the living God" (v. 36). Note, in passing, that in both Chapters 10 and 23, the phrase אלהים חיים occurs in passages missing from 𝔊 (Stipp 2016: 113). For a different view of the meaning of the epithet אלהים חיים, see Kreuzer 1983: 287–292.

18 Compare Ps 10:16, יהוה מֶלֶךְ עולם ועד, "The LORD is king forever and ever" (wherein the phrase עולם ועד is used adverbially).

19 Cf., e.g., Jenni 1952–53: I.240–242.

20 In this usage, the phrase continues into rabbinic liturgy, which makes extensive use of the divine epithet מלך העולם "king of the world."

the linguistic axis around which the passage unfolds, since the two possible senses of עולם explain the content of the two parts of the passage, as well as the connection between them.[21]

The semantic ambiguity of עולם is not a feature of classical Hebrew; rather, it emerges in the transition from classical to late Biblical Hebrew.[22] This feature thus allows one to establish that the poetic passage, in its present form, could not have been composed before the exilic period, at earliest. This conclusion gains further corroboration by textual analysis.

NB. The meaning of the first divine epithet, ויהוה אלהים אמת, requires clarification because it has been somewhat blurred by its syntax. According to the cantillation tradition, וַיהוָה אֱלֹהִים אֱמֶת, the words יהוה and אלהים join into a single name that functions as the subject, while אמת is the predicate. However, this construction results in a perplexing proposition. In biblical literature,

---

21 The *double entendre* of עולם obviously posed a challenge for ancient translators, who normally had to choose which of the two senses would be represented in their translation. Jerome followed the temporal sense of v. 10a, rendering מלך עולם as "eternal king" (*rex sempiternus*), and in his Latin commentary on Jeremiah he explained: *hereticorum umbrae ad tempus praeualent, sed longo tempore corrumpuntur* (ed. Reiter 1960: 104); namely, "the shadows of heretics prevail for a time, but in the long run they fail" (Graves and Hall 2011: 68). 𝕊, ܡܠܟ ܕܥܠܡܐ, "king of the worlds" probably preferred the spatial sense (cf. Nöldeke 1875: 303 n. 4). 𝕮 may be intentionally ambiguous. On the one hand, it renders the phrase as מלך עלמין, seemingly reflecting the temporal sense. On the other hand, in other occurrences of this formula it appears in the emphatic state as מלך עלמיא (Isa 6:5; 30:33; 33:17; Ezek 1:24; Zech 14:16–17); since Jer 10:10 is the only place where the Aramaic phrase is a precise rendition of a Hebrew *Vorlage* (whereas in the aforementioned passages it is a Targumic expansion), 𝕮 may be attempting to faithfully represent its *Vorlage*, without explicitly deciding between the two possible senses.
22 Friedman (2014: 1–116) recently discussed the date of this semantic change (summarizing earlier discussions, especially Jenni 1952–53). I find it difficult, however, to accept his conclusion that the semantic change took place only after the destruction of the Second Temple, in the first century CE, realizing most fully only in Mishnaic Hebrew. To maintain this late date, Friedman has to disqualify a long list of potential occurrences (noted by previous scholars) in late biblical and early post-biblical literature, including Sirach and the Dead Sea Scrolls. Such a sweeping rejection of a variety of passages is unwarranted, and it is pointless to deny the traces left by this semantic change in sources much earlier than the first century CE. The oldest passage testifying to its existence is embedded in a prophecy of Deutero-Isaiah (Isa 40:28), datable to the mid-sixth century BCE. This was perceptively noted by Amir (1997), based – among other things – on the conspicuous fact that the text refrains from the standard word-pair of עולם // דור (ו)דור, preferring instead an alternative parallelism reflecting a spatial interpretation of the term: // אלהי עולם יהוה בורא קצות הארץ. Brin (1997) opposed Amir's observation, arguing that the phrase מלך עולם is to be interpreted as a superlative expression ("the greatest king"), but did not discuss Amir's detailed argumentation.

one may assert that God is רב חסד ואמת, "abundant in goodness and truth" (Exod 34:6, KJV), or that he shows these qualities (2 Sam 2:6), or that his words are truthful (2 Sam 7:28), or the likes; but no other passage insists on defining the divinity itself as "truth."[23] Therefore, the syntax of the text is better interpreted differently: God's name (and the syntactic subject) is יהוה alone, whereas אלהים אמת is his epithet (and the predicate), as the text was indeed rendered by 𝕊 (ܘܡܪܝܐ ܐܠܗܐ ܘܫܪܝܪܐ) and 𝕍 (*Dominus autem deus verus*), both meaning "and the Lord is the God of truth." The syntagm אלהים אמת may alternate with the construct phrase אלהי אמת (2 Chr 15:3), and there is no need to consider the phrase as elliptical,[24] or as a construct phrase with an enclitic *-m*.[25] The two phrases display different syntactic constructions – an appositive in the case of אלהים אמת and a construct phrase in the case of אלהי אמת – but semantically they are both attributive syntagms, in which אמת qualifies אלהים. Compare their use, side by side, in Prov 22:21 (as translated by the KJV):

להודיעך קשט אמרי אמת	That I might make thee know the certainty of *the words of truth*;
להשיב אמרים אמת לשלחיך	that thou mightest answer *the words of truth* to them that send unto thee?

An alternative construal transpires from renditions such as "but Yahweh is God in truth,"[26] which take אמת as an adverbial expression.

§4 Textual development

Why was v. 10 interpolated into its present place, between the polemical depiction of the idols in vv. 8–9 on the one hand and the rhetorical address of v. 11 on the other? In my opinion, it is difficult to supply a satisfactory answer for this question based on the present form of v. 10. As it stands, v. 10 could have been integrated in other places within the prophetic unit just as easily. But the underlying motivation of placing v. 10 in its present immediate context can perhaps be recovered by way of text-critical hypothesis. I propose to consider the possibility that a slight but decisive change took place in one word of this passage.

---

23 Note Qimhi's laborious attempt to make sense of the passage in accordance with the cantillation tradition (ed. Cohen 2012: 70)

24 So Menaḥem of Posquières *ad loc.* (ed. Cohen 2012: 71).

25 So Dahood, cited by Holladay 1986–89: 1.333.

26 Driver 1906: 60. Cf. Giesebrecht 1907: 65; Holladay 1986–89: 1.333.

To be sure, this hypothesis relies primarily on other, independent considerations that pertain to the poetic and stylistic texture of v. 10. At the same time, the main methodological importance of this hypothesis is to be found in the justification it supplies for the given placement of the passage.

Although the passage is characterized by its internal coherence, one may detect in its second part a slight deviation from the norms of biblical poetic diction, in the disharmonious matching between the images of the two concluding cola: "At his wrath the earth quakes, and the nations cannot endure his indignation." Usually in biblical poetry, the image of an earthquake forms part of a parallelism; and since "earth" most commonly pairs with "heavens,"[27] the full parallelism expresses the idea that the entire creation shakes by the power of their divine sovereign. This combined image is particularly typical of theophany, for instance:

Judg 5:4	יהוה בצאתך משעיר	LORD, when you went out from Seir,
	בצעדך משדה אדום	when you marched from the region of Edom,
	ארץ רעשה	the *earth* trembled,
	גם שמים נטפו	and the *heavens* poured.
2 Sam 22:8[28]	ותגעש (ויתגעש) ותרעש הארץ	Then the *earth* reeled and rocked;
	מוסדות השמים ירגזו ויתגעשו	the foundations of the *heavens* trembled and quaked,
	כי חרה לו	because he was angry.
Isa 13:13	על כן שמים ארגיז	Therefore I will make the *heavens* tremble,
	ותרעש הארץ ממקומה	and the *earth* will be shaken out of its place.
Joel 2:10	לפניו רגזה הארץ	The *earth* quakes before them,
	רעשו שמים	the *heavens* tremble.

This state of affairs enables the hypothesis that Jer 10:10 was originally formulated in line with this standard trope of biblical poetry. If so, the passage

---

27 The word שמים may be replaced with its poetic synonym מרום (Isa 24:18; for the phrase אֲרֻבּוֹת ממרום cf. אֲרֻבֹּת הַשָּׁמַיִם in Gen 7:11; 8:2; 2 Kgs 7:2, 19). In addition, the full parallelism may be condensed into a coordinated expression, e.g., ורעשו שמים וארץ, "and the heavens and the earth shake" (Joel 4:16; cf. Hag 2:6, 21).

28 A variant reading of the relevant cola is witnessed by the parallel text of Ps 18:8, ותגעש ותרעש הארץ // ומוסדי הרים ירגזו, "then the earth reeled and rocked; the foundations also of the mountains trembled and quaked". For the word-pair of ארץ // הרים see Ps 104:32; cf. Ps 90:2; 95:4; 104:13 etc.

dealt with God's majestic power as revealed in nature, without any recourse to human or ethnic agents such as the nations:[29]

| מקצפו תרעש הארץ | At his wrath the *earth* shall tremble, |
| ולא יכלו *שמים* זעמו | and the *heavens* shall not contain his indignation. |

This reconstruction of an earlier form of the text remains purely hypothetical, as no recorded variant reading supports it, at least for the time being.[30] Nonetheless, an indirect piece of evidence corroborating it may be deduced from its ability to explain why v. 10 was interpolated in its present place, before v. 11.

As argued above, the secondary insertion of the Aramaic v. 11 into the polemical prophecy may be regarded as the watershed in the compositional history of the prophetic unit.[31] Integrating this segment not only recalibrated the ideological agenda of the text, but also rendered the word-pair of "heavens and earth" into a crucial factor in the subsequent development of the prophecy. This word-pair is completely absent from the original, polemical prophecy (vv. 2–5, 8–9, 14–15), but it plays a pivotal role in the literary structure, stylistic texture, and theological argument of v. 11:

| אלהיא די שמיא וארקא לא עבדו | The gods who did not make *the heavens and the earth* – |
| יאבדו מארעא ומן תחות שמיא אלה | they shall perish *from the earth and from under the heavens.* |

---

29 For the resulting image of inability to contain (יָכִלוּ) God's wrath, compare Jer 6:11, ואת חמת יהוה מלאתי נלאיתי הכיל, "But I am full of the wrath of the LORD; I am weary of holding it in"; cf. Joel 2:10–11, לפניו רגזה ארץ רעשו שמים... כי גדול יום יהוה ונורא מאד ומי יכילנו, "The earth quakes before them, the heavens tremble... Truly the day of the LORD is great; terrible indeed – who can endure it?". The lexical identification of the verb יָכִלוּ as derived from כו"ל "to contain" might seemingly be doubted on the basis of 𝕿, which renders ולא יכלון עממיא לסוברא רגזיה, as if reading ולא יָכְלוּ גוים זעמו <לשאת>, taking the verb as derived from יכ"ל "to be able" (cf. NRSV, "and the nations shall not *be able to abide* his indignation"; see further 𝕿 Gen 36:7; Num 11:14; Deut 1:9; 1 Kgs 8:27). But 𝕿 treats similarly the other occurrences of הכיל (Jer 6:11; Joel 2:11; Am 7:10), so no variant reading needs to be assumed in this case (cf. above, p. 136, n. 69).

30 Unfortunately, this part of the verse did not survive in 4QJer^a, so that it is impossible to ascertain its reading at this point. Still, it is significant to note that v. 10 indeed is witnessed by this scroll, thus testifying to the fact that the long text of Jer 10:1–16 was already extent by the mid-Hellenistic period. See 4Q70, frg. 11 [=col. V, pt. 1], line 2: ו]מֹלֵדָ עולם מקצ[פו (Tov 1997: 158).

31 See above, Chapter 3. As explained there in greater detail, the interpolation of v. 11 represents a crucial stage in the process of supplementing the polemical prophecy with additional literary material. The relatively early date of its addition is confirmed by the fact that v. 11 is already witnessed by the short text of 𝕲 and 4QJer^b. By itself, v. 11 can be dated linguistically to the mid-fifth century BCE.

Once v. 11 has been absorbed into the prophetic unit, the marked appearance of the "heavens and earth" was bound to puzzle ancient readers: how is it possible that this conspicuous element plays such a prominent role in v. 11, although it has not even been hinted at anywhere prior to this point? Moreover, the very picture portrayed by v. 11 is also perplexing: how exactly shall the foreign gods perish? This action is denoted by an intransitive verb (יאבדו), which does not clarify by what way they will meet their destiny. Most crucially, it remains unclear whether YHWH, the God of Israel, plays any role in the process of their destruction. In fact, YHWH is not mentioned at all in v. 11, and the passage nowhere explicates the relation between him and "the gods who did not make the heavens and the earth." Contextually, the implication is that YHWH contrasts with such gods by being the creator of the heavens and earth; but this argument is never made explicitly in the text itself.

The aforementioned hypothesis concerning the textual change that presumably took place in v. 10 allows one to see that the incorporation of v. 10 before v. 11 responds to all these exegetical difficulties by anticipating the appearance of the "heavens and earth" in v. 11. As indicated above (§3), the very poetic structure of v. 10 serves to move from the presentation of God's immanent qualities (v. 10a) to the depiction of his power as manifested in both the earth and the heavens (v. 10b). The picture of nature trembling due to God's potency in v. 10 thus paves the way for the seemingly spontaneous self-destruction of the gods in v. 11. In other words, the insertion of v. 10 (in its hypothetical, original reading) reframes v. 11, supplying ready answers for the potential queries motivated by the latter.[32]

Seen in this light, v. 10 echoes the function of another hymnic passage incorporated within the prophetic unit; namely, vv. 12–13, which now follow v. 11. This passage too accords a prominent role for the heavens and the earth: God is described as the one who "makes the *earth* by his power... and by his understanding he stretched out the *heavens*" (v. 12), and "when he utters his voice, there is a tumult of waters in the *heavens*, and he makes the mist rise from the ends of the *earth*" (v. 13). Since vv. 12–13 are already witnessed by 𝕲 and 4QJer[b], they must have been supplemented earlier than v. 10 (which is not represented by either 𝕲 or 4QJer[b]).[33] In the resulting formation of the text, as witnessed by

---

[32] Obviously, this is not the original function of v. 10, as the passage might well have existed independently, before being interpolated into Jer 10:1–16 – either as a self-standing prayer or as part of a hymn or another liturgical work. The proposal made above concerning the relation between vv. 10–11 pertains only to the secondary employment of v. 10 in its present context.

[33] As indicated above (Chapter 2), vv. 12–13 also differ from v. 10 in their linguistic profile. While v. 10 was probably composed in the exilic period, as the semantics of עולם suggests, vv. 12–13 fit the language of the late monarchic period (though their insertion into their present context may have taken place at a slightly later stage).

𝔐, v. 11 – which speaks against the idols – is framed by two hymnic praises that glorify YHWH by employing the very same trope used for rejecting the idols. In other words, all three supplementations (vv. 10, 11, 12–13) are unified by their effective use of the word-pair of "heavens and earth," which is utilized simultaneously for exposing the inherent weakness of the gods of the nations, on the one hand, and for glorifying the immanent power of YHWH, the God of Israel, on the other.[34]

This reconstruction of the compositional history of v. 10 depends on the assumption that it originally read ולא יכלו *שמים* זעמו, "and the *heavens* shall not contain his indignation," as the word "heavens" pairs with "earth" in the previous colon. However, the reading recorded in 𝔐 is ולא יכלו גוים זעמו, "and the *nations* shall not endure his indignation." Since the hypothetical reading "heavens" is necessary for explaining the very insertion of v. 10 into its place, it seems that the change from "heavens" to "nations" took place at a relatively late stage of the textual transmission of the passage, only after it was fully incorporated into the prophetic unit. Indeed, the textual change may well be explained as resulting from harmonization to another segment of this prophecy; namely, the formulation of another hymnic passage, vv. 6–7, which highlights the divine epithet מלך הגוים. The latter passage is also absent from the shorter text of 𝔊 and 4QJer[b]. Furthermore, its linguistic profile appears to be the latest of all the literary strands and textual segments contained in Jer 10:1–16, pointing to the late Persian period.[35] If this dating holds true, the change of "heavens" to "nations" reflects one of the latest (if not the latest) modifications made to the text of Jer 10:1–16.

It should be underscored that this text-critical hypothesis is purely conjectural, as it has no direct support in the textual evidence. However, it may gain some indirect support from the fact that a comparable change of lexemes is attested in a famous passage of the Song of Moses; namely, Deut 32:43. In that case, the textual modification does not seem to be the result of a scribal lapse but

---

34 The crucial function of the word-pair "heavens and earth" in all three passages does not appear to be incidental; by itself, it may betray the chronological background of the compositional stages during which these texts were gradually absorbed into the prophetic unit. As mentioned above (Chapter 3, §3.5), a divine epithet typical of the Persian period is אלהי השמים, "God of the heavens" (Jon 1:9; Ezra 1:2 ‖ 2 Chr 36:23; Neh 1:4–5; 2:4, 20; cf. Gen 24:7), modelled after the standard Aramaic phrase אלה שמיא (Ezra 5:12; 6:9–10; 7:12, 21, 23; Dan 2:18–19, 37, 44), which was perceived as an abbreviation of the longer epithet אלה שמיא וארעא, "God of the heavens and the earth" (Ezra 5:11; cf. Gen 24:3). Arguably, the place this divine epithet held in the religious terminology of contemporary scribes seemed to motivate not only the insertion of v. 11 but also its reframing by hymnic passages that make prominent use of the keywords comprising this expression.
35 See below, Chapter 5.

rather of a theologically motivated correction, meant to exclude a polytheistic outlook inherent in the original wording of the text. In this case, though, the alternative readings are well-documented in the textual evidence: 4QDeut[q] reads הרנינו שמים עמו, “Rejoice, O heavens, with him” (a reading supported by 𝔊: εὐφράνθητε, οὐρανοί, ἅμα αὐτῷ),[36] whereas 𝔐 reads הרנינו גוים עַמו, “Rejoice, O *nations*, his people.” In the attested original text of this passage, the word “heavens” denotes divine beings summoned by the speaker to praise YHWH, thus acknowledging his dominion over them; in the amended text, in contrast, the nations are summoned, and their praise is no longer directed towards God but rather at his chosen people, Israel, thus purging the passage from any non-monotheistic implication. By contrast, in the hypothetical original reading of Jer 10:10, the “heavens” are mentioned as a cosmographic designation, paralleling “earth.”[37] Still, its change to “nations” similarly diverts the focus of God’s sovereignty from the realm of nature to the historical space of international politics. From this point on, the focus is no longer on God’s dominion over the natural elements but rather on his universal rule over the human nations.[38]

This theological argument is no stranger to biblical prophetic literature; indeed, it takes roots in the prophetic coping with the spiritual challenge posed by the troubling rise of the Neo-Assyrian empire, as manifested in Isaianic prophecies from the eighth century BCE. However, this common motif is given a special form in Jer 10:10. The specific argument made in the passage under discussion here is not a generalized assertion of God’s control over the foreign nations, but rather a concrete expectation for their surrender as part of a renewed

---

36 See 4Q44, frg. 5ii [=col. II] line 6 (Skehan and Ulrich 1995: 141). The various versions also differ in other cola of Deut 32:43, but these differences do not pertain to the present discussion. For the text-critical evidence and the theological trends that transpire from it, see especially Rofé 2000; cf. Goldstein 2005a: 114–124; 2010–11: esp. 11–12.

37 According to the literal sense of the passage; however, it is conceivable that in Jer 10:10, too, the term for “heavens” was interpreted by an ancient scribe as a divine epithet of heavenly beings (cf. Ps 89:6; Job 15:15; note further Jer 14:22, according to Rofé 2012: 41–42, following Cassuto 1971: 122). Note that v. 10 comes after v. 9, which depicts the idols. Read against this background, v. 10 might have been taken as referring to the cult images of the gods of heavens and earth, so that a prudent scribe felt the need to divert its reference to the nations rather than to such divinities. In such a case, there is a full analogy between Jer 10:10 and Deut 32:43.

38 Note also the stylistic result of the textual change: the leading word-pair changed from ארץ // שמים to ארץ // גוים (cf. Isa 14:26; Jer 51:27; Ezek 12:15; Ps 46:11, etc.). A parallel for 𝔐 may be adduced from Jer 50:46, מקול נתפשה בבל נרעשה ארץ וזעקה בגוים נשמע, “at the sound of the capture of Babylon the earth shall tremble, and her cry shall be heard among the nations” – a passage in which the image of an earthquake is similarly matched to the idea that the nations cannot endure the agony involved in the demonstration of God’s power.

world order, to be imposed by God over the cosmic and political reality. The amended reading of the passage thus expresses a view that can be paraphrased with the help of another passage: אבדו גוים מארצו / ועד עולם מלך יהוה, "The LORD is king forever and ever; the nations shall perish from his land" (Ps 10:16). Put differently, the acknowledgment of God's universal kingship is invoked in order to motivate confidence in God's capability to smash the rule of the nations, who currently subjugate the land chosen by God as his special property. Such a perception corresponds well with the exilic or Restoration period – a chronological context that is suggested independently for v. 10 on the basis of linguistic and literary-historical grounds.

§5 Conclusion

The hymnic passage of Jer 10:10 is contained in the long text of Jeremiah, witnessed by 𝔐 and 4QJer[a], but missing from the shorter text, witnessed by 𝔊 and 4QJer[b]. The text-critical evidence thus suggests that this passage was added at a relatively late stage of the formation of the prophetic unit. A close reading of the passage reveals its poetic artistry and enables an appreciation of how and what it draws from the traditional stock of biblical poetic diction and how it reshapes the inherited material within a simple yet effective prosodic pattern.

The textual development of the passage may be partially recovered by way of hypothesis. Although not supported by concrete text-critical evidence, this reconstruction is indirectly backed by its ability to untie several cruxes inherent in the passage in its recorded form. In its hypothetical, original reading, v. 10 forms part of a sequence of supplementary passages (alongside v. 11 and vv. 12–13) that rhetorically and ideologically revolve around the key word-pair of "heavens and earth." The textual and literary development of the passage comprises an aspect of the ideological reworking of the prophetic unit as a whole, following a trajectory that shifts the emphasis from the theological polemic against idolatry to the construction of a group identity in ethno-political terms. In its language, style, and ideological horizon, v. 10 reflects the cultural milieu of the Hebrew literature produced in the Persian period, and it testifies regarding the religious poetry composed during this era.

It stands to reason that the passage originates in psalmic or hymnic literature, and it was incorporated into its present place as part of its gradual, literary growth, and in order to solve exegetical problems motivated by v. 11. If so, analysis of v. 10 sheds light on the multifaceted development of the prophetic unit of Jer 10:1–16, demonstrating the complexity of the processes of formation, transmission, and reception it underwent.

Chapter 5

An orison of incomparability

(Jer 10:6–7)

מֵאֵין כָּמוֹךָ יְהוָה גָּדוֹל אַתָּה וְגָדוֹל שִׁמְךָ בִּגְבוּרָה: 7 מִי לֹא יִרָאֲךָ מֶלֶךְ הַגּוֹיִם 6
כִּי לְךָ יָאָתָה כִּי בְכָל־חַכְמֵי הַגּוֹיִם וּבְכָל־מַלְכוּתָם מֵאֵין כָּמוֹךָ:

> [6] There is none like you, O LORD; you are great, and your name is great in might.[7] Who would not fear you, O King of the nations? For that is your due; among all the wise ones of the nations and in all their kingdoms there is no one like you (NRSV).

§1 Prolusion

Of the three hymnic passages now embedded in the prophetic unit of Jer 10: 1–16, two passages, vv. 6–7 and v. 10, are missing from the short text represented by 𝔊 and 4QJer[b] and recorded only in the long text of 𝔐, as well as the other ancient versions of Jeremiah, which rely on proto-Masoretic *Vorlagen*. This fact strongly suggests that these two passages were added relatively late in the compositional history of the prophetic unit, but it does not imply any positive indication concerning the date, provenance and literary nature of the additions themselves; such information can only be deduced from internal analysis of each passage in and of itself.

The discursive situation of vv. 6–7 is that of a direct address to God in the second person singular, which allows one to define it as a prayer.[1] The present chapter argues that this passage comprises a coherent, self-contained liturgical unit, whose main concern is asserting God's incomparability and universal sovereignty. While couched in traditional modes of expression, in its present form

---

1 In this respect, vv. 6–7 differ markedly from their immediate context, since both v. 5b and v. 8 do not directly address God or even refer to him. Rather, they depict the idols and highlight their nature as inanimate (v. 5b) and perishable (v. 8). Moreover, v. 5b has a different addressee, namely, the human audience of the prophet, referred to in the second person plural.

DOI 10.1515/9783110530162-006

the prayer reflects a late, monotheistic appropriation of an older, monolatrous conceptualization of the divinity.[2] The late date of the prayer is also reflected in its language; as short and stereotypical as it may be, the prayer contains a few markers of post-classical Hebrew, which suggest a date of composition – or at least of formulation – in the Persian period. As such, vv. 6–7 seem to be the latest addition to the conglomerate of Jer 10:1–16. The following discussion thus seeks to explore vv. 6–7 in terms of their literary coherence as an independent piece (§2), to examine its theological outlook by comparison to similar passages (§3), to trace the process by which the prayer grew out of a broader liturgical tradition (§4), and to determine the motivation for its integration into its present context and its literary function within the prophetic unit (§5).

§2 Form and content

Vv. 6–7 constitute a complete literary unit with respect to both form and content. Its formal integrity and internal coherence are marked by the employment of several literary devices. The first and perhaps most conspicuous such technique is the use of an *inclusio* or envelope structure:[3] the same formula, מאין כמוך,

---

2 Arguably, the distinction between "monolatry" and "monotheism" are too simplistic and even artificial. I employ these terms (as well as the term "theology") in a somewhat loose sense, because my concern here is not so much in the abstract theory of divinity but rather in the literary dynamics that produced concrete texts. It goes without saying that biblical literature contains no systematic exposition of any abstract theological doctrine, and biblical authors were more inclined to express themselves in mythopoetic symbols than in methodical treatises. Modern definitions of biblical approaches to the nature of the divinity, including the notion of God's singularity or oneness, are theoretical approximations that are (by definition) remote from the ancients' way of thinking. Such conceptualizations, however, cannot be avoided when conducting typological and comparative research, and they are useful as long as one bears in mind that they are secondary abstractions made from the primary sources. In a sense, "monotheism" is perhaps better accounted for as a rhetorical mode than a religious system. See Smith 2001: esp. 10–14, 149–178.

3 See, e.g., Lundbom 1997: 60–61. Similarly, Hoffman 2001: 1.297 has rightly presented vv. 6–7 as a distinct unit, and he also defined it with the term "psalm." For the use of envelope structure for delimiting poetic units, compare Ps 8, which opens and closes with the praise יהוה אדנינו מה אדיר שמך בכל הארץ, "O Yahweh, our Sovereign, how majestic is your name in all the earth!" (vv. 2a, 10; cf. Segal 1935: 126–127); Ps 103, which employs the self-imperatival clause ברכי נפשי את יהוה, "Bless the Lord, O my soul" for the opening (vv. 1–2) and closure (v. 22b) of the psalm. For the rhetorical technique, see Watson 2001: 282–287.

"for there is none like you," for both opening and closing the prayer, thus delimiting it as a discursive unit.[4] Another device pertains to symmetrical organization of the strophic constituents. The text enclosed between the recurring
formula of incomparability falls into two couplets, each of which opens with
the same word:

- v. 6: גדול אתה / וגדול שמך בגבורה, "*Great* you are, and *great* is your name"
- v. 7: כי לך יאתה / כי בכל חכמי הגוים, "*For* [...] befits you.[5] *For* among all the wise
  ones of the nations" etc.[6]

Between these two couplets, stands a rhetorical question, the only clause
in the passage formulated as an interrogative: מי לא יראך מלך הגוים, "Who would
not fear you, O king of the nations?" Finally, the middle strophe, namely,
the rhetorical question, occupies the strategic, focal point; it is the structural
center of the complete unit – a position that marks the importance of this
particular clause and its function as the core theological message of the
prayer. The unity of the passage is therefore marked by the employment of
a single phrase as a literary frame, within which one finds a description
of divine features. It reiterates God's inherent greatness (v. 6) and kingship
(v. 7), thus leading the audience to acknowledge God's status as the world
sovereign.

The linguistic and stylistic texture of the passage is not easy to define.
On the one hand, it cannot be automatically considered as a piece of
poetry, since it contains not even a single case of semantic-syntactic
parallelism, nor does it exhibit any kind of prosodic regularity. On the other
hand, the passage cannot be considered as 'pure' prose either, since one

---

4 According to the Greek version of Theodotion, the recurring phrase is slightly expanded, as it
includes the divine name in the vocative: πόθεν ὥσπερ σὺ κύριε (Field 1871–75: 2.597–598). This
is probably a secondary expansion, which presupposes that the Tetragrammaton is a direct continuation of the framing call מאין כמוך יהוה, i.e., "there is none like you, O LORD." Syntactically,
however, the Tetragrammaton is perhaps better taken as a different constituent, which connects
with the following clause (see below, n. 7). Interestingly, Theodotion presupposes a syntactic
parsing that is essentially the same as the one encoded by the Masoretic cantillation tradition,
which places the main disjunctive accent in v. 6 under the Tetragrammaton (cf. below, n. 7).
5 See the text-critical discussion below.
6 Syntactically, the words כי בכל חכמי הגוים ובכל מלכותם cannot stand by their own; it is only when
joining the concluding phrase that they constitute a full clause: "For among all the wise ones of
the nations and in all their kingdoms there is no one like you." From the point of view of poetic
structure, however, it is better to consider these two stretches of text as distinct lines. Cf. Cloete
1989: 122, 162.

can detect in it a well-calculated rhythm, which leads the reader through gradually expanding lines. It begins with the single-word address to God (יהוה, "O Yahweh").[7] Then follow two nominal clauses, the first of which contains two words (גדול אתה, "You are great") and the second having three words (וגדול שמך בגבורה, "And your name is great in might").[8] Then the rhetorical questions is posed (מי לא יראך מלך הגוים, "Who would not fear you, O king of the nations?"), and it is followed by a confirmation of the initial declaration, which leads directly to the concluding formula (כי בכל חכמי הגוים ובכל מלכותם מאין כמוך, "for among all the sages of the nations and in all their kingship, there is none like you"). Each clause is longer than the preceding one, until concluding with the short phrase מאין כמוך, "for there is none like you," which harks back to the very opening, thus marking the full closure of the entire unit:

NB. One textual detail in v. 7 requires a more detailed discussion. 𝔐 poses a syntactical problem, since it contains no word that can function as the

---

7 The Tetragrammaton in the vocative is syntactically an independent utterance (cf. above, n. 4). The Masoretic cantillation tradition pulls it backwards: מאין כמוך יהוה, "There is none like you, O Yahweh." In this clause, the Tetragrammaton is an appositive of the 2m.sg pronominal suffix. However, it is much more compelling to consider the vocative as part of the praise that follow ("O Yahweh, you are great" etc.). If so, the Tetragrammaton is in the *casus pendens*, while the independent 2m.sg pronoun אתה refers back to it. Compare the similar structure of another direct address to God, contained in Ezra's prayer: יהוה אלהי ישראל צדיק אתה, "O Yahweh, the God of Israel, you are just" (Ezra 9:15).

8 The greatness motif was apparently placed immediately after the framing formula מאין כמוך since the pragmatic use of the latter in ancient Hebrew was expressing wonder when witnessing a person or an object of exceptional size. For instance, after telling that Saul was taller than everyone else (ויגבה מכל העם משכמו ומעלה, "he was head and shoulders taller than any of them"), Samuel introduces him to the people by saying: כי אין כמהו בכל העם, "*There is no one like him* among all the people" (1 Sam 10:23–24).

subject agreeing in gender with the verb יאתה (3f.sg).[9] The missing, feminine subject is supplied by the two Aramaic versions, namely, 𝕮 and 𝕾, which read here the word מלכותא "kingship." The two versions are not interdependent, as they differ in their exact formulation; most conspicuously, 𝕾 renders the verb יאתה with the cognate Aramaic verb (ܠܟ ܗܘ ܐܪܐ ܦܐܝܐ, "Majesty *befits* you"),[10] whereas 𝕮 replaces the verb with an independent pronoun (דילך היא מלכותא, "For kingship *is* yours").[11] It seems, therefore, that the two Aramaic versions testify to a Hebrew *Vorlage* that contained the word המלוכה (cf. Obad 21; Ps 22:29). It was lost in 𝕸, but its traces are still detectable in the grammatical form of the verb that had once agreed with it.[12]

Support for this reconstruction of the original text of v. 7 – as well as for the very assumption that the relatively late, Aramaic versions can preserve

---

9 A similarly defect text apparently underlies 𝕺: *tuum est enim decus*. The noun *decus* ("ornament, grace, embellishment, splendor, glory, honor, dignity," akin to Greek δόξα) clearly stands for the verb יאתה (and recurs in v. 25 for rendering נֶוֶה), thus attempting to obviate the syntactic difficulty caused by a verb not agreeing with any subject. But this solution did only little to explain the sense of the passage. In his commentary on Jeremiah, Jerome was therefore pressed to supply a somewhat forced explanation, according to which the embellishment referred to is the truth, whereas falsehood – that characterizes idolatry – is represented by ugliness: "*Tuum est, inquit, decus*; in ueritate decor, in mendacio turpitude" (Reiter 1960: 104), that is, "'Yours,' he says, 'is beauty' – beauty is found in truth, ugliness in falsehood" (Graves and Hall 2011: 67).

10 According to Greenberg 2002: 37, 𝕾 at this point reflects a logical supplementation on the part of the translator, based on the immediate context. However, this explanation does not take into account the fact that the same reading is reflected in 𝕮, which also employs the term מלכותא, even though the two versions are not interdependent. Interestingly, the original text was similarly restored by Tur-Sinai 1967: 183. But he reached it by way of quite a complicated conjecture – transferring מלכותם from v. 7 to v. 6, and omitting ובכל מלכותם entirely from v. 7 – and without mentioning the Aramaic versions at all.

11 The English translation of 𝕾 is that of Greenberg et al. 2013: 65; the translation of 𝕮 is that of Hayward 1987: 79.

12 The absence of a subject disturbed other interpreters and translators of 𝕸 (or the proto-Masoretic tradition from which 𝕸 stems), and they attempted to solve this difficulty in a variety of ways. One of the earliest attempts to do so is recorded in Hexaplaric manuscripts of 𝕲-Jer, which come closer to the proto-Masoretic tradition by containing a translation of vv. 6–8 and v. 10 (missing from 𝕲). According to these manuscripts, the curtailed clause לך יאתה was rendered as if reading לך נאה להשתחוות. To be sure, there is much textual variety regarding the Greek verb representing נאה, but the various readings seem to go back to a form of the verb πρέπω (originating, in Jer 10:7, from either Aquila or Symmachus), which renders נאוה in Ps 33(32):1; 93(92):5, as suggested by Rabin, Talmon and Tov 1997: נז, n. 1 *ad loc.*

it – comes from allusions to our passage that are embedded in early *piyyut*, that is, Hebrew liturgical poetry that was composed in Palestine during the Byzantine period. So, for instance, in the opening of a poem that formed part from the service of the New Year by Yosé ben Yosé:[13]

אהללה אלהי / אשירה עוזו / אספרה כבודו / אאפדנו מלוכה
אשגב לפועל / אשר שָׂח ופעל / אאנויהו כי לו / **יאתה המלוכה**

I will praise my God, I will sing his might, I will tell his glory, I will adorn him with kingship.
I will magnify the Creator, who spoke and created; I will extol his beauty, *for kingship befits him.*

And similarly in a poem by Yannai, which reworks poetically a weekly lection from Genesis (Qedushta for Gen 14:1):[14]

כי לך יי הגדולה / ולך היא הגבורה / ולך נאה ממשלה / **ולך יאתה המלוכה**

For to You, O LORD, belongs greatness; and to You, O LORD, belongs might; and to You, the splendor of rule; *and to you, kingship is fitting.*

In the light of both the Aramaic versions and the Hebrew *testimonia*, it seems plausible to hypothesize that a proto-Masoretic text reading כי לך יאתה המלוכה was still available during the first centuries CE.[15] The omission of המלוכה is a textual corruption that took place relatively late in this particular textual tradition (and the Greek and Latin versions that depend on it).

In any case, and regardless of the question whether this particular reconstruction is accepted or rejected, one can easily unpack the rhetorical technique employed in the prayer, which enriches its verbal texture while lucidly communicating its

---

13 Mirsky 1991: 93.
14 Rabinovitz 1985–87: 1.133. For the English translation see Lieber 2010: 420–421.
15 Another indirect witness to such a text of v. 7 is seemingly found in rabbinic literature, in Midrash Psalms on Ps 93:1, which explicates the words כי לך יאתה by the paraphrase לך מלכותא יאתה (in the edition of Buber 1890: 413 one finds the seemingly plural form מלכוותא, but it may be nothing but a typo; in the database of the Historical Dictionary of the Academy of Hebrew Language one finds the expected reading מלכותא). However, I doubt whether anything can be deduced from this quotation. The Aramaic form of the word מלכותא indicated that this is not a reflection of a Hebrew reading but rather an exegetical paraphrase that conflates the Hebrew verse according to 𝔐 with its Aramaic rendering as found in 𝔗.

central themes. It reiterates divine epithets by verbatim repetition of keywords: the word גדול "great" in v. 6, and the words גוים "nations" and derivatives of מלך "king(ship)" in v. 7.[16] This is a discursive strategy (known in discourse analysis as "lexical repetition") that contributes to the internal coherence of the text. At the same time, it also serves as a means for marking subdivision of its contents into two parts, each of which has its own distinct theme: God's greatness in v. 6, and his kingship in v. 7.[17] The careful structuring of the prayer is thus based on an echo pattern, that is, repetition through slight variation, which deepens sounds that had previously been uttered. The structural sophistication of the passage on the one hand, and the lack of obvious poetic features on the other, allow one to locate its style in the grey zone between poetry and prose, which typifies Hebrew liturgical texts throughout the ages.

Thematically, the prayer ties together three motifs of praise: the speaker frames his address by a declaration of God's *incomparability*, and within the address itself he highlights God's *greatness* and this *royal status*. The stylistic device that marks the ideological importance of these motifs is verbal repetition, as each one of them is twice told. At the same time, the speaker gradually expands his praise while also slightly varying its formulation. Noteworthy is the fact that the speaker is content with exaltation alone. The praise is presented in its own right, and there is nothing in the passage to suggest that it has a function beyond it; in any case, it does not introduce a petition or serve as an explanation

---

16 The repetition in v. 7 is even more verbatim according to the Greek version of Theodotion, which reads "and in all their *kings*" (καὶ ἐν πᾶσι τοῖς βασιλεῦσιν αὐτῶν) rather than 𝔐's "and in all their *kingship*" (see Field 1871–75: 2.597–598). This reading was adopted by several critical commentators, such as Duhm 1901: 100 (although he presents it as a conjectural reading, without referring to its source).

17 Identification of this rhetorical technique suggests that no special importance should be attributed to the mentioning of חכמי הגוים, "the wise ones of the nations." Since the motif of wisdom is neither repeated in the prayer, nor occupies a structurally central position, I doubt if it can bear the burden of theological importance attributed to it by Ammann 2015: 131–133. In my opinion, the juxtaposition of wisdom and kingship in this passage is meant to convey the general notion of all human power of whatever sort. In other words, the notion of wisdom is subordinate, in this passage, to the theme of kingship. Indeed, the coupling of wisdom (i.e., intellectual power) and hegemony (i.e., political power) appears to be a rhetorical *topos* that played a role in royal propaganda; see, e.g., 1 Kgs 3:28 (Solomon); Isa 10:13 (the Assyrian emperor); Eccl 7:19 (ironically twisting the same *topos*). Cf. the sapiential proverb quoted in Jer 9:22, in which richness (i.e., economic power) is also mentioned. Cf. below, n. 73.

for a complaint of any sort. If so, the passage is essentially close to the hymnic mode, even though it does not fully comply with the formal characteristics of the *Gattung* of the hymn.[18]

The combination of all these literary features suggests that the passage under consideration is a liturgical piece, even if it is not exactly a psalm in the strict sense of the term. It may be defined as a prayer of praise, for which I suggest the term *orison*.[19] Corroboration for this definition comes from the fact that other biblical passages that parallel Jer 10:6–7 in their formulation and content are also embedded in prayers, or prayer-like utterances, and liturgical contexts: (1) the passage in 2 Sam 7:22 is part of David's prayer, which is presented as the king's reaction to Nathan's prophecy; (2) 1 Kgs 8:23–27 is part of Solomon's prayer on the occasion of the inauguration of the Jerusalem temple; (3) Ps 86:8–10 is part of a psalm of the type of individual lament. The clearest characteristic shared by all these passages, as well as Jer 10:6–7, is the employment of the formula אין כמוך, "there is none like you," which expresses the theological argument that God is incomparable.[20] From a phenomenological point of view, this formula reflects a concept of

---

18 As is well-known, the psalmic genre of the hymn comprises two main parts. It begins with an introit, usually formulated as an imperatival clause, which summons the audience to praise God. Then follows the body of the hymn, which serves as a motive clause, explaining the reason for the praise and normally connecting to the preceding part with the subordinator כי. So, for instance, Ps 117, in which v. 1 is the introit (שבחוהו כל האמים // הללו את יהוה כל גוים, "*Praise* the LORD, all you nations! *Extol* him, all you peoples!"), while v. 2a is the body (כי גבר עלינו חסדו / ואמת יהוה לעולם, "*For* great is his steadfast love toward us, and the faithfulness of the LORD endures forever."). In v. 2b one finds a conclusion that echoes the introit (הללו יה, "Praise the LORD!"). For the hymnic genre and its formal features see especially Gunkel and Begrich 1998: 22–65; Mowinckel 1962: 1.81–105; Koch 1969: 159–170; Crüsemann 1969 (cf. above, p. 155, n. 14).

19 According to the *OED* s.v., the archaic term *orison* is documented in English (or rather Anglo-Norman) since the 13th century, and it was borrowed from French *oraison* 'prayer, discourse,' which was inherited from Latin *ōrātiōn-, ōrātiō-* in the sense of 'speech, language, discourse, formal address,' and in post-classical Latin also 'a prayer to God.'

20 For a systematic exploration of this notion, see Labuschagne 1966. The formula אין כ/-כמו "there is none like…" is discussed *ibid.*, 8–15. Note, in passing, that he also discusses the integration of the orison within the prophetic unit, arguing for the literary unity of the prophecy as a whole and for identifying Jeremiah as its author (*ibid.*, 67–70). These arguments, however, do not stand to criticism, and one can only wonder why Labuschagne does not address the stylistic, form-critical and text-critical data that all speak against his position on this point.

monolatry.[21] With time, however, it was reinterpreted as complying with – and giving expression to – monotheistic conceptions. Comparison of our passage to each of the parallels will illuminate its particular emphases and allow us to better understand its message and the reason for its integration in the prophetic unit of Jer 10:1–16.[22]

§3 Parallels

§3.1 David's prayer (2 Sam 7:22)

David's prayer (2 Sam 7:18–29) is presented in the narrative as a reaction to Nathan's prophecy (2 Sam 7:4–17). It may be divided into two parts: it begins with a series of rhetorical questions that underscore the lowly status of David, the speaker (vv. 18–24); and it continues with a series of three petitions or requests that David asks from the Lord (vv. 25–29).[23] The prayer as a whole reflects a uniform discursive situation: David addresses God in the second person, and refers to himself in

---

21 The original, non-monotheistic nature of declarations coined in the formula (מו)כ ןיא is testified by the fact that close parallels are documented in a variety of liturgical works from the ancient Near East, especially in prayers of Mesopotamian gods. See Labuschagne 1966: 31–63, esp. 55–57, where detailed comparison of the Hebrew and Akkadian formulation of such declarations can be found. According to Labuschagne (*ibid.*, 50–51), the source of such declarations is to be sought in the mythological motif of combat and competition between the gods. Note, in passing, that Labuschagne did not find any parallels from Ugaritic literature (*ibid.*, 62). Yet there seems to be at least one Ugaritic formula that encodes a similar – albeit not identical – notion, in one of Baal's epithets: *in d ʿlnh* "there is none above him" (cf. Ps 16:2, ךילע לב, "there is none above you"); see Rahmouni 2008: 84–85.
22 I will not analyze here other passages that express a similar argument but do so by other means, especially by rhetorical questions such as שדקב ראדנ הכמכ ימ / הוהי םלאֵָב הכמכ ימ, "Who is like you, O Yahweh, among the gods? Who is like you, majestic in holiness...?" (Exod 15:11), ימ ותלחנ תיראשל עשפ לע רבעו ןוע אשנ ךומכ לא, "Who is a God like you, pardoning iniquity and passing over the transgression of the remnant of your possession?" (Mic 7:18) and the like. For such utterances, see Labuschagne 1966: 16–30.
23 Note the transparency of the literary structure of David's prayer. The three main rhetorical questions of the first part begin with the same interrogative: יכנא ימ, "*who* am I?" (v. 18); יתיב ימו, "and *what* is my house?" (v. 18); לארשיכ ךמעכ ימו, "*who* is like your people, like Israel?" (v. 23). Similarly, the three petitions comprising the second part all begin with the same presentative: םיהלא הוהי התעו, "*and now*, O Yahweh God" (v. 25); הוהי ינדא התעו, "*and now*, O Lord Yahweh" (v. 28); ךדבע תיב תא ךרבו לאוה התעו, "*And now* may it please you to bless the house of your servant" (v. 29).

the third person by the deprecatory epithet עבדך, "your servant."[24] Against this background, v. 22 stands out, because it is the only passage in the prayer in which David refers to himself, and to the people he represents, in the first person plural:[25]

על כן גדלת יהוה אלהים	Therefore you are great, O Lord God;
כי אין כמוך	for there is no one like you,
ואין אלהים זולתך	and there is no God besides you,
בכל אשר שמענו באזנינו	according to all that we have heard with our ears.

The stylistic deviation of v. 22 from its context may also be detected in its employment of the divine epithet יהוה אלהים "the Lord God,"[26] whereas in the rest of the prayer the epithet used throughout is אדני יהוה (vv. 18, 19, 20, 28, 29).[27] It is

---

24 The only exception to this rule is v. 18, which is formulated in the first person singular: מי אנכי אדני יהוה, ומי ביתי כי הבאתני עד הלם, "Who am I, O Lord Yahweh, and what is my house, that you have brought me thus far?" The reason for this shift, however, is easy to understand: the rhetorical question employed in this passage is itself a standard, self-deprecatory expression; cf. Exod 3:11; 1 Sam 18:18; 1 Chr 29:14.

25 To be sure, v. 18 is also formulated in the first person (cf. above, n. 24). However, it does not match v. 22, as the two passages differ in their grammatical number: singular in v. 18 (אנכי... ביתי..., הבאתני, "I... my house... you have brought me") vs. plural in v. 22 (שמענו באזנינו, "we have heard with our ears"). The deviation of v. 22 from the discursive situation of David's prayer still holds true, therefore, despite some superficial similarity to v. 18. Note also that v. 22 remains distinct from its context – at least in its greater part – even if one accepts the opinion that the original sequence of passages was v. 22a + 26 (על כן גדלת יהוה אלהים + ויגדל שמך עד עולם), "therefore you are great, O Yahweh the God <...> thus your name will be great forever" etc.), whereas vv. 22b–25 were added later by a Deuteronomistic redactor; see, e.g., McCarter 1980–84: 2.237. According to this analysis, the motif of God's greatness belongs to the pre-Deuteronomistic stratum of the text, while its continuation (כי אין כמוך ואין אלהים זולתך, "for there is no one like you, and there is no God besides you") is a redactional expansion. I am not convinced, however, that this analysis is necessitated by the literary evidence. Furthermore, it does not give sufficient weight to the internal, literary structure of David's prayer (cf. above, n. 23).

26 I follow here the text of the Aleppo Codex (Codex Leningradensis reads at this point אדני יהוה as well). The composite epithet יהוה אלהים recurs in v. 25 (ועתה יהוה אלהים, "And now, O God Yahweh" etc.), but its occurrence there is easily explainable in light of the fact that the surrounding passages employ its constituent components and embed them within detailed theological asseverations: ואתה יהוה היית להם לאלהים, "and you, O Yahweh, became their God" (v. 24); ויגדל שמך עד עולם לאמר: יהוה צבאות אלהים על ישראל, "Thus your name will be magnified forever in the saying, 'The Lord of hosts is God over Israel'" (v. 26). By contrast, no comparable motivation for preferring יהוה אלהים over אדני יהוה in v. 22 can be detected.

27 Alternatively, the divine epithet is sometimes expanded into a full utterance: ואתה יהוה היית להם לאלהים, "and you, O Yahweh, became their God" (v. 24); יהוה צבאות אלהים על ישראל, "The Lord of hosts is God over Israel" (v. 26); כי אתה יהוה צבאות אלהי ישראל, "For you are the Lord of hosts, the God of Israel" (v. 27). Cf. v. 28: ועתה אדני יהוה אתה הוא האלהים, "And now, O Lord Yahweh, you are God."

difficult to find any internal justification – be it literary or theological – for the interchange between the two epithets, and it should be explained in an alternative way. According to the Masoretic tradition, which is encoded in the Tiberian vocalization of the biblical text, the composite name יהוה אדני is a taboo expression, like the name יהוה itself; the composite name is never read as written but rather as אדני אלהים. This relatively late reading tradition explains the shift from אדני יהוה (in most of the prayer) to יהוה אלהים (in v. 22). While the prayer was composed relatively early, when the composite name אדני יהוה was read as such, v. 22 was interpolated later, when scribes tended to employ the alternative name אדני אלהים (though they still wrote the Tetragrammaton, even when actually pronouncing it אֱלֹהִים).

It turns out that the stylistic markers of v. 22 distinguish it from the rest of David's prayer, and they suggest its relative lateness compared to the surrounding text. The interpolator likely intended to assert God's uniqueness in order to prevent readers from drawing too radical conclusions from the theological implications of the following passage, v. 23:

ומי כעמך כישראל גוי אחד בארץ אשר הלכו אלהים לפדות לו לעם ולשום לו שם ולעשות לכם הגדולה ונראות לארצך מפני עמך אשר פדית לך ממצרים גוים ואלהיו

The syntactic incongruences in this passage are so numerous and severe, that it is virtually impossible to supply a literal translation of it into English. A somewhat rough approximation (based on the NRSV, but with some modifications) may run as follows:

> Who is like your people, like Israel? (Is there another) nation on earth whose gods went to redeem it as a people, and to make a name for it, doing great and awesome things for its country, by driving out before your people – which you had redeemed, for your own sake, from Egypt – nations and their gods?

The disturbed syntax testifies to the fact that the text has suffered some mutilation, but even 𝔐 as it stands clearly admits the existence of many gods (הלכו אלהים, "gods went," in the plural), and possibly recognizes the divinity of national gods other than YHWH (גוים ואלהיו, if interpreted as a distributive expression meaning "each nation and its god"). This was enough to motivate the assertion that there is no god other than the Lord.[28]

---

28 A more radical solution to these difficulties was devised by the Chronicler, who removed the syntactic and theological obstacles from the text of the passage: ומי כעמך ישראל גוי אחד בארץ אשר הלך אלהים לפדות לו עם לשום לך שם גדלות ונראות לגרש מפני עמך אשר פדית ממצרים גוים, "Who is like your people Israel, one nation on the earth whom *God went* to redeem to be his people, making for yourself a name for great and terrible things, in driving out *nations* before your people whom you redeemed from Egypt?" (1 Chr 17:21). For a critical treatment of the text of 2 Sam 7:22, see also Driver 1913: 277–278.

The present position of v. 22 has another advantage. Its employment of a derivative of גדל "to be great" at the beginning of the passage (על כן גדלת יהוה אלהים, "Therefore you are *great*, O Lord God") interacts with the surrounding passages, that is, both the preceding (v. 21: כל הגדולה הזאת, "all this *greatness*") and following (v. 23: ולעשות לכם הגדולה, "doing *great* things") verses.[29] These verbal connections enabled a relatively smooth integration of v. 22 into its context.

Still, it is worthwhile to note that v. 22 actually comprises two distinct clauses: the first highlights God's greatness, while the second emphasizes his uniqueness. Moreover, each clause correspond to a different paragraph in the first part of David's prayer and finds an echo in the second part of the prayer (thus illustrating the careful way by which v. 22 was implanted in its present context).

The first clause, על כן גדלת יהוה אלהים, "Therefore you are great, O Lord God," refers back to the first paragraph in the series of rhetorical questions (vv. 18b–21) and to its way in depicting the contrast between human and divine perspectives: God's deeds are great from a human point of view (v. 21: כל הגדולה הזאת, "all this greatness") but small from God's own perspective (v. 19: ותקטן עוד זאת בעיניך, "And yet this was a small thing in your eyes"). An echo of this clause is also found in the first paragraph of the series of petitions (vv. 25–27), which mentions, among other motivations for the request: ויגדל שמך עד עולם, "Thus your name will be great forever" (v. 26).

All these interconnections notwithstanding, the first clause of v. 22 also differs in its discursive form from the other mentions of גדל by applying it to God in the second person. The passage thus expresses God's greatness in a form of prayer (cf. Ps 104:1, יהוה אלהי גדלת מאד, "O Yahweh my God, you are very great"), rather than as a third-person description. There is also a slight difference in theological emphasis between v. 22 and the rest of David's prayer: the

---

29 In 𝔐, the words כל הגדולה הזאת in v. 21 function as the direct object of the verb עשה "to do, make" (בעבור דברך וכלבך עשית את כל הגדולה הזאת להודיע את עבדך, "Because of your promise, and according to your own heart, *you have wrought all this greatness*, so that your servant may know it"), as in v. 23 (ולעשות לכם הגדולה, "and to wrought you greatness"). But Driver 1913: 277 notes that, within the context of v. 22, it remains unclear what exactly is referred to by the term "greatness," as opposed to v. 23, in which it clearly refers to the miracles performed by God during the Exodus. It was therefore conjectured that the text of v. 22 needs to be restored by transposing the crucial words to its end: <את כל הגדולה הזאת> להודיע את עבדך, "to inform your servant of all this greatness." Be that as it may, this emendation does not affect the analysis presented here.

two parts of the prayer give expression to God's greatness indirectly, by way of metonymy: either by describing his great deeds (vv. 21, 23) or his great name (v. 26). In contradistinction, v. 22 asserts that greatness is an immanent feature of God himself.

The second clause contained in v. 22, כי אין כמוך ואין אלהים זולתך בכל אשר שמענו באזנינו, "for there is no one like you, and there is no God besides you, according to all that we have heard with our ears," refers forward to the second paragraph in the series of rhetorical questions (vv. 23–24). It seeks to correct the picture of the relationship between God and the people that transpires from the latter passage, which follows a standard Deuteronomistic definition of this relationship by the act of Israel's salvation from Egypt: ומי כעמך כישראל גוי אחד בארץ אשר הלכו אלהים לפדות לו לעם [...] עמך אשר פדית לך ממצרים, "Who is like your people, like Israel? A nation of earth whose gods went to redeem it as a people... your people, which you had redeemed, for your own sake, from Egypt" (v. 23),[30] following which a covenant was signed by the people and its god: ותכונן לך את עמך ישראל לך לעם עד עולם ואתה יהוה היית להם לאלהים, "And you established your people Israel for yourself to be your people forever; and you, O Yahweh, became their God" (v. 24).[31] This description of the covenant is again evoked in the series of petitions, in the second part of David's prayer: אתה הוא האלהים, "you are God" (v. 28).

From this portrayal, one can deduce that the events were the result of mutual choice: just as the Lord chose Israel from among the various nations of the world, so did Israel chose the Lord from among the many gods of the universe. In other words, as standard and stereotypical depiction as they may be, vv. 23–24 run the risk of admitting the true existence of other gods. The scribe who added v. 22 wished to avoid such a conclusion in the first place, and he therefore insisted unequivocally that YHWH is the God of Israel not because he is the only god who took the trouble of redeeming the Israelites from Egypt, but rather because he is the single existing god in general.

---

30 The verb פדה and its derivatives are typical to Deuteronomic allusions to the Exodus: Deut 7:8; 9:26; 13:6; 15:15; 24:18. Cf. Exod 13:15; Mic 6:4. Note further the intriguing suggestion of MacDonald 2014: 104–105, that the words גוי אחד, "one nation," echo the declaration of God's oneness in Deut 6:4.
31 Compare Deut 26:17–18.

This assertion was formulated in a poetic-like pattern of three lines, whose rhetorical essence and theological message are manifested by the double repetition of the negative particle:[32]

כי אין כמוך	For *there is no* one like you,
ואין אלהים זולתך	and *there is no* God besides you,
בכל אשר שמענו באזנינו	according to all that we have heard with our ears.

It stands to reason that this particular pattern was chosen because it was deemed fitting for being integrated within a prayer. Indeed, a similarly formulated passage is found in Hannah's prayer (1 Sam 2:2):[33]

אין קדוש ביהוה	*There is no* holy one like the LORD,
כי אין בלתך	For *there is no* one besides you,
ואין צור כאלהינו	And *there is no* rock like our God.

In conclusion, the two clauses comprising v. 22 are given in a sequence, and both of them are cast in patterns that are typical to biblical liturgical diction, but they do not merge into a unified utterance. They keep their ideological, stylistic and literary independence from one another, and each clause has a different linkage with distinct sections of David's prayer. It seems, therefore, that 2 Sam 7:22 represents

---

32 Note that the two negated clauses have distinctly different meanings. The clause כי אין כמוך, "for there is none like you," may well be an assertion of monolatry; it contends with the argument that God is incomparable, but it does not explicitly deny the existence of other gods. By contrast, the clause ואין אלהים זולתך, "and there is no god besides you," is a monotheistic proclamation, as it clearly asserts that the Lord is the only god in existence. The following words בכל אשר שמענו באזנינו, "according to all that we have heard with our ears," are not a concessive complement (i.e., restricting the predication 'as far as we know') but rather intend to convey full persuasion in the truthfulness of the factual proposition due to a direct experience of revelation (cf. Deut 5:1). It is perhaps possible to speculate that the monotheistic clause ואין אלהים זולתך, "and there is no god besides you," was added at a relatively late stage, whereas the original text of the passage included only the monolatrous clause together with the affirmation: כי אין כמוך + בכל אשר שמענו באזנינו, "for there is none like you <...> according to all that we have heard with our ears" (see further n. 33), in order to explain the special relationship between the Lord and Israel, which is the concern of v. 26. However, this hypothesis is not supported by the textual evidence, and it is not necessary for the interpretation of the passage as it is.

33 In this passage too there is a tension between the monolatrous clauses אין קדוש ביהוה [...] ואין צור כאלהינו, "there is no holy one like the LORD... and there is no rock like our God," and the monotheistic clause כי אין בלתך, "for there is no one besides you." In this case, however, there might be some clues in the Septuagint tradition that the text of the passage was indeed tampered and the combination of clauses as found in 𝔐 might be secondary. See the text and apparatus of Brooke, McLean and Thackeray 1927: 5; cf. Driver 1913: 24. In any case, there is a noteworthy difference between the two types of clauses in terms of their discursive situation: the monotheistic clause addresses God in the second person, while the two monolatrous clauses describe God in the third person.

a relatively early stage in the history of the liturgical tradition that combines the motif of God's greatness with the assertion of his incomparability.

Another peculiar aspect of this passage – and of David's prayer as a whole – is the complete absence of the motif of God's kingship, which takes pride of place in Jer 10:6–7. In both respects, then, there is a marked difference between the rudimentary form of the tradition as it is found in 2 Sam 7:22 and the much more sophisticated design one finds in Jer 10:6–7. The latter passage still distinguishes between the different motifs of God's greatness (v. 6) and his kingship (v. 7), but both of them were recast in a similar literary form, and they were framed by a unifying structure that expresses the notion of God's incomparability. Jer 10:6–7 thus represent a typologically later stage in the history of the liturgical tradition, a stage in which the older combination was supplemented by the motif of God's kingship and enriched by an extensive literary reworking, which produced a self-contained prayer.

§3.2 Solomon's prayer (1 Kgs 8:23 + 27)

Solomon's prayer in 1 Kgs 8:12–61 is a long piece that generally bears the stylistic and ideological imprints of the Deuteronomistic school.[34] It falls into four parts, which are embedded within a narrative framework that tells about the inauguration of the Jerusalem temple, with each part of the prayer being set at a certain point in the complex, inaugural ceremony. The third part, which is also the longest one (vv. 23–53) describes with much detail the various functions of the temple. It is introduced by an opening paragraph (vv. 23–27), which anchors the building of the temple in God's promise to David:

23 ויאמר יהוה אלהי ישראל אין כמוך אלהים בשמים ממעל ועל הארץ מתחת שֹׁמֵר
הברית והחסד לעבדיך ההלכים לפניך בכל לבם 24 אשר שמרת לעבדך דוד אבי את
אשר דברת לו ותדבר בפיך ובידך מלאת כיום הזה 25 ועתה יהוה אלהי ישראל שְׁמֹר
לעבדך דוד אבי את אשר דברת לו לאמר לא יכרת לך איש מלפני ישב על כסא ישראל
רק אם ישמרו בניך את דרכם ללכת לפני כאשר הלכת לפני 26 ועתה אלהי ישראל
יֵאָמֶן נא דבריך [דבר] אשר דברת לעבדך דוד אבי 27 כי האמנם יֵשֵׁב אלהים על
הארץ הנה השמים ושמי השמים לא יכלכלוך אף כי הבית הזה אשר בניתי

---

34 The Deuteronomistic background of Solomon's prayer has been much discussed in scholarship, but there is no consensus on its exact historical setting. See, e.g., Knoppers 1995, who argues that the prayer reflects the royal propaganda of Josaiah's days; Hoffman 2009, who argues that the prayer was composed in Babylon, by Judean exiles who were deported with King Jehoiachin. This issue, however, does not affect our present concern.

> [23] *He said: O Yahweh, the God of Israel, there is no God like you in heaven above or on earth beneath*, keeping covenant and steadfast love for your servants who walk before you with all their heart, [24] the covenant that you kept for your servant my father David as you declared to him; you promised with your mouth and have this day fulfilled with your hand. [25] Therefore, O Yahweh, the God of Israel, keep for your servant my father David that which you promised him, saying, "There shall never fail you a successor before me to sit on the throne of Israel, if only your children look to their way, to walk before me as you have walked before me." [26] Therefore, O God of Israel, let your word be confirmed, which you promised to your servant my father David. [27] *But will God indeed dwell on the earth? Even heaven and the highest heaven cannot contain you, much less this house that I have built!*

This introductory paragraph may again be divided into two parts: a frame consisting of an opening (v. 23a) and conclusion (v. 27) on the one hand, and the body of the introduction (vv. 23b–26). This division is justified on both stylistic and thematic grounds. The framing passages are united by the repeating use of the keywords "heaven and earth," and it relates divine qualities. The body of the introduction, in contradistinction, focuses on God's promise to David and falls into three subparagraphs (vv. 23b, 24–25, 26), all united by the *Leitwörter* שמר and עֶבֶד.[35]

Our interest lies with the former component, that is, the framing passages. The opening passage establishes the liturgical mode by addressing God directly (v. 23a; cf. Exod 20:4 ‖ Deut 5:8), while the concluding passage is formulated as a rhetorical question, which leads the reader to the main theme of the entire prayer, namely, the temple (v. 27).[36] The literary relation between these two passages is a chiastic one, thus equating between God on the one hand and the temple that represents the divine presence on the other:

---

35 In the third subparagraph (v. 26), the verb אמן substitutes for the semantically close verb שמר, which was employed in the preceding two subparagraphs (cf. Deut 7:9; Mic 7:5, and Ps 89:29, which is part of the poetic retelling of 2 Sam 7).

36 The Chronistic parallel to the opening passage has a shorter text: יהוה אלהי ישראל אין כמוך אלהים בשמים ובארץ, "O Yahweh, the God of Israel, there is no God like you, in heaven or on earth" (2 Chr 6:14). In my view, the longer text of 1 Kgs 8:23a better fits the literary relation between the framing passages (see the analysis below). The short text of Chronicles might be influenced by the standard phrase בשמים ובארץ, "in heaven and on earth" (Deut 3:24; Joel 3:3; Ps 113:6; 135:6), which also recurs in the book of Chronicles itself (1 Chr 29:11).

[23] O Yahweh, God of Israel,	יהוה אלהי ישראל
there is no God like you in *heaven* above	אין כמוך אלהים בשמים ממעל
or *on earth* beneath	ועל הארץ מתחת
[...]	[...]
[27] But will God indeed dwell *on the earth*?	כי האמנם ישב אלהים על הארץ
Even *heaven* and the *highest heaven* cannot contain you,	הנה השמים ושמי השמים לא יכלכלוך
much less this house that I have built!	אף כי הבית הזה אשר בניתי

The two framing passages thus join to a credo that conveys a few theologoumena: God is incomparable on both the heavenly and earthly planes of existence; he cannot be contained in reality, but he is represented therein by the temple; there is a special relation between him and a particular ethnic group, since it is, first and foremost, the "God of Israel."

This credo exhibits a carefully crafted literary structure. As such, it represents a typological stage of the liturgical tradition that is more advanced compared to 2 Sam 7:22 and closer to Jer 10:6–7. Despite some structural differences, 1 Kgs 8:23 + 27 and Jer 10:6–7 also share some literary features. For instance, both of them make use of the echo pattern, in which the crucial keywords are repeated, often with slight variation of the context. Moreover, both texts place at their center a rhetorical question (1 Kgs 8:27a: האמנם ישב אלהים על הארץ, "Will God indeed dwell on the earth?"; Jer 10:7a: מי לא יראך מלך הגוים, "Who would not fear you, O king of the nations?") – a technique designed for promoting the internalization of the message so conveyed and persuading the audience in the inevitability of the answer.

From a thematic point of view, the orison of Jer 10:6–7 highlights God's greatness (v. 6) and kingship (v. 7), and the motif of incomparability frames it all. In the framing passages of the introductory paragraph of Solomon's prayer, the latter motif takes the center stage, whereas God's greatness and kingship are not given explicit expression. Nevertheless, it should be borne in mind that 1 Kgs 8:23 + 27 are only the frame; the body of the introductory paragraph actually integrated the kingship motif (vv. 24–26), since its main theme is God's promise that David will be granted with an eternal royal dynasty.[37] On the other hand, the theme of the temple,

---

[37] If so, the motif of divine greatness is the only one not explicitly mentioned anywhere in the paragraph under scrutiny. From a Deuteronomistic perspective, however, it might be implied in the framing passages; compare the combination of motifs in a Deuteronomic passage such as אדני יהוה אתה החלות להראות את עבדך את גדלך ואת ידך החזקה אשר מי אל בשמים ובארץ אשר יעשה כמעשיך וכגבורתך, "O Lord Yahweh, you have only begun to show your servant your *greatness* and your might; what god *in heaven or on earth* can perform deeds and mighty acts like yours!" (Deut 3:24).

which has such a prominent role in Solomon's prayer, is completely absent from Jer 10:6–7 and 2 Sam 7:22. Obviously, it is not an original part of the liturgical tradition but rather an additional component, which was supplemented in Solomon's prayer in order to fit the liturgical tradition into its specific literary context.

Finally, attention should be given to the ideological function of the liturgical tradition in delimiting a collective identity and in defining the difference between Israel and the other nations. Solomon's prayer addresses the Lord as "the God of Israel," whereas the orison of Jer 10:6–7 refers to him as "king of the nations" and asserts that "among all the wise ones of the nations and in all their kingdoms there is no one like you" (v. 7). Upon first glance, then, Solomon's prayer expresses a particularistic perspective, while the orison reflects a more universalistic outlook. This characterization, however, needs to be refined. On the one hand, the introductory paragraph in Solomon's prayer cannot be detached from its continuation, the third and longest section of Solomon's prayer. While this section indeed makes a distinction between Israel and the nations, and it repeatedly insists that the temple is intended to serve primarily the Israelites, it also affirms that the temple can serve as a locus for worship to be conducted by foreigners, who would come "from a distant land because of your name, for they shall hear of your great name, your mighty hand, and your outstretched arm" (1 Kgs 8:41–42). Solomon even hastens God to accept their prayer: "and do according to all that the foreigner calls to you, so that all the peoples of the earth may know your name and fear you, as do your people Israel, and so that they may know that your name has been invoked on this house that I have built" (v. 43). This idea comes close to the universalistic recognition of God's kingship that transpires from our orison: "Who would not fear you, O King of the nations? ... among all the wise ones of the nations and in all their kingdoms there is no one like you" (Jer 10:7). On the other hand, the reference to "all the wise ones of the nations and in all their kingdoms" in the latter passage signals an ideological distinction between Israel (the 'us' group) and the rest of the nations (the 'they' group), even if this distinction is not explicitly stated but remains merely implicit.[38] If this conclusion is correct, there is another point of contact between

---

[38] Compare Deut 4:6–8, which similarly applies the same terms (עמים "peoples", גוי "nation") to both Israel and the nations, but this does not obscure the ideological and theological distinction between them, which the passage deduces from the special relationship between the people and its god: ושמרתם ועשיתם כי הוא חכמתכם ובינתכם לעיני העמים אשר ישמעון את כל החקים האלה ואמרו רק עם חכם ונבון הגוי הגדול הזה כי מי גוי גדול אשר לו אלהים קרבים אליו כיהוה אלהינו בכל קראנו אליו ומי גוי גדול אשר לו חקים ומשפטים צדיקם ככל התורה הזאת אשר אנכי נתן לפניכם היום, "You must observe them diligently, for this will show your wisdom and discernment to the peoples, who, when they hear all these statutes, will say, 'Surely this great nation is a wise and discerning people!' For what other great nation has a god so near to it as the Lord our God is whenever we call to him? And what other great nation has statutes and ordinances as just as this entire law that I am setting before you today?"

1 Kgs 8:23 + 27 and Jer 10:6–7, as both of them harness the shared liturgical tradition for the ideological purpose of crystallizing a unique ethnic identity.

§3.3 Hymnic addition to individual lament (Ps 86:8–10)

Ps 86 contains two psalms (vv. 1–13, 14–17) that were apparently independent in the first place.[39] From a form-critical point of view, both of them can be classified as individual laments, but they differ markedly in their style.[40] Our concern here is with the first psalm (vv. 1–13), which consists of a series of compound sentences. Typically, the main clause is a cry for salvation, often formulated as an imperatival clause; the following, subordinate clause – normally introduced by the particle כי – supplies the motive for the former call.[41] This basic structure is of course subject to variation, especially by way of expansion,[42] but it is usually maintained throughout the psalm.[43] It is interrupted, however, in vv. 8–10, in which one finds a section that contains no cry for salvation but rather an unconditional praise to the Lord:[44]

---

39 Ayali-Darshan 2005: 331. Although critical commentators are not in agreement concerning the composition of Ps 86, the aforementioned analysis appears to be the most compelling one.
40 Cf. below, n. 43.
41 For instance: כי עני ואביון אני / הטה יהוה אזנך ענני, "*Incline* your ear, O Yahweh, and answer me, *for* I am poor and needy" (v. 1b); כי חסיד אני / שמרה נפשי, "*Preserve* my life, *for* I am devoted to you" (v. 2a); כי אליך אדני נפשי אשא / שמח נפש עבדך, "*Gladden* the soul of your servant, *for* to you, O Lord, I lift up my soul" (v. 4).
42 For instance, see the expanded main clause in v. 5, or the expanded subordinate clause in v. 6, and especially towards the end of the psalm: vv. 11–12 expand the main clause, while v. 13 expands the subordinate clause.
43 By contrast, this recurring structure is completely absent from the second psalm (vv. 14–17), whose poetics is not based on repetition through variation, but rather on piling up thematically similar utterances: first for describing the predicament (v. 14: אלהים זדים קמו עלי / ועדת עריצים בקשו נפשי / ולא שמוך לנגדם, "O God, the insolent rise up against me; a band of ruffians seeks my life, and they do not set you before them"), then for portraying the addressee (v. 15: ואתה אדני / אל רחום וחנון / ארך אפים ורב חסד ואמת, "But you, O Lord, are a God merciful and gracious, slow to anger and abounding in steadfast love and faithfulness"), and finally for asking salvation (vv. 16–17a: פנה אלי וחנני / תנה עזך לעבדך / והושיעה לבן אמתך / עשה עמי אות לטובה, "Turn to me and be gracious to me, give your strength to your servant, save the child of your serving girl, show me a sign of your favor") and depicting the wishful situation that should follow (v. 17b: כי אתה יהוה / יראו שנאי ויבשו / עזרתני ונחמתני, "so that those who hate me may see it and be put to shame, because you, LORD, have helped me and comforted me").
44 Tellingly, even among commentators who defend the unity of Ps 86, one finds some who recognize the special status of vv. 8–10, and at least consider them as an independent strophe. See, e.g., Goldingay 2006–8: 2.617–630, esp. 623–624.

8 אין כמוך באלהים אדני / ואין כמעשיך
9 כל גוים אשר עשית יבואו וישתחוו לפניך אדני / ויכבדו לשמך
10 כי גדול אתה ועשה נפלאות / אתה אלהים לבדך

[8] There is none like you among the gods, O Lord, nor are there any works like yours.
[9] All the nations you have made shall come and bow down before you, O Lord, and shall glorify your name.
[10] For you are great and do wondrous things; you alone are God.

This passage comes very close to our orison, but the conspicuous similarities should be weighed against the subtle differences.

(1) First, there is the issue of literary form. Like our orison, Ps 86:8–10 is thematically similar to hymns, but its formal features do not exactly match this classical *Gattung*. However, Ps 86:8–10 is not identical to Jer 10:6–7 in this regard. While both texts have no hymnic introit, which normally takes the form of an imperatival summon to praise God, Ps 86:10 does include a motive clause marked by כי (v. 10). It thus adopts at least one of the two structural characteristics of biblical hymns, suggesting that it has been appropriated more thoroughly (though not fully) to the formal conventions of hymnic psalmody.

(2) Another issue is the theological arguments embedded in the two texts, particularly in terms of their formulation of the notion of God's incomparability. On the one hand, there is a stark similarity between the opening of the hymnic prayer and the *inclusio* of the Orison:

– Ps 86:8a, אין כמוך באלהים אדני, "There is none like you among the gods, O Lord."
– Jer 10:6a, מאין כמוך יהוה, "For there is none like you, O Yahweh."

But the two texts conclude differently. While the orison concludes in the very same formula, the hymnic prayer employs a different formulation:

– Jer 10:7b, מאין כמוך, "For there is none like you."
– Ps 86:10b, אתה אלהים לבדך, "You alone are God."

Though the opening and closure of Ps 86:8–10 are seemingly synonymous, they actually convey different ideas and have distinct emphases. The opening line, "there is none like you among the gods," argues that God is incomparable, but it does not deny the possibility that it coexists with other gods. By contrast, the concluding line, "you alone are God," insists that there is only one God, namely, the Lord. Put differently, the opening of the hymnic prayer, like the *inclusio* of the orison, is a statement compatible with monolatry, whereas the conclusion of the hymnic prayer is a proclamation of monotheism.

To be sure, the opening and conclusion of Ps 86:8–10 do not overtly contradict each other. Apparently, for the psalmist, they were analogous articulations of the same basic idea, namely, God's uniqueness; it is for this reason that he placed them at the strategic points of the opening and closure of this short prayer. Yet the two statements actually have different interests, so that their combination testifies to a stage in which monolatry was a matter of the distant past, and monotheism took the fore in terms of the theological outlook of the time.[45] The two texts obviously draw from a common liturgical source, but the form of Ps 86:8–10 probably reflects a relatively later reworking of this tradition compared to the form of Jer 10:6–7.

(3) A thematic difference between the two texts lies is in their focus of praise. The orison of Jer 10:6–7 reflect on God's abstract qualities, primarily his greatness and kingship. The hymnic prayer of Ps 86:8–10, by contrast, concentrates on God's actual deeds, that is, on the practical outcomes of his acts in reality.

This is well expressed in the verbal texture of the two texts. In Jer 10:6–7, two keywords are used repeatedly: גדול "great" in v. 6 and מלך "king(ship)" in v. 7. But in Ps 86:8–10, there is a single *Leitwort* that runs through all three verses, namely, the verb עשה "to do, make, work":

- v. 8: ואין כמעשיך, "nor are there any *works* like yours"
- v. 9: כל גוים אשר עשית, "all the nations you have *made*"
- v. 10: ועשה נפלאות, "you... *do* wondrous things"

(4) Finally, it should be noted that the two texts differ remarkably in their prosodic properties. As indicated above, the orison of Jer 10:6–7 has an expanding rhythm, as each line is longer than the preceding one, until being concluded with the short formula "for there is none like you," which echoes the opening. No similar rhythmic organization is to be found in the hymnic prayer of Ps 86:8–10, since its three verses inconsistently vary in their length (v. 8 is the shortest, v. 9 is the longest, and v. 10 has an intermediate length). On the other hand, all three verses rhyme with the same grammatical ending, the 2m.sg pronominal suffix:[46]

---

45 Ayali-Darshan 2005: 331–333.

46 The rhyme is also what stiches the interpolated hymnic prayer into its context, since the continuation of the individual supplication that follows (vv. 11–13) begins with a verse, each poetic line of which ends with the same pronominal suffix: הורני יהוה דרכך / אהלך באמתך / יחד לבבי ליראה שמך, "Teach me, O Yahweh, *your* way / that I may walk in *your* truth / give me an undivided heart to revere *your* name" (v. 11).

- v. 8: כמעשיך, "like *your* deeds"
- v. 9: לשמך, "*your* name"
- v. 10: לבדך, "*your* own"

No such device is employed in the orison of Jer 10:6–7.

But the most outstanding prosodic difference between the two texts is to be found in their adherence to a metrical scheme (or its lack thereof).[47] As mentioned above, no prosodic pattern can be detected in Jer 10:6–7, and this is one of the features that distance it from 'pure' poetry. Ps 86:8–10, however, follows a very clear metrical scheme of double feet, each comprising two accented words. The prosodic analysis thus reveals that the basic scansion is that of dimeter, with each foot consisting of two stresses (line 1, 3, 4, 6),[48] while ends of strophes are marked by a line of a single foot (lines 2, 5) or by a catalectic line (line 7):

Strophe	Line	Text	Scansion
A	1	8 אין כמוך / באלהים אדני	– – / – –
	2	ואין כמעשיך.	– –
B	3	9 כל גוים / אשר עשית	– – / – –
	4	יבואו וישתחוו / לפניך אדני	– – / – –
	5	ויכבדו לשמך.	– –
C	6	10 כי־גדול אתה / ועשה נפלאות	– – / – –
	7	אתה אלהים / לבדך.	– / – –

---

47 I do not share the doubt, expressed by many scholars (e.g., most recently, Dobbs-Allsopp 2015: 95–177), concerning the idea that biblical poetry features regularized prosody. In my opinion, biblical poetry cannot be treated *en bloc*, and the attempt to do so has lead not a few scholars astray. As a matter of fact, "biblical poetry" is nothing but a cover term that actually comprises a variety of approaches to all aspects of poetry, due to the activity of different poetic schools and the textual coexistence of poems originating in different periods. Yet it seems to me impossible to deny that some biblical poems do exhibit a metrical matrix, and the passage under scrutiny is only one out of many other examples. Cf. above, Chapter 4, §2. For a recent survey of select approaches to biblical metrical systems see Vance 2013.

48 The prosodic analysis suggests that the word כי (line 6) is not counted as an independent stress but rather joins to גדול as a single stress unit. This is not because of the cantillation tradition, which places a *maqqeph* on כי, for there are other words in this poem that are still considered metrically independent stresses even though they bear the *maqqeph* sign: אין־ (v. 8), כל־ (v. 9). What matters in such cases is a combination of phonetic and syntactic considerations: function-words such as prepositions and conjunctions – especially monosyllabic particles, and all the more so if they are open syllables – naturally tend to lose their independent stress and become proclitic elements. Close study of biblical poetry demonstrates that in such cases, the prosodic status of these words can adapt to the metrical scheme, i.e., they can be regarded as either independent stresses or part of a larger stress-unit in accordance to the local metrical requirements.

In this respect, too, the two texts evidently draw from a common liturgical tradition, but each passage has reworked it stylistically in its own distinct way. The orison of Jer 10:6–7 transformed the shared tradition into a rhetorical utterance, while the hymnic prayer of Ps 86:8–10 turned it into a piece of poetry. The original independence of the underlying liturgical tradition can still be observed in the fact that it does not fully accord with the norms of biblical poetry. Even in Ps 86:8–10, there is not a single example of *parallelismus membrorum*, in contrast to what one finds in the psalm in which this passage is embedded. This passage therefore stems from a tradition that was not originally poetic in form. Nevertheless, it has been reorganized within a metrical scheme and adapted (more or less) to a poetic framework.

The comparison between the orison of Jer 10:6–7 and the hymnic prayer of Ps 86:8–10 foregrounds the original independence of the liturgical tradition from which both texts stem. The analysis also highlights the different theological emphases of the two works. The orison is still formulated as a monolatrous argument; although this does not automatically mean that the passage was actually authored at an age of pure monolatry, typologically speaking the text as it stands reflects a mode of expression that is relatively conservative. Indeed, this conclusion may be supported by the verbatim repetition of the formula "there is none like you," if it is taken as a relic from an older literary form that is liturgically more primitive, such as a litany. By contrast, in Ps 86:8–10, one finds that the old liturgical tradition has already been explicitly reinterpreted in a monotheistic perspective, thus reflecting a more advanced stage of theological adaptation. This conclusion is in line with the findings relating to the poetic technique of both texts, as the hymnic prayer is clearly a more sophisticated reworking of the verbal texture and prosodic properties of the liturgical tradition than one finds in Jer 10:6–7.

§4 From the shared liturgical tradition to the given orison

All the passages discussed above stem from a liturgical tradition that revolves around the formula "there is none like you," which expresses the notion of God's incomparability. They are also comparable in terms of their secondary position in their respective contexts, since most of them were interpolated into their present place (2 Sam 7:22; Jer 10:6–7; Ps 86:8–10). A changing combination of motifs of praise is weaved around the incomparability formula, so that each passage presents a distinct configuration of motifs, even though its components are standard and even trite by themselves. The unique nature of each passage is also evident in their literary design, and this issue allows one to trace a developmental trajectory that leads from the rather rudimentary deployment – actually, mere juxtaposition – of the various motifs in 2 Sam 7:22, through the attempts to give a more coherent and worked out literary form in 1 Kgs 8:23 + 27 and Jer 10:6–7, to the well-crafted poetic scheme of Ps 86:8–10. The substantial differences in their literary casting and stylistic sophistication demonstrate that these passages do not represent a single or unified redactional stratum but rather a series of local interventions, each with its own peculiar motivation, even though they all apparently draw from a common liturgical tradition.[49]

The various passages also differ from one another in the degree of integration between their themes and theological concerns. The formula "there is none like you" had originally been compatible with a monolatrous argument, but it is evident that it has been reinterpreted through a monotheistic perspective. Nevertheless, the explicit expressions of this perspective are not equally distributed in the various texts, and only some of them unequivocally articulate it (2 Sam 7:22; Ps 86:10). As for the other passages, even if one admits that in terms of their thematic combination and literary form such passages reflect a relatively early stage in the degree of monotheistic reworking of the shared liturgical tradition, this does not yet prove that they intend to articulate a non-monotheistic argument. In other words, when dealing with passages that do not explicate a monotheistic argument (1 Kgs 8:23 + 27; Jer 10:6–7) one cannot escape the question: Do they really represent a pre-monotheistic stage in the history of Israelite religion? Or should we conclude that in these passages too the monolatrous declaration was no longer understood in its original sense but rather taken in an extended way? After all, it is obvious that late biblical authors continued to employ inherited, monolatrous modes of expression, without feeling that originally such formulae actually conveyed a theological content that was quite different from their own conception. If so, one must closely examine each such passage in order to detect in it additional clues for its theological presuppositions.

I propose that Jer 10:6–7 indeed contains an expression – albeit an indirect one – of an essentially monotheistic conceptualization of the divinity. It is to be found in the orison's particular use of the motif of God's kingship. As demonstrated above, the literary construction of the orison guides the reader in identifying the structured hierarchy of its thematic content, with the most important themes being

---

49 According to Ben-Dov 2000: 117–126, the entire hymnic stratum in Jer 10:1–16 belongs to a late layer in prophetic literature, which was identified by Crenshaw in his study on the book of Amos. This layer has three characteristics. (a) Thematically, it concentrates on the motif of God as the creator of the world and the agent responsible for its maintenance. (b) Stylistically, it makes extensive use of participles. (c) It is intimately linked to the employment of the formula יהוה צבאות שמו, "the Lord of hosts is his name" (which occurs in our prophetic unit in v. 16). However, even if these features are detectable in vv. 12–13, they do not fit the orison in vv. 6–7. This difficulty cannot be dismissed by the argument that the latter passage is a secondary expansion of the hymnic stratum, which is late in itself (Ben-Dov, *ibid.*, 123).

expressed in the enveloping statements (God's incomparability) on the one hand, and in the central, rhetorical question (God's kingship) on the other. Both themes evidently polemicize with a henotheistic worldview, whose point of departure is the presupposition that every nation has its own "national god."[50] The *inclusio* argues that there is no entity in the world that resembles the Lord, and this argument leads to a conclusion that is formulated in political terms in the rhetorical question: since there are no other gods, the Lord is the sovereign of all the world's peoples ("king of the nations"). Hence, they all should respect him ("who would not fear you" etc.), that is, exclusively worship him (cf. Ps 22:28–30; 47). The full theological argument, then, is no longer exhausted by pointing out the lack of possibility to compare the Lord to other gods – which is a concept that still admits, at least theoretically, the existence of other such gods, but merely insists that the Lord is superior to them. The theological argument inherent in this passage proceeds to draw the practical conclusion that the Lord's sovereignty is no longer restricted to Israel alone, but rather expands to cover all the nations of the world. The monolatrous foundations of this conception are patent in the very nature of the political argument (that is, in the assumption that if God is a king, and all the more so if he is the king of all nations, then his subjects must worship him). But in its universal enforcement, the theological outlook of the orison is virtually monotheistic.

This conclusion allows one to interpret one detail in the text of the orison that has perplexed all previous commentators. As we have seen, at the heart of the shared liturgical tradition stands the incomparability formula אין כמוך. However, in the orison of Jer 10:6–7 (and in this passage alone), this formula is governed by the preposition מן. Interpreters found it most difficult to comprehend the meaning of the resulting prepositional phrase מאין כמוך, which is repeated verbatim at the opening of the orison (v. 6a) and its conclusion (v. 7b). Already ancient readers were troubled by it. This is indicated, for instance, by the Greek version of Theodotion, who translates, in both occurrences, by the word πόθεν, "whence? where from?" namely, as if reading the form מֵאַיִן.[51] Jewish medieval commentators usually consider the preposition as an added element that is semantically superfluous,[52] while the popular solution in critical scholarship is to delete it as a product of inadvertent dittography (duplicating the final *mem* of אותם in v. 5 and מלכותם in

---

50 For this concept and its ancient Near Eastern roots see, e.g., Block 1988.
51 See Field 1871–75: 2.597–598. This rendition is quite senseless in context, but some modern commentators accepted it nonetheless, attempting to interpret the passage accordingly. For the history of its reception see Barthélemy 1986: 543. Compare the in-depth syntactical analysis of Driver 1885: 34–37 (and, in an abridged form, Driver 1906: 353). For a concise overview of the various opinions concerning this prepositional phrase, see, e.g., McKane 1986–96: 1.223–224.
52 See, for instance, the comments of Isaiah of Trani and Menaḥem ben Shimon *ad loc.* (Cohen 2012: 69).

v. 7).[53] However, it is difficult to believe that such a textual fault will occur twice in a row, within the same passage, but under the influence of two different words. In addition, it has been suggested that the problematic *mem* is not the assimilated realization of the preposition מִן but rather a negative particle, like Arabic *mā* (ﻣﺎ), leading to the interpretation of מאין as a doubly marked negative particle.[54]

As a matter of fact, 𝔐 is not so difficult to interpret. After all, other passages that employ the prepositional phrase מאין use it to mark the reason for the coming about of a certain state of affairs, i.e., it can be rendered as "for (or: since, because) there is no...," for instance:

– Jer 4:7, עלה אריה מסבכו ומשחית גוים נסע יצא ממקמו לשום ארצך לשמה עריך תִּצֶּינָה מאין יושב, "A lion has gone up from its thicket, a destroyer of nations has set out; he has gone out from his place to make your land a waste; your cities will be ruins, *for there will be no* inhabitant."
   Cf. Jer 26:9, והעיר הזאת תחרב מאין יושב, "And this city shall be desolate, *for there will be no* inhabitant."

– Jer 7:32, לכן הנה ימים באים נאם יהוה ולא יאמר עוד התפת וגיא בן הנם כי אם גיא ההרגה וקברו בתפת מאין מקום, "Therefore, the days are surely coming, says the LORD, when it will no more be called Topheth, or the valley of the son of Hinnom, but the valley of Slaughter: for they will bury in Topheth, *for there is no* more room."
   Cf. Jer 19:11, ובתפת יקברו מאין מקום לקבור, "In Topheth they shall bury, *for there is no* more room to bury."

– Jer 30:7, הוי כי גדול היום ההוא מאַיִן כמֹהו, "Alas! That day would be great, *for there will be none like it.*"

---

53 So, for instance, BHK and BHS *ad loc.*, both being edited by Wilhelm Rudolph; cf. his critical commentary, Rudolph 1958: 66. See also Labuschagne 1966: 11 n. 1, and many others. The preposition is not represented in the Syriac and Aramaic versions, but its absence is hardly due to a different *Vorlage*. Admittedly, in other passages of Jeremiah that attest to the prepositional phrase מֵאֵין, it was faithfully rendered by Aramaic מן בלי (Jer 4:7; 7:32; 19:11; 26:9). But when translating the similar phrase מֵאַיִן כמֹהו (Jer 30:7), the two versions again diverge from literal rendition and represent it only with Aramaic לית, the negative existential particle. This fact demonstrates that the different Aramaic renditions are conditioned by syntactic constraints, and it is not to be taken as suggesting a divergent *Vorlage*. According to Hoffman 2001: 1.294, the similarity between Jer 10:6–7 and 30:7 suggests that the former passage was formulated under the stylistic influence of the Book of Jeremiah as a whole.

54 So Dahood 1975. However, as Dahood himself points out, the use of *mā* as a negative particle in Arabic is a late development, the result of grammaticalization of an interrogative particle (akin to Hebrew מָה) that had been employed in rhetorical questions. This is an inner-Arabic development, and there is no solid evidence for suggesting that it took place in Hebrew, or in Central Semitic, i.e., the hypothetical proto-language from which Arabic and Northwest Semitic had presumably developed.

There is no reason to avoid translating, in the same way, this prepositional phrase in our orison too, the only difference being its fronted position in the clause: מאין כמוך יהוה גדול אתה וגדול שמך בגבורה, *"Because there is none like, O Yahweh, you are great, and your name is great."*[55] In other words, the passage clearly explains God's greatness: he is great, because there is no competition with other divine beings. If this interpretation is correct, then one is able to trace the shift from the monolatrous statements to a radicalized, monotheistic outlook already within the very phrasing of the incomparability formula as documented in our orison. The original proclamation is no longer a self-standing statement, but rather syntactically integrated into a broader context, in which it explicates God's greatness and his kingship, thus leading the audience to recognize that God is not only special but also singular.

The above conclusion stands in line with the presence of a few linguistic and stylistic elements, which hint that the time of composition of the orison is to be sought in the exilic period.[56] To be sure, the orison is very short and its language is standard and even stereotypical, so not much chronologically significant data can be extracted from it. Nonetheless, it is certainly noteworthy that the closest parallel to the *pendens* construction יהוה גדול אתה, "O Yahweh, you are great," is attested in Ezra's penitential prayer (Ezra 9:15), which is universally acknowledged as a piece that does not antedate the exilic period.[57] More conspicuous is the form מלכות "kingship" in v. 7, which is a particularly common item in the lexicon of late Biblical Hebrew (although it is sporadically found also in the corpus usually reflecting the classical language).[58]

Finally, it should be noted that the verb יאתה is the only occurrence of יאה in Biblical Hebrew, whereas it is quite common in Aramaic.[59] The clause כי לך [יאתה [המלוכה], "for [kingship] befits you",[60] can be contrasted to classical Biblical

---

55 Cf. Hoffman 2001: 1.297. Already Qimḥi has rightly noted that the sense of the entire phrase crucially depends on the preposition, although he conceptualized the issue in a different way compared to the interpretation presented above: ממה שאנו רואים ויודעים שאין כמוך לא בתחתונים ולא בעליונים ידענו כי גדול אתה וגדול שמך בגבורה, "Based on what we see and know, that there is none like you either on earth or in heaven, we acknowledge that 'you are great and your name is great'" (Cohen 2012: 69).
56 This observation pertains only to the particular textual configuration of Jer 10:6–7. It is not meant to suggest any timeframe for the broader liturgical tradition, from which the orison stems. Indeed, the indications for its internal development preclude any attempt to press this tradition into any fixed date.
57 See above, n. 7. For the genre of penitential prayer, see especially the various contributions in Boda, Falk and Werline 2006–8.
58 Hurvitz et al. 2014: 165–170; Hornkohl 2014: 318–325 §8.6.
59 Forms of יאה are employed in 𝔗 for rendering Hebrew יפה (Gen 29:17; 39:6; 1 Sam 16:12; Zech 9:17; cf. Jer 11:16; 46:20) and sometimes נוה (Jer 6:2; Ezek 34:14; cf. Isa 52:7). They are also attested in Qumran Aramaic (1QapGen 20:3–5, 7–8) and later dialects.
60 For the need to restore here the lacuna in the text of 𝔐 see above, §2.

Hebrew, which expresses a similar idea in a nominal clause, without resorting to any verb at all: כִּי לַיהוה המלוכה, "for dominion belongs to the Lord" (Ps 22:29; cf. Obad 21). Such a borrowing from Aramaic is best explained against the background of the exilic period, when Hebrew speakers came into particularly intense contact with Aramaic speakers, and borrowed from them numerous lexical items, grammatical forms, and syntactical constructions. If so, it stands to reason that the orison of Jer 10:6–7 does not antedate the exilic period.

By the same token, there is no linguistic reason to push the date of the orison to a much later period, such as the Hellenistic period.[61] This is again suggested by perusal of the distribution of יאה. After all, the Greco-Roman period is the historical background of Mishnaic Hebrew, which is richly documented in substantial corpora of texts. Nevertheless, it contains no evidence for productive use of יאה, indicating that this lexeme was evidently obsolete, in Hebrew, by the Hellenistic period.[62] Indeed, many linguistic innovations and Aramaic loans that typify late Biblical Hebrew did not manage to gain hold in Hebrew, and disappeared from later stages of Second Temple Hebrew.[63] If so, the most plausible diachronic conclusion is to date the orison to the Persian period.[64]

Be that as it may, the combination of theological motifs as found in the orison reflects an intriguing stage in the reception history of ancient liturgical formulae

---

61 So, for instance, Duhm 1901:100, who identifies the "wise ones of the nations" (v. 7) with Greek philosophers or sculptors, thus leading him to treat the orison as a very late interpolation ("ein ganz junger Zusatz").

62 *Ma'agarim*, the database of the Historical Dictionary of the Academy of Hebrew Language records only a single occurrence of יאה in Tannaitic Hebrew: יאה תבעו בנות צלפחד, "The daughters of Zelophehad have *rightly* made a claim" (Sifre Num §134). But even this occurrence is not textually secured, since it is attested only by MS Vatican, while all the other manuscripts testify to the alternative reading יפה (the Hebrew equivalent of Aramaic יאה); see the critical edition of Kahana 2011–15: 2.447. Moreover, the reading of MS Vatican may well be influenced by Onkelos's rendering of the Pentateuchal passage that is the subject of the entire homily: כֵּן בְּנוֹת צְלָפְחָד דֹּבְרֹת, "The daughters of Zelophehad *are right* in what they are saying" (Num 27:7), rendered into Aramaic as יאות בנת צלפחד ממללן, "The daughters of Zelophehad speak *rightly*." The linguistic resemblance between the Targum and the Midrash was noted by Kahana, *ibid.*, 4.1134 n. 1. In Amoraic Hebrew, however, the root יאה and its various derivatives are well-documented.

63 For an overview of such items, which set late Biblical Hebrew apart as a distinct chronolect in the history of Hebrew, see Talshir 1987.

64 Another indication, albeit an indirect and circumstantial one, might be gleaned from the fragmentary evidence of 4QJer[a]. Of Chapter 10, only vv. 9–14 are preserved there (col. V), so there is no direct testimony for vv. 6–7. However, calculation of the missing parts (especially at the bottom of col. IV and the top of col. V) suggests that the text of vv. 6–7 is required for filling the space reconstructed for the full height of the columns. If this is correct, then the orison had already been included in a scroll penned by the end of the third century BCE, well into the Hellenistic period.

and their adaptation to the religious thinking of later generations. At the same time, it also reflects an intermediate stage in the history of the liturgical tradition, in terms of the degree of sophistication of the literary design and the level of internal coherence of its constituents.

The liturgical nature of the orison had an effect on the subsequent history of its transmission. For instance, in v. 7, 𝔐 reads the phrase מלך הגוים "king of the nations."[65] But some of the manuscripts of 𝔖 and 𝔗 testify to an alternative phrase: "the king of all eternity": 𝔗 מלך כל עלמיא,[66] 𝔖 ܟܠܗܘܢ ܥܠܡܐ.[67] Previously, this change has been considered to result from a harmonization to the employment of the quantifiers in the continuation of the verse ("among *all* the wise ones of the nations and in *all* their kingdoms"), which took place within the Syriac tradition.[68] But this interpretation only refers to the additional "all" and it does not explain the change of from "nations" to "eternity". Furthermore, it does not give due consideration to the fact that the very same change is testified not only in 𝔖 manuscripts but also by witnesses of 𝔗.

The key for understanding this textual variance is found in the fact that identical phrases typify a liturgical register, which is well rooted in the Second Temple period. This is demonstrated by the peculiar divine epithets employed by the Patriarchs according to the *Genesis Apocryphon*:[69]

---

65 This reading also underlies a rabbinic homily in Midrash Psalms on Ps 93:1, זהו שאמר הכתוב מי לא יראך מלך הגוים – אמר לו הקב"ה לירמיה: אתה קורא אותי מלך הגוים, ומלכיהון דישראל לית אנא. אמר לו: לפי שאמרת לי נביא לגוים נתתיך, אף אני קורא לך מלך הגוים (ed. Buber 1891: 413), "Elsewhere, this is what Scripture says: 'Thou art great and They name is great in strength. Who would not fear Thee, O King of the nations?' (Jer. 10:6–7). The Holy One, blessed be He, asked Jeremiah: 'Thou callest Me King of the nations, but am I not King of Israel?' Jeremiah replied: Because Thou saidst to me, 'I have appointed thee a prophet to the nations' (Jer. 1:5), therefore I call Thee 'King of the nations' also." (Braude 1959: 2.124).
66 Sperber 1959: 160; Ribera-Florit 1992: 95–96.
67 Greenberg et al. 2013: 64; Walter 2006: 243–244. According to Walter's data, both readings ܥܠܡܐ ("eternity," as per MS 7a1) and ܥܡܡܐ ("nations," as per MS 9a1) are also attested in the original text of MS 8a1, prior to its correction (*ibid.*, 243). But it seems that there is a typo there, and one of the two occurrences of the *siglum* 8a1* should actually be corrected to 8a1ᶜ. Moreover, in my opinion, the reading of 9a1 (one of the most important witnesses of 𝔖) is not so clear in a digital image of the manuscript, and it can be deciphered as ܥܡܠܡܐ (sic!); this reading is apparently a mixed form, which reflects uncertainty on the part of the scribe with respect to the question which word should be written at this point.
68 Greenberg 2002: 37.
69 The Aramaic text and English translation are taken from Machiela 2009: 35, 52, 75. The connection between 𝔗 and the *Genesis Apocryphon* was recognized by Hayward 1987: 79 n. 5, who also noted the possible connection to the later employment of the biblical phrase מלך העולם, "eternal king," as a standard liturgical formula in rabbinic prayer. The phrases כל עולמים "all eternity" and מלך עולמים "eternal king" were recently discussed by Friedman 2014: 25–27, 43–56, respectively.

- Lamech: בְּמֶלֶךְ כּוֹל עָלְמִֿים, "by the King of all Ages" (1QapGen 2:7).
- Noah (?): לְמֶּלֶךְ בֹּוֹל עָלְמָֿיא לְעָלֵם וָלְעַד עַד כֹֿוֹל עָלְמִֿים, "to the King of all Ages forever and ever, unto all ages" (1QapGen 10:10).
- Abraham: בריך אנתה אל עליון מרי לכול עלמים די אנתה מרה ושליט על כולא ובכול מלכי ארעא אנתה שליט למעבד בכולהון דין, "Blessed are you Most High God, my Lord, for all ages; for you are Lord and Ruler over everything. You are sovereign over all the kings of the earth, having power to enact judgment on all of them" (1QapGen 20:12–13).

It is well-known that the discursive situation of liturgy follows the legal model of formal petition, presented to the sovereign by his subjects. Obviously, this is a typical formulation of liturgical utterances. The Aramaic and Syriac transmission of the orison thus witness the continued influence of the liturgical phraseology of Jewish (and perhaps also Judeo-Christian) prayers of the first centuries CE.[70]

§5 Function in context

The orison under discussion is a relatively late crystallization of a broader liturgical tradition, and it was integrated into the prophetic unit (Jer 1:1–16) at an advanced stage of its literary growth, as suggested by the fact that the orison is missing from the short text that is fragmentarily preserved in 4QJer[b] and underlying 𝔊. If so, one wonders: why was it interpolated in the first place? And what function does it play in its present place?

In its final form, as witnessed by 𝔐, the orison generally functions like the other hymnic passages that praise the Lord (vv. 10, 12–13), which accumulated by way of gradual accretion and interspersed between the satirical passages that mock idolatry (vv. 2–5, 8–9, 14–16). The two types of passages balance each other thematically and theologically, with the cumulative effect of delimiting sociological borders between the groups of "us" and "them," which are defined both ethnically (Israel vs. the nations) and theologically (believers in the Lord vs. worshippers of idols).[71] The satirical passages critique idol worshippers: they describe polemically how such idols are produced, and identify their worship by the nations as superstitious. By contrast, the hymnic passages laud the Lord as

---

70 For another telling case of contact between the language of Jewish liturgy and a formulation embedded in 𝔖, see Weitzman 2001.
71 For a theoretical outlook of the interconnection between the so-called icon parodies and social formation, cf. Levtow 2008: esp. 33–39, 80–85.

the creator of the universe as well as the God of Israel.[72] The orison highlights the universal dimension of God's rule of the world. In the broader context of the prophetic unit, such a theme contributes to the underscoring of the absurdity of idolatry: if the Lord is feared even by the sages of the nations, then there is really no point whatsoever in "the way of the nations" (v. 2) or "the customs of peoples" (v. 3), thus reaffirming the assertion that their religious worldview is false (v. 3).

It needs to be noted, however, that the interpretation of the orison as part of the overall polemic against idolatry is fully derived from its secondary interpolation into its present context, and it has no actual holding within the orison itself. The theological interest of the orison is in the image of God as a divine king, and it is against this background that it compares God to leaders of the nations – their kings and sages – whereas the contrast to foreign gods, and especially their material representation as idols, is not even hinted in any conceivable way.

It seems, therefore, that the general role of the orison in the prophetic unit as a whole, which is shared by the other hymnic passages, does not exhaust its literary functions. Indeed, in my view, each of the hymnic passages in the prophetic unit has its own distinct features, and they cannot be treated as a single or a unified stratum.[73] By the same token, since the particular realization of the liturgical tradition in vv. 6–7 is different in some essential respects from its formation in parallel passages, it is difficult to argue that all the passages discussed above (§2) represent a well-defined layer. I prefer to consider the orison in vv. 6–7 as a specific realization (integral and complete as a literary piece in itself) of a liturgical tradition that has old roots, even if it is also manifested in late and secondary passages, as it often surfaces in places where scribes felt the need to balance or correct the theological message of the text they inherited and

---

72 This is true, to some extent, not only with respect to the long text of 𝔐 but also to the short text of 𝔊. Even though two of the three hymnic passages are missing from the latter text (i.e., vv. 6–7, 10), it does contain vv. 12–13, which praise the Lord as the creator of the world and ruler of the natural elements. Apparently, the urge to balance the satirical passages (which target the idols) with hymnic passages (which praise the Lord) was operative for quite a while along the textual and compositional history of the prophetic unit. The hymnic passages were not added as a group at a single point in time; rather, they were gradually integrated into an ever-growing text.
73 The original independence of the orison in vv. 6–7 vis-à-vis the other hymnic passages also explains the stark difference in the relative (un)importance of the wisdom motif. In the orison, it plays a very minor role, as indicated by the fact that it is mentioned only once (rather than twice, as found in more prominently marked motifs), as part of the more encompassing motif of portraying God as a royal sovereign (cf. above, n. 17). In contradistinction, the hymnic passage of vv. 12–13 (especially in v. 12) accords much importance to the notion of wisdom, as it is presented as God's most distinctive and unique characteristic.

transmitted, but preferred to do so by patching an existing, perhaps even well-established tradition.

I propose that the orison indeed has an additional, very specific function within its immediate context. In its present place, following v. 5b, it highlights the contrast between the image of the incomparable divine sovereign and the useless idols described beforehand:

אל תיראו מהם	(a)	Do not be afraid of them,
כי לא ירעו	(b)	for they cannot do evil,
וגם היטיב אין אותם	(c)	nor is it in them to do good.

The rhetorical layout of this passage conveys an expressly negative attitude of the speaker toward the idols. It consists of three negated clauses, each of which employs a different negative particle: (a) אַל, (b) לֹא, (c) אֵין. Saying "no" in three different ways is a powerful stylistic device that cannot but underscore a complete denial of any power from the idols.

The passage further foregrounds the logic of the prohibition by a wordplay between the two verbal phrases: (a) אל תיראו and (b) לא ירעו, making effective use of repeating sonorant (/l, r/) and guttural (/ʕ, ʔ/) consonants. Adding the orison in vv. 6–7 amplified this wordplay by echoing the categorical proscription אַל תיראו מהם, "*do not be afraid* from them", in the rhetorical question מי לא יראך מלך הגוים, "who *would not fear* you, O king of the nations?" which, as indicated above (§2), is the heart of the orison both formally and theologically.[74] Seen in this light, readers proceed to identify a contrast between the polemical argument that the idols can do nothing (expressed meristically in v. 5b: כי לא ירעו / וגם היטיב אין אותם, "for they cannot do evil, nor is it in them to do good") and God's omnipotence (v. 6: גדול אתה / וגדול שמך בגבורה, "you are great, and your name is great in might").

---

74 For this reason, I find unconvincing the conjectural emendation of the verb יִרָאֲךָ (from ירא, "to fear") to יְרָאֲךָ (from ראה, "to see, acknowledge"), as suggested by Ehrlich 1912: 270. The verbal point of contact between v. 5b and v. 7, namely, the verb ירא "to fear," has been noted by some commentators, e.g., Lundbom 1999–2004: 1.588 (on v. 7). But it was best illuminated by Qimḥi: אמר 'מי לא יראך' לפי שאמר 'אל תיראו מהם'. אמר: אותם – אין ראוי לירא מהם, אבל אתה – 'מי לא יראך'. אפילו הגוים שעובדים האלילים ראוי להם שייראוך, כי אתה מלך עליהם (ed. Cohen 2012: 69), "He said 'who would not fear you' because he had said 'do not be afraid from them.' Even the nations who worship idols should fear you, because you reign them".

§6 Conclusion

Analysis of the literary features of the orison found in Jer 10:6–7 indicates that this is a coherent and complete piece, suggesting that it had originally existed as an independent literary unit prior to its integration into its present place. As demonstrated above, it is also part of a broader liturgical tradition, which has influenced other biblical passages. In most cases, these are passages that were secondarily interpolated, but they too evince a development in the degree of literary design. For this reason, it is difficult to take them as representing a unified redactional stratum, and they are better accounted for as different manifestations of a long-lived tradition, which was constantly reconfigured by its tradents, and specifically adapted to its various contexts whenever it was felt necessary to evoke it. At the heart of this tradition stands the liturgical formula אין כמוך, "there is none like you," lauding the notion of the incomparability of the God of Israel. While originally compatible with a monolatrous conception of the divinity, it has been adapted to express a different, albeit related concept, namely, a monotheistic outlook. The literary configuration of the orison under scrutiny belongs to an intermediate stage in the process of crystallization of this tradition, so that even though the monolatrous proclamation had already been reinterpreted in it through a monotheistic perspective, the orison is still clinging to traditional modes of expression. At the same time, the language of the orison betrays several markers of post-classical Hebrew, thus allowing one to date it to the exilic or Persian period.

Synthesis and conclusions

> To see a world in a grain of sand
> And a heaven in a wild flower
> Hold infinity in the palm of your hand
> And eternity in an hour
> (William Blake, "Auguries of Innocence," 1803)

The prophecy contained in Jer 10:1–16 is extant in two main textual formations – as attested in the Masoretic text ($\mathfrak{M}$) and its congeners on the one hand, and in the Septuagint version ($\mathfrak{G}$) supported by the fragmentary evidence of 4QJer[b], on the other. When mapped against the form-critical distinction between the satirical (S) and hymnic (H) strands, alongside the Aramaic (A) passage, these formations can be compared as follows:

$\mathfrak{M}$	$\mathfrak{G}$
	Superscription (v. 1)
S_1 (vv. 2–5)	$S_1 + S_2$ (vv. 2–5a→9→5b)
H_1 (vv. 6–7)	—
S_2 (vv. 8–9)	↑
H_2 (v. 10)	—
A (v. 11)	A (v. 11)
H_3 (vv. 12–13)	H (v. 12–13)
S_3 (vv. 14–16)	S_3 (vv. 14–16)

As this comparison clarifies, some of the satirical passages are differently arranged in the two versions: they are separated in $\mathfrak{M}$ (S_1, S_2, S_3) but partly combined in $\mathfrak{G}$ (S_1+S_2, S_3). Furthermore, a stark difference exists between the two versions concerning the number of hymnic passages: $\mathfrak{M}$ has three of them (H_1, H_2, H_3), while $\mathfrak{G}$ has only one (H_3). These differences are best explained as testifying to different stages in the compositional history of the prophecy. However, in my opinion, they cannot be construed as *successive* stages. Rather, they witness two disparate constellations, randomly located along the hypothetical continuum of literary, textual, and linguistic progression, whose compositional trajectory is that of expansion by way of accretion. Put differently, the process of compositional growth can be described as a chain of supplementations, or *Fortschreibung*, at each stage of which a new piece of distinct literary character was integrated into the prophetic unit. If this reconstruction is dependable, it sets an improved model

DOI 10.1515/9783110530162-007

for the compositional history of Jeremiah, considering a broader range of factors than previously acknowledged.

The reconstructed chain of developments discernible in the specific case study of Jer 10:1–16 can be divided schematically into several stages. First, the satirical strand was formed by quoting an existing literary source (vv. 3b–5a→9) and reframing it with polemical statements (vv. 2–3a + 5b→14–16). Second, this formation was soon amplified by breaking the quotation into two fragments and expanding the rhetorical framework so that it would cover both fragments of the cultic source, thus leading to a reshuffle of the earlier formation and the addition of v. 8 (i.e., the change of $S_1+S_2→S_3$ to $S_1→S_2→S_3$). Third, the hymnic passage of vv. 12–13 (H_3) was added later on, in order to balance the negative reproach of idolatry with a positive description of YHWH. Fourth, the Aramaic passage (A), probably quoted from a piece of imperial propaganda, was interpolated, thus matching the formation of the prophecy with the textual constellation represented in 𝕊. But the prophetic unit continued to develop further on, even though the next intermediate stages are not documented independently in the surviving textual evidence. Fifth, the hymnic passage of v. 10 (H_2) was added and textually adapted. Sixth, the orison contained in vv. 6–7 (H_1) was supplemented, supplying the last brick for the construction 𝔐 presents. Moreover, the textual witnesses (primarily the Aramaic ones) attest to even later changes, and the text had a thriving afterlife in apocryphal literature (as demonstrated especially by the *Epistle of Jeremiah*). Notably, not only the ever-changing textual constellations but also the individual segments added at each stage are distinctive literary pieces, produced by their own unique histories; as such, they too are legitimate objects of literary-historical inquiry.

The core of the prophecy comprises of the satirical passages (vv. 2–5, 8–9, 14–16, analyzed in Chapter 1). It may be treated as an original 'document'; i.e., a coherent text that served as basis for all subsequent developments. Significantly, this satirical presentation of idolatry is closer to prose than to poetry, which is a feature that would often be interpreted as indicating a relatively late stage in the formation of Jeremiah. However, it is couched in phraseology typical of the Book of Jeremiah, and there is no essential difference between this prophecy and other literary material compiled in the Book of Jeremiah. Theoretically, the original prophecy could be stemming from the Jeremianic corpus. However, since the book named after this prophet exhibits such a bewildering mixture of original prophecies, intrusive redaction, and excessive reworking, it is unfeasible to differentiate systematically between the prophet's *ipsissima verba* and later adaptations and redactional supplementations – especially, but not exclusively, by Deuteronomistic scribes. Moreover, even the earliest recoverable formation of our prophecy was evidently submitted to modifications of various sorts, including structural reshaping. Thus, the question of authorship of this segment of the text, and of the authorial responsibility for subsequent changes, cannot be given a definitive answer. At any rate, though, the satirical passages comprise the earliest stratum of the prophetic unit under scrutiny.

It must be underscored that even at this initial stage of the prophecy, the text was not an indivisible unity, by any means. On the contrary, the prophecy appears to be part and parcel of an intertextual discourse with other traditions available to the author. Most importantly, the entire prophecy can be read as a polemical treatment of a citation from another literary work of a cultic nature, which depicted the process of manufacturing cult images. The passage quoted admits the inability of such statues to move by their own will (in a manner comparable to statements embedded in an incantation accompanying the Mesopotamian ritual of *mīs pî*). This statement captured the polemicist's attention; he focused on this passage and reframed it with his own rhetorical announcements, insisting emphatically that such cult images are nothing but inanimate idols that cannot perform any action at all, leading to the inescapable conclusion that their worship is a manifestation of human stupidity. The intertextual essence of this prophecy reminds us that no text is an island; it partakes in a multifaceted matrix of cultural negotiation, which renders unrealistic any attempt to recover an 'original text.' Any stage of the compositional process is 'original' in the sense that it presents a textual formation that existed neither previously nor afterward – a formation that is the function of a specific constellation of cultural factors, unique to a particular point in history (even if its exact location along the temporal axis can no longer be fixed in absolute terms).

At a very early stage, the satirical presentation of idolatry was supplemented with a short hymnic passage (vv. 12–13, discussed in Chapter 2), which supplied a positive counterpart for the condemned idols; namely, an image of YHWH the Creator, the real source and the only keeper of all life and fertility. Apparently, this supplementation was motivated by factors internal to the prophetic text (the reference to God as "the creator of everything" in v. 16, which forms the original conclusion of the prophecy) or inherent to the rhetorical matrix of Jeremiah's prophecy at large (as demonstrated by Jer 14:22). Nevertheless, this development set a precedent for future supplementations, by establishing a compositional trajectory of accretion of hymnic passages. This expansive mode continued to be operative in subsequent stages of the literary development of the prophecy.

As in the former stage, the added text cannot be regarded as an 'original,' unanalyzable unity. Close inspection reveals that the hymnic passage is the product of an earlier chain of cultural exchange, manifested as a literary amalgamation of two distinct traditions, representing different genres and social settings. A proverbial saying rooted in wisdom literature was amplified by a fragment from a psalm (perhaps a thanksgiving psalm, possibly designed to mark the end of a drought). These constituents, both separately and in their combined form, were altered several times along their history, with such alterations leaving their traces both in direct textual witnesses and in other biblical and apocryphal texts (Ps 135, the *Epistle of Jeremiah*, and the *Hymn to the Creator*). This analysis illustrates the broad scope of the intellectual and creative resources which prophetic literature in general and Jeremiah's prophecies (or at least prophecies ascribed to Jeremiah) in particular have drawn from along their compositional history.

By the mid-fifth century BCE, Judeans and people of Judean descent were subjects of the Achaemenid Empire. Linguistic, literary, and historical considerations suggest that the imperial propaganda of that period is the most likely source for the Aramaic quotation incorporated into the prophecy as v. 11 (discussed in Chapter 3). While this supplementation was mainly motivated by theological concerns – namely, the wish to recruit a 'self-incriminating' admittance on the part of idol-worshippers that their idols are no gods – this segment also introduced into the prophecy a new element that had a decisive effect on subsequent developments: a language shift that was eventually taken as a marker of ethnic identity and cultural distinction vis-à-vis other ethnic groups. This element recolored existing references to "the nations," reconfiguring this notion as part of an ongoing struggle for cultural and religious dissimilation in an imperial, multinational context.

This new ideological trajectory was reinforced by the textual adaptation of an additional hymnic passage, v. 10 (studied in Chapter 4). While the language of this text suggests that it is a product of the early exilic period, it was apparently supplemented to the prophecy at a later stage, serving as a reaction to the inclusion of v. 11. It appears that this psalmic fragment originally glorified YHWH for his control of the natural elements, thus supplying a positive response to the negative proclamation of v. 11, that gods lacking the power of creation will be destroyed. But a seemingly slight yet crucial change of a single word in v. 10 transformed the text into an exultation of God's sovereignty over the nations. Thus, the text was adapted to the growing need of communities in the exilic period to strengthen their hold against assimilatory pressures practiced by gentiles surrounding them.

The new cultural and political sensitivities came to fruition later in the exilic period, when a complete liturgical piece was interpolated into the prophecy as vv. 6–7 (explored in Chapter 5). This poem evidently stems from a rich theological and literary tradition that underscores God's incomparability to any other entity or deity in the world. At the same time, this particular orison represents a ripe stage in the crystallization of this tradition in terms of both stylistic sophistication and religious thinking. While other components of the prophecy emphasized

God's power and distinctiveness in a variety of forms, this final supplementation adds to the conglomerate a monotheistic view.

The five chapters of this investigation deal with a variety of literary materials, ranging from the hypothetical, narrative-like cultic source underlying the satirical passages to different stages of Hebrew religious poetry as represented by the hymnic passages, passing through imperial propaganda and inner-Judean communication, seasoned with bits and pieces of psalmic and wisdom literature. Therefore, this composite specimen of prophetic discourse may serve as a portal to a surprisingly rich reservoir of cultural heritage, accumulated along many generations of Hebrew creativity. In conjunction, the critical unfolding of this cultural diversity is also the story of theological and ideological evolution. What began as a rhetorical attack of local cults has gradually crystallized into a monotheistic creed, shaping along the way an innovative and flexible model of group identity. As the transmission and reception of the prophecy demonstrate, this model proved to be remarkably helpful and productive for subsequent generations, among a variety of faith communities that transmitted this text while constantly adapting it to new challenges. In this respect, Jer 10:1–16 provides an illustrative example of how the compositional development of a prophetic text, its textual transmission, and its interpretive reception all converge into an ever-flowing stream of tradition, nourishing the spiritual needs of varying communities of readers throughout history.

Bibliography

Ackroyd, Peter R., 1963. "Jeremiah X.1–16," *JTS* 14/2: 385–390.

Adams, Sean A., 2014. *Baruch and the Epistle of Jeremiah: A Commentary Based on the Texts of Codex Vaticanus* (Septuagint Commentary Series), Leiden: Brill.

Adcock, J. Seth, 2017. *"Oh God of Battles! Steal My Soldiers' Hearts!" A Study of the Hebrew and Greek Text Forms of Jeremiah 10:1–18* (Contributions to Biblical Exegesis & Theology 83), Leuven: Peeters.

Aejmelaeus, Anneli, 1990. "ὅτι *recitativum* in Septuagintal Greek," in *Studien zur Septuaginta: Robert Hanhart zu Ehren*, ed. Detlef Fraenkel, Udo Quast, and John William Wevers, Göttingen: 74–82.

— 1993. *On the Trail of Septuagint Translators: Collected Essays*, Kampen: Kok Pharos.

Al-Jallad, Ahmad, 2016. "New Evidence from a Safaitic Inscription for a Late Velar/Uvular Realization of *ś in Aramaic," *Semitica* 58: 257–270.

Althann, Robert, 1989. "The Inverse Construct Chain and Jer 10:13, 51:16," *JNSL* 15: 7–13.

Amara, Dalia, 2015. "Bel and the Dragon: The Relationship between Theodotion and the Old Greek," in *From Author to Copyist: Essays on the Composition, Redaction, and Transmission of the Hebrew Bible in Honor of Zipi Talshir*, ed. Cana Werman, Winona Lake: Eisenbrauns, 125–147.

Amir, Joshua, 1997. "'The God of ʿōlām is YHWH' (Isa 40:28)," *Beit Mikra* 42/2 [149]: 97–103 (Heb.).

Ammann, Sonja, 2015. *Götter für die Toren: Die Verbindung von Götterpolemik und Weisheit im Alten Testament* (BZAW 466), Berlin: de Gruyter.

Amphoux, Christian-Bernard / Aussedat, Mathilde / Sérandour, Arnaud, 2009. "Jr 10,1–10: Les enjeux des deux formes," in *La Septante en Allemagne et en France: textes de la Septante à traduction double ou à traduction très littérale – Septuaginta Deutsch und Bible d'Alexandrie: Texte der Septuaginta in Doppelüberlieferung oder in wörtlicher Übersetzung* (OBO 238), ed. Wolfgang Kraus and Olivier Munnich, Fribourg: Academic Press / Göttingen: Vandenhoeck & Ruprecht, 193–203.

Andrew, M.E., 1982. "The Authorship of Jer 10:1–16," *ZAW* 94/1: 128–130.

Andrews, D.K., 1964. "Yahweh the God of the Heavens," in *The Seed of Wisdom: Essays in Honour of T.J. Meek*, ed. W.S. McCullough, Toronto: University of Toronto Press, 45–57.

Avishur, Yitzhak, 1993. "The Reversed Construct Structure in the Bible, Qumran Scrolls and in Early Jewish Literature", *Leš* 57/4: 279–288 (Heb.).

Ayali-Darshan, Noga, 2005. "The Prayers for 'Fear of God' in Biblical Literature (1 Kgs 8:56–61; Ps 86:1–13; Ps 119; 1 Chr 29:10–19) and the Neo-Babylonian Inscriptions (Nbk. 15; Nbn. 4; Nbn. 5)," *Tarbiz* 74/3: 321–369 (Heb.).

— 2014. "The Question of the Order of Job 26,7–13 and the Cosmogonic Tradition of Zaphon," *ZAW* 126/3: 402–417.

Bar-Asher, Moshe, 2000. "A Few Remarks on Mishnaic Hebrew and Aramaic in Qumran Hebrew," in *Diggers at the Well* (STDJ 36), ed. Takamitsu Muraoka and John F. Elwolde, Leiden: Brill, 12–19.

Barr, James, 1968. *Comparative Philology and the Text of the Old Testament*, Oxford: Clarendon (²Winona Lake: Eisenbrauns, 1987).

— 1989. "'Determination' and the Definite Article in Biblical Hebrew," *JSS* 34/2: 307–335.

Barstad, Hans M., 1978. "*HBL* als Bezeichnung der fremden Götter im Alten Testament und der Gott Hubal," *Studia Theologica* 32/1: 57–65.

DOI 10.1515/9783110530162-008

Barth, Jakob, 1902. *Wurzeluntersuchungen zum hebräischen und aramäischen Lexicon*, Leipzig: Hinrichs.

Barthélemy, Dominique, 1986. *Critique textuelle de l'Ancien Testament*, 2. *Isaie, Jérémie, Lamentations* (OBO 50/2), Fribourg: Editions universitaires.

Baruchi-Unna, Amitai, 2012. "Genres Meet: Esarhaddon's Akkadian Prayers from the 'Washing of the Mouth' Ritual," *Shnaton* 21: 153–173 (Heb.).

— 2017. "Esarhaddon's Prayer in the Inscription AsBbA as Related to the *mīs pî* Ritual," *JCS* 69 (2017), pp. 203–212.

Bauer, Hans / Leander, Pontus, 1927. *Grammatik des Biblisch-Aramäischen*, Halle: Niemeyer.

Baumgartner, Walter, 1927. "Das Aramäische im Buch Daniel," *ZAW* 45 [N.F. 4]: 81–133.

Beck, Pirhiya, 1982. "The Drawings from Horvat Teiman (Kuntillet 'Ajrud)," *Tel Aviv* 9/1: 3–68.

Becking, Bob, 1993. "Does Jeremiah X 3 refer to a Canaanite Deity called Hubal?," *VT* 43/4: 555–557.

— 1999. "Hubal," in *Dictionary of Deities and Demons in the Bible*,[2] ed. Karel van der Toorn, Bob Becking and Pieter W. van der Horst, Leiden: Brill / Grand Rapids, Mich.: Eerdmans, 430.

— 2014. "Coping with Drought and Famine in Some Post-Exilic Texts," in *Thinking of Water in the Early Second Temple Period* (BZAW 461), ed. Ehud Ben Zvi and Christoph Levin, Berlin: de Gruyter, 229–255.

Beentjes, Pancratius Cornelis, 1982. "Inverted Quotations in the Bible: A Neglected Stylistic Pattern," *Biblica* 63/4: 506–523.

Ben-Dov, Jonathan, 2000. "A Textual Problem and its Form-Critical Solution: Jeremiah 10:1–16," *Textus* 20: 97–128.

— 2005. "Treasures of Light," in *On the Border Line: Textual Meets Literary Criticism* (Beer-Sheva 18), ed. Zipora Talshir and Dalia Amara, Beer-Sheva: Ben-Gurion University of the Negev Press, 155–162 (Heb.).

Berlejung, Angelika, 1998. *Die Theologie der Bilder: Herstellung und Einweihung von Kultbildern in Mesopotamien und die alttestamentliche Bilderpolemik* (OBO 162), Freiburg, Schweiz: Universitätsverlag.

Bickerman, Elias J., 1946. "The Edict of Cyrus in Ezra 1," *JBL* 65/3: 249–275.

Block, Daniel I., 1988. *The Gods of the Nations: Studies in Ancient Near Eastern National Theology*, Jackson, Miss.: Evangelical Theological Society.

Boda, Mark J. / Falk, Daniel K. / Werline Rodney A., 2006–8. *Seeking the Favor of God* (3 vols.), Atlanta: Society of Biblical Literature.

Bodel, John / Olyan, Saul M. (eds.), 2008. *Household and Family Religion in Antiquity*, Malden, Mass.: Blackwell.

Bogaert, Pierre-Maurice, 1981. "Les mécanismes rédactionnels en Jér 10,1–16 (LXX et TM) et la signification des suppléments," in *Le Livre de Jérémie: Le prophète et son milieu, les oracles et leur transmission* (BETL 54), ed. Pierre-Maurice Bogaert, Leuven: Peeters, 222–238 (²1997, with addendum on pp. 433–434).

— 2013. "De la *vetus latina* a l'hébreu pré-massorétique en passant par la plus ancienne Septante: le livre de Jérémie, exemple privilégié," in *Revue théologique de Louvain* 44: 216–243.

Borger, Rykle 2005. "Textkritisches zu 'Mundwaschung' zu Walker & Dick, *Induction*", *Bibliotheca Orientalis* 62/5–6: 395–409.

Braude, William G., 1959. *The Midrash on Psalms* (Yale Judaica Series 13; 2 vols.), New Haven: Yale University Press.

Brettler, Marc Zvi, 1989. *God is King: Understanding an Israelite Metaphor* (JSOT Supp. 76), Sheffield: JSOT Press.

Briant, Pierre, 2002. *From Cyrus to Alexander: A History of the Persian Empire*, tr. Peter T. Daniels, Winona Lake: Eisenbrauns.

Bright, John, 1965. *Jeremiah* (AB), Garden City: Doubleday.

Brin, Gershon, 1997. "YHWH is the God of ʿolām," *Beit Mikra* 42/3 [150]: 286–287 (Heb.).

Brooke, Alan E. / McLean, Norman / Thackeray, Henry St. John, 1927. *The Old Testament in Greek*, 2: *The Later Historical Books*, Pt. 1: *I and II Samuel*, Cambridge: University Press.

Buber, Solomon, 1891. *Midrasch Tehillim (Schocher Tob)*, Vilnius: Witwe und Brüder Romm.

Carmignac, Jean, 1970. "Le texte de Jérémie 10,13 (ou 51,16) et celui de 2 Samuel 23,7 améliorés par Qumrân," *RdQ* 7/2 [26]: 287–290.

Carroll, Robert P., 1986. *Jeremiah: A Commentary* (OTL), London: SCM.

Cassuto, Umberto, 1971. *The Goddess Anath: Canaanite Epics of the Patriarchal Age*, tr. Israel Abrahams, Jerusalem: Magnes (originally published in Hebrew, 1951).

— 1973. "On the Formal and Stylistic Relationship between Deutero-Isaiah and Other Biblical Writers," in idem, *Biblical and Oriental Studies*, 1: *Bible*, tr. Israel Abrahams, Jerusalem: Magnes, 141–177 (originally published in Italian, 1911–13).

Cathcart, Kevin, J. / Gordon, Robert P., 1989. The *Targum of the Minor Prophets* (The Aramaic Bible), Wilmington, Del.: Michael Glazier.

Ceriani, Antonio Maria, 1874. *Monumenta sacra et profana ex codicibus praesertim bibliothecae Ambrosianae*, 7: *Codex Syro-Hexaplaris Ambrosianus*, Milan.

— 1876–81. *Translatio Syra Pescitto Veteris Testamenti ex codice Ambrosiano sec. fere VI* (2 vols.), Milan.

Chazon, Esther G., 2000. "Liturgical Communion with the Angels at Qumran," in *Sapiential, Liturgical and Poetical Texts from Qumran: Published in Memory of Maurice Baillet* (STDJ 35), ed. Daniel K. Falk, Florentino García Martínez, and Eileen M. Schuller, Leiden: Brill, 95–105.

— 2003. "The Use of the Bible as a Key to Meaning in Psalms from Qumran," in *Emanuel: Studies in Hebrew Bible, Septuagint and Dead Sea Scrolls in Honor of Emanuel Tov*, ed. Shalom M. Paul, Robert A. Kraft, Lawrence H. Schiffman and Weston W. Fields (*VT* Supp. 94), Leiden: Brill, 85–96.

Churgin, Pinkhos, 1927. *Targum Jonathan to the Prophets* (YOS 14), New Haven: Yale University Press (the book bears the wrong date of 1907; repr. New York: Ktav, 1983).

Cloete, Walter Theophilus Woldemar, 1989. *Versification and Syntax in Jeremiah 2–25: Syntactical Constraints in Hebrew Colometry* (SBL.DS 117), Atlanta: Scholars.

Clendenen, E. Ray, 1987. "Discourse strategies in Jeremiah 10:1–16," *JBL* 106/3: 401–408.

Cogan, Morton (Mordechai), 1974. *Imperialism and Religion: Assyria, Judah, and Israel in the Eighth and Seventh Centuries B.C.E.* (SBL.MS 19), Missoula, Mont.: Scholars.

Cohen, Menachem (ed.), 2012. *Mikra'ot Gedolot 'HaKeter': Jeremiah*, Ramat-Gan: Bar-Ilan University Press (Heb.).

Cohen, Yoram, 2013. *Wisdom from the Late Bronze Age* (WAW 34), Atlanta: Society of Biblical Literature.

Cohen, Sol / Hurowitz, Victor Avigdor, 1999. "חקות העמים הבל הוא (Jer 10:3) in Light of Akkadian *parṣu* and *zaqīqu* Referring to Cult Statues," *JQR* 89/3–4: 277–290.

Crenshaw, James L., 1969. "YHWH Ṣᵉba'ôt Šᵉmô: A Form-Critical Analysis," *ZAW* 81/2: 156–175.

— 1975. *Hymnic Affirmation of Divine Justice: The Doxologies of Amos and Related Texts in the Old Testament* (SBL.DS 24), Missoula, Mont.: Scholars.

Crüsemann, Frank, 1969. *Studien zur Formgeschichte von Hymnus und Danklied in Israel* (WMANT 32), Neukirchen-Vluyn: Neukirchener Verlag.

Dahood, Mitchell, 1975. "The Emphatic Double Negative *m'yn* in Jer 10:6–7", *CBQ* 37/4: 458–459.

Dalman, Gustaf, 1905. *Grammatik des jüdisch-palästinischen Aramäisch*,[2] Leipzig: Hinrichs.

Davidson, Robert, 1973–74. "Jeremiah X 1–16," *Glasgow University Oriental Society: Transactions* 25: 41–58.

Deist, Ferdinand, 1973. "Zu כתמר מקשה in Jer 10:5," *ZAW* 85/2: 225–226.

Dick, Michael B., 1999. "Prophetic Parodies of Making the Cult Image," in *Born in Heaven, Made on Earth: The Making of the Cult Image in the Ancient Near East*, ed. Michael B. Dick, Winona Lake: Eisenbrauns, 1–53.

Dimant, Devorah, 2001. *Qumran Cave 4, XXI: Parabiblical Texts, Part 4: Pseudo-Prophetic Texts* (DJD 30), Oxford: Clarendon.

— 2013. "From the Book of Jeremiah to the Qumranic *Apocryphon of Jeremiah*," *DSD* 20/3: 452–471.

Dirksen, Piet B., 1988. "The Old Testament Peshitta," in *Mikra: Text, Translation, Reading, and Interpretation of the Hebrew Bible in Ancient Judaism and Early Christianity* (CRINT 2/1), ed. Martin Jan Mulder, Assen: Van Corcum, 255–297.

— 1989. *An Annotated Bibliography of the Peshitta Old Testament* (MPIL 5), Leiden: Brill.

Dobbs-Allsopp, Frederick William, 2015. *On Biblical Poetry*, New York: Oxford University Press.

Doering, Lutz, 2005. "Jeremiah and the 'Diaspora Letters' in Ancient Judaism: Epistolary Communication with the *Golah* as Medium for Dealing with the Present," in *Reading the Present in the Qumran Library*, ed. Kristin De Troyer and Armin Lange, Atlanta: Society of Biblical literature, 43–72.

— 2012. *Ancient Jewish Letters and the Beginnings of Christian Epistolography* (WUNT 298), Tübingen: Mohr Siebeck.

Driver, Samuel Rolles, 1885. "Grammatical Notes," *Hebraica* 2/1: 33–38.

— 1906. *The Book of the Prophet Jeremiah*, London: Hodder and Stoughton.

— 1913. *An Introduction to the Literature of the Old Testament*,[9] Edinburgh: T. & T. Clark.

Driver, Godfrey Rolles, 1938. "Linguistic and Textual Problems: Jeremiah," *JQR* 28/2: 97–129.

Duhm, Bernhard, 1901. *Das Buch Jeremia* (Kurzer Handkommentar zum Alten Testament), Tübingen: Mohr Siebeck.

Ehrlich, Arnold B., 1901. *Mikrâ ki-Pheschutô*, 3: *Die Propheten*, Berlin: Poppelauer (Heb.).

— 1912. *Randglossen zur hebräischen Bibel: Textkritisches, sparchliches und sachliches*, 4: *Jesaia, Jeremia*, Leipzig: Hinrichs.

Eichler, Raanan, 2017. "Jeremiah and the Assyrian Sacred Tree," *VT* 67: 1–11.

Enelow, Hyman Gerson, 1933. *The Mishnah of Rabbi Eliezer, or, The Midrash of Thirty-Two Hermeneutic Rules*, New York: Bloch.

Eph'al, Israel, 1986–89. "Isa 40:19–20: On the Linguistic and Cultural Background of Deutero-Isaiah," *Shnaton* 10: 31–35 (Heb.).

Epstein, Isidore (ed.), 1935. *The Babylonian Talmud* (26 vols.), London: Soncino.

Epstein, Jacob Nachum / Melammed, Ezra Zion, 1955. *Mekhilta D'Rabbi Šim'on b. Jochai*, Jerusalem: Meqiṣê Nirdamim (Heb.).

van den Eynde, Ceslas, 1972. *Commentaire d'Išo'dad de Merv sur l'Ancien Testament, V: Jérémie, Ézéchiel, Daniel* (2 vols.; Corpus Scriptorum Christianorum Orientalium 328–329; Scriptores Syri 146–147) Louvain.

Farber, Walter, 2003. "Singing an *eršemma* for the Damaged Statue of a God," *ZA* 93: 208–213.

Field, Frederick, 1871–75. *Origenis Hexaplorum quae supersunt* (2 vols.), Oxford: Clarendon.

Finsterbusch, Karin, 2013. "Gegen die Furcht vor den Göttern der Welt: Eine Art »Psalm« Jeremias für Israel in MT-Jer 10,1–16," in *Ich will dir danken unter den Völkern: Studien zur israelitischen und altorientalischen Gebetsliteratur – Festschrift für Bernd Janowski zum 70. Geburtstag*, ed. Alexandra Grund, Annette Krüger and Florian Lippke, Gütersloh: Gütersloher Verlagshaus, 356–372.

Fischer, Georg, 2005. *Jeremia* (Herders Theologischer Kommentar zum Alten Testament; 2 vols.), Freiburg: Herder.

Fleischer, Ezra, 1977. "Remarks Concerning the Metric System of Ancient Hebrew Liturgic Poetry," *HaSifrut* 7/24: 70–83 (Heb.).

Flesher, Paul V.M. / Chilton, Bruce, 2011. *The Targums: A Critical Introduction* (Studies in the Aramaic interpretation of Scripture 12), Leiden: Brill.

Flynn, Shawn W., 2012. *YHWH is King: The Development of Divine Kingship in Ancient Israel* (*VT* Supp. 159), Leiden: Brill.

Folmer, Margaretha L., 1995. *The Aramaic Language in the Achaemenid Period: A Study in Linguistic Variation* (OLA 68), Leuven: Peeters.

Frankl, Pinkus Fritz, 1872. "Studien über die Septuaginta und Peschito zu Jeremia," *MGWJ* 21 [N.F. 4], Heft 10: 444–456; Heft 11: 497–509; Heft 12: 545–557.

Freedman, Harry / Simon, Maurice (eds.), 1939. *Midrash Rabbah* (10 vols.), London: Soncino.

Freud, Sigmund, 1939. *Moses and Monotheism*, tr. Katherine Jones, Letchworth: Hogarth.

Friedman, Shamma, 2014. *Studies in the Language and Terminology of Talmudic Literature*, Jerusalem: Academy of Hebrew Language (Heb.).

Gabbay, Uri, 2015. "Ancient Mesopotamian Cultic Whispering into the Ears," in *Marbeh Ḥokmah: Studies in the Bible and the Ancient Near East in Loving Memory of Victor Avigdor Hurowitz*, ed. Shamir Yona, Edward L. Greenstein, Maier I. Gruber, Peter Machinist, and Shalom M. Paul, Winona Lake: Eisenbrauns, 185–220.

Giesebrecht, Friedrich, 1894. Das Buch Jeremia (Handkommentar zum Alten Testament), Göttingen: Vandenhoeck & Ruprecht (²1907).

Glanz, Oliver. 2013. *Understanding Participant-Reference Shifts in the Book of Jeremiah: A Study of Exegetical Method and Its Consequences for the Interpretation of Referential Incoherence* (Studia Semitica Neerlandica 60), Leiden: Brill.

Glassner, Jean-Jacques, 2004. *Mesopotamian Chronicles* (WAW 19), Atlanta: Society of Biblical Literature.

Goldingay, John, 2006–8. *Psalms* (3 vols.), Grand Rapids, Mich.: Baker.

Goldstein, Ronnie. 2005a. "From Gods to Idols: Changes in Attitude towards Other Gods in Biblical Literature and the Revision of Isaiah 2:18–21," in *On the Border Line: Textual Meets Literary Criticism* (Beer-Sheva 18), ed. Zipora Talshir and Dalia Amara, Beer-Sheva: Ben-Gurion University of the Negev Press, 113–153 (Heb.).

— 2005b. "Casting Nets and Burning Temples: The Babylonian and Persian Background to Jeremiah 43:8–13," *Tarbiz* 74/4: 483–510 (Heb.).

— 2010–11. "A New Look at Deuteronomy 32:8–9 and 43 in the Light of Akkadian Sources," *Tarbiz* 79/1: 5–21 (Heb.).

Goshen-Gottstein, Moshe H. / Kasher, Rimon, 1983–89. *Fragments of Lost Targumim* (2 vols.), Ramat-Gan: Bar-Ilan University Press (Heb.).

Goshen-Gottstein, Moshe H. / Shirun, Hannan, 1973. *The Bible in the Syropalestinian Version*, I: *Pentateuch and Prophets*, Jerusaelm: Magnes.

Graves, Michael, 2007. *Jerome's Hebrew Philology: A Study Based on his Commentary on Jeremiah* (*Vigiliae Christianae* Supp. 90), Leiden: Brill.

Graves, Michael / Hall, Christopher A., 2011. *Jerome: Commentary on Jeremiah* (Ancient Christian Texts), Downers Grove, Ill.: IVP Academic.

Greenberg, Gillian, 2002. *Translation Technique in the Peshitta to Jeremiah* (MPIL 13), Leiden: Brill.

— et al. 2013. *The Syriac Peshiṭta Bible with English Translation: Jeremiah* (The Antioch Bible), English translation by Gillian Greenberg and Donald M. Walter, text prepared by George A. Kiraz and Joseph Bali, Piscataway: Gorgias.

Greenstein, Edward L., 1982. "The Snaring of the Sea in the Baal Epic," *Maarav* 3/2: 195–216.

Gregor, Barbara, 1988. "'Gold aus Ofir'? Jer 10,9 und eine minäische Inschrift," *BN* 41: 19–22.

Gunkel, Hermann / Begrich, Joachim, 1998. *Introduction to Psalms: The Genres of the Religious Lyric of Israel*, tr. James D. Nogalski, Macon: Mercer University Press (originally published in German, 1933).

Hacham, Noah, 2005. "An Aramaic Translation of Isaiah in the *Rule of the Community*," *Leš* 67/2: 147–152 (Heb.).

Halévy, Joseph, 1885. "Recherches bibliques," *REJ* 11: 60–77.

Hallo, William W. (ed.), 1997–2002. *The Context of Scripture* (3 vols.), Leiden: Brill.

Harshav, Benjamin, 2014. *Three Thousand Years of Hebrew Versification: Essays in Comparative Prosody*, New Haven: Yale University Press.

Hayward, Robert. 1987. *The Targum of Jeremiah* (The Aramaic Bible 12), Wilmington, Del.: Michael Glazier.

Hill, John, 1999. *Friend or Foe? The Figure of Babylon in the Book of Jeremiah MT* (Biblical Interpretation Series 40), Leiden: Brill.

Hoffman, Yair, 1999. *Isaiah* (World of the Bible), Tel Aviv: Davidson (Heb.).

— 2001. *Jeremiah* (Mikra LeYisra'el; 2 vols.), Tel Aviv: Am Oved / Jerusalem: Magnes (Heb.).

— 2009. "The Prayer of Solomon and Jeremiah's Temple Sermon (1 Kings 8:14–53 and Jeremiah 7:1–8:3)," *Studies in Bible and Exegesis, 9: Presented to Moshe Garsiel*, ed. Shmuel Vargon, Yaakov Kaduri (James Kugel), Rimon Kasher, and Amos Frisch, Ramat-Gan: Bar-Ilan University Press, 167–197 (Heb.).

Holladay, William Lee, 1966. "Jeremiah and Moses: Further Observations," *JBL* 85/1: 17–27.

— 1986–89. *Jeremiah* (Hermeneia; 2 vols.), Philadelphia: Fortress.

— 2004. "Elusive Deuteronomists, Jeremiah, and Proto-Deuteronomy," *CBQ* 66/1: 55–77.

Hornkohl, Aaron D., 2011. "The Language of the Book of Jeremiah and the History of the Hebrew Language" (PhD dissertation), Hebrew University of Jerusalem (Heb.).

— 2014. *Ancient Hebrew Periodization and the Language of the Book of Jeremiah: The Case for a Sixth-Century Date of Composition* (Studies in Semitic Languages and Linguistics 74), Leiden: Brill.

Hossfeld, Frank-Lothar / Zenger, Erich, 2005–11. *Psalms* (Hermeneia; 2 vols.), tr. Linda M. Maloney, Minneapolis: Fortress.

Houtman, Alberdina / Sysling, Harry, 2009. *Alternative Targum Traditions: The Use of Variant Readings for the Study in Origin and History of Targum Jonathan* (Studies in the Aramaic Interpretation of Scripture 9), Leiden: Brill.

Hurowitz, Victor Avigdor, 1995. "Do an Image for Yourself," *Beit Mikra* 40/4 [143]: 337–347 (Heb.).

— 2003. "The Mesopotamian God Image: From Womb to Tomb," *JAOS* 123/1: 147–157.

— 2006. "What Goes in Is What Comes out: Materials for Creating Cult Images," in *Text, Artifact, and Image: Revealing Ancient Israelite Religion*, ed. Gary M. Beckman and Theodore J. Lewis (Brown Judaic Studies 346), Providence, R.I.: Brown Judaic Studies, 3–23.

— 2012. "What Can Go Wrong with an Idol?" in *Iconoclasm and Text Destruction in the Ancient Near East and Beyond*, ed. Natalie Naomi May (University of Chicago Oriental Institute Seminars 8), Chicago: The Oriental Institute of the University of Chicago, 259–310.

Hurvitz, Avi, 1972. *The Transitional Period in the History of Biblical Hebrew*, Jerusalem: Bialik Institute (Heb.).

— 1982. "The History of a Legal Formula: *kōl ʾašer-ḥāpēṣ ʿāśāh* (Psalms CXV 3, CXXXV 6)," *VT* 32/3: 257–267.

— 1985. "Originals and Imitations in Biblical Poetry: A Comparative Examination of 1 Sam 2:1–10 and Ps 113:5–9," in *Biblical and Related Studies Presented to Samuel Iwry*, ed. Ann Kort and Scott Morschauser, Winona Lake: Eisenbrauns, 115–121.

— et al. 2014. *A Concise Lexicon of Late Biblical Hebrew: Linguistic Innovations in the Writings of the Second Temple Period* (*VT* Supp. 160), with the collaboration of Leeor Gottlieb, Aaron Hornkohl and Emmanuel Mastéy, Leiden: Brill.

Inowlocki, Sabrina, 2006. *Eusebius and the Jewish Authors: His Citation Technique in an Apologetic Context* (Arbeiten zur Geschichte des antiken Judentums und des Urchristentums 64), Leiden: Brill.

Janzen, J. Gerlad, 1973. *Studies in the Text of Jeremiah* (HSM 6), Cambridge, Mass.: Harvard University Press.

Jenni, Ernst, 1952–53. "Das Wort *'ōlām* im Alten Testament," Pt. I, *ZAW* 64/3–4 (1952): 197–248; Pt. II, *ZAW* 65/1 (1953): 1–35

Joosten, Jan, 2011. "A Neglected Rule and its Exceptions: On Non-Volitive *yiqtol* in Clause-Initial Position," in Ἐν πάσῃ γραμματικῇ καὶ σοφίᾳ: *Saggi di linguistica ebraica in onore di Alviero Niccacci*, ed. Gregor Geiger and Massimo Pazzini, Jerusalem: Franciscan Printing Press / Milano: Terra Santa, 213–219.

— 2012. *The Verbal System of Biblical Hebrew: A New Synthesis Elaborated on the Basis of Classical Prose* (Jerusalem Biblical Studies 10), Jerusalem: Simor.

Kahana, Menahem I., 2011–15. *Sifre on Numbers: An Annotated Edition* (5 vols.), Jerusalem: Magnes.

Kasher, Rimon, 1996. *Targumic Toseftot to the Prophets*, Jerusalem: World Union of Jewish Studies (Heb.).

Kaufmann, Yehezkel. 1937–63. *History of the Israelite Religion* (8 vols.), Tel Aviv: Dvir (Heb.).

Keil, Carl Friedrich, 1873–74. *The Prophecies of Jeremiah* (2 vols.), tr. David Patrick and James Kennedy, Edinburgh: T. & T. Clark.

Kent, Roland G., 1953. *Old Persian: Grammar, Texts, Lexicon*[2] (American Oriental Series 33), New Haven: American Oriental Society.

King, Phillip J., 1996. "Jeremiah and Idolatry," *ErIsr* 25: *Joseph Aviram Volume*, 31*–36*.

Kissane, Edward J., 1952. "Who Maketh Lightnings for the Rain," *JTS* 3/2: 214–216.

Kister, Menahem, 2007. "Back and Forth: Legends and Midrashic Techniques in the Apocrypha and Rabbinic Literature," in *Higayon L'Yona: New Aspects in the Study of Midrash, Aggadah and Piyyut in Honor of Professor Yona Fraenkel*, ed. Joshua Levinson, Jacob Elbaum and Galit Hasan-Rokem, Jerusalem: Magnes, 231–259 (Heb.).

Knoppers, Gary N., 1995. "Prayer and Propaganda: Solomon's Dedication of the Temple and the Deuteronomist's Program," *CBQ* 57/2: 229–254.

Koch, Klaus, 1969. The Growth of the Biblical Tradition: The Form-Critical Method, tr. S. M. Cupitt, New York: Scribner (originally published in German, 1964).

— 1982–83. *The Prophets* (2 vols.), tr. Margaret Kohl, Philadelphia: Fortress.

Kogut, Simcha, 1993. "Alternative Usages of Independent and Suffixed Personal Pronouns to Express Possession in Biblical Hebrew," *Studies in Bible and Exegesis*, 3: *Moshe Goshen-Gottstein in Memoriam*, ed. Moshe Bar-Asher, Moshe Garsiel, Devorah Diman and Yeshayahu Maori, Ramat-Gan: Bar-Ilan University Press, 401–411 (Heb.).

Koller, Aaron J., 2012. *The Semantic Field of Cutting Tools in Biblical Hebrew: The Interface of Philological, Semantic, and Archaeological Evidence* (CBQ.MS 49), Washington, D.C.: Catholic Biblical Association of America.

— 2013. "Ancient Hebrew מעצד and עצד in the Gezer Calendar," *JNES* 72/2: 179–193.

Komlosh, Yehuda, 1973. *The Bible in the Light of the Aramaic Targumim*, Tel Aviv: Dvir (Heb.).

Krašovec, Jože, 1984. *Antithetic Structure in Biblical Hebrew Poetry* (*VT* Supp. 35), Leiden: Brill.

Kratz, Reinhard Gregor, 1991. *Kyros im Deuterojesaja-Buch: Redaktionsgeschichtliche Untersuchungen zu Entstehung und Theologie von Jes 40–55* (FAT 1), Tübingen: Mohr Siebeck.

— 1995. "Die Rezeption von Jeremia 10 und 29 im pseudepigraphen Brief des Jeremia,"
  JSJ 26/1: 2–31

Kraus, Hans-Joachim, 1988–89. *Psalms* (2 vols.), tr. Hilton C. Oswald, Minneapolis: Augsburg.

Kreuzer, Siegfried, 1983. *Der lebendige Gott: Bedeutung, Herkunft und Entwicklung einer
  alttestamentlichen Gottesbezeichnung* (BWANT 6/16), Stuttgart: Kohlhammer.

Kruger, Hennie A.J., 1993. "Ideology and Natural Disaster: A Context for Jeremiah 10:1–16," *OTE*
  6/3: 367–383.

Kugel, James L., 1981. *The Idea of Biblical Poetry: Parallelism and its History*, New Haven: Yale
  University Press.

Kuhrt, Amélie, 1983. "The Cyrus Cylinder and Achaemenid Imperial Policy," *JSOT* 8/25: 83–97.

Labuschagne, Casper J., 1966. *The Incomparability of Yahweh in the Old Testament*, Leiden: Brill.

Lambert, Wilfred G., 2013. *Babylonian Creation Myths* (Mesopotamian Civilizations 16), Winona
  Lake: Eisenbrauns.

Lange, Armin, 2009. *Handbuch der Textfunde vom Toten Meer*, 1: *Die Handschriften biblischer
  Bücher von Qumran und den anderen Fundorten*, Tübingen: Mohr Siebeck.

— 2016. "7.2.1 Ancient Manuscript Evidence," in *Textual History of the Bible*, ed. Armin Lange,
  Leiden: Brill, 1B. 514–542.

Lavee, Moshe, 2016. "Biographic Rehabilitation: Late Rabbinic Readings of Jer 10:1–16 and
  their Christian Context," in *Texts and Contexts of Jeremiah: The Exegesis of Jeremiah 1 and
  10 in Light of Text and Reception History* (Contributions to Biblical Exegesis & Theology 82),
  ed. Karin Finsterbusch and Armin Lange, Leuven: Peeters, 67–87.

Leichty, Erle, 2011. *The Royal Inscriptions of Esarhaddon, King of Assyria (680–669 BC)* (The
  Royal Inscriptions of the Neo-Assyrian Period 4), Winona Lake: Eisenbrauns.

Levtow, Nathaniel B., 2008. *Images of Others: Iconic Politics in Ancient Israel*, Winona Lake:
  Eisenbrauns.

Lewis, Theodore J., 2005. "Syro-Palestinian Iconography and Divine Images," in *Cult Image
  and Divine Representation in the Ancient Near East*, ed. Neal H. Walls, Boston: American
  Schools of Oriental Research, 69–107.

Lieber, Laura Suzanne, 2010. *Yannai on Genesis: An Invitation to Piyyut* (Monographs of the
  Hebrew Union College 36), Cincinnati: Hebrew Union College Press.

Livingstone, Alasdair, 1986. *Mystical and Mythological Explanatory Works of Assyrian and
  Babylonian Scholars*, Oxford: Clarendon.

Loewenstamm, Samuel Ephraim, 1992. "*Naḥ°lat* YHWH," in idem, *From Babylon to Canaan:
  Studies in the Bible and its Oriental Background*, Jerusalem: Magnes, 322–360 (originally
  published in Hebrew, 1987).

Lorton, 1999. "The Theology of Cult Statues in Ancient Egypt," in *Born in Heaven, Made on
  Earth: The Making of the Cult Image in the Ancient Near East*, ed. Michael B. Dick, Winona
  Lake: Eisenbrauns, 123–210.

Lundberg, Marilyn J., 2007. "The *mīs pî* Rituals and Incantations and Jeremiah 10:1–16," in
  Uprooting and Planting: Essays on Jeremiah for Leslie Allen, ed. John Goldingay (LHB/OTS
  459), New York: T. & T. Clark, 210–227.

Lundbom, Jack R., 1997. *Jeremiah: A Study in Ancient Hebrew Rhetoric*,[2] Winona Lake: Eisenbrauns.

— 1999–2004. *Jeremiah* (AB; 3 vols.), New York: Doubleday.

— 2005. "Haplography in the Hebrew *Vorlage* of LXX Jeremiah," *HS* 46: 301–320.

— 2009. "Delimitation of Units in the Book of Jeremiah," in *The Impact of Unit Delimitation
  on Exegesis*, ed. Raymond de Hoop, Marjo C.A. Korpel and Stanley E. Porter (Pericope 7),
  Leiden: Brill, 146–174.

Lunn, Nicholas P., 2006. *Word-Order Variation in Biblical Hebrew Poetry: Differentiating Pragmatics and Poetics*, Milton Keynes: Paternoster.

MacDonald, Nathan, 2014. "The Beginnings of Oneness Theology in Late Israelite Prophetic Literature," in *Monotheism in Late Prophetic and Early Apocalyptic Literature* (FAT 2/72), ed. Nathan MacDonald and Ken Brown, Tübingen: Mohr Siebeck, 103–123.

Machiela, Daniel A., 2009. *The Dead Sea Genesis Apocryphon: A New Text and Translation with Introduction and Special Treatment of Columns 13–17* (STDJ 79), Leiden: Brill.

Margaliot, Meshullam. 1972–74. "Jeremiah's Words against Idolatry," in *Studies in Jeremiah* (3 vols.), ed. Ben-Zion Lurie, Jerusalem: The World Jewish Society of Bible, 3.73–102 (Heb.).

— 1980. "Jeremiah X 1–16: A Re-examination," *VT* 30/3: 295–308.

McCarter, P. Kyle, 1980–84. *I–II Samuel* (AB; 2 vols.), Garden City: Doubleday.

McKane, William, 1985. "The History of the Text of Jeremiah 10,1–16," in *Mélanges bibliques et orientaux en l'honneur de M. Mathias Delcor* (AOAT 215), Kevelaer: Butzon & Bercker / Neukirchen-Vluyn: Neukirchener Verlag, 297–304.

— 1986–96. *A Critical and Exegetical Commentary on Jeremiah* (ICC; 2 vols.), Edinburgh: T. & T. Clark.

Meiser, Martin, 2016. "Reception of Jer 10:1–16 in Early Christian Literature," in *Texts and Contexts of Jeremiah: The Exegesis of Jeremiah 1 and 10 in Light of Text and Reception History* (Contributions to Biblical Exegesis & Theology 82), ed. Karin Finsterbusch and Armin Lange, Leuven: Peeters, 89–106.

Meshel, Ze'ev (ed.), 2012. *Kuntillet 'Ajrud (Horvat Teman): An Iron Age II Religious Site on the Judah-Sinai Border*, Jerusalem: Israel Exploration Society.

Michael, Tony S.L., 2006. "Bisectioning of Greek Jeremiah: A Problem to be Revisited?," *BIOSCS* 39: 93–104.

Miller, Cynthia L., 1996. *The Representation of Speech in Biblical Hebrew Narrative: Linguistic Analysis* (HSM 55), Atlanta: Scholars.

Mirsky, Aharon, 1991. *Yosse ben Yosse: Poems*,[2] Jerusalem: Bialik Institute (Heb.).

Mizrahi, Noam, 2013. "Hebrew of the Dead Sea Scrolls: Liturgy," in *Encyclopedia of Hebrew Language and Linguistics*, ed. Geoffrey Khan et al., Leiden: Brill, 2.558b–561b.

— 2014. "A Matter of Choice: A Sociolinguistic Perspective of the Contact between Hebrew and Aramaic, with Special Attention to Jer. 10.1–16," in *Discourse, Dialogue, and Debate in the Bible: Essays in Honour of Frank H. Polak*, ed. Athalya Idan-Brenner, Sheffield: Phoenix, 107–124.

— 2016. "Writing as Reading: Aspects of the Interpretive Transmission of Isaiah in Qumran – 4QIsa[c] (4Q57) for Isa 24,2.7.15 as a Case Study," in *Transmission and Interpretation of the Book of Isaiah in the Context of Intra- and Interreligious Debates*, ed. Florian Wilk and Peter Gemeinhardt (BETL 280), Leuven: Peeters, 29–59.

Movers, Franz C., 1837. *De utrivsqve recensionis vaticiniorvm Ieremiae, Graecae Alexandrinae et Hebraicae Masorethicae, indole et origine: Commentatio critica*, Hamburg: Perthes.

Mowinckel, Sigmund, 1914. *Zur komposition des Buches Jeremia*, Kristiania (Oslo): Dybwad.

— 1962. *The Psalms in Israel's Worship* (2 vols.), tr. D.R. Ap-Thomas, Oxford: Blackwell.

Müller-Kessler, Christa / Sokoloff, Michael, 1997. *The Christian Palestinian Aramaic Old Testament and Apocrypha Version from the Early Period* (A Corpus of Christian Palestinian Aramaic 1), Groningen: Styx.

Muraoka, Takamitsu, 2011. *A Grammar of Qumran Aramaic* (ANES Supp. 38), Leuven: Peeters.

Muraoka, Takamitsu / Porten, Bezalel, 2003. *A Grammar of Egyptian Aramaic*[2] (HdO 1/32), Leiden: Brill.

Najman, Hindy / Schmid, Konrad, 2016. *Jeremiah's Scriptures: Production, Reception, Interaction, and Transformation* (JSJ Supp. 173), Leiden: Brill.

Nelson, David, 2006. *Mekhilta de-Rabbi Shimon Bar Yoḥai*, Philadelphia: Jewish Publication Society, 2006.

Neusner, Jacob, 1984. *The Talmud of the Land of Israel: A Preliminary Translation and Explanation*, 27: *Sotah*, Chicago: Chicago University Press.

Nöldeke, Theodor, 1875. *Mandäische Grammatik*, Halle: Buchhandlung des Waisenhauses.

— 1904. *Compendious Syriac Grammar*, tr. James A. Crichton, London: Williams & Norgate.

del Olmo Lete, Gregorio / Sanmartín, Joaquín, 2004. *A Dictionary of the Ugaritic Language in the Alphabetic Tradition* (HdO 1/67; 2 vols.), tr. Wilfred G.E. Watson, Leiden: Brill.

Ornan, Tallay, 2012. "Gods and Symbols in the Art of Israel/Palestine c. 1000–600 BCE," in *Ancient Gods: Polytheism in Eretz Israel and Neighboring Countries from the Second Millennium BCE to the Islamic Period*, ed. Menahem Kister, Joseph Geiger, Nadav Na'aman and Shaul Shaked, Jerusalem: Yad Ben-Zvi, 64–89 (Heb.).

Overholt, Thomas W., 1965. "The Falsehood of Idolatry: An Interpretation of Jer. X 1–16," *JTS* N.S. 16/1: 1–12.

Parke-Taylor, Geoffrey H., 2000. *The Formation of the Book of Jeremiah: Doublets and Recurring Phrases* (SBL.MS 51), Atlanta: Society of Biblical Literature.

Parker, Simon B. (ed.), 1997. *Ugaritic Narrative Poetry* (WAW 9), Atlanta: Scholars.

Paul, Shalom M., 1969. "Literary and Ideological Echoes of Jeremiah in Deutero-Isaiah," *Proceedings of the Fifth World Congress of Jewish Studies*, 1:102–120.

Perez, Ma'aravi (ed.). 2002. *R. Judah Ibn Bal'am's Commentary on Jeremiah*, Ramat-Gan: Bar-Ilan University Press (Heb.).

Perles, Felix, 1906. "The Fourteenth Edition of Gesenius-Buhl's Dictionary," *JQR* 18/2: 383–390.

— 1912. "A Miscellany of Lexical and Textual Notes on the Bible: Chiefly in Connection with the Fifteenth Edition of the Lexicon by Gesenius-Buhl," *JQR* N.S. 2/1: 97–132.

Polak, Frank. 2013. "Parler de la langue: Labov, Fishman et l'histoire de l'hébreu biblique," *Yod* 18: *Le Proche-Orient ancien à la lumière des sciences sociales* [http://yod.revues.org/1814].

Porten, Bezalel / Yardeni, Ada, 1986–99. *Textbook of Aramaic Documents from Ancient Egypt* (4 vols.), Jerusalem: Hebrew University, Department of the History of the Jewish People.

Preuss, Horst Dietrich, 1971. *Verspottung fremder Religionen im Alten Testament* (BWANT 5/12 [92]),Stuttgart: Kohlhammer.

Rabin, Chaim / Talmon, Shemaryahu / Tov, Emanuel, 1997. *The Hebrew University Bible: The Book of Jeremiah*, Jerusalem: Magnes.

Rabinovitz, Zvi Meir, 1985–87. *The Liturgical Poems of Rabbi Yannai according to the Triennial Cycle of the Pentateuch and the Holidays* (2 vols.), Jerusalem: Bialik Institute (Heb.).

von Rad, Gerhard, 1972. *Wisdom in Israel*, tr. James D. Marton, London: SCM.

Rahlfs, Alfred, 1935. *Septuaginta, id est, Vetus Testamentum Graece iuxta LXX interpretes* (2 vols.), Stuttgart: Privilegierte Württembergische Bibelanstalt.

Rahmouni, Aicha, 2008. *Divine Epithets in the Ugaritic Alphabetic Texts*, tr. James N. Ford, Leiden: Brill.

Rainey, Anson F., 1996. *Canaanite in the Amarna Tablets: A Linguistic Analysis of the Mixed Dialect Used by the Scribes from Canaan* (HdO 1/25; 4 vols.), Leiden: Brill.

Reid, Garnett, 2006. "'Thus You Will say to Them': A Cross-Cultural Confessional Polemic in Jeremiah 10.11," *JSOT* 31/2: 221–238.

Reimer, David J., 1988. "A Problem in the Hebrew Text of Jeremiah X 13, LI 16," *VT* 38/3: 348–354.

Reiter, Siegfried, 1960. *S. Hieronymi presbyteri opera* (ed. Marcus Adriaen), Pars I: *Opera exegetica*, 3: *In Hieremiam* (Corpus Christianorum: Series Latina 74), Turnhout: Brepols.

Rendsburg, Gary A., 1995. "Linguistic Variation and the 'Foreign' Factor in the Hebrew Bible," *Israel Oriental Studies* 15: 177–190.

— 2002. "Some False Leads in the Identification of Late Biblical Hebrew Texts: The Cases of Genesis 24 and 1 Samuel 2:27–36," *JBL* 121/1: 23–46.

— 2015. "Style-Switching in Biblical Hebrew," in *Epigraphy, Philology, and the Hebrew Bible: Methodological Perspectives on Philological and Comparative Study of the Hebrew Bible in Honor of Jo Ann Hackett*, ed. Jeremy M. Hutton And Aaron D. Rubin, Atlanta: Society of Biblical Literature, 65–85.

Ribera Florit, Josep, 1989. "The Babylonian Tradition of the Targum Jeremiah," in *Proceedings of the Ninth Congress of the International Organization for Masoretic Studies*, ed. Aron Dotan, Atlanta: Scholars, 101–109.

— 1992. *Targum Jonatán de los Profetas Posteriores en tradición Babilónica*, Madrid: Consejo Superior de Investigaciones Científicas.

Rofé, Alexander, 1975. "Studies on the Composition of the Book of Jeremiah," *Tarbiz* 44/1–4: 1–29 (Heb.).

— 1990. "An Enquiry into the Betrothal of Rebekah," in *Die Hebräische Bibel und ihre zweifache Nachgeschichte: Festschrift für Rolf Rendtorff zum 65. Geburtstag*, ed. Erhard Blum, Christian Macholz, and Ekkehard W. Stegemann, Neukirchen: Neukirchener Verlag, 27–39.

— 1991. "The Name YHWH ṢĔBĀ'ÔT and the Shorter Recension of Jeremiah," in *Prophetie und geschichtliche Wirklichkeit im alten Israel: Festschrift für Siegfried Herrmann zum 65. Geburtstag*, ed. Rüdiger Liwak and Siegfried Wagner, Stuttgart: Kohlhammer, 307–316.

— 2000. "The End of the Song of Moses (Deuteronomy 32:43)," in *Liebe und Gebot: Studien zum Deuteronomium – Festschrift zum 70. Geburtstag von Lothar Perlitt* (FRLANT 190), ed. Reinhard G. Kratz and Hermann Spieckermann, Göttingen: Vandenhoeck & Ruprecht, 47–54.

— 2009. "Text-Criticism within the Philological-Historical Discipline: The Problem of the Double Text of Jeremiah," *Tarbiz* 78/1: 5–25 (Heb.).

— 2012. *Angels in the Bible: Israelite Belief in Angels as Evidenced by Biblical Tradition*, Jerusalem: Carmel (Heb.; originally published in 1979).

Rom-Shiloni, Dalit, 2010. *God in Times of Destruction and Exiles: Tanakh (Hebrew Bible) Theology*, Jerusalem: Magnes (Heb.).

— 2013. *Exclusive Inclusivity: Identity Conflicts between the Exiles and the People Who Remained (6th–5th Centuries BCE)* (LHB/OTS 543), New York: Bloomsbury.

Rosenthal, Franz, 2006. *A Grammar of Biblical Aramaic*[7] (Porta Linguarum Orientalium: Neue Serie 5), Wiesbaden: Harrassowitz.

Rosen-Zvi, Ishay, 2016. "What If We Got Rid of the Goy? Rereading Ancient Jewish Distinctions," *JSJ* 47/2: 149–182.

— 2017. "Like a Priest Exposing His Own Wayward Mother: Jeremiah in Rabbinic Literature," in *Jeremiah's Scriptures: Production, Reception, Interaction, and Transformation* (JSJ Supp. 173), ed. Hindy Najman and Konrad Schmid, Leiden: Brill, 570–590.

Rosen-Zvi, Ishay / Ophir, Adi, 2011. "*Goy*: Toward a Genealogy," *Diné Israel* 28: 69–122.

— 2015. "Paul and the Invention of the Gentiles," *JQR* 105/1: 1–41.

Roth, Wolfgang M.W., 1975. "For Life He Appeals to Death (Wis 13:18)," *CBQ* 37/1: 21–47.

Rudman, Dominic, 1998. "Creation and Fall in Jeremiah X 12–16," *VT* 48/1: 63–73.

Rudolph, Wilhelm, 1958. *Jeremia*[2] (Handbuch zum Alten Testament), Tübingen: Mohr.

Sabih, Joshua A., 2009. *Japheth ben Ali's Book of Jeremiah: A Critical Edition and Linguistic Analysis of the Judaeo-Arabic Translation* (Copenhagen International Seminar), London: Equinox.

Saley, Richard J., 2010. "Reconstructing 4QJer[b] according to the Text of the Old Greek," *DSD* 17/1: 1–12.

Sancisi-Weerdenburg, Heleen, 1993. "Political Concepts in Old-Persian Royal Inscriptions," in *Anfänge politischen Denkens in der Antike: Die nahöstlichen Kulturen und die Griechen*, ed. Kurt A. Raaflaub and Elisabeth Müller-Luckner, Munich: Oldenbourg, 145–163.

Sanders, James A., 1965. *The Psalms scroll of Qumrân Cave 11 (11QPs[a])* (DJD 4), Oxford: Clarendon.

— 1967. *The Dead Sea Psalms Scroll*, Ithaca, N.Y.: Cornell University Press.

Schaudig, Hanspeter, 2012. "Death of Statues and Rebirth of Gods," in *Iconoclasm and Text Destruction in the Ancient Near East and Beyond*, ed. Natalie Naomi May (University of Chicago Oriental Institute Seminars 8), Chicago: The Oriental Institute of the University of Chicago, 123–149.

Schniedewind, William M., 2013. *A Social History of Hebrew: Its Origins through the Rabbinic Period*, New Haven: Yale University Press.

Scholz, Anton, 1875. *Der masoretische Text und die LXX-Uebersetzung des Buches Jeremias*, Regensburg: Manz.

Schroer, Silvia, 1987. *In Israel gab es Bilder: Nachrichten von darstellender Kunst im Alten Testament* (OBO 74), Freiburg: Universtätsverlag / Göttingen: Vandenhoeck & Ruprecht.

Seeligmann, Isaac Leo, 2002. "δεῖζαι αὐτῷ φῶς," *Textus* 21: 107–128 (originally published in Hebrew, 1958).

Segal, Moses Hirsch, 1935. "The Refrain in Biblical Potery," Pt. I, *Tarbiz* 6/2: 125–144; Pt. II, 6/4: 433–451 (Heb.).

Segal, Michael, 2002. "1 Samuel 2:3: Text, Exegesis, and Theology," *Shnaton* 13: 83–95 (Heb.).

Seidel, Moses, 1978. *Biblical Studies*, Jerusalem: Rabbi Kook Institute (Heb.).

Skehan, Patrick W. / Ulrich, Eugene, 1995. "44. 4QDeut[q]," in *Qumran Cave 4, IX: Deuteronomy, Joshua, Judges, Kings* (DJD 14), Oxford: Clarendon, 137–142.

Smith, Morton, 1963. "II Isaiah and the Persians," *JAOS* 83/4: 415–421.

Smith, Mark S., 2001. *The Origins of Biblical Monotheism: Israel's Polytheistic Background and the Ugaritic Texts*, Oxford: Oxford University Press.

Smolar, Leivy / Aberbach, Moses, 1983. *Studies in Targum Jonathan to the Prophets*, New York: Ktav.

Snell, Daniel C., 1980. "Why Is There Aramaic in the Bible," *JSOT* 18: 32–51.

Soderlund, Sven, 1985. *The Greek Text of Jeremiah: A Revised Hypothesis* (*JSOT* Supp. 47), Sheffield: JSOT Press.

Sommer, Benjamin D., 1998. *A Prophet Reads Scripture: Allusion in Isaiah 40–66*, Stanford: Stanford University Press.

Sperber, Alexander (ed.), 1956. *Corpus codicum hebraicorum medii aevii*, Pars II: *The Pre-Masoretic Bible*, 1: *Codex Reuchlinianus*, Copenhagen: Munksgaard.

— 1959. *The Bible in Aramaic*, 3: *The Latter Prophets*, Leiden: Brill.

Stadel, Christian, 2008. *Hebraismen in den aramäischen Texten vom Toten Meer* (Schriften der Hochschule für Jüdische Studien Heidelberg 11), Heidelberg: Winter.

Stipp, Hermann-Josef, 2016. "Broadening the Criteria for Clarifying the Textual History of Jeremiah 10: The Pre-Masoretic Idiolect," in *Texts and Contexts of Jeremiah: The Exegesis of Jeremiah 1 and 10 in Light of Text and Reception History* (Contributions to Biblical Exegesis & Theology 82), ed. Karin Finsterbusch and Armin Lange, Leuven: Peeters, 107–116.

Streane, Annesley W., 1896. *The Double Text of Jeremiah (Massoretic and Alexandrian)*, Cambridge: D. Bell.

Swete, Henry Barclay, 1894–96. *The Old Testament in Greek according to the Septuagint*[2] (3 vols.), Cambridge: Cambridge University Press.

Tadmor, Hayim, 2011. "The Rise of Cyrus and the Historical Background of his Declaration," in idem, *"With my many chariots I have gone up the heights of mountains": Historical and Literary Studies on Ancient Mesopotamia and Israel*, ed. Mordechai Cogan, Jerusalem: Israel Exploration Society, 835–859 (originally published in Hebrew, 1983).

Tal, Abraham, 1975. *The Language of the Targum of the Former Prophets and its Position within the Aramaic Dialects*, Tel Aviv: The Chaim Rosenberg School for Jewish Studies (Heb.).

Talmon, Shemaryahu, 1985. "The Ancient Hebrew Alphabet and Biblical Text Criticism," in *Mélanges bibliques et orientaux on l'honneur de M. Mathias Delcor* (AOAT 215), ed. André Caquot, Simon Légasse and Michel Tardieu, Neukirchen: Neukirchener Verlag / Kevelaer : Butzon & Bercker 1985, pp. 387–402.

— 2010. *Text and Canon of the Hebrew Bible: Collected Studies*, Winona Lake: Eisenbrauns.

Talon, Philippe, 2005. *The Standard Babylonian Creation Myth: Enūma Eliš* (State Archives of Assyria Cuneiform Texts 4), Helsinki: The Neo-Assyrian Text Corpus Project.

Talshir, David, 1987. "The Autonomic Status of Late Biblical Hebrew," *Language Studies* 2–3: 161–172 (Heb.).

ter Haar Romeny, Bas, 2005a. "The Syriac Versions of the Old Testament," in *Sources Syriaques*, 1: *Nos sources: Arts et littérature syriaque*, ed. Maroun Atallah, Antélias: CERO, 75–105.

— 2005b. "Hypotheses on the Development of Judaism and Christianity in Syria in the Period after 70 C.E.," in *Matthew and the Didache: Two Documents from the Same Jewish-Christian Milieu?*, ed. Huub van de Sandt, Assen: Royal Van Gorcum, 13–33.

Theodor, Jehuda / Albeck, Chanoch, 1965. *Genesis Rabbah* (3 vols.; Heb.; originally published in 1912–36).

Thiel, Winfried, 1973. *Die deuteronomistische Redaktion von Jeremia, 1–25: Mit einer Gesamtbeurteilung der deuteronomistischen Redaktion des Buches Jeremia* (WMANT 41), Neukirchen-Vluyn: Neukirchener Verlag.

Thomas, Benjamin D., 2008. "Reevaluating the Influence of Jeremiah 10 upon the Apocryphal Epistle of Jeremiah: A Case for the Short Edition," *ZAW* 120/4: 547–562.

Tischendorf, Constantin, 1856. *Vetus Testamentum Graece iuxta LXX interpretes* (2 vols.), Leipzig: Brockhaus.

Tomes, Roger, 1997. "The Reception of Jeremiah in Rabbinic Literature and in the Targum," in *The Book of Jeremiah and its Reception*, ed. Adrian H.W. Curtis and Thomas Römer (BETL 128), Leuven: Peeters, 233–253.

van der Toorn, Karel, 1995. "The Domestic Cult at Emar," *JCS* 47: 35–49.

Tov, Emanuel, 1976. *The Septuagint Translation of Jeremiah and Baruch: A Discussion of an Early Revision of Jeremiah 29–52 and Baruch 1:1–3:8* (HSM 8), Missoula: Scholars.

— 1981. "Some Aspects of the Textual and Literary History of the Book of Jeremiah," in *Le Livre de Jérémie: Le prophète et son milieu, les oracles et leur transmission* (BETL 54), ed. Pierre-Maurice Bogaert, Leuven: Peeters, 145–167 ([2]1997, with addendum on pp. 430).

— 1982. "A Modern Textual Outlook Based on the Qumran Scrolls," *HUCA* 53: 11–27.

— 1989. "The Jeremiah Scrolls from Qumran," *RdQ* 14/2 [54]: 189–206.

— 1997. "Jeremiah," in *Qumran Cave 4, X: The Prophets* (DJD 15), Oxford: Clarendon, 145–208.

Tur-Sinai, Naphtali Herz (Torczyner, Harry), 1950. "Aramaic," in *Encyclopedia Biblica*, 1.584–595 (Heb.).
— 1957. *The Book of Job*, Jerusalem: Kiryath Sepher.
— 1960. "Aramaic in Jeremiah's Prophecy," in *Zvi Carl in Memoriam* (Publications of the Israel Society for the Study of the Bible, 10), ed. Asher Weiser and Ben-Zion Lurie, Jerusalem: Kiryath Sepher, 112–114 (Heb.).
— 1967. *The Literal Sense of the Bible*, 3/1: *Isaiah and Jeremiah*, Jerusalem: Kiryath Sepher (Heb.).
Vance, Donald R., 2013. "Poetic Meter: Biblical Hebrew," in *Encyclopedia of Hebrew Language and Linguistics*, ed. Geoffrey Khan, Leiden: Brill, 3.148–151.
Verbrugghe, Gerald P. / Wickersham, John M., 2000. *Berossos and Manetho: Native Traditions in Ancient Mesopotamia and Egypt*, Ann Arbor: University of Michigan Press.
Vogt, Ernst, 2008. *A Lexicon of Biblical Aramaic: Clarified by Ancient Documents*, tr. and ed. Joseph A. Fitzmyer (Studia Biblica 42), Rome: Gregorian and Biblical Press.
Volz, Paul, 1928. *Der Prophet Jeremia*,[2] Leipzig: Deichert.
Vonach, Andreas, 2009. "Jr 10, 1–10: Crux interpretum für die kürzere LXX-Version?" in *La Septante en Allemagne et en France: textes de la Septante à traduction double ou à traduction très littérale – Septuaginta Deutsch und Bible d'Alexandrie: Texte der Septuaginta in Doppelüberlieferung oder in wörtlicher Übersetzung* (OBO 238), ed. Wolfgang Kraus and Olivier Munnich, Fribourg: Academic Press / Göttingen: Vandenhoeck & Ruprecht, 204–216.
Walker, Christopher / Dick, Michael B., 1999. "The Induction of the Cult Image in Ancient Mesopotamia: The Mesopotamian *mīs pî* Ritual," in *Born in Heaven, Made on Earth: The Making of the Cult Image in the Ancient Near East*, ed. Michael B. Dick (Winona Lake: Eisenbrauns), 55–121.
— 2001. *The Induction of the Cult Image in Ancient Mesopotamia: The Mesopotamian Mīs Pî Ritual* (SAA Literary Texts 1), Helsinki: Neo-Assyrian Text Corpus Project.
Walser, Georg A., 2012. *Jeremiah: A Commentary Based on Ieremias in Codex Vaticanus* (Septuagint Commentary Series), Leiden: Brill.
Walter, Donald M., 2006. "Manuscript Relationships for the Peshitta Text of Jeremiah", in *Text, Translation, and Tradition: Studies on the Peshitta and its Use in the Syriac Tradition Presented to Konrad D. Jenner on the Occasion of his Sixty-Fifth Birthday*, ed. Wido Th. van Peursen and R. Bas ter Haar Romeny (MPIL 14), Leiden: Brill, 231–253.
Waltke, Bruce K. / O'Connor, Michael, 1990. *An Introduction to Biblical Hebrew Syntax*, Winona Lake: Eisenbrauns.
Wambacq, Benjamin N., 1974. "Jérémie, X, 1–16," *RB* 81/1: 57–62.
Watson, Wilfred G.E., 2001. *Classical Hebrew Verse: A Guide to its Techniques*, London: T. & T. Clark (originally published in 1984).
Weinfeld, Moshe, 1972. *Deuteronomy and the Deuteronomic School*, Oxford: Clarendon (repr. Winona Lake: Eisenbrauns, 1992).
— 1976. "Traces of Q^{e}dushat Yoṣer and P^{e}suqê de-Zimra in Qumran Literature and Ben Sira," *Tarbiz* 45/1–2: 15–26 (Heb.).
Weippert, Helga, 1981. *Schöpfer des Himmels und der Erde: Ein Beitrag zur Theologie des Jeremiabuches* (Stuttgarter Bibelstudien 102), Stuttgart: Katholisches Bibelwerk.
Weis, Richard D., 2016a. "Exegesis of Jeremiah 10 in LXX and in MT: Results and Implications," in *Texts and Contexts of Jeremiah: The Exegesis of Jeremiah 1 and 10 in Light of Text and Reception History* (Contributions to Biblical Exegesis & Theology 82), ed. Karin Finsterbusch and Armin Lange, Leuven: Peeters, 117–136.

— 2016b. "7.1 Textual History of Jeremiah," in *Textual History of the Bible* (2 vols.), ed. Armin Lange, Leiden: Brill, 1B.495–513.

Weitzman, Michael P., 1999. *The Syriac Version of the Old Testament: An Introduction*, Cambridge: Cambridge University Press.

— 2001. "The Origin of the *Qaddish*," in *Hebrew Scholarship and the Medieval World*, ed. Nicholas de Lange, Cambridge: Cambridge University Press, 131–137.

Williams, Peter J., 2003. "A Study on Translation Technique in the Peshitta to Jeremiah," *Aramaic Studies* 1/2: 289–298.

Williamson, Hugh G.M., 2015. Review of Koller 2012, *JTS* 66/2: 679–682.

Wolfsohn, Ludwig, 1902. *Das Targum zum Propheten Jeremias in jemenischer Überlieferung*, Halle.

Workman, George Coulson, 1889. *The Text of Jeremiah, or a Critical Investigation of the Greek and Hebrew, with the Variations in the LXX*, Edinburgh: T. & T. Clark.

Yardeni, Ada, 1990. "The Paleography of 4QJer[a]: A Comparative Study," *Textus* 15: 233–268.

Zakovitch, Yair, 1979. *"For Three and for Four": The Literary Pattern Three-Four in the Bible* (2 vols.), Jerusalem: Makor (Heb.).

Zenger, Erich, 2001. "Götter- und Götterbildpolemik im Ps 112–113 LXX = Ps 113–115 MT," in *Der Septuaginta-Psalter: Sprachliche und theologische Aspekte*, ed. Erich Zenger, Freiburg: Herder, 229–255.

Ziegler, Joseph, 1958. *Beiträge zur Ieremias-Septuaginta*, Göttingen: Vandenhoeck & Ruprecht.

— 1976. *Jeremias, Baruch, Threni, Epistula Jeremiae*,[2] Göttingen: Vandenhoeck & Ruprecht.

Index of sources

1 Index of Scripture

DOI 10.1515/9783110530162-009

2 Ancient Near Eastern and classical sources

Aramaic Documents from Egypt

Berossos

Cyrus Cylinder

Enūma Eliš

Esagila Chronicle

Herodotus

5 Rabbinic literature

Mekhilta of R. Shimon Bar Yoḥai

§8 107 n. 91

Sifre Numbers

§134 192 n. 62

Palestinian Talmud

y. Sotah 7:2 21c 111 n. 1

Babylonian Talmud

b. Shabbat 156a 13 n. 29
b. Megillah 15a 91 n. 49

Genesis Rabbah

§5:4 94 n. 57
§13:4 76 n. 6
§74:14 111 n. 1

Exodus Rabbah

§16:2 7 n. 15, 107 n. 91

Canticles Rabbah

§1:3 81 n. 27

Lamentations Rabbah

§1:1 7 n. 15

Midrash Psalms

On Ps 1:18 81 n. 27
On Ps 93:1 170 n. 15

Mishnat R. Eliezer

§11 91 n. 49
§15 76 n. 6

Tanḥuma

Šofṭim, 12 114–115

6 Patristic sources

Eusebius, *Praeparatio evangelica*

VII.11 100 n. 72

Jerome, *Commentary on Jeremiah*

On Jer 10:7 169 n. 9
On Jer 10:9 35 n. 28
On Jer 10:10 157 n. 21
On Jer 10:11 127 n. 50, 146 n. 82
On Jer 10:12 81 n. 27

Ishodad of Merv, *Commentary on Jeremiah*

On Jer 10:2 13 n. 29

Index of authors

(Pre-modern authors are marked by *italics*.)

DOI 10.1515/9783110530162-010

Index of words and phrases

1 Lexicon and semantics

(For word-pairs and Priestly/Deuteronomistic diction see below, §2 Phraseology)

1.1 Hebrew

DOI 10.1515/9783110530162-011

2 Phraseology

3 Grammar and Syntax